THE EXTERNAL ECONOMIC DIMENSION OF THE EUROPEAN UNION

LEGAL ASPECTS OF
INTERNATIONAL ORGANIZATION

VOLUME 35

The titles published in this series are listed at the end of this volume.

THE EXTERNAL ECONOMIC DIMENSION OF THE EUROPEAN UNION

Edited by

PITOU VAN DIJCK

and

GERRIT FABER

Kluwer Law International

The Hague / London / Boston

A C.I.P. Catalogue record for this book is available from the Library of Congress.

ISBN 90-411-1383-5

Published by Kluwer Law International,
P.O. Box 85889, 2508 CN The Hague, The Netherlands.

Sold and distributed in North, Central and South America
by Kluwer Law International,
675 Massachusetts Avenue, Cambridge, MA 02139, U.S.A.

In all other countries, sold and distributed
by Kluwer Law International, Distribution Centre,
P.O. Box 322, 3300 AH Dordrecht, The Netherlands.

Printed on acid-free paper

Printed in the Netherlands.

This book is published under the auspices of:
The Center for Latin American Research and Documentation
The Netherlands Institute of International Relations 'Clingendael'
The Utrecht University

CONTENTS

PART II: REGIONAL DIMENSIONS

PREFACE

ALFRED VAN STADEN

Director of the Netherlands Institute of
International Relations 'Clingendael'
The Hague
The Netherlands

The creation of the Internal Market within the confines of the (European) Economic Community has generated immense economic benefits to all member states of the European Union (EU). The subsequent establishment of the monetary union and the introduction of the single currency enabled them to reap still more fruits of their continuous drive towards economic integration. Whilst further enlargement with the countries of Central and Eastern Europe forces the Union members to devote a great deal of their political energy to internal institutional and financial reforms, there cannot be an excuse for them to turn a blind eye on their economic relations with the outside world. After all, although the weight of the EU in the world economy is somewhat declining, the EU remains the largest trading partner in the world with economic globalization very likely to intensify in the 21st century. It is a hopeful sign that the previous European Commission launched far-reaching proposals for the Millennium Round of trade negotiations in the WTO framework. These proposals are a clear recognition of the need to improve market access throughout the world by reducing tariffs and non-tariff barriers to trade in goods and services. The Commission also emphasized the importance of developing new rules governing trade and investment, trade and competition, and rules aimed at facilitating trade. Its proposals are a welcome antidote against looming protectionism and anti-globalization sentiments in some political quarters.

The main focus of the following study, however, is not on trade negotiations in the global, multilateral setting; it is concerned with the changing position of the EU in the world economy and with the main dimensions of EU's economic relations with different parts of the world. In particular, recent attempts by the Union directed at revitalizing its policy of establishing special and preferential trade relations with countries all over the world are highlighted. The study reaches a balanced conclusion as to the relative advantages of multilateral vs. regional trade arrangements and on their mutual (in)compatibility. It demonstrates that the establishment of a comprehensive, effective and open multilateral trade regime is the preferable avenue to increase welfare in the EU itself as well as in its partner countries. At the same time, it also indicates that the multilateral regime is less than perfect and that regionalism may create additional gains from trade to participants that may not be realized in the multilateral framework. Contrary to popular beliefs (especially prevailing outside the European Union), the study further illustrates that the Internal Market can be taken as a clear case to corroborate the thesis that regional integration may support rather than hinder multilateral liberalization.

In addition to the rich variety of the topics at issue, this volume is extremely valuable for several other reasons. Above all, it is compulsory reading for those who have been affected by demoralizing strikes of pessimism and gloom as far as Europe's overall economic performance is concerned. The picture which is shown in one of the chapters of the potential of the Old World to be the biggest and most important economic area on earth in the next century contrasts sharply with images of Europe projected in the recent past that suggested economic sclerosis and stagnation. The ability of especially the present German government to successfully implement basic economic and social reforms will be crucial to Europe's immediate economic future. From a more analytical point the book is interesting in that it outlines different approaches to the paramount problem of defining and measuring the competitiveness of countries and regions. It is a point of debate to what extent the analysis of a region's capacity to produce a higher standard of living can be separated from that of the region's export performance in world markets. At any rate, several chapters offer a good insight into Europe's relative strengths and weaknesses on these markets. Finally, the interaction of the political and economic dimension of EU's relations with the USA is adequately dealt with. The prospect of monetary bipolarity, with a key role for both the dollar and the euro in the global financial system, increases the likelihood of seeing a more equal partnership between the two sides of the Atlantic.

The value of the book can hardly be overrated. Its publication is very timely not only in view of recent initiatives taken by the Union to strengthen its relations with Eastern Europe, Latin America and Asia Pacific but also in light of the new round of multilateral trade negotiations. The editors deserve credits for bringing a distinguished group of authors (both academics and practitioners) together and for organizing this volume so well.

ACKNOWLEDGEMENTS

The basis of this volume was set during a conference at the Clingendael Institute in The Hague in December 1997, only a few months after the Council of Amsterdam. The initiative to organize the conference and to prepare a volume on its central theme was strongly supported by our two institutions, the Economic Institute at Utrecht University and the Centre for Latin American Research and Documentation (CEDLA) at the University of Amsterdam as well as by the Clingendael Institute. We appreciate the enthusiastic support of Prof. Alfred van Staden, Director of the Clingendael Institute, and Prof. Jan Rood, Director of Studies at the same institute.

We have benefited in many different ways from the highly professional support of Marinella Wallis. Her heroic efforts to tackle all manner of problems with skill and stamina have contributed greatly to the success of this project. Her presence at CEDLA has been appreciated by all members of the staff.

Wil Wassen of the Clingendael Institute has worked closely with us in the past and, once more, facilitated the organization of the conference and the publication of the book, for which we are grateful. We express our gratitude to our publisher for ensuring an undisturbed publication process.

Finally, our appreciation is extended to the Ministry of Economic Affairs for its financial support.

Pitou van Dijck
Gerrit Faber

NOTES ON THE CONTRIBUTORS

Frans Andriessen is Professor of European Integration at the Faculty of Law of Utrecht University, the Netherlands, Special Advisor to KPMG and President of EURO Institute. He was Vice-President of the European Commission, responsible for agriculture and fisheries, and Vice-President of the European Commission responsible for external relations, trade policy and co-operation with other European countries.

Pitou van Dijck is Associate Professor of Economics at the Center for Latin American Research and Documentation (CEDLA) at the University of Amsterdam. His main fields of interest are industrialization and trade policies in Latin America and Asia, and multilateral and regional rule systems for international trade. Among his most recent book publications are *Latin America's New Insertion in the World Economy* (co-edited with R. Buitelaar) and *Challenges to the New World Trade Organization* (co-edited with G. Faber).

Gerrit Faber is Associate Professor of International Economics at Utrecht University, the Netherlands. His main research interests are trade-policy issues related to European integration and development co-operation. Among his most recent book publications are *Challenges to the New World Trade Organization* (co-edited with P. van Dijck) and co-author (with A. Sarma and P. K. Mehta) of *Meeting the Challenges of the European Union - Prospects of Indian Exports.*

Mitsuhiro Kagami is Director-General of the Research Planning Department at the Institute of Developing Economies of the Japan External Trade Organization (JETO) in Tokyo. He worked previously for the United Nations Economic Commission for Latin America and the Caribbean (ECLAC) in Santiago de Chile and served as a Visiting Scholar at the Inter-American Development Bank (IDB) in Washington, D.C..

Michiel Keyzer is Director of the Centre for World Food Studies at the Free University of Amsterdam (SOW-VU) and Professor of Economics at the same university. His main research activities are in the area of mathematical economics and economic model building applied to the projects of the Centre. Among his most recent book publications is *The Structure of Applied General Equilibrium Models* (with V. Ginsburgh).

Jacob Kol is Head of the Erasmus Centre for Economic Integration Studies at Erasmus University, Rotterdam and Professor of Economics at the University of Westminster in London. He has published widely on international economic relations and economic integration.

James Mathis is Academic Co-ordinator of the Trade Law Programme at the Amsterdam Law School of the University of Amsterdam and Visiting Expert at the European Institute of Public Administration.

Max Merbis is Research Associate at the Centre for World Food Studies at the Free University of Amsterdam (SOW-VU) and involved in modelling and analysing the Common Agricultural Policy of the European Union.

Tibor Palánkai is Jean Monnet Professor at the Budapest University of Economic Sciences (BUES) and, since 1997, Rector of BUES. His publications are in the areas of economic integration in Europe and the transformation and integration problems in Central and Eastern Europe. He has been Visiting Fellow at several North American and European universities and institutes and received the Prize of the Hungarian Academy in 1994 and the Order of Merit in 1998.

Jan Rood is Director of Studies at the Clingendael Institute in The Hague and Professor of International Relations and International Political Economy at Utrecht University, the Netherlands. His areas of specialization are the roles of the USA and the EU in international relations, the relationship between the EU and the countries in Central and Eastern Europe and the new world order after the collapse of Bretton Woods.

Jacques Steenbergen is Professor at the Faculty of Law of the Catholic University of Leuven, Belgium, and Visiting Professor at the Europa Instituut at the University of Amsterdam. He has published extensively on topics related to the European Community and economic law.

Christopher Stevens is Fellow at the Institute of Development Studies (IDS) at Sussex University, Brighton, United Kingdom. He has advised and written extensively on the impact on developing countries of the Single European Market, the GATT Round, the Generalized System of Preferences and the Lomé Convention.

Lester Thurow is the Jerome and Dorothy Lemelson Professor of Management and Economics at the Sloan School of Management, MIT, Cambridge, USA. His academic work focuses on international economics. Among his book publications are *Head to Head - The Coming Economic Battle among Japan, Europe and America* and *The Future of Capitalism - How Today's Economic Forces Shape Tomorrow's World*.

Vivianne Ventura Dias is Head of the Division of International Trade, Development Finance and Transport at the United Nations Economic Commission for Latin America and the Caribbean (ECLAC) in Santiago de Chile. She has published extensively in the fields of trade and development.

L. Alan Winters is Professor of Economics at the University of Sussex. He was previously in charge of the department for International Trade at the World Bank. He is a Research Fellow of the Centre for Economic Policy Research in London and Senior Visiting Fellow at the Centre for Economic Performance at the London School of Economics. He has published widely on applied international trade issues. Among his recent book publications are *The Uruguay Round and the Developing Countries* (co-edited with W. Martin).

LIST OF ABBREVIATIONS

ACP	African, Caribbean and Pacific
AFTA	ASEAN Free Trade Area
AIA	ASEAN Investment Area
ANZCERTA	Australia New Zealand Closer Economic Relations Trade Agreement
APEC	Asia-Pacific Economic Cooperation
ASEAN	Association of South East Asian Nations
ASEM	Asia-Europe Meeting
CACM	Central American Common Market
CAP	Common Agricultural Policy
CCP	Common Commercial Policy
CCT	Common Customs Tariff
CEEC	Central and Eastern European Countries
CEFTA	Central European Free Trade Area
CET	Common External Tariff
CFA	Communauté Financière Africaine
CFSP	Common Foreign and Security Policy
CIS	Commonwealth of Independent States
CMEA	Council for Mutual Economic Assistance
CP	Contracting Party (GATT)
CU	Customs Union
CUSFTA	Canada-US Free Trade Agreement
DAC	Development Assistance Committee
DSB	Dispute Settlement Body (WTO)
EA	Europe Agreement
EAEC	East Asian Economic Caucus
EAGCF	European Agricultural Guidance and Guarantee Fund
EBRD	European Bank for Reconstruction and Development
EC	European Community
ECB	European Central Bank
ECIP	European Community Investment Partners
ECSC	European Coal and Steel Community

EDF	European Development Fund
EEA	European Economic Area
EEC	European Economic Community
EFTA	European Free Trade Association
EIB	European Investment Bank
EMA	Euro-Mediterranean Agreement
EMS	European Monetary System
EMU	Economic and Monetary Union
ERM	Exchange Rate Mechanism
ESC	Economic and Social Committee
EU	European Union
FDI	Foreign Direct Investment
FTA	Free-Trade Area
FTAA	Free Trade Area of the Americas
GATS	General Agreement on Trade in Services
GATT	General Agreement on Tariffs and Trade
GDP	Gross Domestic Product
GNP	Gross National Product
GSP	Generalized System of Preferences
IGC	Intergovernmental Conference
IMF	International Monetary Fund
IPR	Intellectual Property Rights
MAI	Multilateral Agreement on Investment
MENA	Middle East and North Africa
MERCOSUR	Mercado Común del Sur
MFA	Multi-Fibre Arrangement
MFN	Most Favoured Nation
MIT	Massachusetts Institute of Technology
NAFTA	North American Free Trade Agreement
NAS	New Asia Strategy
NATO	North Atlantic Treaty Organization
NTB	Non-Tariff Barrier
ODA	Official Development Assistance
OECD	Organisation for Economic Co-operation and Development
OEEC	Organisation for European Economic Co-operation
PAMEFTA	Pan-European-Mediterranean Free Trade Area
PHARE	Pologne, Hongrie et Aide à la Reconstruction Économique

PPP	Purchasing Power Parity
PTA	Preferential Trade Agreement
R and D	Research and Development
REPA	Regional Economic Partnership Agreement
SADC	Southern Africa Development Community
SAFTA	South American Free Trade Area
TAFTA	Transatlantic Free Trade Area
TAM	Transatlantic Marketplace
TEP	Transatlantic Economic Partnership
TRIPS	Trade-Related Aspects of Intellectual Property Rights
UN	United Nations
VAT	Value-Added Tax
VER	Voluntary Export Restraint
WEU	West European Union
WHFTA	Western Hemisphere Free Trade Area
WTO	World Trade Organization

LIST OF TABLES

LIST OF FIGURES

THE EU IN THE WORLD ECONOMY: NEW POLICIES AND PARTNERSHIPS

PITOU VAN DIJCK
CEDLA
Amsterdam
The Netherlands

GERRIT FABER
Utrecht University
Utrecht
The Netherlands

1. Objective of the study

The member countries of the European Union (EU) face new challenges in the world economy. Globalization has created new opportunities but requires also new efforts and initiatives to improve competitiveness and strengthen positions in global markets. Apart from intensified competition with two major economic superpowers, the USA and Japan, the continued dynamism in the Pacific area, the transition of Eastern Europe and the economic recovery of Latin America have created new investment and trade opportunities for European industries, but have as well exposed more and more sectors in the European economies to cut-throat competition.

The world all over, the process of trade and investment liberalization has been intensified and broadened by unilateral, regional and multilateral initiatives. Overall levels of tariff and non-tariff barriers (NTBs) against international trade have

P. van Dijck and G. Faber (eds.), The External Economic Dimension of the European Union, 1–48.
© 2000 *Kluwer Academic Publishers. Printed in the Netherlands.*

been reduced significantly, particularly with respect to manufactured products, and investment regimes have become more liberal and transparent, and less discriminatory towards foreign investors. The implementation of the decisions and concessions made during the Uruguay Round have contributed to that process and will continue to do so in the years to come. A new round of multilateral trade negotiations at the beginning of the new millennium may carry this liberalization process even further.

During the past decades the countries of the EU have taken major initiatives to improve the competitiveness of their industries and to strengthen their positions in international markets separately as well as at the level of the Union. This has been one of the traditional objectives of the EU. The US and Japanese challenges have pushed the deepening and widening of the integration process in Europe.

Whether the EU will be able to establish itself as an influential actor in world markets and in the major multilateral institutions that manage the world economy, depends on its capability to create efficient markets and institutions. More specifically, this requires an effective and integrated external economic policy.

In recent years, the EU has taken major initiatives in the area of its external economic relations. Policy dialogues have been initiated with countries the world all over, and proposals have been made to establish preferential trade and investment areas with the USA and countries in Central and Eastern Europe, the Middle East and North Africa, and Latin America. Also, the traditional special relationship with the large group of so-called ACP countries in Africa, the Caribbean and the Pacific is in the process of being re-arranged. Moreover, the EU has proposed to start a new Millenium Round of multilateral trade negotiations in the World Trade Organization (WTO).

The objective of this volume is to investigate the broad range of recent initiatives taken by the Commission and the Council of the EU to develop a common economic external policy. Essentially, three interrelated topics are investigated: (1) the changing position of the countries of the EU in the world economy; (2) the challenges and problems related to the enlargement of the EU itself, and (3) the prospects and limitations of the new initiatives to establish policy dialogues and preferential trade agreements (PTAs) with countries all over the world.

This chapter is organized as follows. Section 2 will present a brief overview of the changing position of the EU in the world economy. In subsequent sections several aspects of the external economic policies of the EU are investigated. The growth of the EU's external economic powers is the subject of Section 3. The

Economic and Monetary Union (EMU) is potentially an important addition to the EU's external economic powers and is dealt with in Section 4. Recent changes in the role of the EU as an aid donor are studied in Section 5. Changes in three areas of trade policy of the EU are the subject matter of Section 6: the liberalization of the trade regime of the EU; the enlargement of the EU towards Central and Eastern Europe, and the shift from the establishment of non-reciprocal to reciprocal trade agreements with third countries. Section 7 deals with the efficiency and effectiveness of these changes. Finally, Section 8 gives a brief overview of the main issues analysed in this volume.

2. The EU in the world economy

Four economic transitions have had a major impact on global trade and investment relations during the past three decades: the process of economic integration in Europe itself; the emergence of the Pacific Basin as a new trade and investment area in the world economy; the systemic change and the introduction of relatively open market economies in Central and Eastern Europe as well as Asia, and the worldwide process of trade and investment liberalization. These changes have intensified the economic relations among nations, contributed to shifts in the economic centres of gravity in world trade and investment, and consequently changed Europe's position in the world economy.

Many chapters of this volume will deal with specific aspects of these major changes, their consequences for relations between Europe and the rest of the world and the challenges they pose to the external economic policies of the Union. By way of introduction to these analyses, this section will present in a stylized fashion the changing position of the EU in world income, international trade and investment flows.

The EU and the growth of world income

To start with, the dominant position of the group of industrial countries in the world economy has been reduced and new centres of gravity in world production and trade have been created since 1970. These shifts are illustrated in Figure 1.1 which shows annual real growth of gross national product (GNP) in selected regions during the period 1970-97. As shown, real growth in developed countries taken as a group was slower than in the group of developing countries during

Figures 1.1. Growth of real GNP in selected regions, in percentages, 1970-97.

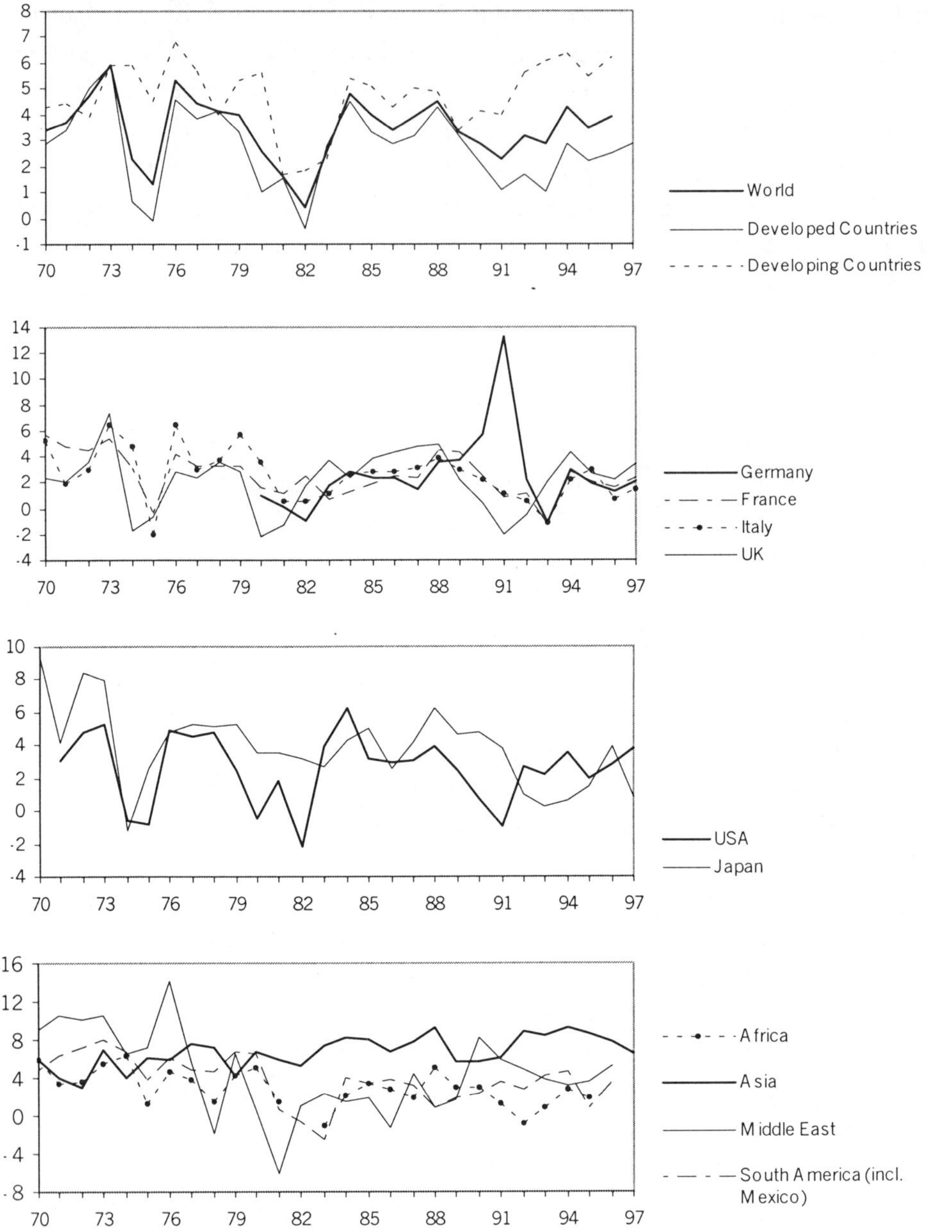

Source: Based on IMF, *International Financial Statistics Yearbook,* Washington, D.C., 1998.

nearly the entire period 1970-97. Within these two groups of countries, however, large differences in dynamism are discernible.

The USA, by far the largest economy in the world and among the countries with the highest income per capita measured at purchasing-power-parity (PPP), has shown a level of dynamism exceeding the average rate of growth of the world economy during several years in this period, particularly during the late 1970s and the first half of the 1980s. From the mid 1980s onwards, however, its rate of expansion continued to be significantly below the average rate of growth of the world economy.

Japan, the second largest economy among the developed countries and the third largest of the world, passed through a remarkable pattern of growth. The so-called Japanese miracle was reflected by growth rates exceeding the average rate of growth of the world economy during most of the years in the 1970s and 1980s. From 1992 onwards, however, the country has progressed at a rate far below the average for developed countries.

Focusing now on the growth performance of the five largest West-European economies that generate over 80 per cent of income of the entire EU - Germany, France, the United Kingdom, Italy and Spain - it appears that these countries, taken as a group, have not been particularly dynamic, although countries recorded exceptional achievements during particular periods. Note that data on Germany are lacking for the 1970s. The rates of growth of these European countries were below the average growth rate for the world economy during the second half of the 1970s and far below the growth performance of Japan or the group of developing countries. Also during the 1980s, growth in the EU was lower than the average growth of the world economy and Japan, but the difference with the performance of the US economy was much less pronounced. Again, in the 1990s growth of the European economies was relatively low compared to the world economy and the US economy. The largest among the European economies, Germany, experienced its so-called *Wirtschaftswunder* after the Second World War but showed little dynamism in the 1980s and 1990s even as compared to the other large economies of the EU and the USA except for the period 1989-1991.

Very significant differences are noticeable among the group of developing countries. First, growth in Africa was below the average rate of growth of the world economy in nearly all years since 1970. Second, growth rates of the Middle East show very large fluctuations: they were the highest of the world in the 1970s, among the lowest in the 1980s, and exceeded the average rate of growth of the world economy in the 1990s. Third, Latin America was a particularly dynamic area during the 1970s, but during the 1980s – the so-called lost decade - the Brazilian economy as well as most other countries in the region stagnated. The 1990s showed renewed growth, be it at a moderate rate. Fourth, Asia, and particularly East and South-East Asia excluding Japan was exceptionally successful in terms of real growth during the entire period of nearly three decades. This truly East Asian miracle resulted in a significant shift in the centre of gravity in the world economy from the North-Atlantic Basin towards the Pacific Basin. Growth rates in East Asia declined sharply during the Asian crisis, particularly so in 1998 but by the very end of the millennium the region was heading for renewed growth. Finally, the group of countries in transition in Central and Eastern Europe have experienced large shocks and went through a difficult adjustment period, resulting in large volatility in their growth performance during the 1990s.

Table 1.1 presents the size of economies and regions as measured according to their GNP measured at PPP expressed in billions of US dollars in 1997. It should be noted that these outcomes differ significantly from presentations based on traditional comparisons of GNP using nominal exchange rates. Overall world income in 1997 measured at PPP exceeds GNP measured according to the World Bank Atlas method by 23.47 per cent. In the case of China, GNP measured at PPP exceeds the value of GNP according to the Atlas method by a factor 3.15.

The selection and presentation of countries and regions in the table links up with the series of initiatives taken by the EU in recent years to establish special or preferential trade and investment relations as studied in Part II of this volume. According to these data, the economy of the USA exceeds the size of the EU by a small margin. Clearly, the group of countries in the North-Atlantic Basin including the members of the North American Free Trade Agreement (NAFTA), the EU and the European Economic Area (EEA) still constitute a centre of gravity in the world economy with a combined GNP of nearly 17,000 billion US dollars. At the same time, however, the countries in the East Asian region, including Japan, China and two generations of tiger economies constitute a new major growth pole. The entire group of countries in the Pacific Basin including the members of the Asia-Pacific Economic Cooperation (APEC) form an economic grouping, the combined GNP of which exceeds 20,000 billion US dollars. In addition to these Basins additional growth poles may be distinguished in South Asia (India) and South America (Mercosur).

Table 1.1 shows that an eastward enlargement of the EU by the full integration of the countries with Europe Agreements may increase the overall size of the EU

Table 1.1. GNP measured at PPP, in billions of US dollars, 1997.

EU	7,466.6	South Asia	2,005.0
EEA	291.6	South-East Asia	1,825.4
Europe Agreements	647.1	China	4,542.1
Rest of Eastern Europe	915.8	Japan	2,950.7
NAFTA	9,122.0	APEC	20,390.6
USA	7,690.1	MENA	992.9
South America	2,429.1	Lomé	591.2
Mercosur	1,421.9	South Africa	286.9

Note: Countries included are listed in Annex 1.A.1.

Source: Based on The World Bank, *World Development Report 1998/99,* Washington,
    D.C., 1998.

by nearly 10 per cent according to the data presented here. Moreover, if eventually the new initiatives of the EU to establish preferential areas with the Middle East and North Africa (MENA) and the countries in Latin America would materialize, this could give a substantial stimulus to the EU economy.

As illustrated above, the size of the European economy relative to the world economy has decreased. This, however, in no way needs to imply that Europe is loosing its economic strength or competitiveness. Competitiveness may become a dangerous obsession if it is not well understood as Krugman indicated (Krugman, 1994). As formulated by Thurow and Kol in this volume, competitiveness is a region's ability to generate a high and rising standard of living. Table 1.2 compares the standards of living in several regions in the world economy as measured by average levels of GNP per capita in US dollars measured at PPP in 1997. According to these World Bank data, the average level of income in the countries of the EMU was over 3.2 as high as the world average level of income per capita, but 30 per cent lower than in the USA. As the table shows, the gap in income levels between the industrialized countries and low and middle-income countries is very wide. This holds particularly for the gap between the EMU countries and Sub-Saharan Africa and South Asia. The group of dynamic East and South-East Asian economies has reduced this gap significantly during the period under investigation but there has not been a general tendency of reduced income inequality between industrialized and developing countries from the 1970s onwards (Barro, 1997, and The World Bank, 1993).

Table 1.2. GNP per capita measured at
PPP, in US dollars, 1997.

EMU	20,230
USA	29,080
Japan	24,400
Sub-Saharan Africa	1,460
MENA	4,630
South Asia	1,590
East Asia and the Pacific	3,170
China	3,070
Latin America and Caribbean	6,730
World	6,260

Source: Based on The World Bank, *World
      Development Indicators,* CD-ROM,
      Washington, D.C., 1998.

The EU in world trade

Gravity models of world trade relate the size of trade flows between countries to the size of the economies, their population and the openness of the trade regime. Hence, the larger economies are, the lower the trade barriers and the larger their population, the more sizable trade flows among them are, particularly so if distances between trade partners are small. In view of the significant differences among regions in the world economy in the growth of their overall income, it may be expected that trade flows have shifted accordingly in the course of time.

Figures 1.2-1.4 show the position of the group of 15 member countries of the EU in world trade during the period 1975-97. During this period the value of world trade expanded from 805 to over 5,525 billion US dollars and world exports to the 15 EU countries expanded from 340 to 1,970 billion US dollars. Note that world exports and imports include intra-EU trade flows. As shown, the second oil price hike of 1980 generated a strong increase in world exports and imports but in subsequent years the value of world trade contracted in nominal terms.

Figure 1.4 shows that in the early 1990s the share of the 15 EU countries in world trade was at a similar level as in the mid-1970s notwithstanding the steep decline at the end of the 1970s and in the early 1980s. However, after 1992, EU

Figure 1.2. World exports to the EU, in billions of current US dollars, 1975-97.

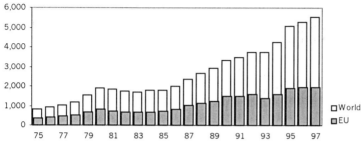

Source: Based on IMF, *Direction of Trade Statistics Yearbook,* Washington, D.C., several issues.

Figure 1.3. World imports from the EU, in billions of current US dollars, 1975-97.

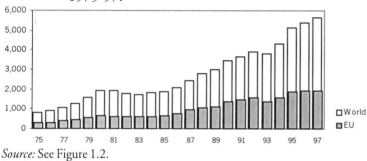

Source: See Figure 1.2.

Figure 1.4. World exports to the EU and world imports from the EU, as percentage shares of world exports and imports, 1975-97.

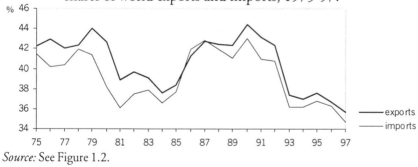

Source: See Figure 1.2.

trade shares declined sharply, which resulted from a strong expansion of world trade combined with stagnation and decline in the EU trade performance in the early 1990s.

Figure 1.5. Shares of intra-EU trade in total EU trade, in percentages, 1990-97.

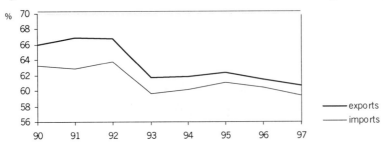

Source: Based on IMF, *Direction of Trade Statistics Yearbook,* Washington, D.C., several issues.

Focusing now more specifically on trade flows between the EU and several major regions in the world economy, a distinction is made between intra-EU and extra-EU trade flows. Growth of intra-European trade has been supported by the growth of the European markets, the progress made in realizing an integrated European market through the abolishment of tariff barriers and non-tariff barriers (NTBs) and the harmonization of standards and rules, the small distances and a well-developed transportation infrastructure connecting the countries in the region. Intra-industry patterns of specialization have been characteristic of the process of European integration and stimulated intra-regional trade in particular. At the same time, however, income in many other regions in the world economy has grown at higher rates and liberalization has progressed more rapidly, particularly in countries that applied comprehensive trade regulations in the past.

Figure 1.5 shows that over 60 per cent of all EU exports and imports are among EU countries but the share of intra-EU trade in total EU trade declined significantly in the period 1990-97. Hence, the EU has become less inward orientated and more dependent on the rest of the world for its trade-related activities.

The direction of EU trade flows to the rest of the world has changed considerably in the 1990s as shown in Table 1.3. The most significant changes may be summarized as follows. First, the traditional strong concentration of trade of the EU to other industrialized countries – inside and outside the EU - has been reduced. Put together, the share of EU exports to industrialized countries excluding intra-EU exports, declined from 46 per cent in 1990 to nearly 39 per cent in 1997. When including intra-EU trade, the share of EU exports to industrialized

Table 1.3. Exports of the EU to selected regions, in percentages (excluding intra-EU exports), 1990-97.

	1990	1991	1992	1993	1994	1995	1996	1997
Industrial countries (excl. EU)	46.40	44.22	43.46	40.42	41.05	39.49	38.87	38.92
USA	20.59	19.20	19.71	19.16	19.42	17.82	18.10	19.20
Japan	6.10	5.96	5.47	5.20	5.47	5.67	5.63	4.90
Developing regions								
Africa	8.56	8.34	8.33	6.99	6.44	6.66	6.15	5.65
Asia	13.04	13.98	14.75	16.32	17.05	17.97	17.71	17.03
China (incl. Hong Kong)	3.20	3.52	3.98	5.09	5.22	5.28	5.07	5.03
Europe	14.46	14.44	13.70	15.18	15.19	17.24	18.78	20.78
Middle East	9.31	10.64	10.92	9.72	8.52	7.90	7.88	8.12
Latin America and Caribbean	5.34	5.98	6.55	6.61	6.64	6.75	6.68	6.54
Mercosur	1.44	1.64	1.80	2.13	2.53	2.93	2.91	3.19

Source: Based on IMF, *Direction of Trade Statistics Yearbook,* Washington, D.C., several issues.

countries declined from nearly 82 per cent to nearly 76 per cent. Thus, the concentration of trade among the so-called Triad powers is still strong but declining and the share of newly industrializing countries in Central and Eastern Europe, East and South-East Asia and Latin America has been increasing significantly.

Second, the USA was and still is by far the single most important trading partner of the EU, absorbing about 20 per cent of extra-EU exports. When including intra-EU trade, exports to the USA amounted to over 7 per cent of total EU exports in 1997.

Third, although Japan clearly is among the most important trade partners of the EU, the size of the bilateral trade flows between the two economies is relatively small, as compared to EU's trade with the USA. Exports to Japan amounted to less than 5 per cent of extra-EU exports and less than 2 per cent of total EU exports including intra-EU trade. Also, from the perspective of the Japanese economy, trade with the EU was of considerable less significance than trade with the USA.

Fourth, among the profound changes in the 1990s has been the transition in Central and Eastern Europe that has boosted trade and financial flows with the EU. Poland, Russia, the Czech Republic and Hungary have become important trade partners of the EU within a very short period of time. Moreover, Turkey –

also included in the category developing Europe in the table – has become an important trade partner of the Union as well.

Fifth, exports to Asia and particularly developing East- and South-East Asia expanded at a high rate. Among the countries in this region, China including Hong Kong has been the single most import destination of EU exports, by now comparable with Japan. Moreover, tiger economies such as South Korea, Singapore, Taiwan, Malaysia, Indonesia, as well as India have become important trade partners.

Sixth, trade relations with Latin America have been intensified, particularly with Mercosur. Over 60 per cent of EU exports to this region are concentrated in the three regional superpowers Brazil, Mexico and Argentina.

Seventh, the value of exports to Africa stagnated and the share of exports to that region in overall EU exports to the rest of the world declined sharply. Even exports to larger traditional trade partners in Northern Africa such as Morocco and Tunisia showed little dynamism or stagnated as was the case with Algeria. Export to the largest export market in the region, South Africa, was relatively dynamic and by now over 23 per cent of EU exports to Africa are concentrated in that country.

Eighth, the share of the Middle East in the total external trade of the Union declined as well. Saudi Arabia and Israel are the two most important destinations of EU exports in this region and trade with Israel in particular has been dynamic. Although the area is exceptionally well endowed with natural resources and has high import requirements, low oil prices, wars and trade embargoes have limited trade with the Union.

So, by the end of the 1990s, the USA, developing Europe and developing Asia have become three major trade partners of the EU of more or less equal size when measured according to EU exports. Altogether, the combined value of EU exports to Latin America and developing Asia now equals the combined EU exports to the Triad powers, the USA and Japan. Not only has the EU become more dependent on world markets, but its orientation has shifted towards the newly industrializing countries of Europe, Asia and America, which creates an entirely new context for the design and execution of a common external economic policy.

Next step in the analysis of the position of the EU in the world trade system is to investigate the position of EU suppliers in the major import markets of the world and compare changes in the EU position with the changing market shares of the USA, Japan and the group of developing countries in these selected markets (see Table 1.4). Changes in these import shares are related to changes in the composition of demand in importing countries and to the structure of supply and the competitiveness of EU producers in world markets, as well as to discrimination in imports that may result from membership of PTAs and other selective import measures. To distinguish these effects, however, a more disaggregated level of analysis is required which is beyond the scope of this chapter.

As Table 1.4 shows, the EU is by far the largest supplier of imports in the world economy, be it that its dominant position was reduced substantially during the 1990s: the share of total world imports, including intra-EU imports, supplied by the EU was 42 per cent in 1990 and 35 per cent in 1997. The position of the EU as a supplier of imports was particularly dominant in the markets of the EU itself, developing Europe, including the Central and Eastern European Countries(CEEC) and Turkey, Africa and the Middle East. EU market shares were particularly small in the rapidly growing market of developing Asia and in Japan. As is the case with the EU, the other two Triad powers have relatively dominant positions in the neigbouring developing regions: the USA in South America and Japan in Asia.

It is striking that the share of the EU in total imports in all regions without any exception declined during the 1990s. The decline was particularly dramatic in Africa, South America and in its own market. To a large extent the loss of market share for a traditional supplier with a dominant market position is inevitable in a period of globalization and export-orientated industrialization in newly industrializing countries. However, the significant decline of import market shares of the EU contrasts sharply with the growing share in supply of the USA and the more or less constant market share of Japan. As illustrated, the USA plays a dynamic role in the process of globalization and is the most successful of the three major industrial economies in penetrating foreign markets, and increasing its share in imports, particularly in South America including Mexico, the Middle East and the EU.

Finally, it may be noted that developing countries as a group increased their share of world supply of imports from 28 to 34 per cent in the course of the 1990s. By the end of the 1990s, their share in import supply in the markets of the USA and Japan exceeded by far their share in the market of developing countries themselves and in the EU market when measured including intra-EU import supply. When excluding intra-EU imports, the share of developing countries (including CEEC) in imports of the EU in 1997 is 54 per cent, nearly equal to

Table 1.4. World imports from the EU and selected regions, in percentages, 1990-97.

Supplier of imports	1990	1991	1992	1993	1994	1995	1996	1997
				World				
EU	42.08	40.90	40.75	36.22	36.18	36.82	36.25	34.74
USA	11.64	12.39	12.38	13.13	13.00	12.56	12.98	13.56
Japan	8.82	9.24	9.36	10.27	9.89	9.33	8.31	8.25
Developing countries	28.13	28.57	28.76	30.89	31.56	32.35	33.42	34.67
				EU				
EU	63.29	62.82	63.77	59.63	60.12	61.06	60.43	59.35
USA	7.34	7.60	7.28	7.86	7.74	7.43	7.70	8.34
Japan	4.37	4.56	4.55	4.76	4.34	4.02	3.68	3.71
Developing countries	18.21	18.68	17.97	20.20	20.31	20.29	21.05	21.86
				USA				
EU	20.00	18.97	18.93	18.18	17.99	17.75	18.03	18.10
Japan	18.00	18.66	18.00	18.40	17.77	16.50	14.42	13.83
Developing countries	41.13	41.37	42.33	41.74	43.01	44.37	45.80	46.83
				Japan				
EU	16.07	14.55	14.48	13.69	14.13	14.55	14.15	13.37
USA	22.46	22.67	22.63	23.15	23.01	22.59	22.86	22.43
Developing countries	49.62	51.17	51.64	52.29	52.25	52.84	53.83	54.79
				Developing Countries				
EU	27.52	25.95	25.65	24.30	23.64	23.67	23.89	22.49
USA	15.19	17.03	17.32	17.28	17.08	16.25	16.84	17.52
Japan	13.54	14.16	14.14	15.01	14.72	14.31	12.49	12.08
Developing countries	36.15	35.85	36.36	37.08	38.29	39.75	40.52	42.05

Source: Based on IMF, *Direction of Trade Statistics Yearbook,* Washington, D.C., several issues.

their share in Japan's imports and much higher than their share in the imports of the USA.

In line with the findings on the changing position of the EU in world import demand are the changes in the position of the EU in export supply of the major regions in the world economy, presented in Table 1.5. As shown, 44 per cent of all exports of the world, including intra-EU exports were destined to the market of the EU in 1990. In particular the exports of Africa and developing Europe

Table 1.5. Exports of selected regions to the EU, in percentages, 1990-97.

	1990	1991	1992	1993	1994	1995	1996	1997
Exporting region								
World	43.72	43.10	42.31	37.37	36.96	37.61	36.68	35.69
USA	26.33	25.71	24.08	21.98	21.03	21.19	20.47	20.48
Japan	20.41	20.36	19.74	16.61	15.48	15.88	15.35	15.61
Developing regions								
Africa	45.27	46.82	45.60	40.76	42.98	44.93	42.91	41.83
Asia	16.59	16.53	15.80	15.40	14.61	14.63	14.53	14.71
Europe	49.50	54.60	54.06	47.51	43.31	42.83	41.74	43.54
Middle East	28.45	26.62	25.03	23.91	23.46	22.99	22.45	20.32
Latin America and Caribbean	24.06	21.09	21.08	17.43	17.53	16.60	14.65	13.87

Source: Based on IMF, *Direction of Trade Statistics Yearbook,* Washington, D.C., several issues.

were orientated towards the EU market. However, the share of the EU in world exports declined to 36 per cent in 1997 and the EU became less dominant in the exports of all regions distinguished in the table.

The EU in world investment flows

Foreign direct investment (FDI) have come to play a critical role in the process of globalization and both outflows and inflows of FDI may contribute in a significant way to the strengthening of the position of countries and regions in the world economy and to their level of welfare. Traditionally, the countries in Western Europe have been major exporters of capital and large investors in each other's economies as well as in economies the world all over. Clearly, during the post World War II period, the USA has been the largest source of FDI outflows and host to foreign investors. However, when seen as an integrated group of countries, the EU has been the world's largest host to FDI since 1970 and the largest source of FDI since the mid 1970s.

Figures 1.6 and 1.7 show the size of total FDI outflows and inflows from 1970 to 1997, and Tables 1.6 and 1.7 show in a more disaggregated manner the positions of several regions in the world economy as home and host of foreign investors. Available data do not permit a presentation of worldwide bilateral flows

Figure 1.6. EU and world foreign direct investment outflows, in billions of current US dollars, 1970-97.

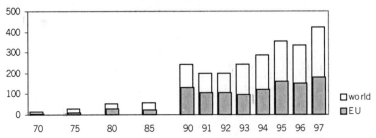

Source: Based on UN, *World Investment Report 1998: Trends and Determinants,* New York and Geneva, 1998 and UNCTAD, *Handbook of International Trade and Development Statistics, 1996/97,* New York and Geneva, 1999.

Figure 1.7. EU and world foreign direct investment inflows, in billions of current US dollars, 1970-97.

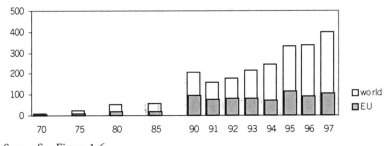

Source: See Figure 1.6.

between countries and regions but a series of observations can be made pertaining to the position of the EU on the basis of the data presented here.

To start with, the position of the EU as a source of FDI became increasingly dominant from the mid 1970s until 1990 and during this interval the EU surpassed the USA as the main source of FDI in the world economy. During the 1990s, however, the position of the EU declined in relative terms while the USA and East Asia contributed in a significant way to the process of globalization as sources of foreign investment. Remarkably, after the spectacular rise of Japan in the 1980s followed a sharp decline in the 1990s and during this decade the group of newly industrializing countries of East Asia surpassed Japan as a source of FDI.

Table 1.6. Shares of regions in world foreign direct investment outflows, 1970-97.

	1970	1975	1980	1985	1990	1991	1992	1993	1994	1995	1996	1997
EU	37.58	37.00	49.77	44.56	54.79	52.92	54.36	40.44	42.42	45.17	45.24	42.44
USA	56.21	50.87	35.10	14.76	11.28	16.68	19.41	31.07	25.77	26.12	22.43	27.03
Japan	2.59	6.29	4.36	11.22	20.96	15.77	8.66	5.74	6.37	6.39	7.02	6.13
Developing countries	0.16	1.1	2.85	8.67	6.73	5.54	10.32	14.50	14.96	12.95	14.74	14.43
North Africa	0.01	0.13	0.16	-0.00	0.05	0.07	0.02	0.01	0.03	0.03	0.01	0.01
Sub-Saharan Africa	..	0.04	0.08	2.37	0.54	0.42	0.24	0.33	0.21	0.14	0.08	0.26
Asia	0.01	0.15	0.82	4.72	5.10	4.16	8.70	12.63	12.51	11.86	14.20	11.84
Central and Eastern Europe	0.00	..	0.04	0.00	0.02	0.02	0.05	0.07	0.09	0.12	0.30	0.78
Latin America and Caribbean	0.14	0.42	0.68	1.39	1.22	1.04	0.69	1.17	1.83	0.67	0.68	2.15
Middle East	..	0.35	1.07	0.16	0.18	-0.17	0.65	0.34	0.38	0.23	-0.26	0.12

Source: See Figure 1.6.

Table 1.7. Shares of regions in world foreign direct investment inflows, 1970-97.

	1970	1975	1980	1985	1990	1991	1992	1993	1994	1995	1996	1997
EU	47.02	42.54	39.10	29.86	47.63	49.59	47.65	37.20	29.64	35.26	27.37	27.01
USA	11.56	11.03	31.01	34.92	23.60	14.31	10.74	20.01	18.56	17.75	22.65	22.66
Japan	0.83	0.99	0.51	1.12	0.85	1.09	1.57	0.10	0.37	0.01	0.07	0.81
Developing countries	19.61	37.74	26.19	27.17	16.78	26.22	29.07	33.33	39.33	31.86	38.45	37.19
North Africa	2.04	-1.91	0.24	2.48	0.54	0.56	0.90	0.73	0.97	0.38	0.39	0.45
Sub-Saharan Africa	0.90	3.62	0.34	2.53	0.61	1.18	0.90	0.95	1.37	1.17	1.04	0.72
Asia	5.48	7.38	5.88	8.02	9.78	13.33	15.83	21.95	24.35	20.57	23.61	21.23
Central and Eastern Europe	..	..	0.02	0.03	0.28	1.58	2.53	2.82	2.43	4.29	3.66	4.60
Latin America and Caribbean	10.50	17.23	13.51	12.61	4.52	9.63	10.02	7.93	11.81	9.64	12.96	14.02
Middle East	0.52	11.24	5.90	1.29	1.13	1.20	1.04	1.58	0.62	0.23	0.09	0.47

Source: See Figure 1.6.

Second, traditionally FDI flows form EU countries have been orientated to a high degree to each other's markets. However, in 1996 EU flows to the rest of the world more or less equalled intra-EU flows for the first time since 1989. It may be that further deepening of the EU integration process and the introduction of the euro may increase the attractiveness of the EU for foreign investors and stimulate intra-EU outflows in the future. The USA has traditionally been the largest receiver of EU FDI outside the EU. During the 1990s, however, the improvement of the investment climate in the CEEC, the strong growth of Asia - apart from the Asian crisis - and privatization programmes the world all over attracted EU investors and stimulated the outward orientation of the overall EU investment performance. According to the World Investment Report 1998 (pp. 156 and 157) the share of developing countries in total EU FDI outflows increased from 10 per cent in 1991 to 14 per cent in 1993 and 17 per cent in 1996 and the EU is catching up in Latin America - particularly Brazil, Mexico and Argentina - and East Asia.

Third, the EU has also been the largest receiver of FDI in the world economy, up to 50 per cent of total world inflows of foreign investment in 1991. Notwithstanding significant progress made in the deepening of the EU market, the lack of dynamism of the EU during the first half of the 1990s made it a less attractive region to invest. During this period, net inflows of FDI even declined in nominal terms and the share of EU in world FDI inflows declined to 27 per cent in 1997. Hence, the very substantial gap between the EU and USA in terms of FDI inflow at the beginning of the 1990s was reduced significantly at the end of the decade.

Fourth, during the 1990s investors diversified their investment, resulting in a strong increase of the flows received by East Asia, Latin America and the CEEC. East Asia has become a new centre of gravity in world investment flows and China including Hong Kong attracted nearly 12 per cent of total world FDI in 1997. Initially, Japanese FDI was strongly concentrated in East Asia but increasingly the region attracted flows from all over the world, most notably from the USA, EU and East Asian investors abroad, particularly Hong Kong, Singapore, Taiwan and South Korea.

Also, the reform programmes in Latin America emphasizing strongly the liberalization of trade and investment and privatization, in combination with intra-regional integration and the establishment of PTAs with the USA and the EU, have contributed to a marked improvement of the investment climate in the region and the attraction of substantial investment flows from the USA and the EU.

Finally, the investment positions of countries in North Africa, Sub-Saharan Africa and the Middle East were marginalized.

These significant long-term developments with respect to the position of the EU in world income, international trade and investment are the context of the policy initiatives and proposals that are the main topic of this book and that aim at the strengthening of the position of the EU in the world economy.

3. The growth of the external economic powers of the EU

The European Community (EC) and its predecessors were traditionally almost exclusively focused on economic issues[1]. The task of the European Economic Community (EEC) was to create a common market between the member states as laid down in Art. 2 of the Treaty establishing the EEC. This entailed:
(1) the abolition of all internal trade barriers and the introduction of a common customs tariff (CCT) with respect to imports from third countries, and
(2) the implementation of the basic freedoms, i.e., the free movement of workers, freedom of establishment, freedom to provide services and the free movement of capital.

Thus, the EC has had the disposal of powers to conduct an external economic policy from the start.

The original EEC Treaty also created special relationships with the dependent overseas countries and territories of some member countries, including reciprocal trade preferences and foreign aid. At a later stage, the CCT was supplemented with many other instruments such as quotas, voluntary export restraints (VERs), tariff preferences, anti-dumping duties, variable levies and export subsidies. The growth of the number of trade-policy instruments has been a reflection of the ongoing integration process. Thus, the introduction of the Common Agricultural Policy (CAP) gave rise to the use of variable levies and export subsidies. Also, the introduction of a common development policy resulted in the establishment of systems of trade preferences for several groups of developing countries. Anti-dumping duties and VERs may be considered instruments of a common industrial policy. Agreements with many countries and groups of countries have been concluded by the EC, most of them containing trade-policy measures as their most important substantive elements.

As the integration process widened in scope, the external powers and instruments of the EC were widened as well, be it that this process was sometimes accompanied by conflicts between the Commission and the Council on questions pertaining to the competence of institutions and on matters of procedure.

The main objective of the Single European Act (1987) was the completion of the Internal Market. It also expanded the competence of the Community in the areas of social, environmental, research and development policies. The programme to complete the Internal Market was a landmark in the sense that it definitely moved the integration process from the abolition of border measures to the removal of administrative barriers to trade in goods, services and capital. As a result, differences among member countries in their national standards pertaining to the protection of workers, consumers and the environment were brought into the orbit of the EC's approximation process, as such differences could mitigate the impact of the abolition of internal borders.

The deepening of liberalization and the widening of the scope of common policies has given the Community institutions parallel powers in the external relations. The European Commission has conducted negotiations on diverse subjects such as international environmental agreements and food standards, although member states often are represented as well. The Community handles the expanding agenda of the WTO, although the European Court of Justice ruled in 1994 that agreements on services are mixed agreements to be ratified by the Community as well as the individual member states. The fact that both the EC and its member states have joined the WTO has given rise to controversy and confusion (Van den Bossche, 1997).

The Treaty on European Union, signed in Maastricht in 1992, gave a boost to the process of economic integration. A timetable for an Economic and Monetary Union (EMU) including convergence criteria and the introduction of a common currency was laid down. In May 1998 the European Council decided to start the final phase of the EMU in 1999 with 11 member countries. Here again, the internal integration will have a large impact on the external competence of the Union. A unified monetary policy and a euro that will take the position of an international currency second only to the US dollar will inevitably increase the impact of the monetary and macro-economic policies in the euro area on third countries, as will be discussed in Section 4 below. In addition, the EU is bound to have the capability and the responsibility to play a crucial role in international monetary co-operation.

The Treaty on European Union expanded the external capabilities of the EU in other areas as well by providing the formal foundation for a common policy of development co-operation. The introduction of Community action in the areas of industry, education, vocational training and youth, public health, consumer protection and culture will give the EC a larger capability to act internationally in these areas. The same holds for the Community policy with respect to the protection of the environment, which was further reinforced by the Treaty on European Union.

The most immediate expansion of the capability of European institutions to act internationally was the establishment of the Common Foreign and Security Policy (CFSP). The CFSP was conceived as the second pillar of the European Union (EU), the EC and the Cooperation in the fields of Justice and Home Affairs being the first and third pillar respectively.

The objective of the CFSP is to assert the identity of the EU at the international level in common foreign and security matters including the eventual framing of a common defence policy, which might in time lead to a common defence, as laid down in Art. 2 of the Treaty on European Union (ex Art. B). The member states will consult each other, define common positions 'whenever necessary', co-ordinate their actions in international organizations and conferences and undertake joint actions, as laid down in Art. 11 and 12 of the Treaty on European Union (ex Art. J.1 and J.2).

An important distinction between the EC and the other two pillars is that decision making in the latter pillars is mainly intergovernmental whereas decisions in the EC are arrived at after a proposal by the Commission has been adopted by the Council - by majority voting in an increasing number of areas - and after consent or consultation of the European Parliament.

After more than 40 years, the EC has developed into a credible international actor, capable to define its goals and to act accordingly. In contrast, in issues of foreign and security policy, the EU has great difficulty in stating its objectives, let alone pooling and using the available instruments (Regelsberger and Wessels, 1996).

As this volume studies the external economic relations of the EU, it will focus in particular on the policies, decisions and procedures in the first pillar, the EC. However, a link may grow between the first and second pillar. As put in Art. 3 of the Treaty on European Union (ex Art. C)

'The Union shall in particular ensure the consistency of its external activities as a whole in the context of its external relations, security, economic and development policies. The Council and the Commission shall be responsible for ensuring such consistency and shall co-operate to this end. They shall ensure the implementation of these policies, each in accordance with its respective powers'.

In a coherent foreign policy, economic instruments will be used as part of a broader policy framework. Economic support including aid and improved market access may stimulate the peaceful settlement of conflicts in and among third countries. Alternatively, economic sanctions can be imposed to influence the behaviour of third countries without using military means. In a coherent foreign policy framework formulated around a set of instruments that can be put on a scale ranging from purely beneficial to third countries - the case of financial gifts - to highly damaging - the case of military intervention - the economic instruments will be more effective than if used in an isolated, haphazard way.

4. The EMU and the world economy

The launching of the EMU on 1 January 1999 and the introduction of the euro as the common currency of the 11 member states participating in the EMU in 2001 may have a profound impact on the external position of the EU. As shown in Section 2 of this chapter, the size of the EU economy is comparable to the US economy in terms of purchasing power and even larger in some other respects. This implies that the euro may play an international role comparable to the US dollar, depending on EMU membership, strength and stability of the euro and the extent to which the EMU members operate unitedly in international economic institutions. Although this subject matter will not be part of the analysis presented in this volume and is surrounded by many uncertainties at this very early stage of the introduction of the euro, the most relevant issues will be referred to briefly in this section.

The effects of the EMU on the international economic relations stem from three sources. First, the euro will fulfil the three economic functions of all national currencies: store of value, unit of account and means of payment. Second, the international monetary system will change from a US dollar-dominated system to a bicurrency system. Third, the EMU will have spillovers to third countries.

It is likely that the demand for euros for portfolio purposes (to use euros as a store of value) will grow in the long run compared to the demand in the pre-EMU stage for the currencies of the countries in the euro area. Private investors will increase their holdings of euro-denominated assets as a result of the deepening and broadening of EU capital markets and the reduction of transaction costs as a result of the substitution of the euro for national currencies (IMF, 1997). However, other forces are at work as well. The economic performance of the EU, the stability of the euro relative to other currencies, and the policy stance of the European Central Bank (ECB) are perhaps even more important factors having an impact on the returns on investment and thus for the attractiveness of holding euros. To the extent that the EMU is a 'safer haven' than before in times of monetary instability, euro-denominated assets will become more attractive.

Central banks demand euros as international monetary reserves, partly in order to make interventions but also to diversify their reserve holdings in line with the currency composition of their trade. The gradual decline of the US dollar as a reserve currency - from 80 per cent of global reserves of foreign exchange in 1975 to 56 per cent in 1996 - will continue or even accelerate.

About half of world trade is invoiced in US dollars, due to the fact that the USA has a large share in world trade and prices of many standardized commodities such as oil are put in US dollars. The absence of exchange-rate risks has large advantages for US companies that invoice in US dollars. Although these traditions and habits will change only slowly, it is likely that the euro will gain importance as an international unit of account. EMU firms are expected to invoice exclusively in euros. Companies in countries that trade mainly with the EU - the CEEC and MENA countries - will probably do the same. Large companies that have a substantial presence in the EU may opt for the euro as the company unit of account. Again, many of these shifts to the euro will take time.

Commercial banks involved in international payments between importers and exporters use the US dollar as a vehicle or intermediate currency, since transaction costs in US dollar exchanges are much lower than in exchanges between less current currencies, as the US dollar market is 'thicker' (Alogoskoufis and Portes, 1997). The euro market will be much 'thicker' than the separate markets of the pre-EMU currencies, and as a result the use of the euro as a vehicle currency is bound to increase. To the extent that the euro is more intensively used as a store of value, the 'thickness' of the euro market will further increase, thus enhancing the opportunities for the euro to be used as a vehicle currency. As the functions of money as a means of payment and a unit of account are strongly linked, it is likely that the euro will eventually become the dominant currency in Europe and its neighbouring regions in the east and south.

For individual EMU countries, international trade – the average of exports and imports - constitutes about 45 per cent of GDP, which characterizes these economies as very open. When considering the EU as one integrated economy, this percentage is reduced to about 15 per cent, comparable to the degree of openness of the USA or Japan. Thus, domestic - that is intra-EU - factors are the most significant to be taken into account when formulating monetary policy at the level of the EMU. Policy makers at the ECB might be less concerned about exchange-rate movements than their colleagues in the pre-EMU era used to be. In that period, however, the currencies of the countries participating in the EMU floated collectively *vis-à-vis* the US dollar and the yen which, after all, makes, the new situation less different from the past and the risk of benign neglect in the future less likely as well (IMF, 1997).

Nevertheless, an international monetary system dominated by two currencies rather than one could be relatively unstable. In theory, macro-economic policy co-ordination between the EU and the USA could produce a higher level of welfare for the participating countries. However, the costs of co-ordination could be very high as the experiences with the Louvre and Plaza Agreements in the 1980s show. To stabilize the exchange rate between the US dollar and the euro, a high degree of transatlantic agreement on macro-economic variables including budget-deficits and the growth of money supply will be required. Because of advancements in technology and communications that have speeded up capital mobility and created global financial markets, those fixed rates may only be defended at very high costs.

The introduction of the euro may have several spill-over effects. First, for the USA, the expected reduction of the international role of the US dollar will reduce the seigniorage from US dollar holdings by non-US residents. It is estimated that these foreign holdings provide annual savings for the USA of 10 to 15 billion US dollar of interest on treasury securities (IMF, 1997). The preference of foreigners to hold US dollar assets makes it easier for the USA to finance balance-of-payments deficits, so-called deficits without tears. On the other hand, the EMU is expected to increase the liquidity of global financial markets, which will lower borrowing costs for all countries, including the USA.

Second, countries that have pegged their currency to an EU currency such as African countries in the Communauté Financière Africaine (the CFA franc zone) and certain CEEC with a peg to or a strong relationship with the deutsche mark, have to decide whether to peg to the euro. Particularly highly indebted countries may suffer from a depreciation of the euro, as the domestic costs of debt service would rise probably without fully offsetting benefits in the trade account.

On the other hand, the EMU offers countries with access to private capital the opportunity of a deeper market in which they can diversify their debts in accordance with their exchange rate peg. For CFA countries that import much more from France than they export to that country, the euro contributes to the reduction of the mismatch between imports and exports in terms of invoice currency.

Regarding the future position of the euro in the world economy the following conclusions are drawn from the observations made above. First, the euro is likely to become a reserve currency in the medium to long run as it fulfils the three functions of international money. Second, as a consequence, the international monetary system will be changed in a fundamental way. The system will probably become less stable while offering a larger potential influence for the EU. Comprehensive co-ordination of macro-economic and monetary policies between the EU and the USA is unlikely. Third, the euro will in all likelihood become the first reserve currency in Europe and its neighbouring countries. Fourth, countries that are pegged to one or more of the pre-EMU currencies - mainly countries in East and Central Europe and Africa - are in a position to peg to the euro which is more stable. Only countries that are highly indebted in US dollar terms and do not have access to private capital markets to float euro-denominated bonds will suffer from a depreciation of the euro.

5. The EU as an aid donor

The EU has become an important donor of financial aid to developing countries over the last 15 years. Table 1.8 shows that the EU disbursements as shares of total official development assistance (ODA) of the members of the OECD Development Assistance Committee (DAC) increased from 5 per cent in 1986/ 87 to nearly 11 per cent in 1997. The EU aid programme increased at an average annual rate of 3.3 per cent during the period 1993 - 1997, while total ODA disbursements decreased by 4.7 per cent annually.

Table 1.8. ODA disbursed by the EU, 1986/87 - 1997.

	1986/87	1994	1995	1996	1997
Millions of US dollars	1925	4825	5398	5455	5261
Shares of total DAC ODA (%)	5.0	8.2	9.2	9.8	10.9
Shares of ODA of member states (%)	10.4	15.9	17.2	17.4	19.8

Source: OECD, *DAC Review 1998*, Paris, 1998.

Also, the share of funds channelled by EU member countries through the EU increased from 10 per cent in 1986/87 to nearly 20 per cent in 1997, which turned the EU into the fifth ODA donor among the 22 members of the OECD DAC.

The geographical distribution of the ODA disbursed by the EU shifted distinctively over the past 10 years. As Table 1.9 shows, the shares of regions bordering the EU - countries in Europe, mainly the CEEC, and the MENA group - increased from 13.7 to 30 per cent, while the share of Sub-Saharan Africa declined from 57.3 in 1986/87 to 42.8 per cent in 1996/97. Although aid to countries in South America increased in relative terms as well, this was far less pronounced, while the share of Asia remained more or less the same. As a consequence of these shifts, the share of the least-developed countries declined from about half to one third of the EU's ODA. This changing emphasis in the distribution of aid reflects the more general and profound changes in the external economic relations of the EU that are analysed in this volume.

6. Changes in the external trade policies of the EU

Major changes are discernable in the ways the EU has been using its trade-policy instruments, be it that these changes have been implemented gradually. This section will focus on three types of change in the trade policies of the EU:
(1) the liberalization of the trade regime of the EU since 1990;
(2) the enlargement of the EU towards Central and Eastern Europe, and
(3) a shift from the use of non-reciprocal to reciprocal regional trade agreements with third countries.

Table 1.9. Regional distribution of gross disburse-
        ments of ODA by the EU, in percentages,
        1986/87 and 1996/97.

Recipient groups	1986/87	1996/97
Europe	6.3	11.2
North Africa	5.9	12.0
Sub-Saharan Africa	57.3	42.8
North and Central America	5.2	8.0
South America	3.9	4.4
Middle East	1.5	6.8
South and Central Asia	10.6	9.1
East and South East Asia	3.8	4.3
Oceania	5.3	1.4
Least-developed countries	50.9	33.2

Source: See Table 1.8.

Liberalization of the trade regime

At the global level, the EU has been one of the main players in international trade negotiations and has been actively involved in the General Agreement on Tariffs and Trade (GATT) and its successor, the WTO. This has resulted in a gradual reduction of barriers to imports from third countries, particularly in a lowering of import tariffs on manufactured products. The simple average tariff rate will be bound by the EU at 3.2 per cent after implementation of the agreement reached during the Uruguay Round, and the applied rate will be at 2.8 per cent, equal to the rates applied by the USA and Japan. Moreover, 100 per cent of the EU import tariffs are bound.

Other barriers to trade appeared to be much more difficult to reduce. During economic downturns in the 1970s and 1980s in particular, new NTBs were introduced by many industrialized countries. The EC introduced an extensive system of VERs, many in the context of the Multi-Fibre Arrangements (MFA). Clothing, textiles, cars, steel were the sectors most frequently and extensively protected by these instruments. In addition EU member states used national quotas, thus breaking up the unity of the Common Commercial Policy (CCP) (Hine, 1985).

The Uruguay Round resulted in a strengthening of the multilateral rule system at the institutional level by establishing the World Trade Organization (WTO) and by liberalizing in a substantial way international economic transactions, not only in the traditional area of tariffs on manufactured products, but in the areas of NTBs, services and agriculture as well. The Round coincided with two remarkable developments in the EU that took place in the early 1990s: the completion of the Internal Market and an economic downturn that hit many member states more than any other post-war recession. These developments inspired many observers inside and outside the EU to predict the emergence of a 'Fortress Europe'. Intensified competition as a result of the introduction of the Internal Market was expected to increase pressures for external protection and the recession would fuel these pressures even more. Contrary to these expectations, however, the external trade barriers applied by the EU decreased in the first half of the 1990s.

The continuous drive towards liberalization may be explained in part by the fact that the Internal Market made trade-policy measures by member countries ineffective while the introduction of compensating and new EU protectionism had become difficult as a result of the institutional arrangements that have created a very strong bargaining position for the member countries with the most liberal preferences in trade policy (Hanson, 1998).

It may be concluded that the completion of the Internal Market constitutes a further example of the thesis that regional integration can support rather than hinder multilateral liberalization (Van Dijck and Faber, 1996). The implementation of the concessions and decisions as laid down in the Marrakesh Agreement of 1994 will result in a further substantial reduction of EU trade barriers and particularly of NTBs and agricultural protection.

Enlargement of the EU

The second important change in trade policy is the enlargement of the EU towards Central and Eastern Europe. Up to the moment of full membership, the EU-CEEC relationships will be part of the external relations of the EU. The process of enlargement changes the Union both in the stage preceding and after accession of the new members. These changes relate to the Union as an institution, its capability to take and implement decisions as well as the substance of the decisions. Increasing the number of member states to 25 or more requires changes in the EU's decision-making structures and procedures that were initially designed for six member states only. The Intergovernmental Conference (IGC) that came to an end in 1997 with the Treaty of Amsterdam, did not bring the required institutional reform. As a consequence of this failure, the capacity to formulate and implement common external actions has declined. Moreover, the accession of CEEC will expand the number of member states at a relatively low level of economic development which will have an impact on the positions the EU will take in international trade negotiations.

More specifically, one may question whether the new members will attempt to make the EU more protectionist regarding sunset industries, such as clothing, shipbuilding and steel, which still contribute in a substantial way to their industrial structures. Some elements of the answer to this question are becoming visible. Although it is likely that the next enlargement will give rise to a further differentiation of membership, as discussed by Andriessen in Chapter 4 of this volume, the Common Commercial Policy (CCP) will remain a unified common policy, as it is one of the foundations of the common market.

The same applies for the CAP. The amendment of the CAP has been inspired to a large extent by the enlargement of the Union. By making the CAP less protectionist, the costs of the policy declines, and even more so in the post-enlargement period as the CEEC have a large potential to produce the traditionally highly protected products such as grains. Moreover, the free trade areas (FTAs) between the EU and the CEEC that have been in force for a number of years, have a large impact on the latter countries by intensifying competition. By the time the CEEC will be full members of the EU, they will be used to the intra-EU level of competition. This makes it likely that protectionist pressures by the new members in the post-enlargement period will focus on those products that are not produced by the present members of the EU and that are highly protected in the CEEC against competition from third countries. To the extent that the CEEC introduce the CCP before they become full members, this possibility is reduced.

Reciprocity in preferential trade agreements

A third major change in EU trade policy is related to the introduction of reciprocity in preferential trade agreements (PTAs). Traditionally, there have been three layers of preferential treatment of third countries. First, 71 countries in Africa, the Caribbean and the Pacific - most of them relatively small former colonies of the member states and known as the ACP group – have had almost free access to the market of the EU under the Lomé Convention, with the exception of temperate-zone agricultural products including fruit and vegetables, sugar, rum and beef, for which special preferential rules have been established. Second, preferential agreements have been concluded with most countries in the Middle East and North Africa - the MENA countries - which provide for free access to the EU market with exceptions for sensitive manufactures and agricultural products. Third, the EU has a unilateral Generalized System of Preferences (GSP) in favour of the exports from other developing countries.

The common characteristic of these trade preferences was non-reciprocity: the developing countries concerned were not required to give the EU preferential treatment in return. This policy is now changing under the influence of the enlargement of EU membership, increasing openness of the EU economy, soaring competition in world markets, stronger rule enforcement by the WTO and disappointment with the outcomes of non-reciprocal preferences. Hence, non-reciprocal systems are giving way to reciprocal arrangements, such as FTAs and customs unions (CU), as illustrated in Table 1.10. If the present trend persists, the GSP could well be the only non-reciprocal preferential system in the end, then mainly benefiting least-developed countries.

It may be argued that reciprocal systems have the advantage of putting preferential access at a firm footing, as withdrawal of preferential access may be reciprocated. Furthermore, the EU hopes to promote development and integration of the partner countries into the world economy. Although the partner countries probably would be better off by liberalizing multilaterally, the political economy of liberalization may make the multilateral road more difficult to follow. Reciprocal trade agreements could function as an anchor for trade reforms, which are often part of a broader reform package.

In a more structural way, the shift to reciprocity should be seen in the context of the changing position of the EU in the world economy. As shown earlier, the weight of the EU in the world economy is declining, the share of Asia and Latin America in EU trade is increasing and trade among the Triad powers - the EU, USA and Japan - is declining in relative terms. The role of the EU as a trader with emerging markets in Asia and Latin America is still relatively limited, while the EU has dominant positions in the stagnating markets of its former African colonies and the Mediterranean region. Introduction of reciprocity in trade agreements is a step to strengthen the position of the EU in international markets.

Table 1.10. The changing nature of preferential trade arrangements between the EU and third countries.

	Reciprocal	*Non-reciprocal*

Discriminating	-Turkey, Malta, Cyprus,
	-New MENA Agreements
	-CEEC (Europe Agreements)
	-European Economic Area
	-EU/South Africa FTA
	-Future: EU-ACP PTAs, PTAs
	  with Mexico, Mercosur, Chile
		-Previous Lomé conventions,
		-Pre-1995 MENA association
		  agreements

Non-discriminating	GATT/WTO agreements	GSP (non-graduated developing countries)

Source: G. Faber, N. Duykers and H. Roelfsema, *The EU Preferential Regime towards Developing Countries: Law versus Economics?*, Utrecht, 1998.

For a long time, the EU was in the comfortable position to protect parts of its own market from foreign competition - mainly from Japan and Asia - while it could open up other segments of its markets in return for improved access to the markets of its most important trading partners in the group of OECD countries. Its preferential partners in the Mediterranean region and the ACP countries were not putting competitive pressure on EU producers.

In the present situation, this strategy does no longer generate the required results. To stay an economic world power, the EU requires good access to fast-growing markets. However, the emerging markets are becoming strong negotiating partners in the WTO and are at the same time establishing PTAs at the regional level. This may result in discrimination against the EU and loss of competitiveness of EU export industries in these markets (Paemen, 1996).

In this context, reciprocal trade arrangements may offer three advantages to the EU. First, they guarantee market access to the emerging markets in Asia and Latin America. Second, they give a secure market access to the traditionally 'preferred' partners that may eventually develop into fast-growing markets in the future. Third, reciprocal regional trade agreements may pave the way for multilateral liberalization.

It may be concluded that the external economic policies of the EU are strongly biased towards neighbouring countries. This regional preference has given rise to a number of regional trade agreements. In the first decade of the 21st century, the

EU will increase its membership to include most of the countries of Central and Eastern Europe. In addition, the geographical distribution of aid disbursements by the EU has shifted in favour of neighbouring areas at the expense of Sub-Saharan Africa. The euro will further cement this regional orientation as firms and public authorities in the neighbouring countries are expected to use the euro as a unit of account and a means of payment at an early date.

At the same time, however, a range of new trade policy initiatives has been taken, involving several groups of countries in Asia, Africa and Latin America. Moreover, the Union has been playing an active role at the multilateral level, thus reducing the risk of 'closed regionalism'. The EU has lowered its external trade barriers substantially in a time of internal liberalization and is preparing for more multilateral liberalization in the Millennium Round of the WTO. The relationship between the regional and multilateral approach in the EU trade policy will be the subject of the next section.

7. Efficiency and effectiveness of EU trade policies

This section will focus on the objectives that the EU pursues in its external economic policies and on the related question whether the policy instruments are appropriate to achieve these policy objectives.

Policy objectives of the EU

The objectives of the EU in its external economic relations derive from the general goal of the EU, viz. 'economic and social progress and a high level of employment' as referred to in Art. 2 of the Treaty on European Union (ex Art. B). According to Art. 131 of the Treaty establishing the EC (ex Art. 110) the aim of the EU's CCP is 'to contribute, in the common interest, to the harmonious development of world trade, the progressive abolition of restrictions on international trade and the lowering of customs barriers'.

It needs no elaboration that the protectionist measures introduced under the Common Agricultural Policy (CAP), the use of NTBs and more specifically the MFA and anti-dumping measures are counterproductive in relation to the general objective of the EU and the more specific CCP objectives, when put in a long-term time frame. The high degree of protection in these sectors reduces overall welfare of the EU and its trade partners. However, the EU has agreed in the Uruguay Round to start liberalizing the CAP and to dismantle the MFA.

It is not entirely clear whether the strong emphasis on reciprocal PTAs in the external economic policies of the EU is an effective way to realize the cited aims of economic and social progress and multilateral liberalization. Bhagwati (1996, pp. 54-55) argues that

'... FTAs seriously damage the trade liberalization process by facilitating the capture of it by extraneous demands that aim, not to reduce trade barriers, but to increase them (as when market access is sought to be denied on grounds such as "eco-dumping" and "social dumping")'[2].

As reciprocal PTAs - and FTAs in particular - play such a predominant role in the external strategy of the EU and are one of the central themes of this volume, these arrangements are analysed in this section in a broader way in terms of their potential economic and non-economic effects.

The aims of the EU's regional initiatives have been laid down in the agreements that form the framework for these regional relations. The Europe Agreements refer in Art. 1 to the development of close political ties as their first aim, together with the promotion of the expansion of trade and harmonious economic relations between the parties, the economic development of the partner countries and integration into the Community.

The Barcelona Declaration mentions the same mix of political and economic objectives: peace, stability and security of the Mediterranean region, the creation of an area of shared prosperity and the promotion of understanding between the peoples and improving their perception of each other.

The stated objective of the Lomé Convention - Art. 1 of the fourth version - is 'to promote the economic, cultural and social development of the ACP states and to consolidate and diversify their relations'.

The EEA agreement puts emphasis on economic objectives of trade and welfare and much less on political aims.

The Interregional Framework Co-operation Agreement between the EU and Mercosur refers to the significance of economic co-operation and the establishment of PTAs as well as to the need of a political dialogue and co-operation in several other areas including education and training. Co-operation aims at the expansion of the economies involved and of their competitiveness, at fostering technical and scientific development, improving standards of living and establishing conditions conducive to employment creation.

Thus, the aims are economic - promoting economic development - and sometimes political - predominantly in the neighbouring regions in the south and in the east - and the instruments are particularly economic - trade preferences, financial aid and technical co-operation. The capability of the EU to use political instruments is still rather weak. As the EU's economic instruments are mainly used to establish PTAs, the issues of the efficiency and effectiveness of trade policies boil down to the question whether these PTAs are efficient and effective instruments to achieve the objectives of their participants. A brief review of the economic literature may be an appropriate way to start answering this question.

Rationale and effects of PTAs from an economic perspective

The economic effects of participation in a PTA are traditionally analysed in terms of the static Vinerian trade-creation and trade-diversion effects under perfect competition. Whereas trade creation contributes to overall economic welfare, trade diversion may be considered the costs of participation in a discriminatory trade-liberalization agreement. In general, empirical analyses that are confined to the quantification of these static effects, show positive but only small welfare effects. This holds particularly for large economies as shown in many *ex-ante* and *ex-post* studies of the integration process of the EC (Winters in Chapter 9 of this volume, and DeRosa, 1998). Such findings make it difficult to comprehend why countries would engage in lengthy and often troublesome negotiations on participation in a PTA.

More sophisticated types of analysis may distinguish additional effects and a larger contribution to welfare. When firms operate under decreasing marginal cost curves rather than increasing costs and liberalization of trade gives rise to intra-industry rather than inter-industry patterns of specialization, different effects may take place. Exploitation of economies of scale may result in price reductions and contribute to the competitiveness of industries. These cost-reduction effects may be added to the production and consumption gains identified in the traditional models of integration. Moreover, the establishment of a PTA may have a 'pro-competitive' effect and may reduce the price mark-up enjoyed by firms operating in less than perfectly competitive markets (DeRosa, 1998).

Also, the PTA may have the effect of contributing to the concentration of production in relatively large markets within the trade area. In sectors characterized by economies of scale, large countries may have a locational advantage over smaller countries. Firms in large countries may operate at a lower cost level per unit of product due to a larger production volume in the pre-PTA stage compared to firms in the small country, even when the production function of the former firm reflects higher average costs per unit of product at similar levels of production. Hence, this is a case of 'perverse' specialization. As indicated by Krugman, concentration of production lowers average costs but may increase the costs of transportation and marketing. Consequently, if a significant share of production is destined for other industries, industries will cluster their activities, presumably in the larger countries (Krugman, 1991 and Baldwin, 1994).

In addition, foreign-investment creation and diversion may be distinguished. Foreign investment may be induced by the increased size of the integrated market, particularly so if tariff reductions on intra-trade are accompanied by complementary measures to deepen the integration of the countries participating in the PTA. These investment flows may be diverted away from non-member countries to avoid the effects of trade diversion (WTO, 1995).

On top of these effects, terms-of-trade effects may be distinguished that may contribute to the welfare of the members of the PTA at the expense of non-member countries.

It is hard to assess which of these potential effects predominate. Recent model studies of the effects of integration processes in Europe and North America show widely differing results depending on the specifications of the models and their time dimensions. Inclusion of the effects of imperfect competition and increasing returns to scale, investments and international transfers of factor incomes may all contribute to the significance of participation in a PTA, as appears from such studies. Gasiorek, Smith and Venables (1992) and Harrison, Rutherford and Tarr (1994) made model studies of integration in Europe, and Brown (1992) and Hinojosa-Ojeda and Robinson (1992) modelled the effects of NAFTA.

However, it should be stressed that many of the effects referred to above such as exploitation of economies of scale and the pro-competitiveness effects are not specifically related to participation in a PTA but may also be realized in the context of multilateral trade liberalization.

Clearly, these models do not intend to quantify broader and non-economic objectives of PTAs. As noted by Winters in Chapter 9 of this volume, large partners in PTAs such as the EU seek particularly political benefits while the smaller partners have economic objectives. More specifically Winters distinguishes four sets of motivations for the EU for its various PTAs including community with its neighbours, stimulation of economic stability and overall development in neighbouring countries, and the defence of markets and reversal of trade discrimination. These benefits are very hard to quantify, which seriously frustrates the making of comprehensive assessments of this critical dimension of the external economic policies of the EU.

Combining membership of PTAs and the WTO

When analysing the preference of a country for participation in a PTA in the context of the country's membership of the WTO, three additional observations may be made on the rationale and effects of membership of a PTA. First, membership of a PTA may add to the concessions made in the WTO with respect to border measures. Second, it may contribute to the deepening of integration and facilitate the exploitation of potential gains from trade. Third, it may help to 'lock in' open macro-economic policies.

To start with, the members of the PTA offer each other tariff concessions on the basis of reciprocity in addition to their GATT/WTO concessions and obligations. In doing so, they have to observe the rules as laid down in Art. XXIV of the GATT and the Understanding on the Interpretation of Article XXIV. The WTO requires that the concessions offered by members of newly established PTAs must be comprehensive, liberalizing 'substantially all the trade' and must be implemented within a reasonable length of time, that is, within ten years (GATT, 1994). In this way PTAs may contribute in a substantial way to the liberalization of trade in areas where the WTO has not yet made much progress such as agriculture and services. This holds particularly for large WTO members.

Second, a PTA may facilitate international trade-related arrangements and the creation of a 'level-playing field' for regional trade, outside and beyond the existing framework of the WTO. Cases in point are product-related and process-related standards, rules pertaining to domestic policies in the areas of agriculture and services, trade-related investment measures and rules pertaining to international property rights. In some cases, such arrangements may anticipate arrangements in a multilateral framework, but this need not always be the case.

Most PTAs focus initially on the reduction of barriers to trade at the border but these trade-related policy measures may be complemented by measures to deepen the process of integration at a later stage. The rationale and impact of deepening integration is hard to assess. Regional as well as multilateral harmonization or unification of standards may contribute to welfare but this is not necessarily the case as has been argued in the literature on the harmonization of labour and environmental standards (Srinivasan, 1996 and Leebron, 1997). It may even be part of the trade strategy of a dominant partner in the PTA to set regional standards and rules in such a manner that they contribute to the diversion of trade to the benefit of the dominant partner and at the expense of other countries inside and outside the PTA. Finally, it need to be observed that a level-playing field may also be established outside the context of a PTA. APEC and ASEM may become cases in point.

The third additional objective of participating in a PTA, distinguished above, is related to the credibility of open macro-economic policies. The PTA may help to 'lock in' liberalization by generating additional revenues of reforms in the short term and increasing the domestic economic and political costs of deviations from the new policy direction in the future. This may hold true particularly in the case of a small country in transition participating in a PTA with a large trade partner such as the EU.

It should be noted, however, that participation in a PTA is not necessarily a first-best policy and need not necessarily reflect the country's priorities. Policies of neighbouring countries or other trade partners may induce a country to opt for bilateral or groupwise rather than unilateral or multilateral liberalization. This may be the case when a potentially major trade partner uses or threatens to use significant import barriers to products for which the country has a comparative advantage. A country may also be induced to participate in a PTA to avoid the trade-diversion effects from which it suffers as an outsider.

Thus, by enforcing and complementing the domestic process of liberalization, and by enlarging the market accessible for producers, PTAs, on top of WTO membership, may improve the macro-economic framework for investors, and by doing so, contribute to the sustainability of overall economic growth. This holds especially for participation in a PTA with one or more countries that pursue stable, open macro-economic policies and have a large domestic market as is the case with the EU and the USA. These effects may be enlarged further by bilateral agreements on investments.

Models to create PTAs and their consequences

Two basic models may be distinguished to establish PTAs among a group of countries. In the first approach, all participating countries have preferential access to the markets of all member countries. Alternatively, not all but just one or some of the participating countries have preferential access to all markets, the so-called hub-and-spoke model. In the latter approach, the hub has access to all

Figure 1.8. Approaches to establish preferential trade areas.

A fully-integrated area.

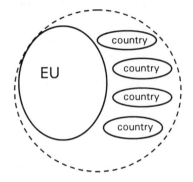

A hub with four spokes.

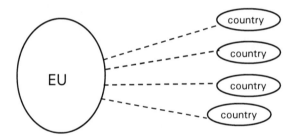

A hub with two types of spokes.

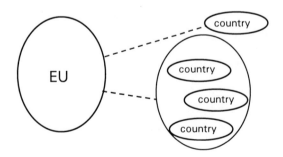

markets and provides all with preferential access to its own market but the spokes do not have preferential access to each other's markets.

The two approaches are illustrated in Figure 1.8. The top figure shows the EU and all other countries participating in a PTA all having free or preferential access to each other's markets. The second figure shows the EU with four separate PTA agreements with individual countries. The unique access the EU has to all markets contributes to its attractiveness as an investment location and supports the potential of industries in the EU market to exploit economies of scale and increase competitiveness. The third figure positions the EU as being the hub in a trade web with individual countries as well as partners in a PTA. Essentially, the EU supports the establishment of PTAs among countries with whom it wishes to establish PTAs as is the case with Mercosur, MENA countries and the CEEC. Seen from a global perspective, the EU will ultimately take a hub position amidst these PTAs.

Notwithstanding the obvious disadvantages of a hub-and-spoke model and the possibility of welfare losses as compared to a comprehensive PTA, countries may be inclined to participate in hub-and-spoke agreements, all the more so if the hub is a large market with significant barriers to imports for the spokes. The agreement provides them with preferential access to a large market, and protects them against future protectionist tendencies in that country. Moreover, not accepting the offer in the presence of rivalling nations that compete in a similar range of product groups, and that are expected to accept or have accepted already such a preferential partnership, brings the risk of competitive disadvantages. A rational way to avoid being manoeuvred into the position of a spoke is to establish a PTA among (potential) spokes. If such an option is not feasible and the costs of trade diversion are substantial, unilateral liberalization may help to reduce the welfare costs of the bilateral PTA, if acceptable to the trade partner.

By way of conclusion it may be indicated that the establishment of a comprehensive, effective and open multilateral trade regime is the preferable avenue to increase welfare in the EU itself and in its partner countries. However, the multilateral regime is less than perfect and regionalism may create additional gains from trade to participants that may not be realized in the multilateral framework. Such a second-best approach does not necessarily inflict more costs than benefits on the multilateral regime. However, there are clearly risks involved in expanding liberalization in the context of PTAs, not only for the multilateral regime but also for the countries participating in such PTAs. These risks are strongly related to the model which is used to establish the preferential market. A combination of comprehensive intra-regional liberalization and low external barriers to trade may be the most risk-averting strategy for establishing PTAs.

To the extent that the EU supports the liberalization process in its member countries and helps to liberalize trade regimes in neighbouring and other countries participating in PTAs in conformity with WTO rules and beyond the concessions made in the WTO, it contributes to its own welfare and to welfare in its partner countries. Moreover, the simultaneous strengthening of the multilateral trade regime and the reduction of barriers to imports in the EU and its partners in PTAs tends to reduce trade diversion and related welfare losses. At the same time, however, the combination of multilateral trade liberalization and proliferation of PTAs reduces the benefits of trade preferences.

8. Organization of the book

This volume is organized in two parts: Part I focuses on general aspects of the position of the EU in the world economy and on specific aspects of its external economic policies, and Part II is exclusively devoted to the regional dimension of the external policy of the EU.

The first two chapters of Part I deal with the international competitiveness of the EU. In Chapter 2, Lester Thurow analyses the competitive position of the EU in broad terms and compares its strength and weaknesses with the other major players in the world economy, the USA and Japan. He considers competitiveness as the ability to generate a high and rising standard of living, which is ultimately related to the capability to increase productivity. After reviewing the major factors that have an impact on productivity growth, Thurow concludes that Europe has the potential of being the biggest and most important economic area on earth in the 21st century. In Chapter 3, Jacob Kol deals with the concepts, measurement and policy implications of competitiveness. Here again, the focus is on the capability of a region to sustain and enhance the standard of living, not the export performance in world markets. Kol distinguishes direct competition among countries through the alteration of national regulations and forms of indirect competition, and reports on country classifications in terms of several performance indicators including economic freedom, competitiveness, readiness to adjust and creditworthiness. The study presents different ways of defining the competitiveness of countries and compares the scoring of the EU with its major rivals in world markets, the USA and Japan.

In Chapter 4, Frans Andriessen deals with the major challenge for the European integration: to accommodate the inevitable substantial extension of EU membership within a relatively short period of time. By now, no less than 13 countries have applied for accession. Andriessen considers different levels of membership and how differentiation may influence decision making and may lead to partial fragmentation. More specifically, he distinguishes four so-called Policy Zones for different groups of countries with a different *acquis communautaire*.

In Chapter 5, Jacques Steenbergen analyses the capacity of the EU to act internationally. He presents an overview of the powers of the EU institutions in external relations as laid down in the Treaties on European Union and on the EC after the IGC of Maastricht in 1991 and the amendments agreed upon in the IGC of Amsterdam in 1997.

In Chapter 6, James Mathis analyses the interaction between the regional dimension of EU trade policy and the multilateral rule system of the WTO. More specifically the chapter investigates the impact of changes in interpretation and implementation that occurred as a result of dispute settlement panels regarding PTAs on the EU regional approach. Moreover, ways to create a more consistent and supportive relationship between EU regionalism and the WTO in the future are investigated.

Agenda 2000 is a broad package of proposals by the European Commission to prepare the EU for the 21st century, including proposals to reform the CAP, which has traditionally been a cornerstone of the Community and still is omnipresent in the actual regional and multilateral policies of the EU. In Chapter 7, Michiel Keyzer and Max Merbis assess the CAP reform proposals in Agenda 2000 and discuss unresolved matters that need to be addressed as well as new developments in international trade policy and agribusiness that need to be taken into account in future CAP reform programmes.

Part II of the volume focuses exclusively on the regional dimension of the external economic policies of the EU. As indicated earlier in this Introduction, the EU has revitalized its policy of establishing special and preferential trade relations with countries all over the world in recent years. Notwithstanding the significant changes in international trade and investment flows that have taken place, the USA is still by far the most important economic partner of the EU.

Moreover, the two Unions are also dominant partners in the formulation and realization of the multilateral trade-policy agenda of the WTO. In Chapter 8, Jan Rood investigates the cohesion of the Euro-American relationship in the new post-Cold War geopolitical setting and the feasibility and rationale of initiatives that have been taken recently to strengthen this relationship, including proposals to establish a special transatlantic economic partnership.

In Chapter 9, Alan Winters analyses the economic and non-economic objectives of the EU and its partners to establish PTAs. The study includes trade agreements - established or in the making - with countries in the EEA, the CEEC, the MENA countries, the ACP countries as well as Mexico, Mercosur, Chile and South Africa. In view of the relatively small economic size of trade partners as compared to the market of the EU, Winters studies particularly the role of non-economic objectives on the side of the EU such as community with its neighbours, their stability and development and most recently the defence of market access. From the perspective of the partner countries, however, seven economic objectives of participation in PTAs with the EU are distinguished.

Traditionally, the most comprehensive and extensive special economic relations of the EU with countries outside Europe has been with the ACP countries. These special relationships involving trade preferences and development co-operation have been formalised in the Lomé Convention since 1975, but this may no longer be the case in the near future. In Chapter 10, Christopher Stevens reviews the Lomé experience and analyses the probable future shape of this special relationship in the context of the new economic priorities of the EU and its declining interest in the ACP group.

The relationships of the EU with its neighbours in the east and south are evolving rapidly. Increasingly countries in both areas are becoming major economic partners of the Union and establishment of stable economic and political conditions in these two areas has become a political priority for Europe. In Chapter 11, Gerrit Faber analyses these recent changes and addresses the question which conditions will have to be met to merge the two separate special relationships of the EU with the CEEC and MENA countries into an integrated Pan-European-Mediterranean Free Trade Area (PAMEFTA). Chapter 12, by Tibor Palánkai focuses more specifically on the rapid change and intensification of the relationship between the EU and its future members in the east and investigates the contribution of the Europe Agreements to the capability of the CEEC to become full members of the Union in the near future.

The recent initiatives that have been taken by the Union to strengthen its relationships with the newly emerging countries in East Asia and Latin America are studied in the next three chapters of the volume. In Chapter 13, Pitou van Dijck studies the economic interaction between the EU and countries in both regions and the competition between the Triad powers to establish beneficial and preferential relationships with these emerging markets. In Chapter 14, Vivianne Ventura Dias focuses specifically on the potential advantages and limitations of PTAs that are in the making between the EU and countries in Latin America, particularly Mercosur, Chile and Mexico. In Chapter 15, Mitsuhiro Kagami gives an overview of trade and investment relations between Europe and East Asia and of the impact of the creation of the euro and the Asian crisis on the nature and intensity of these relations.

The volume is concluded with a chapter by the editors that brings together the main findings of the study and recommendations to change the external economic policies of the EU in order to enhance its efficiency and effectiveness from a global and a European point of view.

Notes.

[1] The Treaty of Maastricht (1992) created the EU. The EU consists of three pillars: (i) the EC, (ii) the Common Foreign and Security Policy and (iii) the Co-operation in Justice and Home Affairs. The differences between these pillars are explained below.

[2] Bhagwati (1996) is more positive on common markets.

References

Alogoskoufis, G. and R. Portes, 'The Euro, the Dollar and the International Monetary System', in: P. Masson, Th. Krueger and B. Turtelboom (eds), *EMU and the International Monetary System*, IMF, Washington, D.C., 1997.

Baldwin, R., *Towards an Integrated Europe*, Centre for Economic Policy Research, London, 1994.

Bhagwati, J., 'The Agenda of the WTO', in: P. van Dijck and G. Faber (eds), *Challenges to the New World Trade Organization*, The Hague, London, Boston, Kluwer Law International, 1996.

Bossche, P. van den, 'The European Community and the Uruguay Round Agreements', in: J. Jackson and A. Sykes, *Implementing the Uruguay Round*, Clarendon Press, Oxford, 1997.

Brown, D., 'The Impact of a North American Free Trade Area: Applied General Equilibrium Models', in: N. Lustig et al. (eds), *North American Free Trade, Assessing the Impact*, The Brookings Institution, Washington, D.C., 1992.

DeRosa, D., *Regional Integration Arrangements, Static Economic Theory, Quantitative Findings, and Policy Guidelines*, Policy Research Working Paper 2007, Development Research Group Trade, The World Bank, Washington, D.C., 1998.

Dijck, P. van, and G. Faber, 'Summary and Conclusions', in: P. van Dijck and G. Faber (eds), *Challenges to the New World Trade Organization*, The Hague, London, Boston, Kluwer Law International, 1996.

European Commission, 'The European Union as a World Trade Partner', in: *European Economy*, Reports and Studies Number 3, Brussels, 1997.

Faber, G., N. Duykers and H. Roelfsema, 'The EU Preferential Regime Towards Developing Countries: Law versus Economics?', Paper for the 15th Annual Conference of the European Association of Law and Economics, 24-26 September, Utrecht, 1998.

Gasiorek, M., A. Smith and A. Venables, 'Trade and Welfare: A General Equilibrium Model', in: L.A. Winters (ed.), *Trade Flows and Trade Policy after "1992"*, Cambridge University Press, Cambridge, 1992.

Gaster, R. and C. Prestowitz, *Shrinking the Atlantic - Europe and the American Economy*, North Atlantic Research, Inc., Economic Strategy Institute, Washington, D.C., 1994.

GATT, *The Results of the Uruguay Round of Multilateral Trade Negotiations, The Legal Texts*, Geneva, 1994.

Hanson, B. 'What Happened to Fortress Europe?: External Trade Policy Liberalization in the European Union', *International Organization*, Volume 52, Number 1, 1998.

Harrison, G., T. Rutherford and D. Tarr, *Production Standards, Imperfect Competition, and Completion of the Market in the European Union*, Policy Research Working Paper 1293, International Economics Department, The World Bank, Washington, D.C., 1994.

Hine, R., *The Political Economy of European Trade*, Wheatsheaf, Brighton, 1985.

Hinojosa-Ojeda, R., and S. Robinson, 'Labor Issues in a North American Free Trade Area', in: N. Lustig et al. (eds), *North American Free Trade, Assessing the Impact*, The Brookings Institution, Washington, D.C., 1992.

IMF, *World Economic Outlook*, Washington, D.C., 1997.

Krugman, P., *Geography and Trade*, MIT Press, Cambridge, 1991.

Lawrence, R., 'Preferential Trading Arrangements: the Traditional and the New', in: A. Galal and B. Hoekman (eds), *Regional Partners in Global Markets: Limits and Possibilities of the Euro-Med Agreements*, CEPR and ECES, London, 1997.

Leebron, D., 'Lying Down with Procrustes: An Analysis of Harmonization Claims', in: J. Bhagwati and R. Hudec (eds), *Fair Trade and Harmonization, Prerequisites for Free Trade?*, Volume 1: Economic Analysis, The MIT Press, Cambridge, Massachusetts, 1997.

Olechowski, A., 'Nontariff barriers to Trade', in: J.M. Finger and A. Olechowski (eds), *The Uruguay Round. A Handbook on the Multilateral Trade Negotiations*, The World Bank, Washington, D.C., 1985.

Paemen, H., 'The EC and the WTO Agenda', in: P. van Dijck and G. Faber (eds), *Challenges to the New World Trade Organization*, Kluwer Law International, The Hague, London, Boston, 1996.

Regelsberger, E., and W. Wessels , 'The CFSP Institutions and Procedures: A Third Way for the Second Pillar', *European Foreign Affairs Review*, Volume 1, 1996.

Srinivasan, T.N., 'International Trade and Labour Standards from an Economic Perspective', in: P. van Dijck and G. Faber (eds), *Challenges to the New World Trade Organization,* Kluwer Law International, The Hague, London, Boston, 1996.

Thurow, L., *The Future of Capitalism - How Today's Economic Forces Shape Tomorrow's World,* William Morrow and Company, Inc., New York, 1996.

UN, *World Investment Report 1998: Trends and Determinants,* New York and Geneva, 1998.

WTO, *Regionalism and the World Trading System,* Geneva, 1995.

Annex 1.A.1. Countries included in the calculations of regional GNPs in Table 1.1.

EU	Austria, Belgium, Denmark, Finland, France, Germany, Greece, Ireland, Italy, the Netherlands, Portugal, Spain, Sweden, United Kingdom.
EEA	Norway, Switzerland (formally not a member).
Europe Agreements	Bulgaria, Czech Republic, Estonia, Hungary, Latvia, Poland.
Rest of Eastern Europe	Azerbaijan, Belarus, Kazakhstan, Kyrgyz Republic, Russian Federation, Tajikistan, Ukraine, Uzbekistan
NAFTA	USA, Canada, Mexico.
South America	Argentina, Bolivia, Brazil, Chile, Columbia, Costa Rica, Dominican Republic, Ecuador, El Salvador, Guatemala, Haiti, Honduras, Jamaica, Nicaragua, Panama, Paraguay, Peru, Trinidad and Tobago, Uruguay, Venezuela.
Mercosur	Argentina, Brazil, Paraguay, Uruguay.
South Asia	Bangladesh, India, Pakistan.
South-East Asia	Indonesia, Malaysia, Philippines, Thailand
APEC	Australia, Brunei, Canada, Chile, China, Hongkong, Indonesia, Japan, Korea, Malaysia, Mexico, New Zealand, Papua New Guinea, Philippines, Singapore, Taiwan, Thailand, USA, Peru, Russian Federation, Vietnam.
MENA	Algeria, Egypt, Israel, Jordan, Lebanon, Morocco, Tunisia, Turkey.
Lomé	Angola, Benin, Botswana, Burkina Faso, Burundi, Cameroon, Central African Republic, Chad, Congo Democratic Republic, Congo Republic, Cote d'Ivoire, Dominican Republic, Ethiopia, Fiji, Gabon, Gambia, Ghana, Grenada, Guinea, Guinea-Bissau, Haiti, Jamaica, Kenya, Lesotho, Madagascar, Malawi, Mali, Mauritania, Mauritius, Mozambique, Namibia, Niger, Nigeria, Papua New Guinea, Rwanda, Senegal, Sierra Leone, Togo, Trinidad and Tobago, Uganda, Zambia, Zimbabwe.

PART I: GENERAL TOPICS

2

EUROPEAN COMPETITIVENESS IN A GLOBAL ECONOMY

LESTER THUROW

MIT
Cambridge
USA

1. Competitiveness

Competitiveness, simply defined, is a region's ability to generate a high and rising standard of living that keeps it abreast of the world leaders in terms of gross domestic product (GDP) per capita.

For any group of people the secret of competitiveness is found in its rate of growth of productivity, as measured by output per hour of work. By augmenting capital per worker, savings and investment play a role in productivity growth, but in the long run major gains in productivity depend upon the adoption of new and better technologies.

To do this a country must have the ability to invent new industries based on breakthrough technologies. New industries and new technologies open up opportunities to employ new skills and new forms of capital equipment. Gains are large relative to gains that may be realized by simply raising capital-labour ratios in existing industries.

The country must also be willing to improve the performance of an industry if it is inefficient and lagging in the implementation of the best practices to be found in the rest of the world. Copying to catch up is simply the fastest way to

P. van Dijck and G. Faber (eds.), The External Economic Dimension of the European Union, 51–70.

advance in this task. This is easy to say, but many are unwilling to do so. 'Not invented here' is a universal human syndrome.

Where becoming world-class is impossible or where world-class levels of productivity are intrinsically low, there are major gains to be made by those countries who are willing to close inefficient industries, import what they need from other countries, and move labour along with other productive resources into higher value-added opportunities. What the Japanese call 'strategic retreats' can lead to a lot of productivity gains.

Competitiveness is often confused with the ability to export. But any country can export more, or even generate a trade surplus, by simply lowering its wage rates. In this sense the poorest, least efficient countries in the world can be competitive. What counts is not the ability to export but the ability to sell goods and services competitively at home and abroad that generate high wages and high profits.

2. Europe

Consider Europe as a man from outer space might see it. Europe is an area roughly equivalent to China in size - it is about 10 per cent bigger. Its population is somewhat smaller, 850-900 million depending upon whether all, or only part, of the Turkish population is allocated to Europe. If one were playing global economic chess and given the choice of any contiguous piece of the globe with approximately one billion people, everyone would choose to play with the European position. It has a far stronger position on the global economic chessboard than any equivalently sized group of people.

Nowhere on earth are there almost one billion contiguous people who are as rich - no region comes even close. Nowhere on earth are there one billion people better educated or skilled - no one comes even close. Nowhere on earth are there one billion people with better infrastructure - no one comes even close.

Europe is composed of peoples with great track records of achievement. European science and engineering is world class. There are areas where Europe dominates in the creation of new knowledge, such as high energy physics at CERN, and there are no major technologies that it has not mastered. Russia has demonstrated its ability to compete with the USA in space, military technologies, and high science including physics and mathematics. Despite wages and fringe benefits 50 per cent above those in the USA, Germany has a large export surplus. London dominates in the trading of international currencies. Italy and France have a flare for fashion and design unmatched in the world. No one is better at starting good small companies than the Italians are. French engineering is some of the world's best. Eastern Europe offers workers with western educational skills at wage levels found only among unskilled workers in underdeveloped countries.

Only Europe has a history of over 40 years in which it has been moving towards economic integration with a momentum on its side that no other part of the world can match. The European common market widens as new countries are added and it deepens as it harmonizes its rules and regulations. Its GDP measured at purchasing power parity prices (GDP PPP) equals that of the USA and is almost three times that of Japan (Morgan Stanley, 1997), as illustrated by Van Dijck and Faber in Chapter 1 of this volume.

Europe has just made a major leap forward with a common currency. In late September 1997, rumours started that the United Kingdom would after all join the euro. In response its stock market soared. Hard-nosed global capitalists understand the gains to be made from integration. In the words of the American investment bank Morgan Stanley

> 'Not only would a single currency revolutionize Europe's capital markets, but it could be accompanied by a massive wave of corporate restructuring sufficient to reshape the global competitive playing field and unlock hidden shareholder value' (Morgan Stanley, 1997).

The same investment bank sees three times as many European as Japanese companies with global competitive advantage.

Europe's two major industrial competitors each have major weaknesses. Japan cannot put together a major trading region with itself at the centre. The Asia-Pacific Economic Cooperation (APEC) does not exist and is unlikely to exist. Differences in levels of development and size are too large for the countries on the Pacific Rim to have a common agenda, harmonize rules and regulation, or share decision-making. And even if APEC were to exist, Japan would have to share the benefits and the leadership with China and the USA.

Japan's financial system is in an advanced stage of melt down. Its stock market crashed in the early 1990s and is still 50 per cent below its previous peak. Property values are 60 to 80 per cent below their peaks - and still falling. Its banks are broke with negative net equity and are now being hit with additional large losses in South-East Asia. Its GDP growth rates used to be among the highest in the industrial world but have been among the lowest in the 1990s. Monetary policies have been exhausted with interest rates near zero, yet no economic recovery is in sight.

Financial deregulation and other structural changes are promised but always at some point in a future that never seems to arrive. Its political system is in gridlock and unable to come to grips with its economic problems.

Japan, as the Japanese themselves recognize, has a creativity problem and has yet to demonstrate that it can make the big breakthroughs in technology that lead to the new industries of the future. Until the Japanese demonstrate this ability, Japan will forever be playing catch-up, and never be the world's economic leader (WuDunn, 1997).

At the time of writing, the rest of Asia with the exception of China, has been in an advanced stage of financial melt down. The collapsing of their financial bubbles, not unusual in the history of capitalism, has been compounded by the fact that their strategy for economic growth, export-led growth, only works when just a few small countries want to play the game.

The USA is also not as strong as it currently looks. The bottom two-thirds of its labour force is poorly educated and skilled by the standards of the developed world. The rapidly rising earnings gaps between the top and bottom quintiles of the work force are in the long run unsustainable. Productivity growth for the USA - 0.8 per cent per year - in the last decade is the lowest in its history. It is a low savings and investment society - Europe invests 45 per cent more - that cannot balance its trading accounts despite having lowered its wages substantially. In contrast, the European Community has a trade surplus with the rest of the world. With the advent of the euro in 1999 the USA will not be able to finance a large trade deficit and will face a very difficult transition.

The North Atlantic Free Trade Agreement (NAFTA) adds nothing to the economic strength of the USA. Canada and Mexico together do not significantly increase the size of America's domestic markets. Neither does it bring complementary industrial strengths or technological leadership in any sector of economic activity. Adding the rest of Latin America to NAFTA does not change either situation.

With the end of the cold war, the Defense Department financed technical system that created the scientific dominance of the USA is being torn up, with nothing visible in the works to replace it. Spending on research and development (R and D) is scheduled to fall substantially.

Viewed from the cosmos, European pessimism about its future economic position is simply unwarranted. In the last ten years real European and US GDP growth rates have been exactly the same at 2.3 per cent per year (President's Council of Economic Advisers, 1997 and IMF, 1997). With slower population growth rates, real growth rates of GDP per capita in Europe have been 50 per cent higher than in the USA, 1.9 and 1.3 per cent respectively.

The pessimism arises, of course, from Europe's inability to create jobs. While the USA has created 16 million jobs in the last decade, Europe has created only 430,000 jobs and none of them in the private sector (President's Council of Economic Advisers, 1997). The size of this difference, however, is grossly misleading. Because of a much slower population growth rate, Europe has to create jobs at a much slower pace once it has brought unemployment down to reasonable levels. To bring its current unemployment rate of 12 per cent into parity with that of the USA (five per cent) the European Union requires nine million jobs. As just mentioned that difference in employment growth is not due to faster American economic growth.

The US unemployment rate of five per cent also is not quite what it seems to be. Like an iceberg only a little of the total mass of underemployment is visible. A five per cent unemployment rate translates into about seven million unemployed US citizenship - only about a third of whom receive any unemployment insurance benefits whatsoever. There are in addition another 5.5 million people who say that they are unemployed but who are not counted as 'officially' unemployed since they do not meet the tests of actively looking for work in the preceding week. The two million people who have just been ordered to leave the welfare roles and find work also are not counted as unemployed. New immigrants, coming at the rate of about one million per year, do not dare call themselves unemployed since lack of work is grounds for automatic deportation. No one knows how many are really unemployed.

Since any amount of work - no matter how few the hours - counts as employment, another 4.5 million people who work part-time but want full-time work are counted as employed rather than unemployed.

In addition there are a lot of US citizens who work in what is called the 'contingent' labour market. Eight million citizens work at temporary jobs, two million work on-call, and eight million work as one person independently employed contractors. Most of them would rather work at regular jobs commensurate with their skills with reasonable wages and fringe benefits such as pensions and health care. They are not employed or unemployed, they are underemployed.

Six million US males aged 25 to 64 have just disappeared from the system. The Census Bureau says that they exist but the Labour Department cannot find them. They are not at work, not unemployed, not in school, and not in jail.

These large invisible reserves of underemployed US workers become visible when employers announce regular job openings with even modest wages and fringe benefits. They are overwhelmed with many more applicants than they want: 20,000 people apply for one hundred fireman's jobs in Los Angeles and 100,000 people apply for 1,000 auto assembly jobs in Michigan.

Viewed from the perspective of US competitiveness all of that employment growth can also be seen as a negative. With equivalent economic growth, employment growth can only have been higher in the USA than in Europe if productivity has advanced at a slower pace than that of Europe, which has been the case (IMF, 1997). Increasing the number of jobs is a problem in Europe, but it is a much smaller problem than the most commonly cited statistics make it out to be.

3. The economic environment

To say that Europe has all of the ingredients necessary to be successful is not to say that it will be successful. In addition to having the necessary inputs, the game has to be played skilfully. To understand what it will take for Europe to succeed in the third millennium, it is necessary to understand the nature of the new economic environment that is being created at the end of the 20th and the beginning of the 21st centuries. Three dimensions are distinguished here.

First, as the one-third of humanity, 1.9 billion people, who used to live under communism join the global capitalistic market economy, a fundamental change takes place in the spatial division of labour. In the oil industry, for example, Central Asia and the region around the Caspian Sea will fundamentally alter global oil supplies while mainland China will be a big addition to the demand side of the equation. The addition of China to the global economy by itself fundamentally changes where light, low-skilled, manufacturing will take place.

Those who succeed will swiftly take advantage of this new economic geography. For those with the necessary flexibility tremendous opportunities exist.

In this context Western Europeans ought to be to Eastern Europe what the overseas Chinese are to China. Conversely Eastern Europe ought to present the booming growth opportunities to Western Europe that China does to South Korea, Taiwan, Hong Kong and other overseas Chinese businessmen. There is nothing to prevent this scenario from happening except a lack of imagination and risk taking in the two halves of Europe.

Eastern Europe is not a drag on Western Europe. It is a tremendous opportunity. Things expensively made in Western Europe ought to be moved to Eastern Europe where they could be made at much lower costs. Western Europe should be replacing the industries that move east with the capital equipment industries, high-tech products, and headquarters functions including marketing, technology development, and global contacts, that Eastern Europe needs to participate in the global economy and catch up with the level of income per capita of Western Europe.

The USA has no similar opportunities lying next to it. Latin America is uneducated. The overseas Chinese have pre-empted and block Japan from gaining this advantage in Asia.

In the future, the south side of the Mediterranean could once again effectively be part of Europe as it was in ancient times. North Africa can do for Europe what Mexico does for the USA - provide large supplies of low cost labour easily integrated with the high wage, highly skilled labour just next door to the north. Europe can, if it wants, have its own NAFTA as well as its unique common market.

Second, an era of natural resource based economies is ending to be replaced by an era of man-made brainpower industries. Microelectronics, biotechnology, new man-made materials, telecommunications, computers, and computer-controlled machinery are the growth industries of the next century. The symbol of this shift is Bill Gates. For more than a century the world's wealthiest man has been associated with oil - starting with John D. Rockefeller in the late 19th century and ending with the Sultan of Brunei in the late 20th century. But today for the first time in human history a knowledge worker is the world's wealthiest human being.

Put simply, skills, education, and knowledge have replaced natural resources as the greatest source of human wealth. There is a skill-intensive technological shift underway. Long-run competitive advantage can only be sustained on the basis of advantages in skills, education, and knowledge. Yet this is precisely where Europe has its largest comparative advantage relative to any group with a comparable size in the rest of the world. It is a human capital-rich continent.

Third, with electrification at the end of the 19th century, in what is sometimes called the second industrial revolution, national economies gradually supplanted local economies. Similarly at the end of the 20th century a revolution in transportation and communications is leading to the development of a global economy that is gradually supplanting existing national economies. Economic historians looking back may well see it as the third industrial revolution.

Everyone is going to be working in a global economy - selling to the rest of the world, buying from the rest of the world, working with labour in the rest of the world. Consider the accelerometer, a 50 US dollar computer chip that replaces 650 US dollars worth of mechanical sensors in controlling car air bags. Made in Boston, tested in the Philippines, packaged in Taiwan, installed in a BMW in Germany, and sold to someone in São Paulo. Skilled workers in Boston working with unskilled workers in the Philippines and medium-skilled workers in Taiwan who are all working with the highest paid labour in the world at the BMW works in Bavaria. And in the end all of their jobs depend upon the prosperity in Brazil that allows someone to afford a BMW.

No one should be better at playing this developing global game than Europeans since they have had, and are having, the experience of a developing regional economy in Europe. Jumping from a national economy to a global economy is much harder than a two-stage jump first to a regional economy and then to a global economy.

In their initial conception of a 'world' car the auto companies envisioned an almost identical car sold around the world to cut development and tooling costs. Experience has taught the auto companies that this world car will never exist. Different groups of customers around the globe do not want the same car. They demand different attributes in their cars. But a new conception of a world car is emerging where every part is made at that point on the globe where it is most cheaply produced and assembled into different configurations in different markets to satisfy different tastes.

Just as large national corporations replaced small family businesses in the second industrial revolution, so even larger multinational corporations are now replacing national corporations in the third industrial revolution. These companies play a global game and in many ways they treat countries in the ways that large national corporations treat US states. Mercedes Benz and BMW were able to negotiate large subsidies: hundreds of thousands of US dollars per job in tax reductions and public expenditures directed at their needs by the states of Alabama and South Carolina in exchange for locating plants in those states. Intel similarly got a huge subsidy from Israel in exchange for building a large semiconductor facility there. Plants are essentially put up for bid. The countries that offer the companies the best deal in wages, skills, transportation costs, markets, taxes, and direct subsidies get them.

The Grand Cayman Islands have become the world's fifth biggest banking centre by becoming the place where one banks if one does not want to follow the regulations of one's local government. Taiwan prohibits many forms of investment in mainland China yet its firms are the biggest investors in China. Investments are organized through dummy companies set up in the Caymans who funnel their funds into China through Hong Kong. And no one ever goes to the Caymans since it is all done electronically.

Put simply, globalization and multinationalization are reducing the powers of government to regulate and to set independent economic policies. Companies simply move their operations to the places where banking regulations, anti-trust policies, and the rules governing intellectual property rights are most favourable to their interests. Citibank does its investment banking in London to get around the American laws prohibiting banks from being both commercial and investment banks. European airlines buy large blocks of shares in domestic airlines - KLM in Northwest, British Air in US Air - that would be illegal if either were an American airline. Drug manufacturers move to India since it does not recognize patents on new pharmaceuticals.

4. The realities of a global economy

By definition an economy is the area over which capitalists arbitrage prices and wages, looking to buy at the lowest possible costs and selling at the highest possible prices. Businesses now arbitrage the globe. With global arbitrage the pressures of factor-price equalization have to mount. Skills rather than geographic location become the prime determinant of wages. Wages depend more upon worldwide supplies and demands for labour and less upon national supplies and demands. The market for software engineers is now a global market. Those in Bangalore (India) will be paid a little less than those in the Netherlands, but not a lot less.

Since unskilled workers are abundantly available in the global economy as compared to the developed countries, wages of unskilled workers in developed countries should be expected to fall relative to wages of the skilled workers in the developed world. Since the globe has a lower capital-labour ratio than the wealthy industrial world, the returns to capital similarly should be expected to rise in a global economy.

All of these expected trends are now visible in the USA. The earnings gap between the bottom and top quintile of workers has expanded sharply. While the real GDP per capita in the USA went up by 40 per cent in the last 25 years, the median real wages for full-time full year workers in the USA are down 13 per cent over the same time period. The lower the skills level, the bigger the decline. Earnings inequalities are compounded since most capital is owned by the very rich and income inequality rises as the share of capital advances.

In Europe this reality has been hidden by government regulations and social practices that prevent the wages of Europe's unskilled workers from falling. But with wages out of line with the rest of the world no business firm wants to expand employment in Western Europe. Unemployment slowly and continually rises into what are now double-digit rates.

Forget the developing world. When European companies can achieve dramatic wage reductions by moving their production to the USA, as is now the case, something is fundamentally wrong. Productivity in the USA on an average is higher than European productivity.

The same problem is dramatically visible within Europe. Average manufacturing wages in Germany are 25 times those in the Czech Republic. Existing productivity differences are not large enough to justify these wage differentials. Volkswagen reports that productivity in its Skoda works is 90 per cent of the productivity in its German plants. In this context any profit-making company will contract its German employment as fast as the law and social realities allow and expand its Czech employment. If the law and social realities interfere to slow the process too much, German companies simply lose market shares to companies in the rest of the world that are not subject to these restrictions.

When production moves to the USA or to the Czech Republic, Europe does not only just lose unskilled jobs, but also some of the skilled jobs that go together with these unskilled jobs, such as managers, engineers, skilled trades. In the end, Europe loses more total earnings than it would lose if it let wages fall and taxed the earnings of those employed in order to compensate those whose wages were reduced.

Europe cannot repeal the laws of economic gravity, but it has to adjust to the realities of a global economy. While the market wages of unskilled workers must fall, there is a short-run remedy that can stop their take-home earnings from falling until they are re-skilled and re-trained. It is what Americans know as an earned income tax credit. Low-wage individuals do not pay taxes, but get a government payment based upon their earnings that might, for example, bring their per hour market wage of 4 US dollars up to a per hour take home wage of 6 US dollars. Earned income tax credits dominate unemployment insurance on every dimension if one is worried about the living standards of those at the bottom.

5. Enhancing European competitiveness

But this does not mean that Europe has to cast aside completely what many Europeans like to call the third way between Soviet communism and American 'survival of the fittest' capitalism. Europe could be far more competitive without having to make major changes in its social market economies. Two priorities will be distinguished.

Priority one: eliminate payroll taxes

The place to start is not by changing Europe's traditional social welfare system or introducing Anglo-Saxon style labour market flexibility but by changing the taxes collected to pay for Europe's social welfare system. Today the system is mostly financed with employment and payroll taxes. These taxes should be completely eliminated and the revenue they now produce should be replaced with an equivalent increase in the value-added tax (VAT). While net tax collections would remain the same, some beneficial economic effects would flow from such a shift in the tax base.

Since the VAT is rebatable on exports while payroll taxes are not, the net price at which Europe's exports could be sold to the world would fall dramatically.

Moreover, since the tax base would expand to include those who consume but who are not in the work force, the elderly, and those whose consumption is financed with non-labour income, the rich, the effective VAT rate that would yield the same revenue would be much lower than the corresponding payroll tax rate. Lower tax rates cause fewer distortions in economic decision-making. Those who wish to invest rather than consume find it much more profitable.

As government is using most of its tax receipts to finance consumption through pensions and health care, consumption taxes are the best way to pay for these expenditures, according to tax theory. By collecting consumption taxes a distortion in the consumption-investment balance, that these government expenditures would otherwise have caused, is prevented.

Most importantly, the shift in the tax base would eliminate the tax wedge. Employers and workers would see the same wage rate. Today employers see wages that are far higher than the wages actually received by their work force. In Germany, payroll taxes effectively double wage rates for employers. When thinking about hiring a new worker employers have to think about whether his productivity justifies a payment of 32 US dollars per hour - half of it to the worker and half to the state - that they will have to make. Without payroll taxes the same German employer faces a charge of 16 US dollars per hour and he can justify hiring more German workers.

The normal argument against the VAT is that they are regressive. But they are less regressive than payroll taxes, especially if these taxes are not collected on all earnings or on unearned income. Substituting a VAT yielding the same revenue for a payroll tax is a movement toward a more progressive tax system. Note however that the VAT can also be made as progressive as one desires with offsetting refundable vanishing income tax credits.

There are economic losers from such a tax shift - the tax bills of the affluent elderly who have left the work force would go up, but such a shift in the tax base provides an enormous win-win opportunity for Europe. Few policies offer more winners and fewer losers.

Priority two: increase industrial flexibility

Institutions like the Organisation of Economic Co-operation and Development (OECD) periodically recommend that Europe deal with its problems of high unemployment by restoring labour-market flexibility (OECD, 1996). While some additional labour market flexibility is needed, this is a mis-identification of Europe's problems. What Europe really needs is an environment more favourable to dynamic new firms. This will require some highly focused labour-market flexibility but the two are not identical.

There are only two ways to create more jobs - increase output or cut wages and as a consequence induce a reduction in productivity levels. Europe has chosen to do neither and the USA has chosen the second option.

Suppose that Western Europe were to introduce an unlimited USA-style right to fire labour - no notice, no severance pay, no justifications necessary. On day number one of this new regime millions of Western European workers would be fired as companies eliminated all of the unneeded workers who are now on their payrolls and those whom they have long wanted to fire. European businesses would probably even fire more workers than they really want to fire since they would suspect, probably rightly, that their new right to fire would not last long and fear that if they did not fire workers now, the law might revert to what it was in the past and they would soon lose the rights that they had just gained.

It is absolutely clear that in the short run unemployment would go up substantially in Europe if USA-style labour-market flexibility were suddenly introduced. If the central banks of Europe, and the European Central Bank (ECB) in particular, did not change their positions on how fast their economies could grow without inflation - and they have not done so even though Europe's unemployment has now risen to 12 per cent - and accelerate growth, unemployment would simply remain at these new higher levels.

Unemployment can only fall if the increased competition among workers for jobs resulting from higher unemployment leads to reductions in real wage rates. With lower wages, business would move to less capital-intensive forms of production and into labour-intensive businesses that cannot profitably operate at the current wage rates. Effectively, either action would raise employment by lowering the rate of growth of productivity.

With lower wages, the USA, for example, uses many more guards and attendants in its parking lots than a higher-waged Europe does where it is more profitable to use card readers and automatic gates. Much of the enormous growth in America's service sector, which explains more than 100 per cent of the employment gains of the last 10 years, would not have occurred if US businesses had had to pay European wages.

Put bluntly, labour-market flexibility by itself is simply an indirect call for lower wages. Any calculation of how much Europe would have to reduce its wage rates to restore full employment will produce a big number, if this were the only measure taken.

One answer to high unemployment in Europe is to recognize that it lives in a very different, deflationary, world in the mid-1990s and that the monetary policies that might have been appropriate for the inflationary world of the early 1980s need to be changed. But Europe's central banks seem stuck in the early 1980s - unable to understand that the world has changed. In contrast, the USA Federal Reserve Board has at least partially adjusted to this new reality.

But something else is needed. If Europe wants to compete successfully in the new growth industries such as microelectronics where it is clearly behind, it needs industrial flexibility - the ability to form and quickly grow new companies into large companies using new break-through technologies.

List the 25 biggest companies based upon market capitalization in the USA in 1960 and again in 1996. Six of the 25 companies either did not exist or were very small 36 years ago (Business Week, 1997). Intel and Microsoft did not exist in 1960, Hewlett-Packard had less than 1000 employees. Do the same for Western Europe. All of the 25 biggest corporations in 1996 were big corporations in 1960. Europe has been completely unable to grow new big companies in the period after the Second World War.

This is important since old big companies are almost never the leaders in big new break-through technologies. They simply cannot cannibalize themselves and take advantages of the new opportunities that now exist. Consider the transistor - independently invented in the General Electric (GE) laboratories shortly after it was invented in the Bell (AT&T) laboratories. GE had a dominant position in vacuum tubes. It gave the plans for the transistor to its vacuum tube division, which then proceeded to sit on its development. The transistor would and did put the vacuum tube division out of business but GE could not drive itself out of business. To this day GE, the largest firm of the USA and many would argue its most successful firm, is not a significant player in the semiconductor industry. GE was not alone. None of the five makers of vacuum tubes were ever successful at making semiconductor chips. This lack of new companies is one of the reasons that South Korea is a bigger maker of semiconductor chips than any European country. Similarly, none of the world's leading pharmaceutical companies played a leading role in the development of biotechnology. They all had to end up buying new biotech companies rather than growing them at home.

For the same reasons old large firms usually do not recognize the value that can be created in new technologies. IBM sold its 20 per cent stake in Intel - a stake that, if it still owned today, would raise its total market value by almost 30 per cent.

Similarly, today's leading retail firms are not going to be the dominant firms in electronic retailing. If they jump into the new technology, they take their own customers away from themselves much faster than any outsider electronic retailer will capture their current customers. In the short and medium term they make more money by sticking with the old technology. The biggest retailer of the USA, Wal-Mart, recently set up an electronic store but it carefully keeps the prices in its electronic store slightly higher than those in its physical stores. Yet the whole advantage of electronic retailing is that costs are intrinsically less and prices can be significantly lower. But Wal-Mart has too much invested in its thousands of physical stores to fully adopt the new technology. If it did so, for a decade or more it would be imposing losses on itself that it can avoid if it does not become a pioneer in the new electronic retailing technologies.

Many European businesses deliberately attempt to remain small to keep below the radar screens of government regulation. If they remain small enough, regulations such as co-determination either do not apply to them or they can cheat a little bit on the regulations and no one is likely to notice. Conversely if they are very large like Fiat and need to downsize, the government will help pay the costs that the regulations impose since the Italian government cannot afford to let Fiat collapse.

But medium-sized firms with too many employees come up on government radar screens. They will have to obey government regulations that make it difficult to grow and are not large enough to be helped by government if they get into trouble because of those regulations. Northern Italy is an example of a part of Europe that is very good at starting new businesses but unsuccessful at growing them into large firms.

To grow small firms into big firms requires simple, easy to follow, equally enforced, rules and regulations that apply equally to firms of all sizes. In addition, each of those regulations has to be vetted to insure that they encourage firms to add employees.

There is some need for labour-market flexibility. If one looks at the firms that have successfully grown into big firms in short periods of time, most of them have had periods when they needed to downsize. If they had not been able to downsize, they would have gone broke during their cyclical or structural down-swings and would not have remained in business long enough to take advantage of the opportunities that were to emerge later. Young firms simply do not have the financial reserves to employ unneeded labour.

The lesson is simple. The ability to downsize is an important part of growth.

Businesses are also often told in Europe that they could afford to pay the existing high wages if they would only use new technologies. This is true in many cases. But the rules needed to use these new technologies profitably are often also not in place. New technologies that would allow Europe's metal working firms to compete in global markets usually involve high capital costs. If these costs are to be recouped, machines must be run three shifts a day, each day of the year. Yet Europe has rules and regulations preventing multiple shifts or round-the-clock operations. If a high-tech, capital-intensive, survival strategy for high wages is to be pursued, that strategy has to include the necessary complementary rules and regulations to make economic success possible.

If one asks why two great high-tech areas of the USA, Silicon Valley and Route 128, exist, the answer is partly found in great educational institutions, Berkeley and Stanford, Harvard and the Massachusetts Institute of Technology (MIT). But there are other places in the USA with great universities. Their real genesis is found in banking institutions that were willing to lend money based upon good ideas and did not require physical assets as security.

They also needed the right sociology. Suppose a young engineer leaves his employer to set up a new business. What happens? Does his old employer and other large employers treat him as a traitor and refuse to buy what he is producing as a matter of principle? If so, he will likely fail in his new business since most new businesses start by selling components to existing firms - often their old firms. Because of brand names, advertising, and the difficulties involved in getting retail shelf space, very few new firms will start by selling directly to the public.

What happens if our entrepreneur's new business fails? Most new businesses will fail and the founder will have to look for work. Will potential new employers see his failure as a permanent mark of failure and refuse to hire him as they do in Japan? Or will potential employers, knowing that most new businesses fail through no personal fault of the founders, see a good hard working, bright, energetic, worker with the drive and initiative that they would like to hire as they do in Silicon Valley or Route 128? If the first set of attitudes prevails, few people will attempt to set up new businesses as this is personally too risky.

Whatever the current degree of entrepreneurial spirit, actions can be taken to enlarge it. MIT graduates and faculty members have founded 4000 companies employing 1.1 million people with sales of 232 billion US dollars (BankBoston, 1997). By themselves MIT-founded companies would be the 24th largest economy in the world. A tradition of entrepreneurship clearly exists and has existed for a long time. But in the last decade that tradition has grown by design. The MIT patent licensing office has shifted its policies from selling its patents to taking an equity position in companies that use its technology. This makes it much less costly to start new businesses using MIT technologies. An MIT Enterprise Forum was organized so that those who had started new businesses could provide tutoring and mentoring for those who wished to start new businesses. Students compete in a new business plans competition with a prize of 50,000 US dollars to the winner. Over time the prize itself has become secondary since many of the plans presented - including many that do not win - are now financed by venture capitalists who attend the competition. Five years ago MIT started to give the Lemelson-MIT prize of 500,000 US dollars for the best American invention of the year. The best MIT student inventor of the year is given a prize of 30,000 US dollars. All have buttressed and expanded an existing tradition of building new companies.

Europe's financial institutions, sociology, social rules and regulations, and universities need to be re-examined from the perspective of creating a better environment for growing new large firms.

Integration should allow Europe to become much better in developing the new break-through technologies of the future. If a big country like the USA puts three per cent of its GDP into R and D it has enough money to be a player in all the hot areas of technology. In many ways R and D spending is like drilling oil wells. If one drills three wells it is a risky business. If one drills 10,000 wells it is just probability. I would argue for example that Spain wastes every dollar that it puts into R and D. It does not spend very much, but not knowing what areas will actually develop into new industries it tries to spread its money around and in doing so does not spend enough money in any area to make a difference. Small countries can concentrate their R and D spending on just one or two areas so that they have a critical mass of funds. However, this is a risky strategy. It is also usually impossible since small countries do not have enough trained people in these narrow areas to spend wisely the money they are allocating. R and D spending in an integrated Europe ought to be more productive than R and D spending in an individual country.

6. Playing the 21st century game

In the past, competitiveness could be viewed as a national game. Individuals in rich countries with high levels of productivity could expect high pay and generous fringe benefits even if they were not individually very productive. Living in a rich country they would work with more capital equipment per worker, enjoy more and better natural resources, and have more skilled co-workers than those with similar skills in poor countries. Highly productive individuals could be taxed to fund generous social welfare benefits for less productive individuals. National governments could and did equalize market outcomes.

However, that world is gone. With world capital markets, capital-intensive facilities can be built in poor as well as in rich countries. Multinational companies take their technologies and their capital to whatever part of the globe serves them best. Natural resources are less important to economic success, sold on world markets, and easily transportable. South Korea and Japan can have world-class steel industries although neither has high quality coal or iron ore deposits. Production can be globally sourced so that a skilled worker in the developed world is essentially working with an unskilled worker in the developing world. Factor-price equalization is a reality. Put bluntly, the unskilled worker in the first-world can no longer automatically expect first world incomes.

Companies who do not want to pay taxes to support generous fringe benefits for today's retirees can move to locations where the taxes to pay for those fringe benefits are not collected. Ordinary workers who do not want to pay social charges disappear into the underground economy. No country's taxes can get too far out of line with those in the rest of the world. If they do, businesses simply will leave.

In the century ahead the economic game will be played on three levels.

First, if geographic areas want all of their citizens to have first-world earnings, they have to insure that each of their citizens are as well skilled and educated as any in the world. These individually well-skilled workers will have to have access to a world-class telecommunications and transportation infrastructure. If they are to participate in the new man-made brainpower industries of the future, their countries will have to be leaders in the R and D that creates these opportunities.

Second, companies will play the game based upon the skills they employ, the capital investments they make, their technical prowess, and their ability to globally source and sell. New start-ups that rapidly grow to become big multinationals will be an important part of success. Social regulations and attitudes will have to permit industrial flexibility.

Third, individuals will play the game based upon their education and skills - and their willingness to change.

There is no reason to believe that Europe cannot play this three-dimensional game. To conclude, no one other billion people starts with a better position on the global economic chessboard than Europe does.

Europe can, if it plays its existing position with skill, be the biggest and most important economic area on earth in the next century.

References

BankBoston, *MIT: The Impact of Innovation*, Boston, 1997.

Bussiness Week, 'The Global 500', July 7, 1997.

IMF, *International Financial Statistics*, Washington, D.C., 1997

OECD, *The OECD Jobs Strategy: Pushing Ahead with the Strategy*, Paris, 1996.

Morgan Stanley Bank, 'The Economics of Competitive Advantage', *International Investment Research*, November 14, 1997.

The President's Council of Economic Advisers, *Economic Report of the President*, Washington, D.C., 1997.

WuDunn, S., 'Japan Cones Another US Idea: Creativity', *International Herald Tribune*, October 10, 1997.

3

THE EU AND COMPETITIVENESS IN THE WORLD ECONOMY

Concepts, measurement and policy implications

Jacob Kol[1]

The Erasmus Centre for Economic Integration Studies
Erasmus University
Rotterdam
The Netherlands

1. Introduction

Krugman (1994) points out that the rise in a country's productivity is related only in a limited way to the performance in international competition. The examples and calculations he presents, show that in the cases of the USA, the European Union (EU) and Japan, the growth rate of the standard of living essentially equals the growth rate of domestic productivity – not productivity relative to competitors. He concludes that national living standards are overwhelmingly determined by domestic factors rather than by some competition for world markets. It should be noted, however, that imports and exports imply exposure of domestic firms to foreign capability and efficiency, with implications in turn for domestic productivity. Krugman (1994) also observes that 'thinking and speaking in terms of competitiveness poses real dangers': it could lead to 'wasteful spending of government money' and to inappropriate public policies both supposedly to enhance a country's 'competitiveness'. He concludes that even the hope to appropriate the rhetoric of competitiveness in order to advocate and implement economic policies that are sound in itself, is misleading.

P. van Dijck and G. Faber (eds.), The External Economic Dimension of the European Union, 71–93.
© 2000 *Kluwer Academic Publishers. Printed in the Netherlands.*

Yet, it is precisely this perspective of policy making to sustain and enhance the standard of living, which provides a constructive angle for the study of the concept and measurement of competitiveness. This is the position taken in Jacquemin and Pench (1997) and likewise in this chapter.

This chapter has been organized as follows. Section 2 describes how countries can be in competition directly through regulatory competition. Moreover, countries can be regarded as competing indirectly through their scores on international ratings of competitiveness and creditworthiness. Increasingly, the rating of creditworthiness of countries has influenced the destination of capital flows and countries are reported to adapt their economic policies in order to improve their credit ratings. Section 3 focuses on the competitive position of the EU in the world economy, notably in international trade. In this context comparisons are made with the performance of Japan and the USA in terms of openness and price and cost competitiveness.

Section 4 studies competitiveness in terms of domestic characteristics of the economy including the standard of living and employment creation. On the basis of the various approaches presented thus far, Section 5 takes a closer look at the variety of definitions of competitiveness that are in use. The connection between competitiveness and economic policy suggests a further analysis of the concept of competitiveness and its measurement in terms of indicators which represent various levels of longevity in the characteristics of economic life. The analysis is illustrated by a 'tree' of competitiveness representing these various levels of economic characteristics with an application to EU-policy making.

2. Countries in competition

Regulatory competition

Regulatory competition can be defined as the alteration of national regulations in response to the actual or expected impact of cross-border mobility of goods, services and factors of production on national economic activity (Pelkmans, 1997). With respect to the EU the regulatory strategy can be considered economically suboptimal, notwithstanding its achievement in reducing regulatory costs. From the perspective of the economics of regulation it may be argued that an optimal strategy would also include the possibility of regulatory competition between EU member states (Pelkmans, 1997).

Sun and Pelkmans (1994) analyse in detail the process of regulatory competition in the EU and describe the complicated interactions between firms and national governments as well as the role of EU institutions. From an analysis of the benefits and costs of regulatory competition and harmonization of regulations they conclude that when regulation is economically justified, regulatory competition and harmonization should be regarded as complements rather than substitutes, with the demarcation between the two being determined on a case-by-case basis.

Fiscal competition tends to work out more rapidly than other forms of regulatory competition. When activities or resources that are very mobile face international differences in tax rates, markets react swiftly, as do governments in turn. Taxation on services may illustrate the point. In 1988 the EU resolved to remove exchange controls, based on a political understanding that a harmonized minimum withholding tax be installed on income from savings and other capital. This would stop the tendency for savings to drift at the margin to zero-tax Luxembourg. Germany however reimposed its own withholding tax as a result of which a capital flight of some 80 billion deutsche mark took effect within a week. The German tax was promptly suspended (Pelkmans, 1997)[2].

Country classifications on competitiveness, economic freedom and creditworthiness

Regulatory competition presents a case where countries compete almost directly, for instance in attracting foreign direct investment (FDI). Countries may also be considered to be in competition in more indirect ways. Nowadays, countries are classified and ranked in a number of ways to show their performance relative to each other on some specific issues. This section reports briefly on country classifications in terms of economic freedom, competitiveness, preparedness to face challenges ahead and creditworthiness. The classifications included in this section testify to the variety of indicators, methodologies and interpretations of the country classifications offered but it is outside the scope of the present study to review and evaluate the various indicators in detail[3].

Since 1994 the Heritage Foundation publishes annually the Index of Economic Freedom. The 1997 Index includes 150 countries and defines economic freedom as '[t]he absence of government coercion or constraint on the production, distribution, or consumption of goods and services' (Heritage Foundation, 1997).

Indices of economic freedom have also been developed by Freedom House and the Fraser Institute[4]. The Fraser Institute Index derives its indicators and their relative weights from a proper definition of economic freedom and covers a relatively long period of time, and is consequently claimed to be more objective than the Heritage Foundation Index and the Freedom House Index, which are considered 'highly subjective' (Gwartney and Lawson, 1997).

Since 1979, the World Economic Forum publishes annually the Global Competitiveness Report, which presents a ranking of the world's most important economies according to their competitiveness, as follows from an analysis of their comparative strengths and weaknesses. Competitiveness is defined as the ability of a country to achieve sustained high rates of growth in gross domestic product (GDP) per capita (World Economic Forum, 1998). The Competitiveness Index is designed to assess the prospects for economic growth over the next five to ten years.

Knack and Keefer (1995) investigate the relationship between institutions and economic performance. Their main conclusion is that the quality of institutions that protect property rights is crucial to economic growth and the evidence suggests that security of property rights affects not only the magnitude of investment but also the efficiency of allocation.

Apart from economic freedom, political freedom has also been investigated in connection with economic performance. In a panel study of 104 countries covering the period 1960-1995 Barro (1997) finds that increases in the standard of living tend to generate a gradual rise in democracy. Moreover, the study observes that an expansion of political freedom – that is, more democracy – has opposing effects on economic growth. Democratic institutions provide a check on the power of governments and thereby limit the potential of public officials to carry out 'unpopular policies'[5]. However, a further increase in political freedom may encourage redistribution of income from rich to poor and typically enhances the power of interest groups[6]. Consequently, Barro (1997) concludes that the net effect of democracy on growth is uncertain.

Recently, the World Economic Forum (1999) introduced an index rating 18 countries according to their 'preparedness to face the challenges of 2050'. The index is developed to assess the capability to face the future, specifically in the 15 EU member states. In order to compare the results with countries outside Europe, the index has been calculated for Japan and the USA as well.

Evaluations of the creditworthiness of countries are a recent phenomenon as compared to the assessments of the creditworthiness of firms and other private institutions. Euromoney and the Institutional Investor publish country ratings on creditworthiness since the early 1980s (Ul Haque et al., 1997). The Economist Intelligence Unit followed later and more of such ratings have been provided by Moody and Standard & Poor.

Worldwide liberalization of capital markets and increased foreign borrowing by governments have stimulated credit-rating institutions to compare countries according to their creditworthiness. From an evaluation of various methods of assessing the creditworthiness of countries, Ul Haque et al. (1997) conclude that credit ratings determine not only whether a country is able to attract loans at reasonable costs but also whether it is able to attract other types of capital. The IMF (1996) observes that the creditworthiness of countries plays an increasing role in determining the destination of capital flows and that developing countries adapt their economic policies to improve their credit ratings. In this way, credit rating results in competition among countries – at least in an indirect way – for flows of international capital and the terms of borrowing.

In connection with the financial crisis in Asia which emerged – outside Japan – in 1997, a curious phenomenon in credit-rating practice could be observed. Within a year the long-term credit rating of South Korea went down from A1 to Ba1 in the categories applied by Moody's, a drop of six grades in a 19 grade classification. Since the rating concerned is meant to reflect the degree of long-term creditworthiness, this casts some doubts regarding the appropriateness of the criteria and indicators in use. To the extent that the financial crisis in Asia is mainly due to the quality of regulations and supervision of financial institutions (Economist, 1997), the eventual shortcomings of South Korea in this respect would have existed long before the financial crisis actually broke out, but were apparently not detected in the procedures for rating creditworthiness in the long term.

Table 3.1 provides a summary of the scores of the EU on various indicators compared to Japan and the USA. The 1997 Index of Economic Freedom ascribes the low score for the EU in particular to a higher degree of government intervention and to less protection of property rights. The 1998 Global Competitiveness Index concludes with respect to the EU to a chronic crisis of declining competitiveness. Among the strong points are outstanding technological capability, management and infrastructure, among the weaknesses are the extensive social welfare provisions and the rigidity of the labour market.

Table 3.1. Classifications of the EU, Japan and the USA.

| | Index | | | |
	economic freedom	global competitiveness	future readiness	credit-worthiness
EU*	25	21	11	15
Japan	11	12	12	13
USA	5	3	8	1
Position EU	behind	behind	equal	behind USA

Note: *In some cases the ranking does not include a score for the EU as a whole. In such cases an unweighted average has been calculated of the scores of the 15 individual EU-member countries.

Sources: Economic freedom: K.R. Holmes, B.T. Johnson and M. Kirkpatrick (eds), *Index of Economic Freedom*, The Heritage Foundation and The Wall Street Journal, Washington, D.C. and New York, 1997.
Global competiveness: World Economic Forum, *Global Competitiveness Report 1998*, Geneva, 1998.
Future readiness: World Economic Forum, *The European Future Readiness Index*, Geneva, 1999.
Creditworthiness: Euromoney, *World Economic Analysis*, September 1997, Supplement, 1997.

3. The EU in competition in the world economy

Openness to world trade

In its report 'The European Union as a World Trade Partner', the European Commission (1997a) analyses the exposure to international competition of the EU, Japan and USA. As illustrated in Table 3.2, there has been a steady increase in the openness of the US economy during the period 1960-96, as measured by the share of international trade in GDP. The trade orientation of the EU and Japan has changed in a somewhat more erratic fashion and peaked in 1975 and 1980, apparently because of the sharp increases in energy prices. By 1996 the EU, Japan and the USA were quite similar in terms of openness. This holds also true when trade in fuel and energy is excluded[7].

The European Commission (1997a) investigated also to what extent the exports of the EU, Japan and the USA have been concentrated in sectors with strong, moderate or weak expansion of world demand[8]. Table 3.3 shows that in

Table 3.2. Trade in goods and services as percentage
shares of GDP, 1960-1996.

	EU	Japan	USA
1960	..	10.5	4.9
1965	8.6	9.8	4.9
1970	9.2	10.2	5.7
1975	10.8	12.8	8.2
1980	11.8	14.2	10.5
1985	12.5	12.8	8.8
1990	9.8	10.4	10.6
1995	10.8	8.7	12.1
1996	11.2	9.7	12.2

Notes: Trade of goods and services is calculated as the average
value of exports and imports, in current prices.
EU is EU-15; only extra-EU trade is considered here.
Source: European Commission, *The European Union as a World
Trade Partner,* European Economy, Reports and Studies
Number 3, European Communities, 1997a.

comparison to the USA and especially Japan, exports of the EU are concentrated
strongly in product groups with a weak expansion of international demand and a
relatively small share of its exports is concentrated in products with a dynamic
international demand. Moreover, the Commission finds that in 1991 25 per
cent of value added in the EU was concentrated in sectors with a dynamic world
demand, as compared to 28 per cent in the USA and 36 per cent in Japan.

International price and cost competitiveness of the EU, Japan and the USA

The main indicator for international price and cost competitiveness used in the
quarterly reports by the European Commission is the real effective exchange rate
which is derived from the nominal effective exchange rate and a trade-weighted
price or cost deflator (European Commission, 1997b). Details about the
methodology are discussed in the Annex to this chapter.

Table 3.4 presents the cost competitiveness of the EU, Japan and the USA
during the period 1988-96, using the unit labour costs in manufacturing as a

Table 3.3. Composition of exports relative to dynamics
of world demand[1], in percentages of total
exports, 1993.

	EU[2]	Japan	USA	Triad
Above average	26.5	34.8	30.0	29.9
Average	48.6	53.5	52.6	51.2
Below average	24.9	11.7	17.4	18.9

Notes: [1] Compared with rates in international demand.
[2] Data relate to Belgium, Denmark, France, Germany, Italy
and the Netherlands only.
Source:: European Commission, *The European Union as a World
Trade Partner*, European Economy, Reports and Studies,
Number 3, European Communities, Brussels, 1997.

deflator and taking 1988 as the base year. The cost competitiveness of the selected
countries and regions has been expressed relative to 23 industrial countries (IC23)
including the 14 EU countries[9], Japan, the USA, Australia, Canada, New Zealand,
Norway and Switzerland as well as Mexico and Turkey. In terms of the real
effective exchange rate the competitiveness of the EU remained nearly constant,
the USA improved and Japan lost.

Within the EU large discrepancies are registered among the member countries.
Substantial gains in cost competitiveness are recorded for Ireland, Finland, Sweden
and Italy, and substantial losses in Portugal, Greece and Germany. The European
Commission (1999) reports on comparable results till the second and third quarter
of 1998. In relation to the group of 23 countries, the EU has gained again
marginally (1 per cent), the USA gained 7.9 per cent and Japan lost 6.6 per
cent[10].

4. Benchmarking the EU economy

A recent report by the European Commission (1998[11]) which assesses the
competitiveness of the EU, observes that '[a] large part of the EU economy heavily
underutilizes its capacity to produce and grow.' To start with, the report observes
that the EU lags behind both Japan and the USA in GDP per capita measured at

Table 3.4. Cost competitiveness of selected countries and regions relative to 23 countries[1], percentage changes, 1988-1996.

	NEER[2]	ULCM[3]	REER[4]
EUR 15	22.1	-18.3	-0.2
Japan	20.9	-6.2	13.3
USA	11.5	-16.9	-7.4
BLEU[5]	16.1	-6.5	8.6
Denmark	15.5	-4.8	9.9
Germany	21.4	-6.6	13.4
Greece	-38.1	114.3	32.6
Spain	-6.8	9.8	2.4
France	19.3	-12.8	4.0
Ireland	5.7	-33.1	-29.3
Italy	-15.5	3.6	-12.5
Netherlands	15.1	-18.6	-6.4
Austria	13.9	-14.5	-2.6
Portugal	-7.9	52.0	40.0
Finland	-7.8	-13.7	-20.4
Sweden	-9.1	-4.1	-12.8
United Kingdom	-13.1	3.9	-9.7

Notes: [1] EUR 15, Japan, USA, Australia, Canada, New Zealand, Norway, Switzerland, Mexico and Turkey.
[2] NEER = nominal effective exchange rate. A minus indicates a depreciation of the NEER.
[3] ULCM = relative unit labour costs in manufacturing, in the national currency.
[4] REER = real effective exchange rate. A minus indicates an improvement in cost competitiveness.
[5] BLEU: Belgium and Luxembourg.

Source: European Commission, *Indicators of Price and Cost Competitiveness,* European Economy, Supplement A, Economic Trends, Number 3/4, March-April 1997.

purchasing power parity (PPP). These levels of income per capita in1997 were aproximately 18,000, 22,000 and 28,000 US dollars respectively. The report considers this a poor performance of the EU.

Analysing the factors explaining the gap in GDP per capita, the European Commission shows that both the EU and Japan lag behind the USA in labour productivity and to a lesser extent in working time per person employed, and that in addition the EU lags behind both countries in the employment rate or participation rate, which expresses the total number of persons employed as a ratio to the total population of working age (15-64 years). In Japan and the USA the employment rate is around 75 per cent and in the EU below 60 per cent. The low employment rate is considered the main factor explaining the income gap with the USA.

The low employment rate reflects the inability of the EU to create new jobs. The annual growth rate of employment has been below 0.5 per cent in the EU since the mid-1970s, as compared to 0.5-1 per cent in Japan and above 1.5 per cent in the USA. Jobless growth in the EU is partly explained by the fact that the growth in labour productivity is to a large extent (40 per cent) the result of capital-labour substitution, whereas this accounts for 25 per cent of labour productivity growth in the USA[12]. This process of capital deepening in the EU relative to the USA can be explained by the higher growth of nominal unit labour costs in the EU as well as by overregulation of the labour market which tends to discourage labour-intensive production. A third factor contributing to jobless growth in the EU is the relatively low degree of specialization in services as compared to the USA, where nearly all net job creation took place in these sectors. In 1995 employment in market services comprised 45 per cent of total employment in the EU against 61 per cent in the USA. Also, the relatively low shares of research- and advertising-intensive industries in total value added as compared to the USA reveal shortcomings in innovation and marketing strategies in the most dynamic markets.

Moreover, the European Commission (1998) finds that in the EU and Japan the costs of important inputs of energy and communications are generally higher than in the USA. Also, the EU lacks adequate risk capital as compared to the USA. There is a lack of funding for start-up firms and technological development, which in turn hampers the growth of employment opportunities.

On the basis of these findings the Commission recommends that the following 'tailor-made' policies be undertaken. First, the elimination of institutional and regulatory barriers in financial, labour and product markets which impede the flexibility of entrepreneurial response required by fast changes in the business environment. Second, the continuous upgrading of European industry in terms of quality and switching to new products early in the production cycle, also in view of the relatively high labour costs in the EU. Also, economic policy in the EU has to promote innovation, adaptability and the upgrading of human capital.

5. The competitiveness of countries: scope and measurement

Krugman's (1994) conclusion in his well-known article 'Competitiveness: A Dangerous Obsession' is

'[s]o let's start telling the truth: competitiveness is a meaningless word when applied to national economies. And the obsession with competitiveness is both wrong and dangerous'.

Krugman argues that countries do not compete, at least not in the way companies do. Two main arguments are put forward. First, countries unlike companies do not go out of business and disappear. As a result 'the concept of national competitiveness is elusive'. However, limiting the concept of competition only to cases with a possibility of ending bankrupt would make it inapplicable to Olympic Games and football matches as well.

Second, in the case of competition among firms, the gain of one firm is at the expense of the others. In the case of countries, the situation in international trade is quite different: 'If the European economy does well, it need not be at the US expense'. The argument could be presented even somewhat stronger: economic growth in one country may have positive spillover effects on other countries through increased demand for imports. Indeed, international trade 'is not a zero-sum game' (Krugman, 1994).

Yet, at the same time, national governments support their national companies also in international bidding against governments of other countries. On the other hand, firms can also be in positive-sum game situations and generally are in such situations as they deliver raw materials, parts and components to other industries. This illustrates that the distinction between competition among firms and countries is less pronounced than suggested by Krugman.

The concept of competitiveness

In previous sections a number of indicators have been presented that are in use to evaluate the economic performance of countries, particularly regarding economic freedom, competitiveness and creditworthiness. A number of institutions has been involved in analysing the performance of countries, using different definitions or descriptions of the phenomena under study, and employing different methodologies and sets of indicators to arrive at specific scores and rankings of countries[13]. It is not surprising therefore that the ranking of countries differs among the rating institutions, sometimes even to a considerable degree, even when countries are evaluated regarding the same dimension of economic performance. This implies that a closer look at the concept of competitiveness is required.

The World Economic Forum (1998) defines competitiveness as 'the ability of a country to achieve sustained high rates of growth'. Similarly in Chapter 2 of this volume, Thurow presents a definition according to which 'competitiveness, simply defined, is any region's ability to generate a high and rising standard of living that keeps it abreast of the world leaders in GDP per capita'. In Thurow's definition the word 'high' connected to 'rising standard of living' and the expression 'that keeps it abreast of the world leaders in GDP per capita' seem inappropriate: a country cannot be blamed *per se* for having a GDP per capita that is lower than that of Switzerland as the level of its income per capita is of course related to its level of development and the scope of its comparative advantage. To be meaningful, the concept of competitiveness should apply to countries at all levels of development.

The Competitiveness Policy Council (1992) uses the following definition
'competitiveness is the ability to produce goods and services that meet the test of international markets while our (the USA) citizens earn a standard of living that is both rising and sustainable in the long run'.

This definition has the advantage that it does not require that the standard of living is 'high' as in the previous definitions but 'rising', which is more prudent, and 'sustainable in the long run' which is different from 'sustained' in the definition of the World Economic Forum. To the extent that 'in the long run' also relates to the aspect of 'rising' this would allow for a country to experience a temporary setback in economic growth, without losing out on competitiveness. The definition also mentions that goods and services should 'meet the test of international markets'. Krugman (1994), however, argued that national standards of living are 'overwhelmingly determined by domestic factors rather than by some competition for world markets'.

A similar definition is quoted from the President's Commission on Industrial Competitiveness (The Council on Competitiveness, 1995)

'competitiveness is the degree to which a nation can, under free and fair market conditions, produce goods and services that will meet the test of international markets, while simultaneously maintaining or expanding the real income of its citizens'.

This definition is cautious as it does not require that real income should be expanding all the time but also allows for real income to be maintained only. The definition introduces a new element when referring to free and fair market conditions, which seems to imply that a specific economic order is required for the concept of competitiveness to be meaningful.

In the definition of the European Commission (1998) the international position has been included as well

'an economy is competitive if its population can enjoy high standards of living and high rates of employment while maintaining a sustainable external position'. Rather than requiring that the test of international markets is met, this definition refers to the sustainability of the external position. In addition, the Commission (1998) refers to 'a high rate of employment' which has been addressed more broadly in the definition of the OECD (1996)

'competitiveness refers to the ability of companies, industries and regions, nations or supranational regions to generate, while being and remaining exposed to international competition, relatively high factor income and factor employment on a sustainable basis'.

One could argue about the proper meaning of 'relatively' in this definition. More significantly, the notion of competitiveness is not confined to nation states, but refers also to regions and to levels of supranational decision making as well as to firms and industries. If it were possible to pursue this line of thinking, the concept of competitiveness would become all the more fruitful.

Jacquemin and Pench (1997) observed in response to Krugman (1994) that the ultimate purpose of analysing the concepts of competitiveness is to show that

' the theoretical inconsistencies underlying the concept of competitiveness should not obscure the significance of the competitiveness debate as an indicator of a far reaching reorientation of policy approaches and policy priorities'.

Moreover, 'instead of focusing on definitions, the analysis should aim at helping policy makers to think about what is important for economic performance.'

Competitiveness and economic policy

The definitions presented in the previous section connect the concept of competitiveness with targets of economic policy. Some targets have been referred to explicitly including a high standard of living, a high rate of growth, high factor income and high factor employment. Moreover, a variety of indicators is used in several of the approaches that relate to widely different dimensions of the societies under investigation. This may be illustrated by referring to the indicators used by the World Economic Forum (1998) to arrive at a value of its index of competitiveness: the quality of the political system; flexibility of the labour market, and openness of the economy. The first of these indicators is a fundamental characteristic of the organization of society; the second indicator represents a policy and the third indicator can be related to a statistic which may change every year. Hence, these indicators represent various degrees of changeability in the economic and political reality.

This distinction is used by Jacquemin and Pench (1997) in their typology of competitiveness, in which indicators are distinguished under the headings of performance, factors and policies. The performance indicators represent the more volatile characteristics of the economy, factors represent the more fundamental aspects of the economy and policies have an intermediate position. Jacquemin and Pench (1997) apply these three levels of indicators at three levels aggregation in economic life: the enterprise, the industry and the economy as a whole. The distinction according to various levels of changeability and of aggregation closely resembles the approach adopted by Tinbergen (1967). The distinction between fundamental and less fundamental characteristics according to Jacquemin and Pench (1997) reflects two ways of looking at competitiveness: *ex-post* and *ex-ante*; the *ex-ante* approach would be based on an analysis of the fundamentals, the *ex-post* evaluation of competitiveness would be based on the performance variables.

At this stage it may be recalled that Balassa (1965) introduced the concept of revealed comparative advantage to be distinguished from the concept of comparative advantage itself. The latter concept is more fundamental and relates to the availability of factors of production in an economy relative to other economies, resulting in differences in relative scarcity and prices comparative advantages in production processes in line with the differences in factor availabilities. As these differences are difficult to observe, Balassa (1965) proposed to analyse comparative advantage from the other side as revealed by the trade performances of countries. After all, the - intrinsic - comparative advantage was bound to show up in a country's revealed performance and product-pattern of trade.

Finally it will be recalled from Section 2 that in a short period of time in 1997 the long-term credit rating of South Korea went down six grades in a 19 grade classification. Apparently, in the assessment of the long-term creditworthiness the balance between long-term indicators (fundamentals) and short-term indicators (performance variables) had not been appropriate, in terms of numbers, weights or both.

In this connection the approach by Tinbergen (1967) is very fruitful, not only because of the distinction between fundamental characteristics and other variables, but also because of the different weights that can be attached to various targets of economic policy according to the preferences given to them in the decision-making process and, as a consequence, as well as to the instruments of economic policy, according to their relative contribution to reaching the targets.

The tree of competitiveness

The observations presented above have been combined in a single framework, the so-called tree of competitiveness, presented in Table 3.5. This tree has the following characteristics. First, economic competitiveness is related to economic policy making. Second, various levels of changeability of the indicators are distinguished, representing fundamentals, instruments or targets in economic policy making. Also, the analysis extends to the various levels of aggregation in economic life including the level of the firm, industry, country and group of countries. Examples are given for the case of policy making at the macro-level or the (multi) country-level.

An example related to international trade may illustrate the usefulness of this approach in analysing the relationship between policy and competitiveness. The EU adheres to the principles of non-discrimination, underlying the General Agreement on Tariffs and Trade (GATT) and the World Trade Organization (WTO), and national treatment, as a consequence of the 1992 programme for the Single Market (Pelkmans, 1997). On the basis of these fundamentals one would expect the EU to apply low, uniform and bounded tariffs and to use non-tariff barriers (NTB's) only by exception. At the level of revealed characteristics one would expect internal EU prices to be close to world-market prices. Clearly, the EU in many respects adheres to the fundamentals of non-discrimination and

Table 3.5. Tree of competitiveness.

	Competitiveness	policy making	Macro-level (country)	
			example: money	example: trade
Foliage	Revealed competitiveness	targets	- inflation - credit rating	- domestic prices vs. world prices - growth of trade vs. output
Trunk	Competitiveness policies	instruments	instruments of monetary policy - interest rates - money supply	instruments of trade policy - tariffs - non-tariff barriers - trade agreements
Root	Fundamentals of competitiveness	fundamentals	Central Bank - independence - supervision over commercial banking	principles of - non-discrimination - domestic treatment

national treatment in its trade policy, but significant exceptions may be noted in this regard. Internal EU prices of a number of agricultural products are much higher than corresponding prices in the world market[14]. Also, the EU applies a variety of NTBs targeted at individual countries and even at individual firms within a country[15]. Moreover, the EU has concluded a number of preferential trade agreements (PTAs) (Pelkmans and Carzaniga, 1996), that are studied in Part II of this volume. These observations on revealed characteristics and trade policies show that there may be more fundamentals that play a part as well. Wolf (1988) has analysed the factors that underlie the apparent discrimination in EU trade policies and has suggested that the EU has a preference for managed trade for two basic reasons. First, because of a general fear of being uncompetitive, initially *vis-à-vis* the USA, and at later stages *vis-à-vis* Japan and the newly industrializing countries in East Asia. Second, a resistance to change and adjustment resulting from the evolving pattern of comparative advantage in the world economy.

In this way the tree of competitiveness provides a framework for searching methodically for the concurrence between revealed characteristics, instruments and fundamentals within an area of policy making, and allows for a search for hidden fundamentals, when revealed characteristics and instruments are not in accordance with the fundamentals proclaimed.

Notes

[1] I would like to thank Dr. G. Faber, Dr. P. van Dijck and Professor D. McAleese, for their advice and comments. I would also like to thank Mr. B. Kuijpers, MA, at the Erasmus Centre for Economic Integration Studies, for his co-operation and Mrs. F. Ackermans at the same centre for her assistance.

[2] Pelkmans (1997) comments: 'By refusing to agree to minimum harmonisation or to adequate reporting obligations to the tax authorities of other member states, Luxembourg causes negative externalities to other member states, because it imposes another tax revenue structure than they want'. To what extent the externality is negative, can only be judged from the point of view of an optimal or preferred rate of taxation.

[3] A more extensive presentation is presented in Kol (1999).

[4] Messick (1996) and Gwartney and Lawson (1997).

[5] This refers probably to policies constraining economic growth as often found in dictatorships.

[6] The former would seem to be a less relevant factor in influencing economic growth than the latter.

[7] In explaining the erratic movements in openness of the EU and Japan compared to the USA, the European Commission (1997a) attaches much weight to the movement in the exchange rates of the US dollar against the yen and European currencies. This is not convincing to the extent that in the ratio of openness of the EU and Japan both the numerator and denominator are expressed in US dollars. However, the ratio of exports to GDP of Japan shows a decline from 13 per cent in 1984 to 9 per cent in 1996, which may reflect *inter alia* the position of the yen against other currencies.

[8] Strong, moderate and weak refers to above average, average and below average growth in international demand, respectively.

[9] BLEU includes Belgium and Luxembourg.

[10] The European Commission (1999) also reports on cost competitiveness using unit labour costs for the economy as a whole (UCLE) rather than for manufacturing only (ULCM). The results for the EU remain the same, but are reversed for Japan and the USA registering a gain and a loss of 12 per cent each respectively against the IC23.

[11] The economy-wide assessment of EU competitiveness is followed by a more specific analysis of the competitiveness of the EU manufacturing sector; this study concentrates on the former part.

[12] The remainder is attributed to total factor productivity growth.

[13] For a detailed overview see e.g. Kol (1999).

[14] Examples are sugar, beef and milk, for which the internal EU prices in 1997 were 203, 193 and 176 per cent, respectively, of the corresponding world-market prices (OECD, 1998).

[15] Pelkmans and Carzaniga (1996) and the WTO (1998) conclude however that the protective strength of the NTBs applied by the EU is gradually being reduced.

Annex 3.A.1. The real effective exchange rate as an indicator for international competitiveness

The main indicator for international price and cost competitiveness is the real effective exchange rate (REER). It is derived from a combination of the nominal effective exchange rate (NEER) and a trade-weighted price or cost deflator (European Commission 1997b).

$$\ln (REER_t / REER_{t-1}) = \ln (NEER_t / NEER_{t-1}) + \ln (Deflator_t / Deflator_{t-1}),$$

the NEER shows the changes in the value of a currency with reference to a given base or reference period and is calculated as a trade-weighted geometric average of bilateral exchange rates against the currencies of the competing countries considered. With respect to trade weights there are various possibilities for using data on imports and/or exports. The European Commission (1997b) uses double bilateral export weights, which reflect the shares of the exports of the country under consideration in the home markets of the various competing countries, as well as in export markets elsewhere. Various price and cost deflators can be used to transform nominal into real exchange rates. The European Commission (1997b) lists the consumer price index (CPI), the GDP deflator, the price deflator of exports of goods and services, unit labour costs in the economy (ULCE), unit labour costs in manufacturing only (ULCM). Empirical evidence shows that the choice of the deflator may strongly affect the outcome of developments in the REERs. Therefore, the European Commission (1997b) rightly advises that the choice of the deflator is to be made carefully and in line with the objective of the analysis. For example, an analysis of world-market shares would use the export price deflator, while an investigation of employment growth would focus on indicators for cost competitiveness based on unit labour costs. Another important choice is that of the reference period. The European Commission (1997b) investigates this choice in detail. Ideally, the period of reference represents years in which the economy is in internal and external balance. An internal balance would represent a situation in which output growth is near the potential maximum in combination with a low and sustainable rate of inflation, and an external balance would imply that the current account would be sustainable in the medium term, together with the exchange rate. On this basis the European Commission (1997b) has rejected 1979 as a year of reference and has selected 1987 and 1988 instead. This selection is also related to the conclusion of the Louvre Agreement which has marked the beginning of a period of exchange-rate stability that ended with the crisis of the Exchange Rate Mechanism (ERM) in September 1992 (European Commission, 1999).

Finally, in a comparative analysis of cost competitiveness between the EU and the USA, it might be preferable to include the EU as a single economic entity rather than as 15 separate countries. In that case intra-EU exports would be regarded as part of domestic production, not as exports competing with USA exports in the markets of various EU member countries. Treating the EU as a single entity implies further the design of an imaginary currency for the EU as a whole. The bilateral exchange rate of such a currency against the US dollar would be defined as an indexed weighted average of the dollar exchange rates of the currencies of the EU countries with the shares of the member states in extra-EU exports being used as weights (European Commission, 1997b). In the empirical analysis however it turns out that the difference between the outcomes for both options are only marginal. The development over time of US cost competitiveness relative to the EU as a whole appears to be practically identical to the US competitiveness when measured relative to the 15 EU member countries individually (European Commission, 1997b).

As to alternative indicators, the European Commission (1997b) observes that next to the REER, two indicators for competitiveness merit attention. Both indicators measure profitability economy-wide. The effective profitability of the economy compares trade-weighted changes in price and in unit labour costs to indicate the development in productivity of the economy relative to its competitors. The effective export profitability of the economy is the ratio of trade-weighted changes in the export price index and in unit labour costs. Calculating these two alternative measures for the period 1979-1997, the European Commission (1997b) concludes that the EU relative to the IC23 group of countries has gained in profitability of the economy as a whole as well as in exports. Also, EU exporters have preferred to raise profit margins rather than to increase their shares in world markets. On the other hand, exporters in Japan and the USA have been willing to sacrifice profitability in order to maintain or raise their market shares. In the USA this took place against a general economy-wide decline in profitability, whereas in Japan general profitability rose but far less than in the EU.

References

Balassa, B., *Trade Liberalization and 'Revealed' Comparative Advantage*, The Manchester School of Economic and Social Studies, Volume XXXIII, 1965.

Barro, R.J., *Determinants of Democracy*, Research Memorandum 9706, OCFEB, Erasmus University, Rotterdam, 1997.

Brittan, L., *The Europe We Need*, Hamish Hamilton, London, 1994.

Competitiveness Policy Council, *Building a Competitive Advantage*, First Annual Report to the President and Congress, Washington D.C., 1992.

Council on Competitiveness, *Competitiveness Index 1995*, Washington D.C., 1995.

Economist, The , *Asia's Economic Crisis*, November 15, 1997.

Euromoney, *World Economic Analysis*, September 1997, Supplement, 1997.

European Commission, *The European Union as a World Trade Partner*, European Economy, Reports and Studies Number 3, European Communities, 1997.

European Commission, *Indicators of Price and Cost Competitiveness*, European Economy, Supplement A, Economic Trends, Number 3/4, March/April 1997, 1997b.

European Commission, *The Competitiveness of European Industry*, European Communities, Luxembourg, 1997c.

European Commission, *The Competitiveness of European Industry*, European Communities, Luxembourg, 1998.

European Commission, *Price and Competitiveness Report*, Q 2-3, 1998, The European Commission, Brussels, 1999.

Gwartney, J.D. and R.A. Lawson, *Economic Freedom of the World*, Annual Report, The Fraser Institute, Vancouver, 1997.

Holmes, K.R., B.T. Johnson and M. Kirkpatrick (eds), *Index of Economic Freedom*, The Heritage Foundation and The Wall Street Journal, Washington, D.C. and New York, 1997.

IMF, *International Capital Markets: Developments, Prospects and Key Policy Issues*, Washington, D.C., 1996.

Jacquemin, A. and L.R. Pench, 'What Competitiveness for Europe? An Introduction', in: A. Jacquemin and L.R. Pench (eds.), *Europe Competing in the Global Economy*, Edward Elgar, Cheltenham, UK, 1997.

Knack, S. and Ph. Keefer, 'Institutions and Economic Performance: Cross-country Tests Using Alternative Institutional Measures', *Economics and Politics*, Volume 7, Number 3, 1995.

Kol, J., *Competitiveness of Nations, An Overview of Concepts and Measurement*, Research Memorandum, Erasmus Centre for Economic Integration Studies, 1999.

Krugman, P., 'Competitiveness: A Dangerous Obsession', *Foreign Affairs*, Volume 73, Issue 4, March/April, 1994.

Messick, R.E., *World Survey of Economic Freedom: 1995-1996*, Transaction Publications, New Brunswick, 1996.

Ministry of Economic Affairs, *Benchmarking the Netherlands*, Ministry of Economic Affairs, The Hague, 1997.

OECD, *Industrial Competitiveness*, Paris, 1996.

OECD, *Agricultural Policies in OECD Countries: Monitoring and Evaluation 1998*, Paris, 1998.

Pelkmans, J., *European Integration. Methods and Economic Analysis*, Addison Wesley Longman Ltd, Harlow, UK, 1997.

Pelkmans, J. and A.G. Carzaniga, 'The Trade Policy Review of the European Union', The *World Economy*, Volume 18, Supplement, 1996.

Sun, J.M. and J. Pelkmans, *Regulatory Competition in the Single Market*, Centre for European Policy Studies, Brussels, 1994.

Tinbergen, J., *Economic Policy: Principles and Design* (4th rev. printing), North Holland, Amsterdam, 1967.

Ul Haque, N., D. Mathieson and N. Mark, 'Rating the Raters of Country Creditworthiness', *Finance and Development*, March, 1997.

Wolf, M., 'An Unholy Alliance: the European Community and Developing Countries in the International Trading System', in: L.B.M. Mennes and J. Kol (eds.), *European Trade Policies and the Developing World*, Croom Helm Ltd., Beckenham, UK, 1988.

World Economic Forum, *Global Competitiveness Report 1998*, Geneva, 1998.

World Economic Forum, *The European Future Readiness Index*, Geneva, 1999.

WTO, *Trade Policy Review: European Union* 1997, Geneva, 1998.

4

ENLARGEMENT OF THE EU: INTEGRATION AND FRAGMENTATION

FRANS ANDRIESSEN
Utrecht University
Utrecht
The Netherlands

1. Introduction

Public opinion regarding the European Union (EU) has predominantly focused on the establishment of the Economic and Monetary Union (EMU) of late. Not surprisingly so, as this undertaking may be considered the most significant monetary operation of the 20th century. This is at least how it is experienced in the EU. Granted, the International Monetary Fund (IMF) in particular has become significantly more important as a global monetary authority, but the operation aimed at unifying countries ranked among the world's most important economies into a single monetary union with a single common currency is an unparalleled achievement, even though the United Kingdom keeps clear of this operation, at least for the time being.

At the same time, this final stage of the European economic integration provides an interesting example of the proposition that major decisions or major steps forward in the European integration process are impossible without either consensual decision-making - which often implies indecisiveness on vital policy areas - or differentiation in the sense that exceptions of a transitory and sometimes even structural nature are anticipated. In the case of EMU this invoked the opting-

P. van Dijck and G. Faber (eds.), The External Economic Dimension of the European Union, 95–113.
© 2000 *Kluwer Academic Publishers. Printed in the Netherlands.*

out for the United Kingdom and Denmark and an accepted Swedish derogation that cannot be legitimated on the basis of the generally held interpretation of the convergence criteria laid down in the Treaty of Maastricht. It even goes a little further, as it is anticipated that member countries that fail to meet the convergence criteria, may obtain the status of a derogated member state, which enables them to stay outside the EMU temporarily. Hence, differentiation has been made possible for countries that do not want to participate fully as well as for countries that are not yet capable to.

From the perspective of European integration, the EMU may be the largest operation of the century, but it is not the major challenge. For that consists in extending the European integration after the collapse of the Berlin Wall, the reunification of Germany, the dissolution of the Warsaw Pact and the implosion of the Soviet Union, up to the boundaries of this subcontinent or even beyond. The recognition of that mission has not come about without due resistance. Even the inclusion of countries that were never excluded from the Western European cultural sphere, met with hesitation and even occasioned the creation of the European Economic Area (EEA) which extended the *acquis communautaire* by a number of countries without offering them full membership of the Union. Maybe it is an irony of history that the creation of this zone accelerated the membership of a number of the countries concerned. All the stronger was the initial hesitation towards the Central and Eastern European countries (CEEC) that had been part of the Soviet bloc. This becomes apparent from the initial refusal of the EU to consider the so-called Europe Agreements (EAs) a preliminary but definite step towards their entry into the EU. That hesitation was overcome at the European Council of Copenhagen in 1993. From that moment on, the prospect of access to the Union under certain conditions was held out to all CEEC with whom association arrangements in the form of EAs have been concluded. In the meantime the enlargement has become a top EU priority for the years ahead. The way in which the enlargement will take place and the changes it will bring about in the structure and homogeneity of the EU will be the subject matter of this chapter.

The chapter is organized as follows. Section 2 defines the concepts of deepening, widening, enlargement and differentiation and examines to what extent they are already finding application. Section 3 deals with the question whether differentiation will also lead to fragmentation of membership. In Section 4, the enlargement of the EU is considered, and Section 5 discusses the time schedule for the enlargement and the differentiation related to it. Sections 6 and 7 analyse the conditions for enlargement to be met by the EU and the new member states respectively. Section 8 outlines what differentiated membership could look like. Section 9, finally, elaborates on the institutional embedding of differentiated membership.

2. Deepening, widening, enlargement and differentiation

The enlargement is a major step in the European integration process, which, in its consequences, even surpasses the establishment of the EMU. It is different in nature, as well. The EMU typically is an integration measure. It confirms and consolidates the existing integrated economic order in the Union and as such it is part of the *acquis communautaire*. In due course, the *acquis communautaire* will also apply to the new entrants to the Union.

Enlargement, however, involves something else. The EMU may be seen as a form of deepening - it reinforces integration in existing common policy areas and widening - it creates new common policy areas with the concomitant institutions and powers. Enlargement should rather be considered as a means of broadening the geographical area where Community law and institutions apply (Pelkmans, 1997). The debate about deepening which was held intensively in the Union some time ago, resonates in this approach, although the debate certainly was not merely about deepening of the *acquis*, but primarily about strengthening the institutional structure, in order to avoid conflicts between enlargement and the actual functioning and deepening of integration.

Section 6 will point out that a deepening, widening and enlargement in the sense of a strengthened institutional and budgetary structure has not materialized. In this respect there is another fundamental difference with the EMU. After all, the deepening and widening which is required for the establishment and functioning of the EMU was fully detailed in the relevant articles of the Treaty of Maastricht. As noted earlier, even the respective exceptions were provided for. Put differently, the conditions that would enable this form of deepening and widening of the integration to be successful were basically complied with in full.

As shown in this chapter, the conditions for enlargement have not been met. The Intergovernmental Conference (IGC) of Amsterdam, intended as an evaluation of the Treaty of Maastricht, but meanwhile upgraded to the occasion where conditions for enlargement of the Union were to be realized, only satisfied these objectives in the eyes of some government leaders. Generally speaking, it is observed that Amsterdam indeed achieved improvements in some respects, but that the vital objective could not be realized.

The proposition that major steps in the integration process are impossible without an often-paralysing unanimity or differentiation found an interesting confirmation in the Amsterdam Treaty. First, according to the so-called flexibility clause stating that a group of member countries that prefer to integrate faster should be allowed to do so under relatively stringent conditions. Decision-making in this respect involves a qualified majority vote, unless a member country opposes it invoking a plea of national interest. A second form of differentiation may be equally interesting indeed. It pertains to Art. 23 of the EU Treaty (ex Art. J13) in the second pillar - foreign and security policy - stating that a member country that withheld its vote can make a formal statement which enables it not to apply the decision, which is, for all other purposes, binding. Here, this is about differentiation towards less integration, whereas the flexibility clause discussed earlier is about a differentiation towards more integration.

It is beyond any doubt that the highest institution of the EU, the European Council, has recognized the generally felt need for more nuance by allowing for differentiation. At the same time it is obvious that this body emphatically continues to see differentiation as a deviation from the principle according to which acceptance and absorption of the *acquis* is the rule and will remain so. For the foreign and security policy the option to derogate seems to be of a more structural nature. In that case it concerns derogation from the rule of unanimity, which is upheld as the principal element in foreign and security policy. Other examples of structural derogation will be elaborated later on.

3. Differentiation and fragmentation

From the above it follows that differentiation is already inevitable in the EU of the 15. It would not be difficult to draw numerous examples from previous treaties, such as the Single European Act, but it is beyond the scope of this chapter to go into a full consideration of this issue as such. It was merely mentioned, because solutions to the issue of enlarging the EU towards the boundaries of Europe will of necessity be even less able to be realized without differentiation.

The question that then imposes itself is how far this differentiation may go. Is it only tolerated as an unavoidable but by definition temporary derogation of the *acquis*, or could it be considered to be a more structural instrument, which could lead to partial fragmentation? Fragmentation would mean that countries are not bound to parts of the *acquis*, and as a result entail no rights or obligations and thus they would have a less far-reaching form of membership.

At first glance, this seems to be inconceivable and unacceptable. This line of thought is indeed at odds with the approach that, at least in theory, has been followed so far. Yet, the development that took place with respect to the West European Union (WEU) may be relevant to the approach of this issue. It is true that the attempt made in Amsterdam to integrate the WEU into the EU in due course, failed. Still, the WEU remains integral to the development of the Union and the instrument to become operative in security policy. At any rate, integration over time is no longer out of the question. The WEU, then, has four ways of participation: as a member, an associate member, an associate and an observer. These four forms of participation have their own substance and meaning. Obviously, the more limited the degree of participation, the smaller the 'substance'. Members are in a different position from observers. The four forms of partnership, however, have been formalized.

The impression can hardly be avoided that the more complex and delicate the issue, the more variation in forms of membership and participation is acceptable. It may not be without good reason that especially in the area of security policy, differentiation should have taken its most far-reaching form. Differentiation as a structural instrument, and not as a - by definition - temporary measure *vis-à-vis* an existing *acquis*, appears to be accepted in this field. It looks as if, in order to reach a set objective, pragmatic solutions have been sought and found to emerging handicaps that contribute to realizing the set goal - in this case: more security - without unnecessarily hampering the functioning of the institution concerned.

4. Enlargement

The enlargement of the EU has gained momentum, in terms of membership and pace. By now, 13 countries have applied for accession, which is nearly the number of countries in the current Union. It took the Union 34 years - from 1952 to 1986 - to double its membership from six to 12. The political pressure to accede, however, is so enormous that for the great majority of the present applications the process will in all likelihood be wrapped up within ten years. At least, that is the general expectation. The political capability of the Union to lay down a time schedule considerably in excess of about ten years, is probably inversely proportional to the degree of internal, and particular external pressure exerted. The last word has yet to be spoken on this matter, however.

An enlargement up to the boundaries of Europe has been discussed earlier in this chapter. This was for a simple reason: after all, the preamble of the Treaty of Rome expresses that European countries that endorse the objectives of the Union, are invited to participate in this integration process. Yet one thing is for sure: what constitutes the boundaries of Europe is not defined by historical events, such as the Iron Curtain or a former allegiance to the Soviet Union. There is no sensible geographical rationale why we should consider the Baltic states to be European countries, but the Ukraine or Belarus as non-European countries. Likewise, one can hold different views about the Caucasian Republics, even more so now that for political reasons Turkey is considered to belong to the European family. And at some stage in the past a president of the Council of Ministers offered Israel a conditional place in the European Economic Area.

The issue whether or to what extent the Russian Federation is part of Europe, is not a serious issue for debate on where to draw the limits of Europe at this time - no doubt in part owing to its delicate character - although the current president, Mr. Yeltsin, expects the Russian Federation to become part of the EU, if in due course. An EU that has devoted itself to the enlargement towards other European countries for predominantly historical, cultural or political reasons, simply cannot halt at those countries falling into its lap as the upshot of recent European history.

This issue is not broached here to complicate matters. However, the fact that the Union will, sooner or later, be confronted with this issue will have to be accounted for and in part, this may well be sooner than later. It might be one more reason to allow more radical solutions to be considered in the debate on how to solve the complications already posed by the 13 that have presented themselves so far. It involves a political decision, after all, as has become clear from the present state of affairs.

5. Time schedule and differentiation

Virtually the most simple solution would be a multi-stage accession of new members in accordance with the moment they have fully prepared themselves for accepting and absorbing the *acquis*. This solution is unrealistic, though. At the highest political level expectations have been raised for a more rapid accession, which will strongly increase the external pressure, certainly when the first countries in the region will have become members.

In this context it is not insignificant either, that the phased approach chosen for the enlargement of the North Atalantic Treaty Organization (NATO) has already led to quite a number of tensions in the Baltics, as well. The decision-making at the 1997 Luxembourg Summit reflects this political fact: a phased approach to the negotiations was opted for, and at the same time countries not yet part of the first group were offered to be involved in the process of enlargement as intensely as possible (European Commission, 1998). For certain the pressure will increase enormously after the first few sheep have leapt over the ditch.

On the other hand, there is a possibility that the material conditions under which the first accessions will be allowed, notably with respect to derogations from the *acquis*, will heighten the resistance in the existing Union against further enlargement, as such derogations will almost certainly lead to frictions in the market. Moreover, it remains difficult to foresee how new entrants in the region will respond to exceptions, if any, made for other CEEC. It might be, that they will wish to consolidate as much as possible the benefits they enjoy, certainly in the early years, and share them with as few others as possible.

The budget may have a delaying influence. It goes without saying that the issue, which is mainly about reforming agricultural policy and the regional funds, will need to be solved before the first accessions. The way in which solutions for this delicate problem will be found, however, is related to the amount of money that will be made available for the pre-adherence strategy and to its effect on the means available to the present member states. Nevertheless, it seems wise to assume that a number of countries in the region will certainly enter sooner than would be objectively desirable from the point of view of the classical theory of applying the *acquis*. After all that has happened, waiting-periods of up to 15 years do not seem to be politically realistic any more, all the more so as after the wave from Central and Eastern Europe, another wave will emerge from the Balkans and more remote European areas. This implies an increasing inevitability of differentiation.

Countries in the region that qualify most for membership, have forwarded appeals for substantial derogation with respect to the movement of capital and financial services. Presumably, this derogation will have to be granted and this implies the acceptance of a long-term derogation of the EMU. Note that this is only about the most qualified countries. Thus, one should not harbour any illusions.

The official negotiators are understandably reticent about taking radical positions in this respect for reasons of negotiating tactics. These tactics, however, should not make us lose sight of the strategic aspects, and certainly not internally. These strategic aspects relate to the problem of combining the political inevitability of accession at relatively short notice with an acceptable functioning of the Union, both in its present and its future form.

6. Conditions for enlargement

Strikingly, discussions about further integration mostly mention the conditions for accession, meaning the conditions made on the countries that wish to become EU members. Far less mention is made of the conditions for enlargement that is to say, the conditions that the Union should meet to admit new members in a balanced way. The latter, however, is at least as important as the former. After all, one should not just be concerned with the interests of the newly entering countries, but also with securing the interests of the countries that are already EU members. It is not in the interest of the new entrants to become a member of a Union that - whether or not as a consequence of this accession - will go on functioning less effectively.

As for the conditions for enlargement, it can be argued that enlargement actually has not been prepared internally. True, the Declaration of Copenhagen emphatically mentions the absorptive capacity of the Union, but in practice hardly any attention has been paid to it, and the discussion seems to narrow down too much to the question how and for whose benefit the regional funds of the Union are to be restructured. The *acquis communautaire* is slowly changing from a rather rigid and formal system of rules into a system in which the market dynamics are stimulated by a progressive degree of deregulation and liberalization as is the case in the sectors of telecommunications, informatics and energy supply. This is the kind of *acquis* the entrants will have to anticipate, and more often than not people seem hardly aware of this fact.

In addition to the internal issue of the *acquis*, there are budgetary issues. Unfortunately, the discussion mainly focuses on the budgetary side, as has often been the case. Some accuse the European Commission of having misled the member states by proposing an explicit 'catch-all scenario' in its enlargement strategy, Agenda 2000, which incidentally assumes particular willingness to make concessions on the part of the richer member states than with those countries that are less prosperous (European Commission, 1997). Spain for one has taken a strong position, not only raising the issue of redistributing the regional funds but also of the cohesion fund in a fundamental way.

In the 'catch-all scenario' the large majority of transfers in the coming budget period will be allocated to the actual members of the Union. Nevertheless, there is substantial resistance. Yet, there would be every reason to seize a major opportunity - the enlargement with such a large number of new and less prosperous countries - for fundamental debate on the allocation method of the regional funds. It looks odd that it is proposed to maintain the existing course of action for the 15, whereas a kind of national limit is set which applies for the new members. This national limit is derived from the actual results of a regional assessment method in the group of 15. It would stand to reason to start from the objective national need for transfers expressed in entities that apply to all member states, existing and new, and specify them for each region. Subsequently, this might lead to a drastic cut back in expenses on that account and at the same time to a far more accurate allocation of means. It is regrettable that the European Commission has seen no reason for definitely raising this budgetary issue fundamentally. Hence, a thorough budgetary preparation for the enlargement has not taken place.

It is generally agreed upon that in terms of decision-making the Treaty of Amsterdam has underperformed. In a number of areas where decision-making by majority vote had been proposed, this could not be attained, mainly because the Federal Republic of Germany let itself be spoon-fed by its *Bundesländer*. The decision-making about rule-setting has been simplified, which is no doubt an advantage. But the principle that a qualified majority vote will be allowed except for very exceptional circumstances, could not be realized.

Also, the questions of weighing votes in the Council of Ministers where, after all, decision-making takes place, and of the balance between larger and smaller countries, could not be resolved. This issue is linked to the composition of the European Commission in which - sooner or later - large countries will have to give up their second commissioner. One cannot expect this problem to be readily solved when even the smaller countries fail to come to terms over this point, e.g. the Netherlands vs. Belgium. Still, this should be hammered out with considerable speed as the next round of enlargement of the Union will push the number of commissioners beyond the number deemed acceptable for the time being, i.e. 20. Then, something might come of these preparations.

More in general, the position of the European Commission in the total institutional framework has weakened. It involves a very gradual process that already became manifest in Maastricht and proceeded considerably in Amsterdam. As legislation and enforcement become more complicated - which will be the case in the framework of accession - the executive power needs to be strengthened rather than weakened. Moreover, as mentioned before, the nature of the work carried out in the EU is changing. More and more the work shifts from the issuing of rules towards execution, deregulation, co-ordination and support, all of which requires a well-equipped and strong authoritative Commission. There will be a High Authority for foreign policy, but the Commission itself will not be repromoted to be the High Authority as was the case in the European Coal and Steel Community (ECSC).

Finally, there is the matter of the ongoing democratization. It looks as if this is solely broached by the European Parliament, as yet. National parliaments are more concerned about their role in the European complex than about a fuller involvement of the European Parliament, which is after all, where the democratization of Europe has to develop. With respect to the issuing of rules, the position of the Parliament has been strengthened, albeit at the expense of the Commission, but there has been no palpable strengthening of the controlling authority of the Parliament. However, this is where the continuation of Europe's democratization has to be realized. In sum, the preparations for the enlargement are wholly unsatisfactory and do not bear any relation to the political priority accorded to the enlargement.

7. Preparation for entry and increasing differentiation

On the part of the Union, a significant transfer of financial means has existed for many years. Analogous to the course of affairs with regard to the accession of Spain and Portugal this may be considered a form of pre-adherence support since the EAs, and has come to be extended into a pre-adherence strategy since the 1993 European Council of Copenhagen. This strategy can be taken to include the formal objectives laid down in the EAs, e.g. the establishment of Free Trade Areas (FTAs). In 1997, jointly with Agenda 2000, country assessments were published by the Commission, on the basis of which definite choices were made about starting the negotiations.

On the part of the acceding countries as well, the preparations are well under way. The results are regularly monitored and in some cases spectacular progress can be reported. The main uncertainty existing in this respect is not so much about the formal acceptance of the *acquis* as to its actual implementation in the administrative, political and legal systems of the countries concerned. As noted earlier, the approach of these preparations is classical, that is to say that the main focus for negotiations is the acceptance and absorption of the entire *acquis communautaire* as expressed in formal regulations, decisions, directives and international treaties. It is precisely in this area that difficulties will arise.

These difficulties are bound to arise frequently. Questions related to agriculture, the regional funds and the budget have already been reviewed. Different studies have presented a more or less exhaustive inventory of the issues and there is no need to review them at length in this chapter (see European Commission, 1997). For sure the *acquis communautaire* cannot possibly be immediately adopted in its entirety. Important exceptions will have to be made, some areas requiring lengthy periods of transition. That will be the first and - theoretically speaking - maybe the most fundamental violation of the *acquis*. When Austria, Finland and Sweden acceded, an emphatic starting point for negotiation was that no new internal borders could be accepted, implying that no transitory stipulations were acceptable which would give reason to internal border checks. The Internal Market without internal borders had to be respected wholesale. It must be added that internal borders are still in place with regard to passenger travel, even now that 'Schengen' has been incorporated into the Treaty of Amsterdam as part of the *acquis*. The United Kingdom and Ireland still remain outside, though.

In the framework of the coming enlargement, new internal borders will be created with the new entrants. Probably, the impact in the various entrants will be dissimilar but that does not need to be a problem technically. In case of the accession of Spain and Portugal, different border checks, between countries were also in place for various products over a long period of time. The Union does become more complicated by this, however.

The many comments on these necessary exceptions and transitory stipulations reflect the view that the functioning of the internal market must not be affected. That condition, however, is unrealistic in many areas. It is unthinkable, for example, that the countries concerned will be able to meet the environmental norms of the Union instantly. The higher environmental standards and the higher costs these would entail, would impair the competitiveness of the acceding countries. Thus, it is generally anticipated that, certainly in the case of environmental norms, transition periods will be required. With regard to monetary policy the same observation holds true. As the Treaty reads right now, the new member countries will have to meet with demands of the second stage of the EMU at once, implying the reduction of excessive budget deficits and a specifically designed policy to meet the other convergence requirements. More generally, these countries will have to meet the requirements as laid down in Art. 4, Section 2 of the EC Treaty (ex Art. 3a, Section 2) stipulating that the activities of the member countries and Communities shall include

> 'the irrevocable fixing of exchange rates leading to the introduction of a single currency, the ECU, and the definition and conduct of a single monetary policy and exchange-rate policy, the primary objective of both of which shall be to maintain price stability and to support general economic policies in the Community in accordance with the principle of an open market economy with free competition'.

In addition, this policy includes price stability, sound public finances and monetary conditions and a sustainable balance of payments. It seems inconceivable that a number of CEEC will be able to realize these objectives of economic policy within the time span allotted them. In any case, it is clear that during a long period of time an exchange-rate mechanism will have to be maintained in addition to the EMU. It is not cast in stone that this should be the same mechanism that was designed for some of the countries among the 15 that will not be joining the EMU for the time being. One may wonder whether an intensive and forcible monetary co-ordination can be imposed on those countries, all the more so because they will no doubt need derogations from the free movement of capital as well.

Major disparities will also persist in the area of social policy. So far these differences did not pose insurmountable difficulties to the Union of the 15, although their influence on the choice of investment locations gave rise to some internal tensions. Those tensions may increase significantly in the context of enlargement if the relocation of productive activities to the countries concerned will not be sufficiently accompanied by new employment opportunities in the former host countries. This question may become more pressing if the creation of the EMU in itself will trigger the relocation of investments. This has always been considered a real threat by the weaker economic regions in the Union and has led to a considerable increase in financial transfers to these potentially threatened areas. The relationship between socio-economic aspects of enlargement and the introduction of the euro has not been investigated sufficiently. Here, again, a timely investigation of the implications and, if necessary, measures to alleviate the negative effects, seem desirable.

Finally, it needs to be noted that the implementation of the accepted *acquis* may give rise to problems as well. Such problems are already present in the Union of the 15. The enforcement of sometimes complicated legislation presupposes a certain homogeneity of administrations in the various countries. It is, however, generally doubted whether those conditions can be met at short notice. Nevertheless, inadequate enforcement of communitary legislation will bear its effects on the operation of the market.

Taking all this into account, it seems obvious that with so many new members entering in such a short time span there is more at hand than just some well-described exceptions to the existing *acquis*, which is still regarded nearly unanimously as a strict precondition. Increasing heterogeneity as a consequence of accession can only result in more heterogeneity of the rule system, the consequences of which have not been sufficiently recognized so far. Should it not be recognized that with such extensive derogation and differentiation, which are inevitable, the *acquis* as such can no longer be the only starting point for negotiations, or merely as an objective for such a distant future and that more radical provisions will need to be made? It can, of course, be argued that while acceptance and eventual absorption of the *acquis* remains the objective, there will be a differentiation with respect to policies, but not membership. But that does not seem to be any more than a semantic solution to the tension between theory and practice. In actual practice, there will indeed be question of differentiated memberships.

This is at odds with classical theory, but is it unacceptable? As mentioned above there is no essential difference between flexibility in the sense of more integration, and flexibility in the sense of less integration. This occurs in nearly all areas of the *acquis*, if mostly with a view to its eventual abolishment, but certainly not in all cases. In the areas of monetary policies, foreign and security policy, and passenger travel, differentiations have been allowed for that are intended to be structural. Formally this is not the case for the movement of goods, but ever since the establishment of the Community infringements on this rule have existed, e.g. in the energy market. Coal still is not a freely tradable good in the ECSC. However, the EU has managed to live with it, be it in a suboptimal manner. It is hard to see why infringements could not be allowed for in other areas as well, where goods are concerned.

8. Differentiation of membership

Structural exceptions on the *acquis* are always based on delicate reasons such as constitutional freedom, the nature of international politics, imputed vital economic interest, public health and crime fighting. In fact, it is a recognition of the existing heterogeneity which, however, is not allowed to stand in the way of integration in numerous other areas. The question then is how to go about this differentiation. One can continue to treat differentiation frenetically as a temporary exception to the rule. In that case, it will be unnecessary to make special provisions to deal with differentiation, but the tensions resulting from it will not be taken away. However, it can also be decided that as a rule structural exceptions are conceivable, and to make the necessary specific provisions. In my opinion, the latter is preferable, since it would allow the exception to be 'managed' better, one would clarify the situation to those involved; they would not be made responsible for things they are not qualified for, or for which they cannot bear responsibility. No doubt, this will lead to a certain fragmentation of the *acquis*.

Given the existing diversity inside and outside the Union, one possibility would be to have a number of policy zones for different groups of countries with a different *acquis*. This would obviously have to be conditional on each zone or group being open to all qualified member states. In addition, it would only be possible for a country to join such a zone if it accepted the entire *acquis* of the group.

One advantage of this idea is that it would be compatible with the current discussion in the Union of the 15 and with the complications resulting from the creation of a continental Union. It would result in a number of *de facto* zones in which countries could be divided according to the degree to which they qualify. The situation might look as follows.

Policy Zone One would be the core group which has accepted the entire *acquis* as well as the EMU, a compulsory Schengen, an adequate social policy, and possibly more far-reaching rights of citizenship. The pillar structure would disappear, and the zone's institutional orientation would obviously have to be Community-based. It might also have its own democratic legitimacy. This group would serve as an example to the others, and would have a more pronounced degree of identity. However, the big problem here would be France, which has now moved even closer to the idea of an '*Europe des Patries*'. At the same time, France and Germany would have to be part of such a zone, along with perhaps one other major country. Both in terms of monetary union and political union, a critical mass would be needed to achieve the desired effect both internally and externally.

In Zone Two, membership would involve acceptance of the current *acquis* as well as any changes made as a result of the IGC. The Zone One countries, which would have their own separate status, would also be part of this zone together with the other member states of the Union. It would have to be accepted that some or all of the pillars in Zone Two would remain in place, and that the combination of Community and intergovernmental elements would remain.

Zone Three could consist of a number of new entrants which are essentially willing to accept the *acquis*, but require derogations from important parts of it, such as full civil rights, the Internal Market - perhaps with some notable exceptions - the unimpeded movement of people and capital, compulsory monetary co-ordination, general convergence targets, social and environmental policy and other areas.

If necessary, a Fourth Zone might be established for countries which still have a long way to go, though this would require further analysis and evaluation. But the structure suggested here does not rule out differentiation among the new member states.

A brief comment is in place pertaining to some key aspects. Recognizing the reality of differentiation does not imply opting for a Union *à la carte* in which each member state can make up its own menu on a 'pick and choose'-basis. It should be determined by negotiation how this differentiated membership should be arranged for each specific case. Some grouping of member states that are homogeneous to a specific degree is, of course, necessary. In addition to this, it could be outlined how the 'content' of membership can be modified in the future.

Of course, the institutional matter is key to this approach. The classical approach holds that the unitary structure of the institutions should be upheld. However, in practice even now this maxim is deviated from. In the protocol to the Treaty of Amsterdam with regard to the position of the WEU it is mentioned specifically that the responsibility and formal influence of the various kinds of partners is restricted to the content of their partnership. In the flexibility clauses introduced in the Treaty of Amsterdam, non-members to the flexibility groups are allowed to attend the deliberations, but not the decision-making. The vehement discussions in the 1997 European Council of Amsterdam come to mind, when the British made frantic efforts to gain admission to the club of Finance Ministers (Euro-x) of the countries that will have joined the EMU. When accepting differentiation leading to fragmentation, the principle will have to be upheld that member states or institutions only have a say in matters in which they have fully accepted the *acquis*. In relation to the existing *acquis* of the 15 it means an increasing say in the flexibility and, for new entrants, a decreasing say in conformity with the necessary differentiation. This rule should be applied to the Council of Ministers and its associated bodies, and the European Parliament. This implies, for example, that if countries fail to introduce the Common Agricultural Policy (CAP), those countries cannot take part in setting agricultural prices in the framework of the CAP. The same holds for the advisory function of the European Parliament.

As for the European Commission, matters are a bit more complicated. The Commission will have to be charged primarily with monitoring the entire integration process and it has also been assigned a task in applying the flexibility clauses. In addition, the Commission soon can be expected to be composed in such a way that not all member states are represented. Consequently, the activities of the Commission will have to extend to the whole, to groups heading for more and less integration. The previous paragraphs have identified four zones and the Council of Ministers and the European Parliament as well could be specified in accordance with the composition of these zones.

The Treaty of Maastricht has introduced subsidiarity as a legal regulatory principle. This is not a conscious choice for more differentiation, but it is most certainly a choice for a very critical reflection on the necessity of rule-setting. It is clear that less regulation automatically leads to less differentiation with regard to regulation, but to more differentiation in the daily practice of the Union. It stands to reason that a consequent and strict application of the subsidiarity principle is an inevitable condition for an EU of about 25 member states to remain manageable. In this context it may be useful to point out that subsidiarity does not merely imply fewer regulations as such, but also to regulate more on the basis of general policy guidelines. That too, will enable less differentiation with regard to the regulations, but at the same time result in more differentiation in daily practice. As such, this fits the increasing heterogeneity of the Union. In an expanding EU the meticulous precision with which regulators tried to structure the internal market in the past, will become more and more outdated. A critical review of the existing regulations seems inevitable.

The above is no plea for unlimited fragmentation. There are, of course, a number of areas in which no derogation can be allowed. In this respect, antitrust policy, the customs union (CU), trade policy, crime and presumably migration policy come to mind. Regarding the principles of democracy and the constitutional state, human rights and discrimination with respect to race, sex, religion, age etc. this principle holds *a fortiori*. For constitutional and human rights no transition periods or differentiation would be appropriate. In an EU preparing for enlargement towards the boundaries of Europe, and in view of the increasing cultural diversity this will imply, it would be desirable to consider adding stipulations to the Treaty that guarantee the upholding of those basic human values within the context of the Union by the bodies of the Union.

Everyone who considers such an enlargement of the EU a historic necessity and therefore a challenge, to be addressed constructively, would be well-advised to recognize that new ways will have to be found to move from separation and discord towards integration. Accepting fragmentation *vis-à-vis* the ideal seems inevitable. Unity in diversity and diversity in unity is the answer to the need for integration coming from so many centuries of historical disintegration.

Note

[1] I phrase this as 'basically complied with in full' as particularly the infrastructural provisions for the behaviour of member countries after entering the EMU are dealt with unsatisfactorily in the Treaty.

References

European Commission, *General Report on the Activities of the European Union 1997*, Brussels/Luxembourg, 1998.

European Commission, 'Agenda 2000', *Bulletin of the European Union, Supplement 5/97,* 1997.

Pelkmans, J., *European Integration. Methods and Economic Analysis*, Addison Wesley Longman, Harlow, 1997.

5

THE DECISION-MAKING CAPACITY OF THE EU AFTER THE TREATY OF AMSTERDAM

Jacques Steenbergen

Loeff Claeys Verbeke
Brussels
Belgium

1. Introduction

The Treaty of Amsterdam (1997) is the result of the Intergovernmental Conference (IGC) that started in 1996. The IGC's objectives were to bring the Union closer to the citizens, to improve the European Union's (EU) ability to act internationally and to reform the institutions. With respect to the institutional reform, in particular the rules for majority voting and the number of commissioners, it was decided to resume the negotiations after it will have been decided to expand the membership of the EU to more than 20.

This chapter will discuss the powers of EU institutions in external economic relations. As a result, it will concentrate on the EU's first pillar or the European Community which consists of the common market and the economic and monetary union (EMU). However, it follows from Art. 3 of the Treaty on European Union (ex Art. C)[1] as agreed upon in Maastricht in 1991 and amended in the Treaty of Amsterdam in 1997, that it is necessary to consider the external economic relations of the EU in relation to the Common Foreign and Security Policy (CFSP): '[t]he Union shall in particular ensure the consistency of its external

P. van Dijck and G. Faber (eds.), The External Economic Dimension of the European Union, 115–125.
© 2000 *Kluwer Academic Publishers. Printed in the Netherlands.*

activities as a whole in the context of its external relations, security, economic and development policies'.

The chapter is structured as follows. The second section will give a brief overview of the powers of the EU institutions in external relations as laid down in the Treaty on European Union after the IGC of Maastricht. Section 3 presents the amendments that have been agreed upon in the IGC of Amsterdam. The final section puts forwards some general observations on these issues.

2. The decision-making capacity after Maastricht

Since the Treaty on European Union was signed in Maastricht in 1991, the process of European integration takes place in a three-pillar construction. The Union consists of the European Community (EC), the CFSP and the co-operation in the fields of justice and home affairs. The Union's international objective is (Art. 2 of the Treaty on European Union, ex Art. B)

> '(..) to assert its identity on the international scene, in particular through the implementation of a common foreign and security policy including the eventual framing of a common defence policy, which might in time lead to a common defence'.

More detailed goals and the way to realize the specific goals of the CFSP are given in the Art. 11 to 28 of the Treaty on European Union (ex Art. J to ex Art. J.11) . For the present time, the emphasis on the CFSP in the Union's objectives should not hide the fact that the main powers of the EU in external policies are in the area of economic relations, mainly covered by the EC. The external powers of the EC are to be found in different fields of common policies.

First, the EC may enter into international monetary agreements for the ECU in relation to non-Community currencies (Art. 111 of the EC Treaty, ex Art. 109)[2].

Second, as a customs union (CU) constitutes the basis of the EC, a Common Commercial Policy (CCP) has gradually been established from the start of the Community. The objectives of the CU are formulated in Art. 131 of the EC Treaty (ex Art. 110)

> 'By establishing a customs union between themselves member states aim to contribute, in the common interests, to the harmonious development of world trade, the progressive abolition of restrictions on international trade and the lowering of customs barriers'.

The procedures to take decisions on the CCP are given in Art. 133 of the EC Treaty (ex Art. 113). For areas where the EC has exclusive powers, the Council decides by qualified majority voting on proposals of the Commission. If an insufficient harmonization of the external trade regime causes distortions of trade, member states may be authorized to take protective measures, as stipulated in Art. 134 (ex Art. 115).

Third, the Community may co-operate with third states and international organizations in many areas. This applies for culture (Art. 151.3, ex Art. 128.3), public health (Art. 152.3, ex Art. 129.3), trans-European networks (Art. 155.3, ex Art. 129c.3) and the environment (Art. 174.4, ex Art. 130r.4).

Fourth, in the field of development co-operation, the IGC of Maastricht decided on the formal basis for and the objectives and instruments of this policy (Art. 177, ex Art. 130u)

'Community policy in the sphere of development co-operation, which shall be complementary to the policies pursued by the member states, shall foster:
- the sustainable economic and social development of the developing countries, and more particularly the most disadvantaged among them;
- the smooth and gradual integration of the developing countries into the world economy;
- the campaign against poverty in the developing countries'.

These objectives are to be realized by appropriate measures to be taken by the Council, by co-ordination, consultation and joint action and by co-operation with third countries and competent international organizations. A potentially far-reaching article is Art. 178 (ex Art. 130v) which says that 'The Community shall take account of the objectives referred to in Article 177 in the policies that it implements which are likely to affect developing countries.'

The EC Treaty provides a general procedure for the conclusion of agreements between the Community and third countries or international organizations (Art. 300, ex Art. 228). The Commission makes a recommendation to the Council for the opening of the negotiations. The Council will act by a qualified majority, unless the procedure for the adoption of internal rules uses a different voting rule. This brief overview of the areas of EU external powers as agreed in the Treaty on European Union in Maastricht, gives rise to the following conclusions.

First, since Maastricht, the Union can act internationally - from the point of view of its internal attribution of powers by the member states - in virtually all domains which are relevant to the scope of the Union's domestic policies and the traditional fields of external relations

(1) with regard to the external economic relations, the existing provisions with respect to the CCP and especially the regime organized under Art. 133 of the EC Treaty (ex Art. 113) has been complemented by the above-mentioned provisions on international monetary agreements;

(2) this is also true with respect to the traditional fields of international relations as the Union is empowered to act in the areas of foreign and security policy by the Art. 11 to 28 of the Treaty on European Union (ex Art. J); and

(3) and in respect of development policy, the Union received its own powers to act under Art. 177 to 180 of the EC Treaty (ex Art.130u to 130y).

It should be added that the Maastricht Treaty did not contain any provision that suggests that the pre-existing case law in respect of the parallelism between internal and external powers and the implied external powers of the EC is no longer valid[3].

Second, while there remain few if any gaps with regard to the type of measures the EU can take or can be involved in after the Maastricht Treaty, there remain significant differences with regard to the extend to which the Union can act effectively with regard to the various aspects of international relations. The main differences can be summarized as follows

(1) with regard to all measures that can come under the heading of the CCP, the EC has its own exclusive powers[4], even though negotiations may often be concerned both with exclusive powers of the Community and with areas where the member states may still claim the power to enter into agreements. The more relevant negotiations such as multilateral trade negotiations are therefore mostly negotiated according to the mixed delegation formula (Kapteyn and VerLoren van Themaat, 1998 and J.H.J. Bourgeois et al., 1997). The Council and the Commission do not need to consult the European Parliament about commercial policy agreements;

(2) with regard to international monetary agreements, Art. 111 of the EC Treaty makes a distinction between exchange-rate agreements concerning the ECU[5] and parity agreements within the framework of exchange rate agreements. Depending on the qualification of the agreement, the Council can decide by qualified majority or with unanimity on the proposal of the Commission or the European Central Bank (ECB), and after consultation of the European Parliament or only by informing the Parliament;

(3) in matters for which the EC has powers but which fall outside the scope of the CCP and the monetary agreements, the Council can decide to enter into agreements upon a proposal of the Commission, and after consultation of the European Parliament;

(4) it should however be added that while the Community now has unquestionably powers to enter into development-aid agreements in its own name, and while the procedure to enter into such agreements is no different from the procedure described under the previous indent, Art. 177 of the EC Treaty contains an unusually detailed description of the objectives of the Union's development policy which can be interpreted as limiting the discretionary powers of the Union in this respect;

(5) a completely different regime applies in the area of foreign and security policy: these fields remain strictly intergovernmental, also after Maastricht. The regime agreed upon in Maastricht can be summarized as empowering the Union to participate in nearly any action, but limiting the actions that can be taken to what can be decided by consensus. The member states are, however, no longer authorized to act independently once an area has been dealt with in a common action. It follows that the Union could often act more efficiently and with more flexibility if it was decided that a joint action of member states did not qualify as a common action in the meaning of the European Union Treaty because it meant that they could manage such action without the constant need of consensus among all member states.

The regime organized by the Maastricht Treaty can be summarized further - in a way which may not be kind but is still fair - as a regime whereby the Union can participate in international economic agreements and policies, and which entitles the Union to deal with virtually all other aspects of international relations. However, it remains nevertheless unlikely that the Union will have the decision-making capacity that enables it to act effectively in any area outside the international economic relations that enter into the scope of application of the European Community Treaty (EC or first pillar).

3. The Treaty of Amsterdam

The amendments to the Treaty on European Union as agreed upon in the IGC of June 1997 in Amsterdam cover several areas of external policy making. In this section these changes and their relevance and political impact will be reviewed.

The co-ordination of the external economic policy and the other external policies of the Union

Pursuant to Art. 3 of the Treaty on European Union (ex Art. C) after Maastricht, the Union needs to ensure the cohesion of its external action. The Council and the Commission are each, according to their respective powers, responsible for the coherence of these policies. The text of Art. 3 has been reworded in the Treaty of Amsterdam. The Council and the Commission continue to be responsible for the coherence of the various aspects of the Union's external policies, and the text adds that they need to co-operate in that respect while both are responsible for the implementation of the Union's policies according to their own powers.

The new text does not significantly alter the regime organized by the Maastricht Treaty, but it gives a better description of the division of powers and responsibilities between the two institutions.

The Common Commercial Policy

As the main external powers of the EU are in the field of international economic relations in which trade policy plays a very important role, it is relevant to analyse the amendments in the CCP made by the Treaty of Amsterdam.

The main amendment is concerned with the question whether agreements and measures with respect to the international trade in services can be dealt with under Art. 133 of the EC Treaty (ex Art. 113) and the CCP. This question has been fiercely debated in the margin of the Uruguay Round and has given rise to the request for an opinion of the Court of Justice under Art. 300 of the EC Treaty (ex Art. 228)[6]. The Court of Justice considered in its opinion that the Community was empowered to enter into agreements under Art. 133 of the EC Treaty in respect of cross-border supplies of services. It held, however, that the Community could not conclude international agreements under Art. 133 in so far as these agreements were concerned with trade in services whereby either the service provider or the user went to another Member State.

This opinion of the Court of Justice disappointed the European Commission which considered it illogical that it would be unauthorized to deal with major aspects of the external dimension of the services markets at a time that international trade negotiations increasingly focus on services, and for several member states services have become a more significant contributor to the gross national product than the sectors of trade, agriculture and industry.

The Court's opinion probably gives a conservative interpretation of what member states considered at that time to be part of their commercial policy in view of the fact that services were one of the most hotly discussed topics during the multilateral trade negotiations of the Uruguay Round. It would not have been inconsistent with the Court's previous case law[7] if the fact that services were negotiated in the Uruguay Round were seen as an indication that trading nations considered that services needed to be dealt with in the main commercial policy forum. In that case, services should be incorporated into the scope of the CCP as referred to in Art. 133 of the EC Treaty in accordance with the above-mentioned case law. The Court had, however, also good reasons to refrain from such a conclusion in view of the fact that there was at that time still strong opposition to the proposal to deal with services in the framework of GATT.

The Commission and several member states concluded after the Opinion of the Court that it would not be wise to wait until the Court should consider that it had been sufficiently established that negotiations both on trade in goods and in services were generally qualified as trade-policy negotiations. The Commission sought an amendment of Art. 133 of the EC Treaty (ex Art. 113) in order to incorporate services explicitly into the scope of this provision.

The above-mentioned dispute has, however, not been resolved by the Treaty of Amsterdam. Art. 133.5 now only states that the Council can decide, by unanimity, upon a proposal of the Commission and after consultation of the European Parliament, that the paragraphs 1 to 4 of Art. 133 will also apply to international negotiations and agreements concerning services and intellectual property rights in so far as they do not come under the scope of the above-mentioned provisions.

The Treaty of Amsterdam thus creates an alternative route to resolve the discussion by an explicit decision that services and intellectual property rights can be dealt with under Art. 133 of the EC Treaty. It made it unlikely at the same time that this route will be chosen in the near future by stipulating that such a decision can only be taken by unanimity.

It should be added that the wording of the Treaty of Amsterdam has not closed the route of the evolving concept of commercial policy which keeps the scope of Art. 133 in line with international state practice as indicated in the earlier case law of the Court of Justice. However, it is nevertheless to be feared that the organization of an explicit procedure will make it even less likely that the Court will decide in the future that measures with respect to the trade in services have become part of the CCP, even in case no such explicit decision has been taken.

International agreements

It is also important to note that decisions with regard to the signing of agreements by application of Art. 300.2 of the EC Treaty (ex Art. 228. 2) are to be taken by the Council with a qualified majority unless the agreement is concerned with a subject matter of an internal nature on which the Council can only decide by unanimity, or in respect of association agreements as referred to in Art. 310 of the EC Treaty (ex Art. 238) .

Other aspects of the external economic policies

The Treaty of Amsterdam has not changed the regime of the Maastricht Treaty in respect of monetary agreements or other external economic policy measures and agreements that do not come within the scope of application of Art. 133 of the EC Treaty and the CCP.

Foreign and security policy

The Treaty of Amsterdam has introduced several new provisions in respect of foreign and security policies. The key amendment is to be found in Art. 11 of the Treaty on European Union (ex Art. J.1.1) and repeated in Art. 17 (ex Art. J.7.1) where it is stated that the Union has a common foreign and security policy that covers all areas of foreign and security policy, or, respectively, all issues that are concerned with the security of the Union. It appears from these provisions that the Union has moved from a period where it could decide to deal with issues collectively if there was a consensus to do so, to a period where the Union should have an all-embracing foreign and security policy. From the obligation to co-ordinate policies provided for in Art. 3 of the Treaty on European Union (ex Art. C), it follows that there is a virtual obligation to have an integrated external policy, covering all these aspects of external relations. This is a significant change of the Union's external relations regime.

When acting in the intergovernmental framework of the 'second pillar' of the Maastricht construction, the member states have always received input from the Commission with respect to any matters that may affect the 'first pillar', as well as the coaching of the Presidency of the Council. Art. 26 of the Treaty on European Union (ex Art. J.16) further facilitates - but does not guarantee - the co-ordination of external policies by the introduction of the High Representative, the Secretary General of the Council. The High Representative will contribute to the formulation, preparation and implementation of policy decisions and may deal with third parties on behalf of the Council at the request of the Presidency.

It is also important that the Treaty of Amsterdam has altered the decision making provisions in the CFSP, be it to a limited extent. Art. 23.1 (ex Art. J.13.1) still stipulates that Council decisions in the field of foreign and security policy are to be taken by consensus (unanimity of the present and non-abstaining members)[8]. However, the impact of this principle has been limited by organizing an opt-out regime: in accordance with Art. 23.2 of the Treaty on European Union (ex Art. J.13.2), member states representing up to one third of the weighted votes can opt out of a common action by abstaining, with the qualification that they do not wish to be bound by the decisions. In that case the Member State concerned accepts that the Union undertakes a common action, but it will not be obliged to take part in such action.

Art. 23.2 also stipulates that implementing decisions concerning actions and other implementing measures decided within the framework of a strategy determined by consensus, can be taken by qualified majority.

The combined effect of Art. 23.1 and 23.2 remains unclear. Art. 23.1 does not stipulate how many member states may abstain unless they qualify their abstention in the option not to be bound.

4. Final observations

The Treaty of Amsterdam has often been criticized by senior politicians such as Mr. Delors as well as by other commentators. In the field discussed in this chapter it does not organize the great leap forward few expected but many hoped for. It also falls short of what figured on technical agendas (Duff, 1997, XXXIII et seq.). However, the Treaty of Amsterdam has safeguarded to some extent the ability of the Union to act, while stimulating at the same time the continued development of the Union's foreign policy, aiming at a gradual integration of all foreign policy actions by member states into an integrated presence of the European Union on the international scene. The direct impact of the Treaty on the Union's foreign economic policy is nevertheless likely to be limited. But given the fact that this area was already reasonably well covered since Maastricht, this does not need to be interpreted as a major criticism.

Notes

[1] Article numbers refer to the integrated versions of the Treaty on European Union and the Treaty establishing the EC, after incorporation of the Treaties of Maastricht and Amsterdam. In Section 2 the original numbers as can be found in the Maastricht Treaty, are given in brackets. Section 3 gives the original numbers as can be found in the Treaty of Amsterdam.

[2] The name of the EMU's common currency was decided to be euro in 1995, many years after the conclusion of the Maastricht Treaty, cited here, when the ECU was the currency unit in the European Monetary System. The ECU ceased to exist on 1 January 1999.

[3] See on implied powers Case 22/70, AETR, 1971 ECR 263 and Kapteyn and VerLoren van Themaat, 1998.

[4] See Case 41/76, Donckerwolcke, 1976 ECR 1921.

[5] This should read as euro; see note 2.

[6] Opinion 1/94, WTO, 1994 ECR 5267.

[7] Opinion 1/75, Common Commercial Policy, 1975 ECR 1355.

[8] The text of Art. 23 of the Treaty on European Union uses the term 'unanimously' but stipulates explicitly that abstentions do not stand in the way of taking a decision.

References

Bourgeois, J.H.J., J.L. Dewost and M.A. Gaiffe (eds), *La Communauté Européenne et les Accords Mixtes*, P.I.E. Collège d'Europe, Brussels, 1997.

Duff, A. (ed.), *The Treaty of Amsterdam*, London, 1997.

Kapteyn, P.J.G. and P. VerLoren van Themaat, *Introduction to the Law of the European Communities. From Maastricht to Amsterdam*, third edition incorporating the fifth Dutch edition, edited and further revised by L.W. Gormley in co-operation with the editors of the fifth Dutch edition, London, The Hague, Boston, 1998.

6

THE COMMUNITY'S EXTERNAL REGIONAL POLICY IN THE WTO

JAMES H. MATHIS

University of Amsterdam
Amsterdam
The Netherlands

1. Introduction

The European Union (EU) has been taking initiatives to develop its external regional policy towards trade agreements of a more comprehensive nature as studied in several chapters in this volume. This dimension of the external economic policy of the EU has been developed and extended rigorously during the Uruguay Round negotiations and in subsequent years. If Viner's recital of 'propinquity' as justifying regionalism in 1950 was accurate, then 'nearness' also takes on some expanded meaning in the global economy, as the Union can define its regional interests nearly anywhere on the globe[1].

The economic and political rationale for such an active EU regional programme has been analysed by several authors in this volume and will not be the focus here. Rather, this chapter will discuss points of interaction between prospective EU regional agreements and the World Trade Organization (WTO). Without seeking to present a legal study, one can outline some legal developments and attempt to describe a trend for the rules in the WTO as they may be applied to new EU trade agreements. While the Union's concept of regionalism is being seen to evolve, the WTO legal system which will be called upon to validate

P. van Dijck and G. Faber (eds.), The External Economic Dimension of the European Union, 127–150.
© 2000 *Kluwer Academic Publishers. Printed in the Netherlands.*

preferences is also evolving. Although the final outlines are hardly clear, the case can be made that a more disciplined system of reviewing regional formations is on its way, and unless frustrated by regional proponents, will likely have the capacity to impose a more narrowly prescribed gateway for regional preferences to deviate from most-favoured nation (MFN).

Any WTO development that reaches for more precise standards for regional trade agreements is bound to influence the design of later regional trade agreements and the manner in which proponents go about declaring them in the WTO. However, the reverse can also be the case, that the quality of agreements submitted, as declared expressions of compatibility with the rule system of the General Agreement on Tariffs and Trade (GATT) and the WTO, can either reinforce or undermine the prospects for understandable interpretations of the rules. In no area is this more evident than in the declarations for free-trade areas (FTAs) between developed and developing territories, and certainly including those earlier formations to which the European Economic Community (EEC) or European Community (EC) was a party.

Therefore, it is not unreasonable to inquire whether the next round of formations between the Union and partners will see the presentation of agreements to the WTO which, once again, raise intractable points of interpretation for the GATT rules and the WTO members who attempt to apply them. Another way of asking the same is to inquire whether the Union and its less-developed partners will submit FTA plans which demonstrate a commitment to exchange a complete set of preferences. The alternative is to insist again that reviewing parties will deadlock over whether partial agreements between parties of unequal economic development should be judged consistent with the GATT rules. This second course would naturally lead the proponents to argue anew for retaining flexibility in the interpretation and application of the rules, exactly the opposite of what the MFN clause and the principle of non-discrimination should be receiving in the form of legal support at this precarious stage of multilateralism. However the European Commission chooses to finally advance its arguments for new regional compatibility with the WTO in light of the agreements actually advanced, one would prefer to finally observe that the goal of one evolution, the EU regional system, was not necessarily accomplished at the expense of the multilateral rules.

With this purpose of discussion in mind, the following questions will be addressed in turn. First, what changes have occurred as a result of dispute resolution panels regarding FTAs and what impact will these legal developments have on the EU regional system? Second, in light of these changes, which GATT/WTO provisions remain most important in qualifying the regional proposals and how rigorous might they be applied in respect of the legal developments? Finally, how can the Union and its partners act to frame their regional plans in such a manner so as to endorse the emerging interpretations?

2. Dispute settlement

The EU regional system of associations and FTAs was built upon the premise that a notification of regional preferences as determined by them was sufficient to secure an MFN exception. Since the GATT working group review process was and still is consensus-based, any division of opinion between proponents and outsiders led to an absence of recommendations as to whether a trade agreement was compatible with the GATT rules permitting the MFN exception. In the absence of recommendations, there was little basis for the larger GATT Council to base any action of its own in the form of decisions or resolutions, even though the power to direct amendments to an agreement has always been available in the rules. The treatment of the regional exceptions as an inherent self-declaratory exercise through the 1960s and 1970s led to the precipitous presumption, never really tested, that any plan notified to GATT must be 'legal' for the purpose of the MFN exception, at least in the absence of any GATT Council decision or other resolution to the contrary.

That the legal status of the preferences offered in the Lomé Convention are now trapped within the confines of a GATT Art. XXV waiver rather than Art. XXIV, should indicate that there was something seriously amiss with this view of how preferential trade agreements (PTAs) are legitimated in the GATT. This is especially apparent if one contrasts this current position of Lomé with the long asserted Community opinion that the Convention was a fully-qualified Art. XXIV FTA. The loss of this legal cover for the Convention's preferences is not to be attributed to the WTO banana cases, which have raised interesting legal issues of their own, but all within the context of the GATT Art. XXV waiver. Rather, the two earlier and unreported GATT panel cases, also about ACP bananas (originating from the African, Caribbean and Pacific countries, known as the ACP group), that were conducted in 1993 and 1994 under pre-WTO GATT rules, are the source of the EU's difficulties in seeking to return the Convention to the FTA exception. These earlier reports form the first point of reference to determine the parameters that the EU must confront in establishing any future FTAs between the EU and ACP countries or any other formations involving developed and developing territories. Moreover, the treatment of issues in these reports demonstrate just how far legal developments have progressed in granting to other WTO members a legal basis to challenge others' regional preferences[2].

The problem of reverse preferences

The question of whether or not reverse preferences must be required of a developing country within an FTA with a developed partner is a long standing and controversial aspect of EU external arrangements. In the Overseas Association (1958) review, most parties understood Art. XXIV to require the removal of barriers to trade *between* the constituent territories forming an FTA. The express provisions of the Rome Treaty which permitted the Overseas Territories to reimpose barriers on the trade of the EEC for development goals raised the issue between the requirements of the GATT article and the expressed development needs advocated by the proponents. While the proponents could reasonably argue that it was draconian to require parties at different levels of development to exchange preferences in full, others took the view that Art. XXIV was being re-tailored to accommodate formations that should not have been brought within its provisions in the first place. Haight (1972, p. 394) looked back in 1972 and described this sentiment from the earlier period as follows

'[b]ut how many delegates could have foreseen that these provisions would be used also for forging closer commercial ties between developed and developing countries? Such a colonial-type pact was surely a thing of the past ... One would not expect independent developing countries to enter voluntarily into such a new-colonial arrangement, thereby limiting their freedom to protect their own industrial development'.

For the Overseas Association, there was no resolution to be had on the question as the proponents held to the opinion that full reciprocity would eventually be achieved within the Association, or that it was not necessary in any case to provide for reverse preferences due to the GATT's own development articles[3]. These commitments to not require reciprocity in the multilateral negotiations from less developed territories could be 'read in' to GATT Art. XXIV requirements to allow for deviations otherwise not specified within the text of Art. XXIV. Much later in 1976, the pretext of forming an ACP agreement with reverse preferences was simply dropped as a condition to the formation of the first Lomé Convention. At this time, it was reported that only one GATT working group member objected to the elimination of a reciprocity requirement[4].

However sympathetic parties may have been then to the notion of partial exchanges between developed and developing countries, this view was not confirmed at the time by any decision that the first Lomé Convention was compatible with the coverage requirements of Art. XXIV.

The right to challenge

Thus it came to pass 15 years later that the EU and the ACP beneficiaries found themselves in a GATT panel challenge directed to the banana preferences on the basis that they violated MFN and other GATT articles. As recounted by the EU's position in the first report, the importance of the challenge was not merely that it was directed to the issue of market access, but rather, as it was claimed to constitute an attack on the contractual scheme of preferential arrangements made in the Lomé Convention, and perhaps more important, could establish the principle that other GATT parties could invoke dispute resolution procedures to challenge a regional agreement which had already been subject to the review procedures of Art. XXIV. As the EU presented this view of the issue

'[t]he legal certainty with respect to international contractual relations duly notified to the GATT would be severely affected, if many years after the coming into effect of an international convention which was examined by the appropriate GATT bodies, its conformity with the general agreement could be questioned anew'.[5]

According to the EU, this re-examination of a well-established practice would breach the legitimate expectations of the parties to be able to maintain trade agreements without risk of later modification.

The Lomé parties fared poorly on this first critical point. Where an earlier and also unreported panel regarding citrus products[6] had concluded that it would refrain from examining bilateral agreements which were otherwise subject to special review procedures, the new panel reversed by concluding that such a holding would mean that dispute resolution procedures in GATT would never be available for matters upon which the Contracting Parties (CPs) had the power to take decisions. The result would be that '[i]f preferences granted under *any* agreement for which Article XXIV had been invoked could not be investigated under Article XXIII, any contracting party, merely by invoking Article XXIV, could deprive other contracting parties of their rights under Article XXIII.'[7]

As this question was raised again in the second banana panel, that finding is instructive not only as it reiterated the first ruling, but by also emphasizing the right of a panel to review the agreements themselves which were being claimed to fall under the Art. XXIV provisions. Thus

'[t]he Panel could not accept that tariff preferences inconsistent with Article I:1 would, by notification of the preferential arrangement and invocation of Article XXIV against the objections of other contracting parties, escape any examination by a panel established under Article XXIII ... The Panel concluded therefore that a panel, faced with an invocation of Article XXIV, first had to examine whether or not these provisions applied to the agreement in question'.[8]

Since the EU had been implementing regional trade agreements without obtaining affirmative recommendations or decisions for over 35 years, the absence of so many decisions for so many FTAs in the interim now suggested a new vulnerability for agreements which had already been placed into effect. In this light one can appreciate the importance of a ruling like this upon EU contemporary regional practice. Not only would other GATT parties have a right to apply for dispute resolution procedures to challenge preferences, but then once formed, panels could actually derive some basis to examine a regional agreement, at least on the surface, to determine whether Art. XXIV should apply to grant the MFN exception.

Although unreported, these two rulings must remain at the core of the EU's problems for both its existing and prospective regional trade arrangements, whether notified under GATT or WTO. It also provides the opportunity to drive the process of reform of the EU regional system. However, at this juncture it is not yet clear whether proposals being developed for regional reforms will be determined to be sufficient if and when challenges arise.

Resolution on reverse preferences

A remaining glimmer of hope for self-declaratory regionalism can be found in the facts before the unreported banana panels in reference to the degree of review that a future panel may choose to exercise over any particular arrangement. At first impression, this question was resolved narrowly on the facts. Since the provisions of the Lomé Convention clearly stated that there was no obligation on behalf of the ACP parties to provide for reverse preferences on behalf of the EU, it was not difficult for the second panel to use this most visible defect as the basis to determine that the Lomé agreement was not of a type contemplated by the FTA provisions of Art. XXIV. As the panel held

> '[t]his lack of any obligation of the sixty-nine ACP countries to dismantle their trade barriers ... made the trade arrangements set out in the Convention substantially different from those of a free trade area, as defined in the Article XXIV:8(b)'[9].

However, this may not lead to a conclusion that an FTA declaration which purports to cover substantially all trade between the parties is necessarily sufficient to pass muster in a later panel challenge. Since the Lomé proponents had also attempted to defend the absence of reverse preferences in the Convention by making reference to the development articles of the GATT, an opening for a broader ruling was granted for the panel to address the old Overseas Association question, that being whether Art. XXIV would permit formations including developed and developing countries to utilize a lower level of exchange in deference to the development articles of the GATT. Here the second panel seemed to dismiss this other important foundation upon which the ACP system had been constructed.

> 'Had non-reciprocal agreements between developed and developing parties been considered justifiable under Article XXIV and Part IV, the decisions of the CP on the GSP [Generalized System of Preferences] and the Enabling Clause would have been largely unnecessary. Developed countries could simply have formed a "free-trade area" with selected developing countries by reducing barriers unilaterally on imports from those countries'.[10]

Implications for WTO review practice

An implication for future practice may be drawn from this. Since GATT has already provided for a system of non-reciprocal development preferences in the form of the GSP, a burden may be seen to rise with regional proponents to justify in some detail any occasion where they have chosen to not exchange a complete set of preferences. At the least, it appears no longer possible to claim that free trade formations between developed and developing countries are somehow entitled to a lesser exchange solely by making reference to GATT's trade and development provisions.

Whether or not a free trade declaration which purports to make a complete exchange will be sufficient to avoid an examination by a panel remains to be answered. As for the troubled Lomé 'free-trade area', we have already noted that the EU and ACP parties submitted the arrangement to the WTO and obtained a waiver under Art. XXV. The conditions of this waiver for the banana regimes have been the subject of the WTO actions which have caused so much recent excitement. However, for any return to the FTA exception for future EU-ACP arrangements, the earlier panels discussed above have the greater bearing on the questions of qualification.

Finally, the panel developments discussed above may begin to shift the burden to the proponents in an institutional sense as well. If one can now say that the legal status of trade agreements remains an open question in the absence of recommendations or decisions by GATT bodies, then proponents should want to seek affirmative recommendations and decisions for their agreements in order to secure legal certainty for the regional preferences. Although the weakness of a consensus-based process has worked against stricter interpretations in the past, perhaps this same consensus approach may work against proponents in the future. If a recommendation or decision is necessary to secure an agreement from legal challenge, then every party with a vote must be satisfied of the agreement's compatibility. This would suggest that proponents might need to be more flexible themselves in amending provisions of trade agreements being subject to review. It also might suggest that regional proponents could support the development of more clear compatibility guidelines within which they can make their arguments for recommendations.

This raises the next topic. If it comes to pass that affirmative recommendations or decisions will be advantageous to regional proponents, then query whether this would also strengthen the position of those members advocating that GATT Art. XXIV should grant the MFN exception only for complete preferential formations. It is from this view that we turn to some of the substantive requirements of Art. XXIV to examine what may be on offer if those advocating a higher bar for the exception were favoured by such developments.

3. The GATT regional requirements: the legacy of a misconstruction?

MFN and the foundations of the GATT exception

Both the GATT and the General Agreement on Trade in Services (GATS) of the WTO are governed centrally by the contractual promise of the parties to adhere to the MFN obligation. While MFN is often cited to support the goal of the reduction of tariffs and other trade barriers, it is also the primary mechanism which secures another expressed goal of the WTO. That is, to achieve the 'elimination of discriminatory treatment in international trade relations ...' as put in the Marrakesh Agreement establishing the WTO (GATT, 1994, p. 6).

This places the nature of preference within its proper context as a deviation from non-discrimination, irrespective of any welfare implications generated by one preference or another. The primary exceptions for MFN as they relate to the granting of preferences are established according to GATT Art. XXIV. Besides establishing the territorial application of the General Agreement, this article permits an exception from the MFN clause for certain frontier traffic, for customs unions (CUs) and for FTAs.

Identifying an internal trade requirement

FTAs and CUs are legally distinguishable in regard to the nature of their external trade regimes, as a completed CU is treated for the purposes of the General Agreement as a customs territory and therefore a CP. However, as to the degree of trade to be liberalized within either type of formation, there is no distinction in the text between the two forms as both require the identical removal of barriers, so that ' ... the duties and other restrictive regulations of commerce ... are eliminated with respect to substantially all of the trade between the constituent territories ...'[11].

In addition, it is not very difficult to establish that the internal trade requirements of the FTA exception were intended to be aligned with those which were already understood to apply to pre-GATT CU practice. For the new FTA exception introduced at Havana, the changes to the proposed article were forwarded with the following notation, that

'[t]he text of Article 42 has been redrafted on the basis of proposals by the French delegation, the main change being *to extend to* free-trade areas the provisions relating to customs unions, as requested by the delegations of Lebanon and Syria'[12].

At least from the point of view of the drafters and by mere reference to the provisions, one would conclude that the quality of internal free movement to be obtained in an FTA was not in any way intended to be somehow lesser than that to be obtained in a CU. Instead, a legal approximation between the two formations in respect to the trade to be covered appears to have been intended[13].

How much coverage is required?

For both formations permitted by Art. XXIV, the GATT does not appear to encourage partially preferential or otherwise incomplete formations, even if such agreements may pose a lesser risk of external trade diversion[14]. The revised preamble of the 1994 Uruguay Round Understanding on the Interpretation of Article XXIV now acts to re-enforce this interpretation by recognizing not only that a contribution to the expansion of world trade may be made by the closer integration of regional parties, but that

> 'such contribution is increased if the elimination ... of duties and other restrictive regulations of commerce extends to all trade, and diminished if any major sector to trade is excluded ... '

While this preamble will not be identified here as a new legal requirement, it certainly has the capacity to inform the reviewing parties as to the orientation to be applied in enunciating an interpretation of the article in favour of more complete preferences to be exchanged by the parties to a regional formation.

As to the coverage within any particular agreement, the devil shall always remain in the details, and this is particularly so for those details which concern sensitive and/or traditional sectors of trade between developed and developing territories. However, what can be seen to emerge is a notion that a 'major sector' of trade should refer to those categories of goods which are recognizable as distinct sectors of principle economic activities such as agriculture, textiles, autos and steel as compared to generally recognized sub-categories within such sectors such as cereals, men's suits or compact autos.

As to the quantity of trade to be covered, this raises the question of whether a guideline percentage at the outset should finally be settled and applied. Review parties have turned on this problem for years and one can be reminded of Kenneth Dam's 1970 quip that 'substantially' must mean more than some of the trade, but less than all of it. However, one can also note that the preparatory work indicates that the term reflected a conscious choice (Jackson, 1969, p. 608, note 2; Dam, 1970, pp. 274-75). What may be arising for reviews is an understanding that coverage has both elements of quality, as outlined above, and quantity. The easier sectors may not be relied upon to complete quantity where major sectors remain uncommitted. A percentage guideline - not less than the EU's traditional position of 80 per cent but perhaps as high as 95 per cent - can act as a starting point by which individual reviews apply such a measure and then go on to outline deviations for particular formations where the structure of trade or the position of the parties involved suggests flexibility. Similarly, the quantitative indicators can be designated as a range, say from 80-95 per cent, and guidelines could develop over a series of individual reviews to designate which types of formations should be permitted to form at the lower end and which should be treated more strictly.

A final aspect of coverage is raised by an older suggestion of criteria, again from the Overseas Association, whereby

> ' ... a matter to be considered was whether the provisions of a free-trade area pointed towards a gradual increase of barriers affecting the trade between the constituent parties or a gradual reduction of such barriers'[15].

In combination with the article's new provision which limits the interim period for formations to ten years[16], a gradual decrease in barriers over this reasonable period should result in a formation in which no major sector has been excluded from the commitment, and that a significant percentage of internal trade according to some benchmark be covered. Additionally, what may also be suggested for a modern review process is that FTAs are not static even after formation. The imposition of a biennial review for trade agreements - a requirement said to be mandated by the Singapore WTO Ministerial - should be applied so that later contingent measures between partners would also be subject to reporting and eventually be considered in determining whether or not substantially all trade was continuing to be covered in the formation.

While this would not require the prohibition of trade measures between regional partners, an enhancement that could also be defended from the Art. XXIV text, it nevertheless would serve as a significant departure from earlier practice. In the 1972 Yaoundé II review, some working-group members suggested that safeguard, budgetary and development measures, all capable of restricting trade between the parties, should be reported on the interim review. The EEC response then was that it was up to the regional parties and not the CPs to determine if later introduced measures degraded trade coverage below the 'substantially all trade' level[17]. The parties to the Convention promised to report to the GATT if such a lowering of trade occurred. It would be a meaningful indicator of progress to contemplate whether such an approach to continuing disclosure will be tolerated in the WTO.

The Lomé REPAs: Overseas Association redux?

Given the long history of EU-ACP trade relations in the GATT, it is doubtless the case that coverage questions will be examined carefully in any proposal to re-establish preferences within the FTA exception. As indicated by the history, the question of reverse preferences on the part of the ACP parties will be at the heart of this examination. At such a juncture, the proposals now circulating to provide for distinct FTAs for different groupings of ACP territories, known as the concept of 'differentiated reciprocity', will also likely surface as the centre of attention. By merely raising the term 'differentiation' in relationship to ACP obligations, the primary question as to why separate regimes are required in order to comply with Art. XXIV will be raised.

Proponents should therefore be prepared to clarify early and precisely the goal that is sought to be achieved by differentiated market access provisions between groups of developing ACP countries, particularly as they would otherwise qualify for GSP and its already established graduation levels within the autonomous EU legal regime. One source of descriptive advocacy for the establishment of differential regimes is found in an Economic and Social Committee (ESC) Opinion made in reference to the Commission's 1997 Green Paper on relations between the EU and the ACP countries[18]. From this it appears that between the options of GSP and a single FTA for all ACP territories, there is a determined need to provide for differentiation in respect of either the different development levels of the ACP parties or in respect of their own geographical clusters. According to the ESC Opinion, the EU and ACP countries, 'must press the WTO to retain a number of nonreciprocal preferences for the *least*-developed ACP countries on a temporary basis'[19]. Likewise,

> '[t]he phasing-in of these arrangements would allow the least developed ACP countries to maintain, for a limited period, protection to support the development of a number of *their* economic sectors'[20].

One draws from this the consolation that differentiated access to the EU market is not apparently a component of the concept, a feature which, if included, would likely doom the proposals quickly. If only development concerns are at issue on behalf of the ACP territories, and assuming for now that an FTA arrangement is not avoidable as evidenced by the parties' declaration to form one, the question should turn on whether deviations from one ACP group to another cannot be accommodated within a single FTA agreement. Since the indication is made above that the non-reciprocal preferences are intended to be temporary, then the review parties would likely inquire whether differentiation within a ten year interim would be sufficient for this accommodation, or if it was not, whether extensions beyond ten years for the least-developed parties would not be unreasonable in the facts, and given the alternative of separate permanent FTAs.

However, an additional objective in support of differentiation is also raised by the ESC Opinion. By establishing separate FTAs, regional co-operation between the ACP countries can also be promoted

'insofar as such programmes to open up markets would, as a matter of priority, include an internal chapter dealing with the region concerned, providing for accelerated free trade and increased co-operation between countries ... '[21].

Here is a suggestion that regional FTAs would seek to provide for some type of cumulation - regional or full - between the ACP partners within any single arrangement, and assumedly including the EU as to each formation. Since the prospects for area-wide treatment are raised as an aspect of the benefit to be derived from differentiation, the discussion will now turn to address this aspect and in the larger context of the EU regional universe.

4. The greater European space: what is a region and how should larger EU external regions be viewed in the WTO?

Although it was indicated above that the internal trade requirements for FTAs and CUs are not distinguishable according to the GATT rules, the functional distinction imposed by rules of origin is nevertheless persistent in the choice of formations as these rules are a required aspect in any formation in the absence of a harmonized tariff[22]. While rules of origin have long been criticized for the ability to provide a protective effect as to trade with outsiders, as they can act to raise new barriers to trade, there is also an aspect of the rules which can serve internal protective purposes. Since rules of origin define which products receive preferential treatment, '[t]he solution to these problems will not only condition the functioning of a free trade area; it will also, to some extent, govern its actual scope. The volume of goods which can circulate free of duty within the area will depend on whether these "mixed" products are given exemption from duty in a more or less liberal manner'(OEEC, 1957, pp. 11-12).

As the EU has learned in previous and recent experiments, and as suggested by Faber in Chapter 11 of this volume in the context of the EU-CEEC relationship, the development of full cumulation among pre-existing free-trade partners is a difficult task, perhaps subject not only to internal protective pressures which oppose mixing in the larger destination market, but also within the partner markets where even a lesser diagonal treatment can conflict with certain objectives of industrial and investment policy. It would appear that a pre-commitment to engage in the necessary harmonization would not only be advisable from the perspective of justifying in the WTO the rationale for differentiation on the basis of cumulation, but would probably be advised in order to secure the commitment to achieve it between the parties concerned[23].

The possibility to review the quality of cumulation intended within a proposed formation may not be so far beyond the purview of WTO review as to be disregarded. This argument follows if one acknowledges that the design of the rules determines whether a declared FTA is in fact an 'area' within which duties and other restrictive regulations of commerce have been removed to support free movement on at least a diagonal basis, if not fully cumulative. If a single agreement with more than two parties is proposed without diagonal cumulation, then this might negatively infer that a free-trade 'area' could not be intended to be created by the declaration, since in such a case even originating obtained products from one territory could not be mixed in all of the other constituent territories, except of course by MFN rates.

It is more difficult to see the capacity for review extended to require a full cumulation among FTA declarants to a single agreement, even though true 'area' treatment does more closely resemble the quality of movements provided in a completed CU. However, between three parties to a single agreement, a type of objection could be raised if the arrangement was internally bilateral, i.e., if only one territory retained cumulation with two others and they did not provide for cumulation between themselves. This formation could be treated de facto as two FTAs posing as one.

The most difficult scenario upon reviews, but pressing as a systemic issue, is the resulting 'area' which occurs or fails to result from multiple (bilateral) FTAs with members common to more than one arrangement. The power to examine the overall structure of resulting arrangements, including previously examined formations, would be resisted by proponents, since each review is limited to an analysis of the single agreement at hand. However, when one country is a party to more than one FTA the resulting structure of overlapping FTAs can also provide for protective effects on trade and may have distortive effects on investment as well[24].

The greatest implicit challenge in such formations is probably directed to that regional proponent that is common to all agreements. Here, an allegation of sorts is made that such a system has implications for reinforcing the dominance of one party as,

' ... a strong hub like the United States or EU will have its already dominant bargaining power increased if it is negotiating with one partner at a time, and may use this to maintain more protection (perhaps contingent protection) against its spoke partners - at a cost not only to the spokes, but also in many cases, to the hub itself' (Enders and Wonnacott, 1995, p. 4).

This insight also finds its origins in a European context, as the same argument was made in support of a multilateral European area in light of the EEC formation[25]. A desire to avoid individual OEEC country bilateral agreements with the newly formed EEC was a paramount goal as,

'[i]nstead of a broad free trade area in which each country maintained similar relations with every other country within the group, a new pattern of trading would be established based on an inner group of countries (the Six) at the centre of the web with ties radiating out to the surrounding countries' (Dunlap and King, 1974, p. 24).

This is not to suggest that the EU is exercising hegemony, or that a review process is going to rule on questions of dominance, as characterized above. However by way of caution, there is a view that has long disfavoured preferences between developed and developing countries on this basis and which finds support in the GATT objective to eliminate discrimination in international trade. Since the choice of geographical formations is not accidental, and where one country has bargaining power and is common to all arrangements, then it can follow that the choice of bilateral arrangements rather than a multilateral framework for regional trade is already an exercise of this power for some purpose. As interest in these aspects develops in international trade, and not only in reference to the regional plans of the EU, such considerations can be expected to linger in the background as other WTO members attempt to discern what is at the core of EU differential FTAs with the ACP. Therefore, as the expressed goal of the EU is to pose differentiation as the legitimate mechanism to respond to the longer-term development needs of the regions themselves, this should be made clearly apparent in the construction of the formations and in the cumulation possibilities designated within them.

Finally, the EU maintains a complex and extensive series of regional trade agreements, most of which are bilateral with individual territories but some of which are with groups of countries including the Lomé Convention. Any movement to simplify this universe and integrate these formations into a smaller number of larger 'regional' FTAs is generally acknowledged to be a worthy goal which would promote uniformity of rules of origin, simplify trade operations, and serve economic development in regions. However, as larger regions of cumulation may develop, one also wishes to discern whether such regions are the ultimate goal of the policy, or whether a single cumulation reality for all of the preferential agreements of the EU is ever possible or desirable from the viewpoint of the EU itself.

While such questions are beyond the scope here, one can at least pose the question whether the creation of separate regions, while favouring intraregional trade, may tend to diminish over time the larger potential of developing countries in a global economy. Likewise, where contiguous regions are identified for separate cumulation regimes, there is also a possibility foregone that trade could develop naturally across such regional borders. Thus, while one can support the benefits that may be derived from broader cumulation within the Mediterranean region and as to the EU, who is to say that Central and Northern Africa do not share as much potential propinquity between themselves as 'regions' as they may share individually with Europe in the present. Similarly, while Turkey may be treated to be a part of a greater Mediterranean region which will benefit from its economic power there, does this option not forego opportunities to develop with its natural trading partners in Central and Eastern Europe?

5. EU regionalism in a Millennium Round

The conclusion of the Uruguay Round in 1994 found the new WTO operating in a dramatically different regional environment then when the Round commenced in 1986. Not only had the USA become a major regional actor by concluding FTAs with Canada and Mexico but the decline of state trading systems unleashed a major foray of regional agreements in Central and Eastern Europe. Additionally, new rounds of agreements among Central and South-American countries were initiated.

While the Uruguay Round produced the changes noted above for the GATT rules for regional exceptions, the first WTO Ministerial Round in Singapore sought to respond more directly to the new environment by creating a standing committee to review agreements as they were proposed, as opposed to the GATT practice of forming ad hoc reviews for each agreement. This committee was also granted an authority to tackle systemic issues, an area of discussion which is said to have already borne some fruit. However, while the committee has received a large number of declarations from regional proponents, the reviews made for individual declarations have not been appearing to result in recommendations that particular agreements are consistent with the requirements of the regional exception article. While it may be possible that the requirement of consensus in reaching such decisions will prove too weak to allow recommendations to come forth, it has been suggested here that proponents of agreements are the real risk-takers in a process where recommendations do not come forth and decisions are not made.

The European Commission is now advocating a new round of multilateral trade negotiations. While the WTO members attempt to frame terms of reference for presentation at a WTO Ministerial Round before the end of 1999, there has not yet been heard a call from either the EU or the USA to include the GATT/WTO rules governing regional agreements on this agenda. Perhaps this indicates satisfaction with progress made thus far to close the Art. XXIV loopholes. It may unfortunately also suggest that parties have calculated a benefit in the status quo whereby maximum regional flexibility is preserved for future regional plans. If so, the Community for its part might also consider in its calculations this additional prospect: that a continuing absence of guidelines for FTAs increases the latitude for conflicts with trading partners who have chosen to become active on the same third territories where the Community is itself active, either in seeking new preferences or in attempting to reform existing preferential arrangements.

In such regional contests, the EU can not always claim to hold a superior hand. For the USA certainly exerts some greater influence and advantage on certain territories than does the EU, whether these advantages be locational by proximity, economic by reliance upon US trade, or a mix of political and cultural factors. Given that an active policy on regionalism has been enunciated by two successive presidents, the domestic politics of congressional fast-track approval appear to operate now as the only deterrent to a new round of US FTA declarations. Besides the USA, Japan can also emerge as competitor for regional preferences within Asia. For now, Japan remains the only quad party that has not initiated a formal regionalism strategy. This self restraint can not however be presumed to be a permanent policy, and there are already suggestions from Japan that bilateral FTA formations in the region are being actively considered.

These factors should inform the Community's policy toward regional agreements in the WTO. At the least, the Community will benefit from framing its external regional policy by taking into account not only the prospects for its own projects, but also the implications which flow from the regional projects of other WTO members. For a more severe characterization, if the Community and its partners now pass upon the opportunity to settle the reforms that are possible for Art. XXIV, this choice may be seen in retrospect to have framed the moment when the major WTO members escalated a contest to secure regional zones of influence as based upon preference both for trade and investment opportunities. For all parties concerned, this outcome can not be seen to be superior to that provided by MFN.

The Commission's expressed advocacy for a development-orientated round should also be viewed in the light of the regionalism issues. If all can agree that the stake of the least-developed territories in the WTO needs to be enhanced and can see a better multilateral system occurring as a result, then the market leaders' regional plans with developing countries should also be viewed in this light. At this juncture, it is apparent that a large number of WTO's least-developed members are reluctant to start a new round without seeing first a substantial down payment on the market-access issues left over from the Uruguay Round. If the Community diverts its energy for concessions to the formation of agreements with only a select group of developing countries, a conflict with the interests of the larger set of similarly situated WTO territories will be hard to ignore. This includes not only the question whether the regional plans will undermine the EU's ability to deliver a larger set of concessions undertaken in a multilateral round towards all developing countries, but also the future role of the GSP in the WTO, as these preferences will be alleged to be further marginalized by a new round of FTAs.

A consistent approach between these posts would look again at the prospects for the GSP as from a purely non-discrimination standpoint, GSP can always be criticized for its preferential nature. However, it is certainly 'multilateral' in the sense that it is already an endorsed GATT mechanism for granting preferences to less-developed countries without reference to regions, permits for graduation in respect of development levels, and does not require reverse preferences on behalf of the recipients.

Given the legal developments described above, the possibilities of a new round of negotiations and the ongoing development of new disciplines in the WTO, it is possible that the historical approach to regional formations by the EU can be seen to stand at something of a legal, if not historical, juncture. At the extremes, in one direction lies a continuation of an older policy of establishing incomplete preferential systems by declaration in the absence of clear guidelines in the WTO, and perhaps without third parties ever challenging these preferences. This route provides most flexibility for the Union to conduct its external regional system to its liking and assumedly, to the liking of its regional partners. However, it also grants the same policy flexibility to other major regional actors which are also learning their way in the world of regionalism. The implications for the flexible approach may include the prospect of a more strenuous competition between major actors for the formation of preferential agreements with developing and transitional markets, and a resulting large number of developing territories seeking to become installed as primary hubs formed by overlapping FTAs with their developed partners.

An alternative to the traditional approach would be to close the chapter on the long and troubling legacy of the Overseas Association episode once and for all by supporting a new WTO discipline over preferential deviations from the MFN clause. Building upon the GATT 1994 Understanding on the Interpretation of Article XXIV, this avenue would seek to finally generate a set of interpretative guidelines to give substantive definition to the Uruguay Round Art. XXIV preamble declaration, that the compatibility of regionalism with the multilateral system is better insured when no major sector of activity is excluded.

In these choices, one also sees the Union playing two roles: one as a party like any other, seeking to implement its notion of regional systems in a manner it believes to be in its commercial and political best interests, and in the interests of its regional partners; the other, as a large territory member of the WTO that is called upon to exercise leadership, which together with other members, assumes responsibility for the direction of activities and reforms to be considered in the WTO. While perhaps it is unfair to place any heightened burden of leadership upon the Union when it comes to the issues of regionalism, it is also a fact that the status of regionalism within the multilateral system today is quite attributable to previous Community practice and policies. No other party in the GATT system has had as much to say about the qualifications of agreements as a proponent, and arguably, no other party has a higher stake in how others will assert these similar interpretations in the future.

Although a middle way which favours some reforms but not others, depending upon the requirements of the particular regional agreement being advanced, can appear as the most practical course to take, the opportunity for some bolder initiative in the Millennium Round can also be considered.

Notes

[1] The concept of 'regional', ' ... frequently reflect(ing) little more than a sentimental contemplation of the desirability in the abstract of closer economic relations with countries with which there were - or it was pleasant to think that there were, or could be developed - specially close ties of sentiment and interest arising out of ethnological, or cultural, or historical political affiliations' (Viner, 1950, pp. 5 and 19).

[2] *EEC - Member States' Import Regimes for Bananas.* DS32/R 3 June 1993; *EEC - Import Regime for Bananas,* DS38/R, 11 Feb. 1994. GATT panel reports (reported or otherwise) do not have the legal value of precedence in later cases, but even unreported reports have been cited and quoted in later panels to support the parties' arguments or the panel's own findings and conclusions.

[3] This occurred before the enabling clause and the advent of the GSP. See generally, GATT 1947, Part IV, Trade and Development, Art. XXXVI, Principles and Objectives.

[4] The ACP-EEC Convention of Lomé, Report 15 July 1976, 1977 BISD, L/4369, para. 10.

[5] DS32/R, para. 220.

[6] *EEC-Tariff Treatment of Imports of Citrus Products from Certain Countries in the Mediterranean Region,* L/5776, Feb. 7, 1986, para. 4.16.

[7] DS32/R, para. 366 and 367, emphasis added, citing Citrus Panel, ibid., at para. 4.16.

[8] DS38/R, para. 158.

[9] DS38/R, para. 159; Lomé Convention, Title I, Art. 174, ' ... the ACP States shall not be required to assume ... obligations corresponding to the commitments entered into by the Community ... '.

[10] DS38/R, para. 162. The EEC's own declaration on the Yaoundé Convention was also raised, which stated Part IV could not modify Art. XXIV. BISD 14S/100, para. 14, ibid., para. 162.

[11] Art. XXIV:8(a) for CUs, and Art. XXIV:8(b) for FTAs.

[12] C.3/11, Item 13. E/CONF.2/C.3/78, p. 5, emphasis added. As Viner (1950, p. 124) noted regarding the term free-trade area: '[t]his term is introduced, as a technical term, into the language of this field by the Charter, and its meaning for the purposes of the Charter must therefore be sought wholly within the text of the Charter'.

[13] Partially preferential agreements were permitted in the Havana Charter, but not for the FTA exception: '[p]referential Agreements for Economic Development and Reconstruction', available for contiguous territories or those belonging to the same 'economic region', as necessary, 'to ensure a sound and adequate market for a particular industry or branch of agriculture which is being, or is to be, created or reconstructed or substantially developed or substantially modernized.' (Havana Charter, 1948, Art. 15:4, (a)-(f).

[14] Art. XXIV:5 has been relied upon to suggest that less than complete formations which do not raise new barriers to the trade of outsiders should be consistent with the article's requirements. The difficulty with this view is that the examination of external barriers which occurs under Art. XXIV:5 is limited to those formations which are already defined as qualified by Art. XXIV:8, i.e., FTAs and CUs and interim agreements leading to either.

[15] 1958 BISD, Report 29 November, 1957, para. 34.

[16] 'In cases where Members parties to an interim agreement believe that 10 years would be insufficient they shall provide a full explanation to the Council for Trade in Goods of the need for a longer period' (GATT 1994, Understanding on the Interpretation of Article XXIV:5(3)).

[17] 1972 BISD, L/3465, para. 11 and 12.

[18] European Commission, 1996; ESC Opinion, 1997. The author apologizes if later sources containing clarifications as to these elements are available for citation.

[19] ESC Opinion, para. 5.3.2., emphasis added.

[20] ESC Opinion, para. 5.4., emphasis added.

[21] ESC Opinion, para. 5.5.

[22] 'This is a special problem, therefore, which does not arise in the Customs Union when the common external tariff has come into force.' (OEEC, 1957, p. 11). For a theoretical view, see generally for the EC, Forrester, 1980.

[23] 'Diagonal' referring here to where the use of materials which is designated as already *originating* in any of the partner countries is permitted. 'Full' cumulation referring here to where *processing* is permitted to be cumulated between the free trade parties. Both terms can apply to one agreement with more than two parties, or where separate agreements are linked.

[24] ' ... the cost to spokes of a H&S (hub and spoke) is the opportunity lost to liberalize their spoke-spoke trade. But there is also a second cost because a H&S damages that spoke-spoke trade, since each spoke's exports face discrimination in other spoke markets in competition with duty-free exports from the hub ... (Finally), spokes would be at a severe disadvantage in competing with the hub in attracting investment, since

only firms locating in the hub acquire free access to markets in - and duty-free inputs from - all participating countries' (Enders and Wonnacott, 1995, pp. 4-5).

[25] ' ... Because several OEEC members were anxious to counterbalance the formation of the EEC common market, the (OEEC) Council established a working party to examine the feasibility of forming a free-trade area in Europe' (Dunlap and King, 1974, p. 208). The EEC would have functioned as one territory within this.

References

Dam, K W., *The GATT: Law and International Economic Organization*, The University of Chicago Press (Midway Reprint), 1977.

Dunlap, J., and R. King, 'Regional Economic Integration and GATT: the Effects of the EEC EFTA Agreements on International Trade', *Law and Policy in International Business*, Volume 6, 1974.

Enders, A., and R. Wonnacott, *How Useful is the NAFTA Experience for East-West European Integration?* (draft), 1995.

Forrester, I.S., 'EEC Customs Law: Rules of Origin and Preferential Duty Treatment-Part One', *European Law Review*, Volume 5, pp. 167-197, 1980.

GATT, *The Results of the Uruguay Round of Multilateral Trade Negotiations, The Legal Texts*, Geneva, 1994.

Haight, F.A., 'Customs Unions and Free Trade Areas Under GATT', *Journal of World Trade*, Volume 6, Number 4, 1972.

Jackson, J.H., *World Trade Law and the Law of GATT*, the Mitchie Company, Charlottesville, Virginia, 1969.

Viner, J., *The Customs Union Issue*, Carnegie Endowment, 1950.

Documents

European Commission, DG-VIII, *Green Paper on Relations between the European Union and the ACP countries on the Eve of the 21st century*, Com(96)570 final, 20 November 1996.

European Communities, ESC Opinion, OJ C296, 29.09.97.

GATT, *EEC - Member States' Import Regimes for Bananas*, DS32/R, 3 June 1993.

GATT, *EEC - Import Regime for Bananas*, DS38/R, 11 Feb. 1994.

GATT, *EEC-Tariff Treatment of Imports of Citrus Products from Certain Countries in the Mediterranean Region*, L/5776, Feb. 7, 1986.

GATT, *The ACP-EEC Convention of Lomé*, Report 15 July 1976, BISD, L/4369, 1977.

OEEC, Special Working Party for the Council, *Report on the Possibility of Creating a Free Trade Area in Europe*, C(57)5, Paris, 1957.

7

CAP REFORM IN AGENDA 2000: LOGIC AND CONTRADICTIONS

MICHIEL KEYZER
MAX MERBIS

Free University
Amsterdam
The Netherlands

1. Introduction

The Common Agricultural Policy (CAP) underwent significant reform in 1992, as the European Commission moved the agricultural policy into a new direction. The thrust of the reform was a shift from price support to direct income support, achieved by lowering the intervention prices, while compensating farmers via acreage and headage premiums. As a means to reduce the production of cereals and oilseeds, a set-aside scheme was introduced, and professional farmers were only eligible for compensation payments if they participated by keeping a specified fraction of their land fallow. With the benefit of hindsight, it can be concluded that the measures relieved international tensions on agricultural export markets, and virtually saved the Uruguay Round, resulting in a new General Agreement on Tariffs and Trade (GATT, 1994). Furthermore, the compensation payments turned out to be generous, as market prices became higher than anticipated.

Subsequently, the CAP essentially remained unchanged, although pressures for further reform have been building up. The European Commission argues in its Agenda 2000, as part of a broad package to prepare the European Union (EU) for the next century (CEC, 1997a,b), that a deepening and widening of the 1992

P. van Dijck and G. Faber (eds.), The External Economic Dimension of the European Union, 151–173.
© *2000 Kluwer Academic Publishers. Printed in the Netherlands.*

reform is called for, in view of the developments in the agricultural sector itself, the upcoming international trade negotiations under the World Trade Organization (WTO) and the planned accession of Central and Eastern European countries (CEEC). The agricultural chapter of Agenda 2000 contains a first version that was subsequently elaborated upon in the draft regulations published in March 1998 (CEC, 1998a).

In a nutshell, the 1992 reform is pursued with a further lowering of internal prices and increase of headage and acreage premiums as compensating payments. The proposals seek to improve market conformity by cutting the set-aside rate to zero, and by allowing for some expansion of milk quotas. In addition, food quality and safety concerns figure more prominently, in response to the recent spread of animal diseases, and rural policies are to be strengthened (see also CEC, 1997d).

Since the proposals basically amount to an extension of the 1992 reform, they are best characterized by the elements that are kept unchanged: compensation through premiums that are not fully decoupled, strong restrictions on the import side, and no reform for sugar. It is noteworthy that the Commission has opted for such an extrapolative approach, rather than presenting a clear vision of the future of European agriculture. This is presumably because the EU member states appear to have widely diverging views on the matter. Indeed, the Agenda 2000 proposals found little endorsement by the various member states and yet, no alternatives have been formulated that can count on a majority of votes in the Council of Ministers. Ultimately, the European Council in Berlin in March 1999 adopted the Commission proposals, be it in a weakened form: smaller cuts in prices and implementation of reforms at a later date than originally proposed.

The aim of this chapter is to look over the edge of Agenda 2000. It is argued that the measures adopted in Berlin will soon need more substantial modification: although all the steps follow logically from the earlier reform, they nonetheless strengthen the inherent contradictions of the CAP. Their contribution to trade liberalization is unlikely to appease the negotiating partners of the coming WTO round.

In particular in countries such as Germany and the Netherlands that are net contributors to the EU budget, taxpayers and financial authorities find it hard to accept the proposed increase in compensation payments. The planned accession of countries from Central and Eastern Europe will only make it more difficult to finance the CAP.

Agenda 2000 also fails to draw the policy consequences of recent shifts in consumer concerns and the ongoing concentration in agribusiness. More generally, by choosing an extrapolative approach the Commission cannot look ahead to policies for a rural sector that will increasingly receive income from non-agricultural activities and whose agricultural operations will be integrated more closely within the processing chain. These developments and their effects on developing countries will be analysed. The position taken in this chapter will be that the contradictions of a CAP that claims to become more liberal while keeping its internal prices isolated from the world market and asking for more budgetary support, create artificial tensions. It will be argued that such tensions can be avoided if the policies become more market-orientated combining openness in trade with a good financial reward for environmental and other services rendered by farmers.

The chapter starts with a brief assessment of the current proposals in Section 2. Section 3 discusses a number of unresolved issues that need to be addressed as well as recent developments which the CAP will eventually have to account for. Section 4 deals with the implications of regionalization and Section 5 with vertical integration within the agribusiness. In Section 6 the policy implications are sketched.

2. CAP-reform in Agenda 2000

The Agenda 2000 proposal bears a strong resemblance to the 1993-95 reform. The proposal is a further step towards liberalization: the internal price of wheat is reduced to the world-market level; for coarse grains, beef and dairy products the gaps become smaller, and refunds decrease.

Effect on the EU

According to an impact study published by the Commission (CEC, 1998c, see also Keyzer and Merbis, 1998), the effects of the Agenda 2000 proposal at the level of the EU can be summarized as follows. The total premium amount will rise by 8.2 billion euros in 2005 in real terms, as compared to the business-as-usual scenario. Export refunds will decrease by 2.3 billion euros, keeping the budget of the European Agricultural Guidance and Guarantee Fund (EAGGF) below the official spending guideline. Average farming income in the year 2005 will be lowered by 5.3 per cent per worker. Consumers will gain as their tax burden increases by 5.9 billion euros, while they will save 13.6 billion euros on food expenditures. The gain from the reform could be higher, if it results in improved efficiency in the non-agricultural sector.

As regards the commitments in the GATT, it appears that if world-market prices for cereals by the year 2000 have returned to the 'generally predicted' level - by the end of 1998 the US export price for wheat was 15 per cent below this level - it should be possible for the Community to export wheat without refunds. For coarse grains, export subsidies are still required, and for dairy products and beef the price reductions generate savings on export subsidies. Overall, the product-related subsidies - premiums per hectare and per animal - increase, while for crops the premium levels tend towards harmonization. Whether this harmonization will be sufficient to ensure GATT-compatibility will have to be settled during the next trade round.

It must be emphasized that the effect of the current price proposals critically depends on world-market prices. If conditions are not 'normal', that is: if world market prices for cereals remain below the level of the proposed intervention price of 95 euros per tonne (Figure 7.1 shows that they actually did so in the past), the EU will still have to provide export subsidies and raise the set-aside, or pay compensation premiums. Both options are costly.

Effect on world markets

The main effect of Agenda 2000 on the world market is an increase of EU wheat exports. Table 7.1 shows production and export data of some major trading blocs. This increase occurs because once internal prices have reached the world-market level, no export subsidies are required and restrictions such as set-asides, that were needed to constrain exports, can be lifted. According to FAPRI (1998), the world-market price for wheat and coarse grains will fall by five and two per cent, respectively, with respect to baseline projections, and the USA will lose about three per cent points of its world market share in wheat. Other products and countries are only marginally affected. The expansion in milk quota that was subsequently proposed, points in the same direction for dairy. Given the proposals, the outcome is not surprising. Yet the prediction of a fall in price is interesting, since during the Uruguay Round negotiations all parties seemed to agree that trade liberalization would cause world-market prices to rise, mainly because of a reduction in the dumping of surpluses.

It is hard to judge whether these predictions were right. Indeed, starting in 1994-95 cereal prices started to rise, peaking in May-April 1996, but this was

Figure 7.1. Wheat prices per tonne, in ECUs, 1980-97[1].

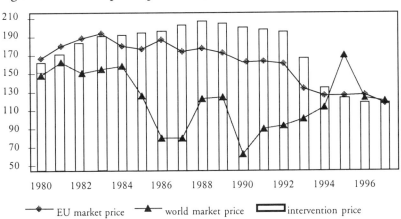

Note:[1] EU market price is French soft wheat price, taken from SPEL database, Eurostat;
World-market price is Argentina Trigo Pan, taken from FAO;
Intervention price is taken from European Commission.

also caused by other factors including El Niño, imports by Russia, and income growth in Asia, as well as the set-aside programmes of the EU and the USA.

Conversely, the Asian crisis and bumper crops caused cereal prices to plunge in 1998. These major shocks dominate so much that it becomes impossible to isolate statistically the effect on the world market of the 1992 reform. Be this as it may, it seems realistic to expect that the Agenda 2000 will *ceteris paribus* cause a modest fall in price, as shown in the FAPRI study.

This discussion illustrates the typical situation when analysing the international implications of CAP reforms. First, the direction of the effect differs from one reform to the other, as set-asides are phased in and out again. CAP reforms only reveal the effect of the change, not the effect of the CAP itself.

Second, although the EU is not a negligible player on the market for dairy and cereals, and its policies on other commodities can have important effects on third countries, the policy has been in place for so many years and the reforms that are implemented are so moderate and gradual, that it becomes very difficult to measure empirically the effects of the CAP on world markets.

Finally, in international fora the bone of contention is the CAP itself, whereas the eventual reform is only what comes out after years of resistance on the part of

Table 7.1. Agricultural production and trade of four trading blocs, 1990-1996 averages.

	EU	NAFTA	Mercosur	ANZCERTA
Wheat (1000 mt)				
production	89,731	95,771	14,342	15,385
net exports	17,719	49,823	584	10,780
Coarse grains (1000 mt)				
production	95,633	285,367	44,142	9,068
net exports	3,870	58,157	4,495	3,553
Refined sugar (1000 mt)				
production	16,312	9,500	22,088	4,255
net exports	3,405	-2,662	3,246	2,912
Vegetable oils (1000 mt)				
production	4,972	16,354	8,696	312
net exports	-4,970	4,011	5,249	-155
Dairy (1000 mt milk eq.)				
production	126,158	83,915	25,382	16,400
net exports	11,310	-2,277	-836	8,672
Beef (1000 mt)				
production	8,861	13,270	7,680	2,366
net exports	199	1,194	785	1,569
Pork (1000 mt)				
production	15,721	9,711	1,574	380
net exports	614	985	18	140
Bovine meat (1000 mt)				
production	1,206	225	3,138	1,199
net exports	-212	-51	57	582

Note: Export figures contain derived processed products, like wheat flour, cheese, butter, milk powder, etc. Sugar includes beet and cane sugar. Vegetable oils from oilseeds only. ANZCERTA is the Australia New Zealand Closer Economic Relations Trade Agreement.
Source: Own computations from FAO supply utilisation accounts.

the EU. For these reasons, subsequent sections will abstract from the specifics of Agenda 2000 and its quantitative effects, and evaluate the proposals in a broader perspective.

3. Issues pending

The European Commission has presented its Agenda 2000 proposals for CAP reform as a widening and deepening of the 1992 reform and hence as a natural and logical step in the direction initiated during the Uruguay Round. The proposals are succinct and operational. They build on the consensus view that something has to change, not so much to meet the challenges of the future as to effectuate GATT commitments made in the past. The approach has the advantage of conceptual simplicity. Even though some aspects are technical, the interest groups that are directly concerned can trace relatively easy the implications for their own operations. By the same token the proposals fail to convince outsiders and the public at large, since no attempt is made to present a coherent vision of the future of European agriculture. This section reviews a number of issues that remain unresolved and will have to be addressed in the years to come.

Import access

Agenda 2000 focuses on further reduction of export subsidies and keeps the import regimes unchanged. Export subsidies are mainly a concern of the EU itself, in view of the budgetary costs, and the competing exporters, such as the USA. As consumer demand in the EU has been almost stagnant for several years, large exporters find it more important to challenge the EU in international markets than domestically. Yet several smaller players, particularly from the developing world, would gain from improved access, especially for fruits, vegetables, and possibly sugar. At present the EU implements market-access commitments via tariff quotas, the modalities of which were agreed in GATT (1994). This is a cumbersome procedure that discriminates exporters and is in need of improvement. Yet the EU's current external policy, formally not part of the CAP, is to grant country groupings preferential access through special agreements.

Price transmission

The Commission continues to view price stabilization on the internal market as an important policy objective, and proposes to maintain the present system of protection through variable import tariffs and tariff quotas. Figure 7.1 shows that the EU wheat price basically follows the intervention price, and is unrelated to fluctuations in the world market. Similarly, the internal price of animal feed grains will not rise when there is a shortage outside the EU. This lack of transmission intensifies the price fluctuations in the world cereals market and shifts the full burden of short-term adjustment to traders and consumers outside the EU. Price transmission would reduce these fluctuations and improve world-market integration, and thus strengthen the role of prices as scarcity indicators. It would also remove the artefact that the EU keeps prices of wheat and feed grains at the same level, while at world markets they are moving in parallel at a distance of 30-50 US dollars per tonne.

Acceptability of blue-box measures under WTO

The introduction of the so-called blue box was a novelty of the 1994 agreement. The blue box 'contains' measures of support that are acceptable under the agreement although they are not fully decoupled. Decoupled measures are supposed to have no effect on production decisions and hence on trade. Research and development (R and D) and extension services qualify as such. The blue box covers among others the deficiency payments in the USA and the premiums per hectare and per head of the EU. It is uncertain whether such exceptions will be made in the coming round. By harmonizing the per hectare premiums for arable crops, the EU evidently hopes that the measures will qualify for the green box, or allow for the blue box to be maintained.

CEEC-accession

The price reductions proposed in Agenda 2000 significantly reduce the price gap between the EU and the CEECs, and this facilitates their accession. However, it remains questionable whether the reduction is sufficient to avoid an important increase in consumer prices in CEECs upon accession (CEC, 1998b). If the current slump in world markets persists, these countries might have lowered their internal prices by the time so as to let their consumers benefit, and in that case the gap would still be wide.

Moreover, it is unlikely that the CEECs will eventually be offered the full price package of Agenda 2000, as some of these countries have to cope regularly with devaluation of their national currencies relative to the euro. Since it is highly unlikely that these countries will soon join the European Monetary System (EMS), let alone the euro zone, these devaluations cause the revival of the old problem that countries with strongly depreciating currencies receive agricultural payments in euros and benefit too much. The mechanism operates as follows.

While the CAP specifies all intervention prices and premiums in a common currency, actual payments are in the national currency, based on the green exchange rate. After a devaluation, agricultural prices and subsidies rise overnight, while other prices and costs often adjust more slowly or only in part. This implies that farmers in countries that devaluate benefit temporarily, while consumers suffer. The current proposals do not indicate how the EU intends to deal with this issue, although the Commission recognizes the problem when announcing that "they [the new member states] are expected to participate in an exchange rate mechanism and avoid excessive exchange rate changes" (CEC, 1997a, Part Two, I.3). This might be asking too much.

In short, the Agenda 2000 proposals make the accession of the CEECs easier, because they lower the existing price differences, but it may be questioned whether the reforms go far enough. It seems likely that the new member states will need a significant transitional period before they can fully harmonize their prices. Furthermore, the system of premiums per hectare and per animal implies an inherent budgetary risk, as the newly admitted countries could eventually claim these subsidies as well, on top of the aid they are already receiving from the structural and cohesion funds.

Finally, by extending membership, the EU makes it more difficult for itself to design a CAP that meets the interests of all member countries. In the early days it was possible to satisfy members in the northern zone with sheep premiums, and high prices for dairy and beef, while the countries in the middle zone were more interested in support for cereals and sugar, and countries in the southern zone received premiums for olives and wine and protection for fruits and vegetables. With the extension from six to 15 members, and the WTO-induced reduction of price support, it has become necessary to include direct payments through structural and cohesion funds to keep some balance in the distribution of benefits. With the accession of the new members it will only become more difficult to maintain this balance.

Sharing the budgetary cost

Not surprisingly, the increase in budgetary outlays that results from further replacement of price support by premiums has met with resistance of the Ministers of Finance in various member states. Some of them have advocated (partial) financial renationalization of the CAP, whereby the budgetary costs are being shared among member states in proportion to the benefits enjoyed. As argued in

Folmer et al. (1987, 1995), Kjeldahl and Tracy (1994), and Keyzer (1995), this mode of financing offers several advantages. First, member states can avoid negotiating on petty details of the CAP. Provided the compensation payments satisfy basic principles of decoupling, i.e. avoid subsidization of specific commodities, countries can decide by themselves how much they wish to spend and who should benefit.

Second, the regulation becomes more transparent, since it becomes clearer what the taxpayer's money is used for. Whereas structural and cohesion funds can channel funds across member states, the market-related policies of the EAGGF are no longer used for this purpose, although the implicit transfers that result from the remaining market protection are not eliminated. Consequently, the enlargement to the east can be achieved more easily, as the compensating transfers to these countries are not subject of the negotiations.

In short, financial renationalization maintains the CAP with respect to market regime, but the financing is no longer out of the common budget, to which countries contribute in proportion to their tax base. Financial renationalization has been resisted mainly by the southern member states, and so far with success. Yet the issue will presumably be tabled time and again, as long as the costs of the CAP remain so high.

4. A changing external environment: regionalization

As mentioned in Section 3, the EU's current policy with respect to market access is to grant preferential access through special agreements that are being concluded with a large number of country groupings. The current WTO rules allow for such reciprocal arrangements, and the EU is in the process of negotiating such arrangements with groupings from all over the world. For example, the current EU mandate for negotiations with the group of countries in Sub-Saharan Africa, the Caribbean and the Pacific, known collectively as the ACP countries, specifies that the earlier set of Lomé countries should be redefined and split into regional groupings (CEC, 1997c). This would seem to be at odds with the EU's stated goal of promoting free trade (CEC, 1997a). This issue is discussed in more detail by Stevens in Chapter 10 of this volume.

In this connection, it is important to distinguish the issue of regionalization itself from the modalities of agreements between the EU and other regions. Regionalization commonly takes the form of preferential trade agreements (PTAs) whereby members of the region are being granted access at lower tariffs than non-members. In some instances the PTA takes the form of a customs union (CU), whereby members gain free access, impose a common external tariff (CET) and establish a rule for sharing tariff proceeds to ensure that, say, landlocked members benefit as much as others.

Whether regionalization actually brings benefits to developing countries remains hotly disputed, as discussed by Van Dijck and Faber in Chapter 1 and by Winters in Chapter 9 of this volume. Bhagwati (1993), Bhagwati et al. (1998) and Srinivasan (1998) view PTAs as 'stumbling blocks' to multilateral liberalization, which slow down development since they divert imports from the most efficient producers and distort domestic specialization. On the other hand, Lawrence (1996), Frankel (1997) and Ethier (1998) view PTAs as 'stepping stones' towards free trade, which enable developing countries to open up for trade at first with competitors within the same region, who often share similar cost structures and will therefore not wipe out domestic production. In addition, Collier and Gunning (1995) argue that by their international nature PTAs tend to strengthen a lasting commitment to policy reform and provide a more stable and secure policy environment, which is conducive to foreign direct investment.

As far as EU agriculture is concerned, the PTAs of the EU define a reciprocal access that necessarily is heavily restricted by quotas (Duponcel, 1998, Tangermann, 1997 and Davenport et al. 1995). Under a more liberalized regime the EU markets would be flooded with imports and the CAP would be incapable to function. The PTAs can also be seen as a device to maintain support for the CAP itself, on the part of the participating countries. They may as well serve to define preparatory stages of accession for potential EU members.

In short, for the EU the PTAs have the advantage of organizing the world into a limited number of geographical units between which it becomes easier to conclude further PTAs. Whether this adds to the stumbling-block or to the stepping-stone nature of these arrangements remains a matter for debate.

The EU policy of exclusively linking its PTAs to regional groupings definitely adds to the attractiveness of these groupings, but also makes them more dependent on the EU's willingness to maintain the preferential access in the future. Nonetheless, somewhere along the path to trade liberalization, all preferences should vanish eventually. Then, the PTAs are to be treated as transient phenomena, that do not deserve elaborate institutional embedding. On the other hand, by opting for a regionalized approach the EU keeps its options open. In case the

WTO process fails, the EU can resort to managed trade (Krugman, 1990) by adjusting its own exports as well as the concessions to other regions.

Mercosur

Let us briefly turn to Mercosur, a region of special relevance in the present volume. Major aspects of the relationship between the EU and Mercosur have been reviewed by Van Dijck in Chapter 13 and Ventura Dias in Chapter 14 of this volume. Through the 1991 Treaty of Asunción, the Mercosur countries went a long way in creating a CU. They have established a CET and proclaimed that internal free trade should be achieved by 2005. So far, some sensitive products such as sugar and automobiles are still protected by higher tariffs but the harmonization of external tariffs has been substantial (Laird, 1997), although the rates differ among sectors (Olarreaga and Soloaga, 1998).

Mercosur offers a good illustration of the controversies around the issue of regionalization. Yeats (1998) argues that trade diversion has contributed significantly to the growth of trade among Mercosur partners, but Nagarajan (1998) concludes differently. Yet this was before Mercosur raised its external tariff on thousands of items by 25 per cent at the onset of the Asian crisis in the second half of 1997.

Mercosur has announced further reductions of its external tariff and is in the process of expanding its membership and international linkages. Both the USA and the EU expressed their interest in association and possibly free-trade agreements with Mercosur, evidently allured by the large and strongly growing consumer markets in the Southern Cone of America. In practice, enlargement proves difficult to accomplish, even with neighbours at a similar stage of development. Chile has been admitted as an associate member, but attempts to upgrade to full member failed. Negotiations with the Andean group have been unsuccessful, so far. Deals with the USA, as any attempts at far more ambitious projects like a free trade zone for the entire hemisphere (known as the FTAA, see Lee, 1995 and FTAA, 1999) floundered. Similarly, a deal with the EU was halted, as it was incompatible with the CAP. The present agricultural policy regime in the EU does not allow to absorb large imports, as the EU is a large diversified agricultural producer with substantial net imports only for oilseeds and beverages such as coffee, tea and cocoa. Mercosur also has large export potentials, as illustrated in Table 7.1, and is known to be a low-cost producer of products such as cereals and beef. Not surprisingly, the EU Ministers of Agriculture blocked the negotiations on a free-trade deal with Chile and Mercosur (Agrafocus, August 1997).

5. A changing external environment: vertical integration within the agribusiness

The CAP is largely concerned with prices and premiums at the farm level, which is the primary level of production, and with the markets for these products in raw form. Almost all measures relating to products at a higher level of processing are derived on the basis of the raw-material content. There is no explicit policy with respect to agribusiness and the relationship between agribusiness and the farm sector beyond the sponsoring of investment projects in the context of regional development activities. Similarly, when assessing the effects of policy changes on countries and regions, the Commission focuses on incomes from farming, neglecting other sources of income for farmers as well as the effect on incomes earned in the agribusiness.

This is somewhat surprising in an economic environment where members of farm households are often engaged in non-agricultural activities and the relations between the farm and the agribusiness become ever tighter both upstream in the provision of inputs, and downstream in processing and marketing. The present section discusses some developments in the agribusiness that explain this shift towards further vertical integration and identifies three forces that contribute to a further vertical integration in agriculture: consumer concerns, economies of scale in the industry, and intellectual property rights.

Consumer concerns

Consumer concerns play a role of increasing importance in the EU, both at the political level and on the food markets themselves (Barkema, 1993, Van Ravenswaay and Hoehn, 1996). The BSE crisis for beef is a case in point. Changes in technology and the growing interdependence among farms, i.e. feeding ruminants with animal proteins, has allowed the mad-cow disease to spread. Medical research establishes a link between BSE and the fatal Creutzfeldt-Jacob syndrome in humans. Government authorities establish regulations whereby the feeding of animal proteins is being prohibited and every cow can be followed from stable to table. Yet, cases of fraud are detected. Consequently, supermarket chains are looking for ways to establish their own labels and product quality control, implemented through direct contracts with farmers whose feeding practices and livestock trade are being controlled very tightly. Similar developments take place in other branches of the livestock sector (e.g. in the Dutch pork industry, den Ouden et al., 1994).

Hence, the agribusiness has to meet new demands with respect to food quality, including phytosanitary requirements, convenience and the emotional impact, and to modes of production, including animal welfare, labour standards and environmental sustainability. Products that satisfy the requirements acquire special labels and fetch a higher price but to guarantee the various qualities it becomes necessary to follow virtually every unit throughout the processing chain. For some products, such as meat, this implies tight vertical co-ordination while for others, such as vintage wines it has so far been possible to 'seal' the product and 'freeze' its qualities before it leaves the farm or the region of origin.

Clearly, within the food markets of the EU, these developments reinforce the increasing dominance of the marketing and processing parts of the chain. For example, the relative weight of this part of the chain can be assessed by comparing food expenditures and agricultural production. In the EU (15 member states), annual final consumption of households amounts to 3,450 billion euros on an average during the period 1990-94, of which 19 per cent is spent on food, beverages and tobacco (Eurostat, 1996). Agricultural gross value added is only 18 per cent of the spending on this food package, while the share is 33 per cent when using agricultural output. Implementation of Agenda 2000 may cause these shares to drop even more.

Consumer concerns have far-reaching implications for exporters from developing countries, who, in addition to the existing tariff barriers and phytosanitary requirements also are required to provide evidence of the appropriateness of their modes of production. While the WTO has so far been very explicit in banning special import tariffs that would 'punish' deviations from the domestic standards in the importing country, it can hardly counter the trend towards more labelling and the resulting price differentiation.

Yet, agribusiness will soon find it profitable to outsource much of its raw-material production to countries with good land, reliable transportation, and low wages. The preferential trade agreements of the EU provide focus areas for the European food industry to penetrate both in terms of market outlets as well as outsourcing. Why raise pigs in overpopulated areas of the EU where environmental costs are being charged in full, if it is possible to produce them at lower costs elsewhere?

Yet as food safety has become a major concern, the produce has to be followed throughout the production chain, from farm to retail level. Consequently, for this type of product a form of vertical co-ordination is unavoidable. This does not necessarily imply full integration. Although all segments of the chain have to fit very tightly, they might be organized as separate firms. The product will have to be of homogeneous quality and characteristics, but there could be several alternative units supplying it (Porter, 1985 and Perry, 1989).

Economies of scale

Consumer concerns are not the only cause of stronger vertical co-ordination. For several decades, European agriculture has been characterized by sustained growth and increases in efficiency through specialization of farms (Folmer et al., 1995) with less on-farm labour and processing and more intensive use of agricultural inputs such as fertilizers, seeds, plant protection, animal feed and veterinary services. The possibility to exploit increasing returns to scale in processing and marketing led to further vertical co-ordination of agro-industry, often through farming contracts that bypass local agricultural markets. Examples are the barley-malt-beer chain (Jansen and van Roekel, 1994), the Dutch hog sector (den Ouden, 1996), and the Spanish citrus industry (Poole et al., 1998). Lawrence et al. (1997) demonstrate that also in the US pork industry the number of slaughter and processing firms halved in less than 15 years.

The advantages of this integration process are clear: reduction of transaction costs, an improved ability to differentiate products and to market them under a brand name, and more bargaining power for these brands (Johnston and Lawrence, 1988). Among the disadvantages are lack of competition and flexibility as well as dulled incentives, especially at farm level.

Intellectual property rights

Consumer concerns and economies of scale are not the only forces to foster concentration and imperfect competition in the agribusiness. Technological innovation plays a role on its own in this process, through the intellectual property rights it creates in the form of patents, licenses and breeders rights. These enable the inventors to receive a reward for their efforts. In relation to agriculture, the difficulty with an intellectual property right is not so much the recognition of the right itself but the adequate pricing of the 'product' that is being sold. Since a full monopoly is being granted and the marginal costs - the costs of issuing and servicing the license - are almost zero, the intellectual property right offers a market power that is only mitigated through the pricing of competing products. Hence if all close substitutes come into a single hand, the owner acquires large powers to extract rents.

Recent development in biotechnology have led to a fast and poorly monitored expansion and cumulation of intellectual property rights in the agro-industry, on the input side as well as in the processing. While such changes are essential in generating the technical progress in food production that is necessary to maintain growth in food production worldwide, in the future the CAP will have to consider the associated competition issues seriously and avoid concentration of patents for close substitutes.

Summing up, it is evident that the process of vertical integration causes a fundamental change in the relationship between farmer and agribusiness. If, as a result of trade liberalization or under the pressures of consumer concerns, the European farmer can no longer be assured of a stable and rewarding price on the markets for his raw materials, he has no other choice but to recur to contract farming, and accept the terms offered by the processor. In the past this led to the creation of farm co-operatives for processing and marketing, but the current trend is that under pressure of competition, these co-operatives are being dismantled or converted into private firms. While it seems unlikely that this restructuring towards vertical integration can be reversed through any meaningful EU policy, the EU is able to use its regulatory power in the field of competition law to prevent excessive concentration. In addition, its rural development programmes will be important to guarantee sufficient alternative or supplementary employment to the farmers under the restructuring process.

Yet the same problems will arise in the non-member countries, where the rural sector could turn into colonial plantations that subjugate their workers. Fortunately, if consumer awareness proves sufficient, it will be possible to implement a code of conduct to avoid excesses in these countries as well. After all, the issue shows many similarities with the question of labour standards.

While developing countries have relatively little sophisticated agricultural processing, the issue of intellectual property rights is nonetheless highly relevant to them. The EU and other developed countries protest that developing countries should improve their protection of intellectual property rights, yet these countries generally want shorter periods of patent protection than developed countries to enable them to engage in imitation. The next WTO round will include further elaboration of the trade-related intellectual property rights (TRIPS) agreement, now under evaluation (Downes and Stilwell, 1998), and especially of its application in developing countries. Although at present opinions differ, no strong arguments can be made for international harmonization of intellectual property rights (Deardorff, 1990 and Mayer, 1998).

6. Policy implications: how to change the CAP?

This review of a large number of issues and changes in the external environment may be summarized as follows. The Agenda 2000 proposals amount more or less to a mechanical extension of the 1992 Reform. They do not implement any specified vision on the future of European agriculture. This makes it easier to quantify their short-term impact but also more difficult to assess the viability of the measures proposed, even over the seven-year period which has been covered. Moreover, the approach remains ambivalent with respect to external trade policy. While professing its support for trade liberalization and the WTO, the proposals maintain import protection and expand the number and depth of blue-box measures. The EU has also formulated a mandate for the negotiations on the new Lomé Convention that defines preferential agreements with new regional groupings, and has been actively involved in negotiations with existing groupings such as Mercosur. In this way, the EU seems to keep all options open for the coming WTO round and in case this round fails, the EU can resort to trade agreements to promote its interests.

However, there are several issues that will make it difficult to abandon the path of liberalization. First, it is unlikely that the WTO negotiations can be successful without further CAP reform. Some developing countries will also challenge the conservatism with respect to import access but countries enjoying preferences might favour it. The WTO will call for further tariffication, and hence for restoring the link between world-market prices and internal prices, especially for cereals. Virtually all trading partners will resist maintenance of blue-box measures, but for different reasons. Developed countries resist as the support is insufficiently decoupled and developing countries as even the green-box measures are too costly for them (de Zeeuw, 1997).

Second, the tendency towards further decoupling of support creates additional strains on the EU budget, especially in the wake of the accession of new members. The annual agricultural budget of around 40 billion euros still comprises half of the total EU budget, and will move up by more than 10 per cent once the new proposals will be fully implemented, and if world prices remain as low as in 1998 there will be an additional 2-3 billion euros to be spent on export subsidies. Not surprisingly, a considerable number of EU Ministers of Finance call for stabilization of the agricultural budget at the pre-reform level, and it seems unlikely that EU consumers will be willing to continue paying these vast sums indefinitely.

From this it can be concluded that the CAP will have to proceed towards further trade liberalization and decoupling of support. Moreover, the publicly funded farm-income support of the CAP will have to be replaced by a system of payments for services which the consumer is willing to pay, either indirectly through the price of labelled products that meet consumer concerns, or directly, through entrance fees in parks, or again as tax payer, via contribution to landscape preservation. At the same time, farmers will have to pay for environmental damages caused. In such a setting, the countryside becomes much more than a production area of raw materials, and offers a variety of alternative jobs. This asks for a reassessment of the system of headage and area premiums the CAP is handing out currently, and of the environmental constraints that are being imposed.

In this perspective, the premiums become rewards for services, that are linked to the mode of production of the farm. In this way a remuneration arises for characteristics such as animal welfare and preservation of rural life and natural amenities. This goes beyond the 'cross-compliance' requirements proposed in Agenda 2000, according to which farmers also comply with environmental objectives in return for payments received. The proposed regime calls for explicit and independent assessments of the contributions made and the damages caused by a given farm operation. The assessors could even provide grades that the processing industry can subsequently report on its labelling, comparable with grading systems for restaurants.

This has strong international ramifications, as European agribusiness will outsource a large part of its agricultural production, especially if import access is improved. In that case, consumers could ask the agribusiness to supply evidence on the sustainability of its mode of production worldwide, its respect for labour standards and its allegiance to free competition.

However, it is important to mention that in such a world of standards moral monopolies must be avoided as well. Standards should meet the interests of those they are supposed to protect. For example, labour standards should primarily benefit the workers concerned, not to help the competitor. In such a system the main role of a European Common Agricultural Policy is supervising the labelling and inspection process to safeguard standards and transparency. The food industry will presumably be able to organize these institutions by itself since in view of the emerging consumer concerns worldwide it has strong incentives to maintain a solid reputation for its products.

References

Agra-Europe, *AgraFocus, The Monthly Report for European Agribusiness Executives,* Bonn, various issues.

Barkema, A., 'Reaching Consumers in the Twenty-first Century: the Short Way around the Barn', *American Journal of Agricultural Economics,* Volume 75, 1993.

Bhagwati, J., 'Regionalism and Multilaterism: an Overview', in: J. de Melo and A. Panagariya (eds), *New Dimensions in Regional Integration,* Cambridge University Press, Cambridge, 1993.

Bhagwati, J., D. Greenaway and A. Panagariya, 'Trading Preferentially: Theory and Policy', *The Economic Journal,* Volume 108, 1998.

Commission of the European Community (CEC), *Agenda 2000: for a Stronger and Wider Europe,* DOC/97/9, Strasbourg/Brussels, 1997a.

CEC, *Long-term Prospects: Grains, Milk, and Meat Markets',* CAP 2000 Working Document, DGVI, Brussels, 1997b.

CEC, *Policy Guidelines for Future EU-ACP Relations,* Communication to the Council and the European Parliament, DGVI, Brussels, 1997c.

CEC, *Rural Developments,* CAP 2000 Working Document, July 1997, DGVI, Brussels, 1997d.

CEC, *Draft Agenda 2000 Regulations on Cereals, Beef, and Dairy,* available at http://europe.eu.int/en/comm/dg06/ag2000, 1998a.

CEC, *Agricultural Situation and Prospects in the Central and Eastern European Countries,* Working Document, June 1998, DGVI, Brussels, 1998b.

CEC, *CAP Reform Proposals. Impact Analyses,* CAP Reports, October 1998, DG VI, Brussels, 1998c.

Collier, P. and J.W. Gunning, 'Trade Policy and Regional Integration: Implications for the Relations between Europe and Africa', *The World Economy,* Volume 18, 1995.

Davenport, M., A. Hewitt and A. Koning , *Europe's Preferred Partners? The Lomé Countries in World Trade,* Overseas Development Institute, London, 1995.

Deardorff, A.V., 'Should Patent Protection be Extended to all Developing Countries?', *World Economy,* Volume 13, 1990.

Downes, D.R. and M. Stilwell, *The 1999 WTO Review of Life Patenting under TRIPS: Revised Discussion Paper*, Centre for International Environmental Law, Washington, D.C., 1998.

Duponcel, M. , 'The Poor Impacts of the Liberalisation of EU Agricultural Imports from Central and Eastern Europe: Failure of the Preferences, or Failure of the Associated Countries', *Food Policy*, Volume 23, 1998.

Ethier, W.J., 'The New Regionalism', *The Economic Journal*, Volume 108, 1998.

Eurostat, *National Accounts ESA, Detailed Tables by Branch (1970-1994)*, Luxembourg, 1996.

FAPRI, *FAPRI Analysis of the Proposed 'Agenda 2000' European Union CAP Reform*, FAPRI Working Paper 98-WP 191, Iowa State University, Ames, USA, 1998.

Folmer, C., M.A. Keyzer, M.D. Merbis, E. Phimister, H.J.J., Stolwijk and P.J.J. Veenendaal, *Budgetary Consequences of Changing Rules for Financing EC farm Support*, 5th Congress of European Association of Agricultural Economists, Balatonszéplak, Hungary, 1987.

Folmer, C., M.A. Keyzer, M.D. Merbis, H.J.J. Stolwijk and P.J.J. Veenendaal, *The Common Agricultural Policy beyond the MacSharry Reform*, Amsterdam, North-Holland, 1995.

Frankel, J.A., *Regional Trading Blocs in the World Economic System*, Institute for International Economics, Washington, D.C., 1997.

FTAA, *Declaration of Principles and Plan of Action*, available at internet http://alca-ftaa.org, 1999.

GATT, *The Results of the Uruguay Round of Multilateral Trade Negotiations, the Legal Texts*, GATT secretariat, Geneva, 1994.

Jansen, M.G.C. and J. van Roekel, *Strengthening Agro-industrial Chains; the Barley-malt-beer Case*, NEHEM Consulting Group, Rosmalen, 1994.

Johnstone, R. and P.R. Lawrence, 'Beyond Vertical Integration - the Rise of the Value-adding Relationship', *Harvard Business Review*, Volume 66, 1988.

Keyzer, M.A., 'Gevolgen van Financiële Renationalisatie van het GLB', in: *Toekomst van het Europees Landbouwbeleid* ('Consequences of Financial Renationalisation of the CAP' in: *Future of the CAP*), LEI-DLO mededeling 544 , Den Haag, 1995.

Keyzer, M.A. and M.D. Merbis, 'CAP Reform in Agenda 2000: Implications for European Agriculture', in: *CAP Reform Proposals, Impact Analyses*, European Commission, DG VI, Brussels, 1998.

Kjeldahl, R. and M. Tracey (eds.), *Renationalisation of the Common Agricultural Policy?*, Agricultural Policy Studies Publications, La Hutte, 1994.

Krugman, P.R., *Rethinking International Trade*, MIT Press, Cambridge, Mass., 1990.

Laird, S., *MERCOSUR: Objectives and Achievements*, WTO Staff Working Paper TPRD-97-02, WTO, Geneva, 1997.

Lawrence, J.D., V.J. Rhodes, G.A. Grimes and M.L. Hayenga, 'Vertical Coordination in the U.S. Pork Industry: Status, Motivations and Expectations,' *Agribus*, Volume 13, 1997.

Lawrence, R.Z., *Regionalism, Multilaterism, and Deeper Integration*, The Brookings Institution, Washington, 1996.

Lee, D.R., 'Western Hemisphere Economic Integration: Implications and Prospects for Agricultural Trade', *American Journal of Agricultural Economics*, Volume 77, 1995.

Mayer, R.N., 'Protectionism, Intellectual Property, and Consumer Protection: was the Uruguay Round Good for Consumers?', *Journal of Consumer Policy*, Volume 21, 1998.

Nagarajan, N., *MERCOSUR and Trade Diversion: What do the Import Figures Tell Us?*, European Commission, DGII, Economic Paper Number 129, CEC, Brussels, 1988.

Olarreaga, M. and I. Soloaga, 'Endogenous Tariff Formation: the Case of Mercosur', *World Bank Economic Review*, Volume 12, 1998.

Ouden, M. den, A.A. Dijkhuizen, R.B.M. Huirne and P. van Beek, 'Pork-production-marketing Chains in Economic Perspective', *Tijdschrift voor Sociaal Wetenschappelijk Onderzoek van de Landbouw*, Volume 9, 1994.

Ouden, M. den, *Economic Modelling of Pork-production-marketing Chains*, Mansholt Studies 4, Wageningen University and Research Centre, 1996.

Perry, M.K., 'Vertical Integration: Determinants and Effects', in: R. Schmalensee and R.D. Willig (eds.), *Handbook of Industrial Organization*, Volume 1, Amsterdam, North-Holland, 1989.

Poole, N.D., F.J. Del Campo Gomis, J.F.J. Igual and F.V. Gimenez, 'Formal Contracts in Fresh Produce Markets', *Food Policy*, Volume 23, 1998.

Porter, M.E., *Competitive Strategy: Creating and Sustaining Superior Performance*, The Free Press, New York, 1980.

Ravenswaay, E.O. van, and J.P. Hoehn, 'The Theoretical Benefits of Food Safety Policies', *American Journal of Agricultural Economics*, Volume 78, 1996.

Srinivasan, T.N., *Developing Countries and the Multilateral Trading System: from the GATT to the Uruguay Round and the Future*, Westview Press, Boulder, 1998.

Tangermann, S., *Access to European Union markets for Agricultural Products after the Uruguay Round, and Export Interests of the Mediterranean Countries*, INT/93/A34, UNCTAD, Geneva, 1997.

Yeats, A., 'Does Mercosur's Trade Performance Raise Concerns about the Effects of Regional Trade Arrangements?', *World Bank Economic Review*, Volume 12, 1998.

Zeeuw, A. de, 'International Agricultural Trade Negotiations under GATT/WTO: Experiences, Future Challenges and Possible Outcomes', *European Review of Agricultural Economics*, Volume 24, 1997.

PART II: REGIONAL DIMENSIONS

8

TRANSATLANTIC ECONOMIC RELATIONS IN A NEW ERA

JAN ROOD

The Netherlands Institute of International Relations 'Clingendael'
The Hague
The Netherlands

1. Introduction

Although bilateral consultations between the European Union (EU) and the USA had started on an informal basis in the 1970s, the practice of consultation and co-ordination acquired a new dimension from the 1990s onwards. In particular the Transatlantic Declaration of 1990 and the subsequent agreement in 1995 on a New Transatlantic Agenda and a Joint EU-US Action Plan constituted a new framework for consultation and co-operation between both sides of the Atlantic. An essential element of this framework, which came to be known as the Transatlantic Dialogue, is the Transatlantic Agenda, which established an institutionalized mechanism for regular meetings at various levels of official representation of the EU and the USA. The Agenda and Action Plan have given substance and direction to the process of consultation by formulating a comprehensive series of projects for co-operation and co-ordination on a broad range of topics.

The Agenda and Action Plan emphasized the need for a closer, broader and more institutionalized relationship between the EU and the USA in the post-Cold War era. In both documents the parties commit themselves to initiate an

P. van Dijck and G. Faber (eds.), The External Economic Dimension of the European Union, 177–193.
© 2000 *Kluwer Academic Publishers. Printed in the Netherlands.*

intensive process of joint action to promote peace and stability, democracy and development around the world, to respond to global challenges such as posed by international crime and terrorism, and to build bridges across the Atlantic; all this in addition to the issue of closer co-operation in the field of economic affairs and trade, which has dominated EU-US relations from the 1960s onwards. Moreover, the Agenda and Action Plan reflect the perceived need for a more or less permanent framework for consultation and co-ordination between the EU and the USA, which was absent until then.

Despite the introduction of this broad and ambitious framework, it is obvious that, also after the Cold War, trade and economic issues still dominate 'bilateral' EU-US relations. This is at least partly the result of the state of European integration. The EU still is first and foremost an economic and trade entity, pursuing a common trade policy and, since 1 January 1999, possessing a common currency. The importance of the economic dimension is illustrated by the European Commission proposals of March and September 1998 respectively to create a Transatlantic Marketplace (TAM) and a Transatlantic Economic Partnership (TEP) as the first steps in the process of implementation of the Agenda and Action Plan, as well as the suggestion to establish a Transatlantic Free Trade Area (TAFTA) as a logical sequel to the intensification of EU- US consultation and co-ordination. From the perspective of the EU such a development would underline the 'special relationship' between the Union and the USA as the two main trading blocs in the world economic system. For the USA, the creation of a TAFTA would provide the 'missing link' in the system of hub and spokes, that may result from a series of initiatives including the Canada-US Free Trade Agreement (CUSFTA), the North American Free Trade Agreement (NAFTA), the Asia-Pacific Economic Cooperation (APEC) and the Free Trade Area of the Americas (FTAA).

This chapter focuses on the impact such a development might have on the functioning of the multilateral trade regime which was created after the Second World War. In this respect the main issue is whether it would be in the interest of the EU to establish a more or less exclusive bilateral relationship with the USA.

2. The EU-US relationship: dominance and asymmetry

Such a development would seem natural in view of the strong relationship that has existed between the EC/EU and the USA since the beginning of the European integration process in the 1950s. The USA played a crucial role in the creation of the bodies for integration that developed into the EU. Mainly for security reasons it was one of the strongest proponents of European integration, specifically in the economic field. The USA was prepared to support European economic integration in spite of the risk of trade diversion. Moreover, as a result of the creation of the Common Agricultural Policy (CAP) and the establishment of the customs union (CU) during the 1960s, the Community's trade policy developed in particular in relation with its major trading partner, the USA, and to some extent its former colonies.

In this respect one may also consider the position of both the USA and EU within the world trading and economic system. Although their share in world trade has declined as a result of the rise of Japan as a trading nation followed by other South-East Asian countries, the Union and the USA still dominate the world trade system, as shown by Van Dijck and Faber in Chapter 1 of this volume. The EU's share in world trade (excluding intra-EU trade) is about 20 per cent, and the share of the USA is about 13 per cent. If one looks at other dimensions of international economic relations, the dominance of the EU and the USA is even more apparent. They are the most important exporters and importers of services, and with regard to foreign direct investment (FDI), the member states of the EU and the USA hold dominant positions in the world economy as investors and as hosts to foreign investments.

In the increasingly 'triadic' pattern of world trade flows between the USA, Europe and Asia-Pacific, the transatlantic trade relation has lost the top position it held until the beginning of the 1980s and at present has to settle for the third position. But from a 'qualitative' point of view there is an intense and, according to some observers, more stable trade relationship between Western Europe and the USA than between the USA and the Pacific area. While US trade with Asia is in deficit and has become the source of much political tension - particularly in the relationship with Japan and China - transatlantic trade has been much more balanced. Moreover, the USA is the EU's most important trade partner, while the Union, in its turn, follows Canada as the second trade partner for the USA. Western Europe and the USA are also by far the most important investors in each other's economies, while the degree of technological co-operation and participation in joint development programmes is much more intense between American and European companies than between American and Asian companies. In a recent study Gaster and Prestowitz (1995, p. iv) conclude that 'the link between Europe and the USA is central to US economic relationships. In most areas, relations with Europe are much more important quantitatively than are similar relations with Asia. The evidence strongly suggests that this will remain true well into the next century'.

Even more important than their weight in terms of trade and investment volumes are the positions of the EU and the USA in the multilateral trade regime. Agreements on a further liberalization of trade in goods and services or the introduction of a multilateral regime for investments have very little effect if the USA and EU do not participate. Put differently, any progress on such issues prerequisites bilateral agreement between the EU and the USA. This became clear during the Uruguay Round negotiations on the liberalization of trade in goods and services, which could only be concluded after a compromise had been reached between the EU and the USA on, specifically, trade in agricultural products. The negotiations on the so-called 'loose ends' of the Uruguay Round agreement - especially in the field of services - show as well that a preceding compromise between the Union and the USA is a strict precondition for an agreement. The other side of the coin is that such a compromise constitutes an accomplished fact for the other parties in the negotiations.

To summarize, the relationship between the EU and the USA is characterized by a high degree of interdependence, especially in the field of trade and invest-ment. This relationship is expected to expand into the fields of monetary and macro-economic affairs after the introduction of the euro. Given the dominance of both parties, their relationship is crucial for the way in which the international trade system will evolve. For instance, the functioning of the WTO, in particular the effectiveness of its trade dispute-settlement panels, depends to a large extent on the willingness of the EU and USA to refer trade conflicts to those panels and to accept their decisions. In this context it is noteworthy that from the perspec-tive of the EU the relationship with the USA is very different from the relation-ships with other countries or groups of countries in Central and Eastern Europe or in the Mediterranean. While those relations are characterized by a certain asym-metry in favour of the EU, the relationship with the USA is much more sym-metrical, or even slightly asymmetrical to the Union's detriment.

This asymmetry resulted from Western Europe's reliance on US protection, in particular on its policy of extended nuclear deterrence during the Cold War. It could well be argued that until the fall of the Berlin wall, EU-US trade relations were subordinated to the strategic relationship as developed in the framework of the Atlantic Alliance. One might even agree with Joan Gowa, that the relatively open trade regime between the EU and the USA could only develop within the geo-strategic setting of the post-Second World War bipolar alliance structure under American leadership (Gowa, 1989). It is in this broader geo-political context that the course of EU-US trade relations and the efforts to develop a new institutional framework should be explained.

3. The geo-political setting of the EU-US relationship: friction, cohesion and change

From the outset it is important to keep in mind that crises, confrontations and conflicts have been an integral part of the post-war Euro-American relationship. As a result, there have always been strong doubts about the cohesion of Euro-American relations, in particular about the solidity of the Atlantic Alliance. Almost immediately after the creation of NATO the Europeans began to express doubts about the American commitment to European security and insisted on a larger share of control over the use of nuclear weapons. As early as 1962, Robert Osgood wrote about an 'entangled alliance', while in 1965 Henry Kissinger characterized the relationship between Western Europe and the USA as a 'troubled partnership' (Osgood, 1965). In the 1960s, moreover, the inflationary spillover of American domestic economic policies - President Kennedy's and President Johnson's 'Great Society' - and foreign policy, particularly the Vietnam war, put great strain on transatlantic co-operation, especially on US relations with France and Germany. The 1970s and 1980s showed a series of confrontations and conflicts about 'burden sharing' within NATO, differences of opinion on the approach towards the crisis in the Middle East, on energy policies and the optimal mixture of détente and deterrence towards the Soviet Union, in particular the need for modernization of theatre nuclear forces. The 'Year of Europe', proclaimed by Henry Kissinger in 1972 as a benchmark of American foreign policy, turned out to be a complete failure.

Friction and co-operation were not only characteristic of the strategic relationship between the EU and the USA but also of commercial and trade policies: conflicts arose on nearly everything that was traded across the Atlantic. It started as early as the beginning of the 1960s, when the creation of the EC's Common Agricultural Policy (CAP) led to the so-called 'chicken war' between the EU and the USA. It proved to be the forerunner of a long and extensive series of conflicts and disputes, on all sorts of topics, ranging from trade in steel and pasta, the use of gelatine in medicine and hormones in meat, and the effects of the EU's external and enlargement policies on third countries, to the complex and very sensitive issues of the extra-territorial effects of US-legislation with regard to the treatment of so-called rogue states - the d'Amato and Helms-Burton Acts concerning Cuba, Libya and Iran - and to competition policy dimensions, especially concerning the position of Airbus and the merger between the American aircraft manufacturing companies Boeing and McDonnel-Douglas. The last two examples show that current EU-US economic diplomacy concerns more than just trade. But more important in this respect is to note that on several occasions the spectre of a trade war was looming in European-US relations.

The ongoing conflicts between both sides of the Atlantic have led many to predict a fragmentation of the transatlantic system. In 1987, François Heisbourg (1987, p. 413) wrote that

> '[a]s a result of a number of recent developments the Alliance is now exposed to a new, more diffuse peril: senility, possibly leading to death from natural causes (...) it faces the possibility of gradual, spontaneous disintegration after a period of growing incoherence'.

But, as in the case of Mark Twain's death, the announcements of the Alliance's demise seem to have been rather premature. Perhaps more striking, therefore, is the fact that despite these continuous frictions and disputes, foremost in the field of trade, the relationship between Western Europe and the USA did not collapse.

In explaining this continuity and persistence many observers point to the geo-strategic setting during the Cold War era. From the 1950s onwards, US membership of NATO and the presence of American troops on European soil were the clearest expressions of unconditional American commitment to European security. Through its policy of extended nuclear deterrence the USA acted as the protector of Western Europe against the threat of Soviet aggression. The Americans regarded this protection as crucial in view of the global balance of power. A Western Europe dominated by the Soviet Union was perceived a direct threat to America's security and economic interests. The presence of a common enemy, therefore, was one of the main elements cementing the Atlantic Alliance. During this period, the need to maintain political and military cohesion acted as a break on conflicts between Europe the USA. In the words of Philip Gordon (1996, p. 34), 'a common purpose held the allies together even when their economic, political or even military interests temporarily diverged'.

This also applied to economic frictions. There too, the necessity to maintain unity in the face of a common enemy forced Europe and the USA to look for compromises in their trade disputes, to avoid real trade wars and to refrain from protectionist policies. A different view would be that during the Cold War, security ties between Europe and the USA were so strong, that whatever the gravity of their mutual trade frictions, the prerequisite to maintain Atlantic security cohesion would always prevail.

This implies that a change in the geo-political setting underlying the EU-US partnership might have a very negative effect on the relationship. Even without accepting the view that alliances will inevitably disintegrate in the absence of a common enemy, it is clear that the presence of the Soviet threat gave the transatlantic partnership its special strength, and that as a result of changes in the geopolitical situation a persistence of the European-US relationship is less certain than in the past (Walt, 1992). This view was expressed in 1992 by Heisbourg (Heisbourg, 1992, p. 666) in a follow-up to his 1987 article in International Affairs quoted above: '[w]hat in 1987 was a largely hypothetical question (...) has now become an urgently practical issue'. Actual practice seemed to prove his point: in 1993 the prospect of a failure of the Uruguay Round on trade liberalization led to lively speculation about a falling apart of the transatlantic system.

There are several reasons to fear such a development. One is that with the end of the Soviet domination of Central and Eastern Europe and the collapse of the Soviet Union itself, the geostrategic realities which underpinned American foreign, security and defence policy as phrased after the Second World War, have fundamentally changed. In the absence of a direct threat to the territorial integrity and security of Western Europe, the American and West-European security interests do no longer need to coincide to the same extent as in the past. Paricularly in Europe, a strong feeling emerged that as a result of the diverging security interests, the Atlantic relationship had already lost its foundation and that both sides would inevitably drift apart. Although that view dominated in the aftermath of the collapse of the Berlin wall, some scholars warn that even at present there is a considerable risk of Europe and the USA growing apart (Weidenfeld, 1997).

To these forces of Atlantic fragmentation may be added the fear that with the end of the Cold War, transatlantic economic relations would become a source of intra-alliance friction and conflict. As argued earlier, during the period of bipolar confrontation, the frequent economic and trade conflicts did not pose a threat to transatlantic political and military cohesion. With the end of the Cold War, there was no longer reason to subordinate economic interests to strategic objectives. On the contrary, in a world where the rivalry between states was perceived to have shifted from the strategic-military realm to the field of trade and investment, there was no longer reason to maintain such a rather altruistic policy. The domestication of America's foreign policy during the first years of the Clinton administration seemed to prove this point. Its strong emphasis on America's economic interests increased the risk of a spillover of transatlantic economic frictions into the security field.

A third reason for concern about the Euro-American relationship was the alleged strategic reorientation of American foreign policy from the Atlantic to the Pacific. In particular the statement of November 1993 of US Secretary of State Warren Christopher that '[n]o area of the world will be more important for American interests than the Asia-Pacific region', gave Europeans reason to assume that the USA was turning from a 'European power' into a 'Pacific power' (Marini and Rood, 1996). And it seemed only too natural that America's strategic and economic focus would be adapted to the shift of the centre of world economic activity from the Atlantic to the Asia-Pacific region, which according to many observers was taking place. For the Europeans, such a development would increase the risk that security and economic ties with the USA would loosen further.

As a final point in this respect the following observation may be made. In the first post-Cold War years, a rather fundamental shift in orientation seemed to have taken place in American trade policies. Although the USA was the founding father of the post-war multilateral trade regime, from the 1980s onwards it turned more and more to a policy of aggressive unilateralism in its trade relations, in particular towards Japan. Furthermore, the USA began to pursue a policy of bilateral and regional preferential trade agreements, in 1985 with Israel and at the end of the 1980s with Canada (CUSFTA). Yet, more important from the perspective of the EU were the American initiatives to establish regional trade arrangements. In 1990, president Bush launched his Enterprise for the Americas initiative which aimed for an all-American free trade zone. This initiative got a follow-up during the Summit of the Americas in Miami, where the parties agreed to work on a Pan-American free trade zone, the FTAA. In 1989, the USA, moreover, joined the Australian initiative to establish the APEC. According to the agreement of the APEC Summit of Bogor (1994), this initiative should lead to an area of free trade and investment in the region by the year 2020. Most important, however, was the ratification in 1993 of a NAFTA between the USA, Canada and Mexico, which aims at the establishment of a zone of free trade and investment in North America between 2003 and 2009.

In response to these initiatives and developments, Europeans openly started to question the American commitment to Europe, and to express their fear that in strategic and economic affairs the USA might turn away from Europe. The American preference for regionalism led to increasing doubts about US support for the multilateral trade regime. Those doubts were specifically raised at the beginning of the 1990s, when both the EU and the USA had great difficulties in reaching a final agreement on further liberalization of world trade during the Uruguay Round negotiations. A stalemate had emerged on the issue of trade liberalization in the agricultural sector and the liberalization of trade in services and a total collapse of the Uruguay Round looked imminent. Under those circumstances the American interest in NAFTA and APEC seemed to signal that the USA had an alternative to a multilateral free trade regime, in case the Uruguay Round should fail. For the Europeans this was not a very attractive perspective[1].

4. The initiative to strengthen EU-US relations

In the context discussed above the recent efforts to strengthen transatlantic ties and to establish direct formal links between the EU and the USA can be explained. The first proposal to develop a new framework for EC-US co-operation was launched by the former American Secretary of State James Baker during a visit to Berlin in November 1989. In his view, stronger EC-US relations were necessary in order to address the fundamental changes that were taking place in Europe

'[w]e propose that the EU and the USA work together to achieve, whether it is in treaty or some other form, a significantly strengthened set of institutional and consultative links' (Gardner, 1997, p.10).

Baker's call was followed by a number of suggestions, proposals and initiatives aimed at building a new foundation for transatlantic co-operation, ranging from the proposal to create an Atlantic Community to the call for a New Atlantic Charter. These proposals reflected the view that in response to the forces of fragmentation the development of a new institutional setting for consultation and co-ordination between the EU and the USA was called for. At the same time, they underlined that, paradoxically, with the end of the Cold War the two issues that had always dominated European-US relations, security and trade could no longer be considered separate topics. This implied that in addition to consultations within NATO, a direct link between the EU and the USA on economic affairs was necessary, thereby correcting the institutional imbalance at which many observers had pointed, i.e., that in the field of security NATO provided the West-Europeans and the Americans a framework for consultation, while, apart from the OECD, such a framework was lacking in the field of trade and economics.

The European response to the initiatives aimed at strengthening EU-US co-operation was very positive. One reason for this was the fear to become isolated. From the European perspective, strengthening transatlantic ties was primarily a means to reaffirm and guarantee US commitment to Europe, in particular its commitment to European security. In addition it was seen as an opportunity to influence US trade policy and specifically to restrain the inclination for unilateralism and regionalism, and to commit the USA once more to the rules and procedures of multilateralism.

But there was also support from the other side of the Atlantic. From the US perspective, the post-Cold War world was - and is - a more complicated world, with unexpected security risks, new global challenges for the economy, environmental risks and an increasing threat posed by international crime and terrorism. In this increasingly complex and interdependent world, even the USA as the only remaining superpower must be able to rely on allies in order to realize its goals and protect its interests. It is fair to assume that compared to other possible alliances, the EU-US relationship is potentially 'a winning coalition', and that Western Europe is America's most stable and 'natural' ally. As Peterson and Ward (1995, p. 146) put it

> 'US-EU relations are stronger and more institutionalized than relations between any other major players in international politics. US-EU political relations are themselves multidimensional: they are rooted in strong cultural, historical and economic ties'[2].

In particular the Transatlantic Declaration of 1990 can be seen as an expression of the concern that both sides of the Atlantic share about the state of cohesion of their relationship in the field of security. The Agenda and Action Plan of 1995 reflect the broader agenda of EU-US consultation, with the formulation of four major goals:

(1) promoting peace and stability, democracy and development around the world;
(2) responding to global challenges;
(3) contributing to the expansion of world trade and closer economic relations;
(4) building bridges across the Atlantic.

Since the agreement on the Agenda and Action Plan the issue of trade and economic relations has been the main topic of the transatlantic dialogue. This appears from the proposals made during the process, in particular by the European Commission. In March 1998 the European Commission launched its proposal for a New Transatlantic Marketplace (TAM) agreement. The main elements are the elimination of all tariffs on industrial goods by the year 2010, negotiations on a free-trade area in services, and liberalization beyond WTO rules in areas such as government procurement, intellectual property and investment. Due to the stern opposition from France in particular, the Commission's proposal was not accepted by the Council. In September 1998, the Commission made a second attempt with its proposal for an 'action plan for transatlantic economic partnership', which envisaged a number of bilateral and multilateral initiatives to strengthen EU-US trade and economic relations.

As yet the provisions concerning transatlantic consultations on security matters have produced hardly any results and consequently the emphasis has been on trade-related issues and economic policy. The expectation of some Americans that, as a result of the Maastricht Treaty, the EU would be able to develop its own security and defence identity, and that security matters could be included in the transatlantic consultation process, has not materialized. On the contrary, during the past years NATO has been affirmed as the main organization for European security and defence matters.

5. The case for and against an 'exclusive' EU-US relationship

As noted above, the discussion about the need to strengthen EU-US relations originated from a concern about the transatlantic security links, but in practice the consultation process has mainly focused on economic and trade issues. Subsequently, an important question is whether closer links between the EU and the USA in the field of trade and economics should be welcomed and whether it would be a sensible policy, from the perspective of the Union and the world trade system, to institutionalize these links in a free-trade agreement (FTA) such as TAFTA or an economic partnership.

A case in favour of stronger EU-US economic ties could be made on the basis of the dominant position of the two unions in the world economy and the pivotal role they play in world trade matters, and it should be beyond dispute that their co-operation is of utmost importance for the world trade system to function effectively, and hence crucial to world prosperity. To the extent that a closer relationship helps to prevent the escalation of trade conflicts, the initiative for the new transatlanticism seems to deserve support.

Another consideration is that closer transatlantic co-operation may function as a breeding ground for further liberalization of trade on a global level and for increased co-ordination and harmonization of policies in the so-called new fields of trade policy including taxation policy, social policy and competition policy. Such harmonization would be the next step in a globalizing world economy in which in addition to the free movement of goods, movement of capital, technology and knowledge have become of paramount importance. Such harmonization will, however, be difficult to achieve at a global level, and with the exception of Japan, these dimensions of globalization have so far been limited mainly to countries belonging to the Transatlantic Community. Therefore, it makes sense that both sides of the Atlantic take the lead in developing a transatlantic framework of public policy. Initiatives taken within the framework of the transatlantic dialogue enable the EU and the USA to join forces in stimulating the process of multilateral economic liberalization, and in particular in developing common economic policies that go far beyond trade liberalization.

Such co-operation seems to be particularly crucial to the outcome of the new round of trade negotiations - the Millennium Round - that is due to start at the WTO Ministerial Meeting in Seattle in November 1999. The new trade-related topics will be high on the agenda, apart from other issues that have not yet been properly dealt with in the Uruguay Round. A successful outcome of the Millennium Round will depend mainly on the ability of the EU and the USA to co-operate. Another topic that may divide the Union and the USA, and therefore requires close consultation, is the enlargement of the EU with countries in Central and Eastern Europe. Although the USA supports accession of these countries to the EU for reasons of security and stability in Europe, this accession may be seen in Washington as detrimental to US trade and economic interests, as has been the case with earlier enlargements. Finally, the recent financial turmoil in Asia and its spillover to other parts of the world economic system have laid bare the fragility of the world financial system. The Asian crisis has already caused irritation on both sides of the Atlantic - especially in the USA - on the question of who is to bear the burden of the bail-out of the Asian economies. Such crises emphasize the need for the EU and the USA to co-ordinate their policies, not only their trade policies, but also their monetary, macro-economic and financial policies.

This final perspective will especially appeal to those who consider that the EU and the USA are natural partners in coping with new security risks and new global challenges concerning not only the international economy, but also the environment, international crime and terrorism. According to this view, the stability of the world system will depend upon the ability of the West-Europeans and the Americans to be partners in leadership or, as only American writers are able to express it, leaders in partnership. In that case, a new transatlantic relationship will have to be established that will indeed go far beyond the security arrangement of the Cold War.

Others, however, strongly oppose closer transatlantic relations, i.e., relations that go beyond regular consultations and that aim for the establishment of more formally institutionalized bilateral arrangements on trade, investment and other economic issues. As they argue, first, it is false to assume that closer economic relations will strengthen security ties between Europe and the USA. The Atlantic cohesion will ultimately be decided by the ability of the EU to play its own role in security matters, in close co-operation with the USA. In other words, closer economic relations are not an alternative to or a remedy for the lack of balance in the transatlantic security relationship.

Second, in order to reach agreement on a TAFTA or on other substantial arrangements, difficult and sensitive issues between the EU and the USA concerning trade in agricultural products in particular, will have to be solved. Without agreement in those areas TAFTA would be rather purposeless, certainly when the present high degree of liberalization of transatlantic trade is taken into account. In view of those ramifications, TAFTA may cause more problems and will not contribute substantially to cohesion in EU-US relations. Here it should be emphasized that the delay in concluding the Uruguay Round was precisely caused by frictions between the EU and the USA (Barfield, 1998, p. 209).

Third, the establishment of a more or less exclusive partnership or trade agreement between the world's two most important economic powers would be a threat to the functioning of the multilateral trade system. Although the views are still divided as to the specific effects bilateralism and regionalism will have on trade patterns - in terms of trade creation and diversion - the main effect of such a development would be on the functioning of the multilateral trade regime as a system of principles, rules and procedures. It is rather difficult to imagine this system to function effectively at all, if next to the WTO multilateral regime, a patchwork of regional, bilateral and inter-regional arrangements would exist. Such a system will create its own logic and dynamics, which need not necessarily be in agreement with the rules of multilateralism. In other words, where regionalism and bilateralism are considered a threat to the multilateral trade regime, this would even more so apply to an inter-regional arrangement between the EU and the USA as the two dominant powers in international trade. It would most definitely be interpreted by other countries as proof of the lack of commitment of these economic blocs to the multilateral trade regime.

Finally, there is the question whether the establishment of a structural 'bilateral' economic relationship between the EU and the USA would be in the interest of the EU. Given the American propensity for unilateralism in its trade policy, it seems to be in the interest of the EU to retain the option of multilateralism, specifically to counter the US inclination to a more aggressive trade policy.

The conclusion, therefore, is that notwithstanding the good reasons to support initiatives to intensify bilateral EU-US consultations, especially in the fields of trade and economics, one should object efforts to transform this relationship into an exclusive partnership. From the perspective of the viability of the post-war multilateral trade, monetary and financial regimes, such a step is potentially damaging, and not in the interest of the EU.

Notes

[1] For instance Vernon underlines that the 'mixed strategy' of multilateralism, regionalism and bi- and unilateralism that the USA was (and is) following in trade matters, was meant to put pressure on the EU during the Uruguay-negotiations, in order to make it more flexible on certain issues, in particular the issue of trade in agricultural products (Vernon, 1996).

[2] See for a discussion of the reasons why a prolongation of the US commitment to Europe is likely for the near future Marini and Rood (1996). To this should be added that from the American point of view there may be reason to strengthen the relationship with the EU, as important American strategic and economic interests may be affected by the outcome of the European integration process. For both security and economic interests, therefore, the USA has reason to be involved in European affairs.

References

Barfield, C. E., 'The Deceptive Allure of a Transatlantic Free Trade Agreement: A US Perspective', *Intereconomics*, 1998.

Gardner, A.L., *A New Era in US-EU Relations? The Clinton Administration and the New Transatlantic Agenda*, Aldershot, Avebury, 1997.

Gaster, R. and C. Prestowitz, *Shrinking the Atlantic; Europe and the American Economy*, North Atlantic Research, Inc., Washington, D.C., 1995.

Gilpin, R., *The Political Economy of International Relations*, Princeton University Press, Princeton, New Jersey, 1987.

Gordon, P.H., 'Recasting the Atlantic Alliance', *Survival*, Volume 38, 1996.

Gowa, J., 'Bipolarity, Multi Polarity, and Free Trade', *American Political Science Review*, Volume 83, 1989.

Heisbourg, F., 'Can the Atlantic Alliance Last Out the Century?', *International Affairs*, Volume 63, Number 3, 1987.

Heisbourg, F., 'The European-US Alliance: Valedictory Reflections on Continental Drift in the Post-Cold War Era', *International Affairs*, Volume 68, 1992.

Heuser, B., *Transatlantic Relations: Sharing Ideals and Costs*, Chatham House Papers, Royal Institute of International Affairs, London, 1996.

Kissinger, H.A., *The Troubled Partnership; a Re-Appraisal of the Atlantic Community*, McGraw-Hill, New York, 1965.

Marini, G. and J. Rood, 'Maintaining Global Dominance: the USA as a European and Asian Power', in: M. van Leeuwen and A. Venema (eds), *Selective Engagement: American Foreign Policy at the Turn of the Century*, Netherlands Atlantic Commission/Netherlands Institute of International Relations 'Clingendael', The Hague, 1996.

Osgood, R.O., *NATO, The Entangled Alliance*, Chicago University Press, Chicago, 1962.

Peterson, J. and H. Ward, 'Coalitional Instability and the New Multidimensional Politics of Security: a Rational Choice Argument for US-EU Cooperation', *European Journal of International Relations*. Volume 1, Number 2, 1995.

Vernon, R., 'Passing Through Regionalism: the Transition to Global Markets', *The World Economy*, Volume 19, 1996,

Walt, S.M., 'Why Alliances Endure or Collapse', *Survival*, Volume 39, Number 1, 1997.

Weidenfeld, W., 'America and Europe: Is the Break Inevitable?', *The Washington Quarterly*, Volume 20, Number 3, 1997.

9

EU'S PREFERENTIAL TRADE AGREEMENTS: OBJECTIVES AND OUTCOMES

L. ALAN WINTERS[1]

University of Sussex
Brighton
United Kingdom

1. Introduction

This chapter examines the preferential trade agreements (PTAs) of the European Union (EU) with third countries. It speculates on what the parties to them might hope to achieve and whether such hopes are likely to be vindicated. Implicitly the question is why, given the theoretical arguments in favour of non-discriminatory trade policy, the EU and its partners should put so much effort into and set so much store on signing discriminatory agreements. In part the answers are Europe-specific - particularly the absence of other instruments of international diplomacy at the EU level - and partly they reside in the general economics and politics of regional integration between large and small countries, or more usually rich and poor 'North-South' partners. Viner (1950) observed in his classic work on customs unions (CUs) that in these asymmetric cases the larger partner was almost always seeking political benefits while the smaller partner had economic objectives, and this is basically what has also been found in this contribution.

For the EU four sets of motivations are distinguished for its various PTAs: community with its neighbours, the stability and development of the partners concerned, and, most recently, the defence of markets. These motivations are mixed in different proportions in the various agreements. For the partners seven

P. van Dijck and G. Faber (eds.), The External Economic Dimension of the European Union, 195–222.
© 2000 *Kluwer Academic Publishers. Printed in the Netherlands.*

sets of objectives are distinguished: export markets, import liberalization, credibility, investment and growth, institutions and domestic policy, financial support, and political security. The discussion of these latter factors draws on a major World Bank project (Winters, 1997, Schiff and Winters, 1998, and The World Bank, forthcoming).

2. The agreements

The analysis in this chapter has been confined to formal PTAs between the EU and various partners. The agreements go beyond merely guaranteeing 'regular' most-favoured-nation (MFN) treatment in trade to offer partners reductions in most tariffs and freedom or more relaxed application of certain non-tariff barriers (NTBs). They also often go beyond border measures to consider other factors affecting trade such as standards and competition policy and in nearly all cases contain provisions for financial transfers. In general, only reciprocal agreements are considered in this chapter. However, because of its importance in EU policy-making and as it will likely become reciprocal in due course, the Lomé Convention has been included in the analysis.

To be specific, the PTAs considered here include those with the countries of the European Economic Area (EEA), the Central and Eastern European Countries including the Baltics (CEEC), the countries of the Mediterranean excluding Libya, and the African, Caribbean and Pacific Countries (ACP). This chapter also briefly considers a series of other actual and potential partners with which the EU has or is negotiating reciprocal trade agreements - Mexico, Mercosur, Chile and South Africa, which will be referred to as non-traditional PTAs.

Table 9.1 summarizes the various arrangements, while Annex Table 9.A.1 presents some economic statistics on the various partners. The table shows that compared to the EU itself, all the traditional partners are individually economically small. Not only do the traditional partners take relatively small shares of EU total exports (final column), but also their markets are small (total imports of goods and services) and even their incomes. Thus it is quite easy to believe that the EU is not seeking economic benefits from its traditional PTAs, whereas the partners would expect to find preferential access to the EU market, which could absorb all their output, quite attractive. The non-traditional partners are somewhat larger, especially in terms of total trade and income if not current imports from

Table 9.1. EU preferential trade arrangements, 1996.

Agreement	Type	Partners
European Economic Area (EEA)	Single market	Iceland, Liechtenstein, Norway
EEA-like	free-trade area (FTA)-plus	Switzerland
Europe Agreements (EAs)	FTA, eventual accession	Bulgaria, Czech Republic, Estonia, Hungary, Latvia, Lithuania, Poland, Romania, Slovak Republic, Slovenia
Euro-Med Agreements (EMAs)	CU	Turkey
	FTA	Algeria*, Cyprus, Egypt*, Israel, Jordan, Malta, Morocco, Lebanon*, Syria*, Tunisia
Lomé Convention	Currently non-reciprocal; prospective FTAs?	ACP countries
Other	FTA	South Africa**, Mexico*, Mercosur*, Chile*

Notes: *Under negotiation
   ** Signed in 1999

the EU. It will be argued in this contribution that this is what lies behind the EU's recent interest in them.

Probably the deepest of the EU's PTAs are those with the countries of the EEA - Iceland, Liechtenstein and Norway[2]. These PTAs bring the partners under the *acquis communautaire* except in agriculture, which, in accordance with restrictiveness on both sides, is excluded. The EEA is intended to deliver the economic benefits of the single market without the political ties that bind EU members. It was originally expected to cover other Scandinavian and Alpine partners, but some found it politically so unattractive that they sought full membership of the EU, while Switzerland found it too intrusive for its decentralized traditions and pulled back. CEPR (1992) and Baldwin (1994) analyse the various economic and political trade-offs in the original conception. The countries that chose to remain with the EEA see themselves as structurally sufficiently distinct from the EU to warrant this arms-length association, Iceland because of fish and Norway because of oil. Switzerland is still constitutionally unwilling to enter a deep and binding relationship with other countries, but it maintains an industrial free-trade area (FTA) with the EU supplemented with a good deal of informal co-operation in other commercial areas. Perhaps the most interesting challenge for Baldwin's (1995) theory of domino regionalism will be whether the Swiss can resist the gravitational pull of the EU indefinitely.

The Europe Agreements (EAs), which date from 1994-1996 (and from 1992 for the Interim Agreements), are also deep by the standards of North-South PTAs. They do not apply the full *acquis* to the partners, but do require them to adopt EU competition and intellectual property regimes and to make efforts to converge in other dimensions. Trade is relatively free within the agreements, but there are potential or actual exceptions; investment and services are also liberalized.

The Euro-Mediterranean Agreements (EMAs) cover a wide variety of forms. A long-standing PTA with Cyprus and Malta was seen as a precursor to accession, but has not yet developed this way because of Greek-Turkish political sensitivities and because of the complexities of integrating very small countries into the EU's current political structure. The latter problem also besets Malta's request for accession, made in 1990 and revived in 1998. The CU with Turkey is essentially a consolation prize for rejecting her membership of the EU. The CU was chosen as the route for economic integration, as opposed to an FTA, because it had prior legal cover under the Association Agreement of 1963, and so sidestepped the political friction that might arise from creating a new agreement. The CU is prospectively far-reaching in its treatment of Turkish trade policy with the EU and third countries and in several aspects of the *acquis*, e.g., competition policy, standards and intellectual property rights. Some frictions remain, however, such as facility for levying anti-dumping duties on EU-Turkish trade and the absence of a timetable for freeing agricultural trade. Transition periods of up to 22 years are permitted in other elements of the agreement, so 'no time-table' does indeed look very slow. Additionally neither capital or, of course, labour mobility is allowed for, and neither is the liberalization of the Turkish service market required.

The 'ordinary' FTAs among the EMAs concern Israel and the Arab countries. That with Israel dates from 1975 and was updated in 1995, whereas the others are more recent: Morocco and Tunisia switched from non-reciprocal arrangements to an FTA in 1995 and Jordan in 1997. FTAs with other countries have yet to be signed. These FTAs have their origins in the Barcelona Declaration of 1995, which sought to offer the Mediterranean countries and their Latin champions among the EU membership levels of commitment similar to those offered to the CEEC under the EAs. Relative to the PTAs discussed so far, the Tunisian FTA, and by inference the others, do not look very far-reaching: EU market access in agriculture is not substantially liberalized, and services, investment and establishment are effectively not included[3].

The Lomé Convention defines the EU's relationship with 71 small and mostly poor developing countries in Africa, the Caribbean and the Pacific (ACP), nearly all of which were formerly colonies of one of its members. It currently offers them, non-reciprocally, access to EU markets duty free and subject to no quantitative restrictions except for some tariff quotas. The current Convention runs until 2000 and its successor is under negotiation. Major changes will be required, since the current arrangements have been ruled to be inconsistent with obligations under the World Trade Organization (WTO). The EU plans for renegotiation are to grant all least-developed countries, not just those in the ACP-group, non-reciprocal preferences, as is permitted, at least implicitly, by the WTO, and to require other ACP countries to sign a series of regional FTAs with the EU. There are no models for these, but given the ACP countries' lack of development, the nature of the EMAs and the difficulties encountered in the non-traditional PTAs, one should not expect anything too far-reaching.

Finally, the EU has started to negotiate a series of FTAs with more distant partners. South Africa was deemed too large to enter the trade arrangements of Lomé and so has been negotiating a separate FTA. Mexico and Mercosur are also formally negotiating FTAs with the EU while Chile is doing so informally (on the EU side - where the Commission does not yet have formal negotiating authority). These FTAs are restricted in coverage to goods and even here both sides have lists of sensitive products they wish to exclude - mainly agricultural in the EU. These lists have been a major issue in negotiation and may yet scupper the deals. The FTAs make no attempt to extend the *acquis* to the partners and, unlike the 'traditional' PTAs, there are no effective financial protocols. These are simple FTAs aimed at securing preferential market access.

3. What's in it for the EU?

This section considers what the EU hopes to achieve and is actually achieving from its main external relationships - i.e., its PTAs, which go deeper than co-operation agreements. As noted above, they are all rather similar, varying in degree rather than nature. They are structured around international trade relationships and the ancillary requirements for efficient trade, have recently been extended into areas such as investment, and frequently include an aid or financial component. This similarity might *prima facie* suggest similar objectives, but in fact arises from the constrained choice of tools. Almost regardless of the ultimate objective, the EU has only commercial diplomacy at its disposal.

Commercial instruments such as PTAs lie firmly within the ambit of the Commission, the body charged with furthering the idea and the ideal of European integration. This has two effects. First, the Commission is happy to use commercial instruments because partners automatically have to deal with Brussels on commercial matters and recognize that what they receive is genuinely European or Europe-wide rather than, for instance, French or British. Second, it is very much easier to use commercial diplomacy than other tools. It is true that even for the use of commercial instruments most or all national governments must concur through the Council, but the Commission has the power to propose policies in these areas and is also responsible for implementing them. In other areas in which countries use to influence each other, such as diplomatic support in world fora, monetary affairs and security arrangements, the member governments are more or less wholly independent and tend to resent Commission coaching or suggestions.

If the EU can maintain no other than commercial relationships, it is not surprising that these relationships actually stem from several different motives. Four broad classes of goals are distinguished here. Most actual arrangements derive from a combination of such motives but they are, nonetheless, useful as an organizing framework.

Community

For close neighbours in Europe the EU is prepared to contemplate accession or, if partners wish, some slightly looser relationship. This is the area over which the *acquis communautaire* potentially extends. It most obviously includes the EEA and Switzerland, and the countries with EAs since they are seen as eventual candidates for accession.

The motivation here for the EU is basically cultural and political - what Luyten (1989), a former senior EC negotiator, refers to as an axiomatic 'natural vocation to unify'. The EU countries recognize a historical, geographical and cultural affiliation with these partners that dominates simple economic calculation, in the same way as did German reunification or, for some advocates, does maintaining the national integrity of, for instance, Canada or Belgium. This is not to say that such views transcend economics, for some prices would be too high to pay for union, but there is undoubtedly a strong emotional weight on the pro-union side of the scale[4]. There is also an element of political legitimization in this motive. A European Union that explicitly rejected culturally similar neighbours as members would be seen to be exclusionary and discriminatory. This would tend to undermine the EU's legitimacy not only with the neighbours themselves, who could then turn hostile, but also internationally in fora such as the WTO or the United Nations (UN).

There may also be economic benefits from bringing these closely neighbouring countries into the Union, but given their small size relative to the Union these are likely to be minor. For example, Haaland and Norman (1992) suggested that extending the EC-12 into the EEA by including all the then European Free Trade Association (EFTA) member countries would add around only 0.1 per cent to the EC-12's real income. Similarly, Baldwin, Francois and Portes (1997) see EU-15 gains of only 0.2 per cent of real income from admitting the CEEC-7 - Bulgaria, the Czech Republic, Hungary, Poland, Romania, the Slovak Republic and Slovenia.

The reasons for the small size of these benefits are well understood. The benefits of economic integration stem mainly from larger markets (allowing more economies of scale) or greater competition stemming from either closer interaction and rivalry between firms in different member countries and/or significantly different factor proportions between members. Neither EFTA nor the CEEC increase the size or factor diversity of the European market very much and, besides, in many areas even without the EEA or EAs these countries would have relatively good access to the EU market. By the same token, EFTA and CEEC markets, while attractive, are not large enough to offer EU producers large increases in earnings.

The main exceptions to the lack of economic benefits would be from liberalizing agriculture and sensitive manufactures, such as clothing and steel; but these are the very areas where integration is least complete. The EFTA countries are even more restrictive about agricultural liberalization than the EU and the CEEC still face barriers to agricultural exports and formal or informal export restrictions on goods such as clothing and steel. In other words, the very sectors which could generate economic gains, albeit at the costs of temporary adjustment stresses in the EU, are excluded or attenuated in the integration.

Stability

The second motive for signing PTAs is to foster a band of stability around the EU borders. This was clearly evident in the initial set of EAs negotiated over 1990-92, for, at that time, there was no commitment to eventual membership[5]. It is also now evident further east, in the promises of agreements with Ukraine and Russia if they reform sufficiently. Most of all, however, it is the characteristic of the EU's Mediterranean policy, which envisages binding virtually every Mediterranean country into a PTA with the EU.

The reasons for seeking stability on one's borders are not particularly complex. Serious disruption could disrupt economic and social conditions in the neighbouring parts of the EU, but more seriously could spillover into them in the form of violence or migration. The last is probably the most pressing in EU policy-makers' minds. The EMAs, including the CU with Turkey, ostensibly address the issue in two related fashions. First, a simple reading of trade theory would suggest that if, for instance, Morocco can increase its exports to the EU, this will raise the returns to its abundant factor of production, labour, and thus reduce the incentive for workers and their families to migrate.

Second, if the EMAs foster and support reform in the Mediterranean partners by, for instance, liberalizing their imports, reforming their institutions and transferring capital and know-how, there will be both social modernization and increasing economic prosperity. These, it is hoped, will curtail the spread of Islamic fundamentalism and cement in place more liberal pluralistic western institutions (which are held *a priori* to be better for human welfare). On the economic front they will create prosperity, which, as well as fostering political development, will discourage migration.

For several reasons, the success of the EMAs in these dimensions is far from assured. First, while increasing exports to the EU is likely to induce some tendency towards raising labour returns, the effects may well be mixed. For example, Falvey (1995) has argued that partial liberalizations might have perverse effects. Increasing exports to the EU is not the same as increasing total exports, and, similarly, may not increase the prices of exportables overall; and if factors outnumber goods, simple trade theory results may not hold, and even if they do, exports may be intensive in labour that is relatively skilled in Mediterranean terms, rather than the very unskilled labour that the Europeans fear most. This latter problem is likely to be exacerbated if exports come mainly from enclave firms created by foreign direct investment (FDI) rather than from indigenous production in sectors such as agriculture. Thus the second reason to fear disappointing results is that the EMAs have not liberalized all Mediterranean exports: agriculture, in particular, remains heavily constrained.

Third, the Agreements do not show much signs of generating deep reforms in the Mediterranean partners. For example, transition periods for tariff reforms are long and have, on occasions, been perverse such as in Tunisia where tariffs on inputs were cut first, raising effective rates of protection until the tariff rates on final goods eventually follow. Services are excluded from the agreements and hence from reform, agriculture remains protected in some cases, and the agreements have no direct effects on sclerotic labour markets or public ownership (Djankov and Hoekman, 1996, Galal and Hoekman, 1997). Thus, one could be forgiven for seeing these agreements less as a first step on the road to fundamental reform than as a tactical retreat in the effort to resist change. Of course, if one sees reform as disruptive and likely to stimulate political and social unrest in the short run this may be sensible, but it does not correspond with the rhetoric nor bode well for the longer term.

Fourth, migration specialists have argued that increasing prosperity might foster rather than discourage migration in the short run. If migration requires capital in advance to pay for tickets and a period for settling into the new location, and if capital markets are imperfect, then increasing prosperity could push more people into the migratory group, as has been argued by Martin (1993) and Lopez and Schiff (forthcoming).

As noted in the case of community, the EU will see relatively little general economic benefit from the EMAs. There will, of course, be some lucky exporters and investors and some lucky importers and consumers, but overall these benefits would hardly warrant the fanfare and effort accorded to the agreements.

Development

The third broad category of motivations for PTAs is development: the EU's concern, for humanitarian and geo-political (as opposed to Euro-political) reasons, that poverty be alleviated and economic development encouraged. This lies behind the EU's unilateral trade preferences under the Generalized System of Preferences (GSP), which are not treated here, and is evident at least in part in its relations with the CEEC and Mediterranean countries. Most obviously, however, it is the defining characteristic of the Lomé Convention governing relations between the EU and 71 ACP countries. This too involves unilateral trade preferences but here of a contractual nature: unlike GSP preferences the EU can not unilaterally withdraw Lomé preferences during the life of an agreed Convention (five to ten years). The Lomé Convention also involves special protocols for certain commodities - bananas, beef, sugar and rum - an aid protocol and a good deal of political co-operation.

The Lomé Convention and its preceding Yaoundé Convention and Association Agreements stretch back to the inception of the European Economic Community (EEC) in 1957, at which time many current ACP countries were colonies. The policy basically represented the continuation of French colonial policy on an EEC scale. Through time the number of associates has expanded, most dramatically through UK accession in 1973, when much of the Commonwealth was permitted to join.

Continuing these neo-colonial links was probably motivated in part by altruistic concerns about development and poverty alleviation. However, if these had been the dominant motive, one might have expected to see a stronger developmental focus to the policy, especially in later years when the original model was manifestly failing to deliver development and theories of development evolved to move the stress away from policies such as commodity stabilization and protected markets[6]. Grilli (1993) suggests two main EU objectives in the relationship with ACP countries: increasing the security of access to raw materials and maintaining global political influence in a world increasingly dominated by one or two superpowers.

In the last two decades the first objective has seemed unnecessary and anachronistic. Moreover, it flies almost directly in the face of the ACP countries' principal aim of the relationship which is industrialization. Thus, overall this objective does not figure very strongly in EU thinking about the renewal/ replacement of Lomé in 2000.

The second objective, on the other hand, continues to be relevant, receiving several mentions in EU documents about replacement (Commission of the European Communities, 1997). It is reinforced by the argument that developing countries are becoming increasingly important in the global economy both in terms of size - although the ACP group is still tiny economically - and institutions, in which case a set of 71, albeit small, votes probably is a useful adjunct to EU diplomacy.

Colonial and neo-colonial markets are sometimes seen as useful dumping grounds for exports that are not globally competitive. This is probably still true of the ACP market for the EU - at least, EU exports to ACP countries are significantly higher than one would predict on objective criteria (Winters and Wang, 1994) - but, again, these markets are so small that the increments are hardly significant as a source of income in the EU[7].

Defensive

So far, the various motivations adduced for EU PTAs have referred to 'natural' partners (in the political sense): countries which for reasons of history or geography lie within EU members' traditional spheres of interest. The last motivation, proposed here, shifts the focus to more distant partners and more recent arrangements. It is to defend EU access to distant markets in the face of the attempts of the latter group of countries at regional integration. This motivation is most obviously present in the arrangements recently concluded or currently under negotiation with Mexico, Chile and Mercosur and the FTA with South Africa may also be included in this group[8]. It also applies to the Asia-Europe Meetings (ASEM) with the members of the Association of South East Asian Nations (ASEAN) and to the Transatlantic Market Place (TAM) proposal with the USA, which are analysed elsewhere in this volume.

Until the 1990s, the EU had grown up and pursued its trading arrangements with other countries in a world in which it was the only major regional bloc. Among other things, this gave it a relaxed attitude to Art. XXIV of the General Agreement on Tariffs and Trade (GATT) and meant that it was rarely on the exporting end of the trade diversion (Nagarajan, 1998). That is, it never had to worry about market access except in an MFN fashion at the GATT. In return, through a slightly vague agreement with the USA in 1974 (the Casey-Soames Agreement) the EU agreed not extend its PTAs beyond its traditional borders. All this changed in the 1990s as regionalism took hold in a number of the world's major economies, leading to blocs such as the North American Free Trade Agreement (NAFTA), Mercosur and the ASEAN Free Trade Area (AFTA).

Although one can already identify some trade diversion in these blocs - see Yeats (1998) on Mercosur and USITC (1997) and Nagarajan (1998) on NAFTA - the concern is more for the future, as the blocs come to the end of their transition periods and, potentially worse from the EU perspective, consider ever deeper or wider forms of integration. By negotiating FTAs with these various blocs or their members, the EU can reverse the discrimination it faces on tariffs and make a stronger case for concerning itself with their future development. Thus, as a formal FTA partner of Mercosur or Mexico the EU feels that it may more legitimately comment on, or even participate in, talks on the evolution of Mercosur, NAFTA and the Free Trade Area of the Americas (FTAA). A good parallel is the US demand for 'a seat at the table' as the Europeans discussed their Single Market Program, and, similarly to that case, although the EU will not obtain full access to Western Hemisphere talks, the more active its prior engagement, the more influence it is likely to be able to wield in regional talks. Exactly the same arguments apply to the ASEM relationship, which is basically an attempt at entryism to the Asia-Pacific Economic Co-operation (APEC).

It is less obvious that EU relations with South Africa fall mainly under the defensive heading. On balance, however, it is likely that the main motive was to bind the major political force and market in Africa into the European sphere rather than risk President Mandela's internationalist sentiment and the evident interest of the USA leading it elsewhere. Whether the strategy will be successful remains to be seen, however, given the difficulty of and the perceived EU stinginess in the negotiation.

4. The partners' objectives

The partners in the various EU PTAs also have differing objectives, or at least place different weight on a common set of objectives; and as with the EU itself, it is not obvious that they get all that they hope for. In this section, the aims that countries generally appear to have in forming a PTA with a large and affluent partner are briefly dicussed.

Export markets

The most obvious benefits that a PTA partner seeks is tariff-free access to EU markets. A small partner can expect that if it alone gets such access, it will be able to increase its export prices by the extent of the tariff which it is exempted from and so earn some rents. Its firms might choose to raise prices a little less and expand their sales, but, if so, this is because they prefer doing so to the straight price increase and so the latter represents a lower bound on the export benefits of the PTA.

Clearly these benefits exist and can be considerable, but for several reasons they are not necessarily as princely as is sometimes thought. First, the EU's MFN tariffs (what exporters pay if they do not get preferences) are not very high for industrial goods and non-agricultural primaries: Finger, Ingco and Reincke (1996) put the EU's post-Uruguay Round average tariff facing developing country exporters at 4.5 per cent and 1.5 per cent respectively and at 11.2 per cent for agriculture.

Second, developing countries would qualify for the GSP rates for many of their exports, and these rates are usually significantly lower than MFN rates.

Third, as noted above, the EU insists that temperate agricultural products be largely excluded from its arrangements and frequently either formally or informally restricts sensitive manufactures such as clothing or steel.

Fourth, the EU has preferential arrangements with many countries. These frequently compete to provide the same goods and so, rather than the individual exporter pocketing the tariffs that are forgiven, they are passed onto to EU consumers in the form of lower prices. Sometimes the resulting expansion of demand will provide compensation for exporters, but only if they are efficient and competitive enough to increase supply.

Fifth, a major motive for smaller countries seeking PTAs with larger partners is the so-called 'insurance' motive. Whalley and Perroni (1994) see this as securing a friendly market in case a trade war breaks out, and they identify large benefits from it, albeit in very unlikely circumstances. An alternative view - Hindley and Messerlin (1993) - is that it is an attempt to avoid the major partners' contingent protection - safeguards, countervailing and, most significantly, anti-dumping duties. This was quite obvious in EFTA's desire for the EEA, and was achieved; but in all other cases, the EU has retained the right to exercise anti-dumping against its partners. The grudging admission to the CEEC at the Essen Council in 1994 that the EU

> 'should be ready to consider refraining from using commercial defence instruments for industrial products [conditional on the] satisfactory implementation of competition policy and control of state aids ... together with the wider application of other parts of Community law linked to the internal market, providing a guarantee against unfair competition comparable to that existing inside the internal market'

shows just how far the EU is from surrendering this instrument.

One can argue that *de facto* the use of anti-dumping against partners declines when a PTA is signed. Hindley (1997) offers some *prima facie* evidence to that effect in that fewer cases were initiated against the CEEC in the 1990s than before, but he does not seek to establish causality. One should also recognize that the joint political bodies overseeing the various PTAs - e.g., the Association Councils for the EAs - offer an additional review and appeal procedure. However, by their very nature, political consultations tend to become managed trade solutions that effectively constrain market access, even if at higher levels of imports than the EU might have permitted unilaterally. Thus overall, contingent protection (and the threat of it) does curtail the export benefits of PTAs with the EU.

Import liberalization

Given the now widespread understanding that openness is good for growth, governments do frequently aspire to open their import markets, but usually slowly, selectively and with 'adequate' safeguards, what has been called 'managed liberalism' (Winters, 1993). The PTAs with the EU appear to offer developing countries a reasonable route for this in several ways.

The transition periods are typically long - e.g., 12 years for the EMAs - and the EU is fairly relaxed about what occurs in them, as when Tunisia raised its effective protection rates. In return for maintaining its own sectoral foibles, the EU understands about the partners' wishes to exclude certain sectors and to have 'suitable' safeguards built in. Similarly the EU is not particularly pressing on services or investment - at least relative to the USA, the only comparable PTA partner - and the EU is not fiercely competitive in many of the more labour-intensive industries that partners wish to protect.

While all these reasons ease the political strains of adapting to the PTA - and may, it is sometimes argued, be necessary to allow the developing partners to liberalize at all - they also reduce the value of the liberalization as a stimulus to competition and efficiency. Whether the PTAs allow net benefits in this dimension depends on a number of trade-offs.

It is well understood that trade preferences cause trade diversion - the switching of the demand for imports from the most efficient (cheapest) source to the partner which can now undercut other suppliers because it is exempted from the tariff. This is costly, but how costly depends on how much trade is diverted and how much less efficient the partner is than the least-cost source, which, in turn, is bounded by the tariff that the latter faces. It is commonly argued that large open economies such as the EU can not be far from least costs in virtually all goods and thus that the costs of each unit of trade diversion are small. Moreover, if the EU is the partner country's principal source of imports, there is little trade to divert. On this view signing a PTA is fairly close to adopting free trade multilaterally and is likely to be strongly beneficial.

The contrary view, however, starts by observing that the efficiency of EU production is far from guaranteed, for instance in the sectors of textiles, steel and vehicles. Moreover, if the EU does not wholly replace all other imports, the partner continues to import from the most efficient sources outside the EU. If these suppliers charge price p and face tariff t, the partner's internal price will be $p+t$ and this is the price that EU firms will charge regardless of their costs. In this case every unit of diverted trade entails national welfare forgone, equivalent to t: the unit could have been bought by paying p to the efficient producer and t to the government rather than $p+t$ to the EU producer. Worse, imports from the EU originally cost the country p (with t going to the government) but now cost $p+t$. Thus, on every unit of imports that was previously bought from the EU, the partner will transfer the tariff revenue t to an EU producer. Quantitatively speaking this is likely to be the major effect on partner welfare, and will be larger the higher the volume of imports from the EU initially (Schiff, 1997).

The argument of the previous paragraph ceases to hold if the EU becomes the only supplier of the good in question. If EU supply is competitive, prices will be bid down to the level of marginal costs. There will still be losses from any trade diversion and from revenue transfers to EU producers if EU costs rise as a result of supplying larger quantities; but at least the partner's internal prices will fall to some extent, allowing the possibilities of gains from trade creation. If EU goods are unique because of product differentiation, then by definition the EU is the only supplier and there is a larger presumption of benefits.

Trade creation - the replacement of inefficient domestic production by the newly liberalized EU imports or increases in consumption as internal prices fall - is a benefit of a PTA which depends partly on the extent of restructuring which is induced in the economy of the partner.

The non-European partners of the EU typically have rather high external tariffs, which tend to be associated with high values of both trade creation and diversion. On balance, the latter probably dominates at high tariffs, meaning that in the dimension of import liberalization partners probably lose. A number of modelling studies of the EMAs tends to confirm this. For example, even allowing for improved market access to the EU, Maskus and Konan (1997) suggest that Egypt will hardly gain any welfare as a result of its EMA.

Credibility

An important benefit of a PTA is often asserted to be improved policy credibility, which can be particularly valuable to an economy trying to reform after years of poor economic management or in a different system as was the case with the CEEC. Careful analysis, however, suggests distinct limits to the scope of this argument (Fernandez and Portes, 1998, Schiff and Winters, 1998).

A PTA can create credibility if either the partner - here the EU - has sufficient interest and power to discipline policy defections, or if the PTA changes the incentives for governments to mismanage their economies.

Consider trade policy on imports from the EU. Here the EU has a direct interest in enforcing the PTA and, by threatening retaliation, the means to do so. Thus here the PTA almost certainly increases credibility. Trade policy towards other suppliers however, looks less secure. The EU has little interest other than altruism in reducing the margins of preference it receives in its partners' markets and seems unlikely to risk trade frictions on its own exports to keep tariffs on third countries low[9]. For the partners, having zero tariffs on the EU induces some pressure to keep tariffs on other suppliers down to reduce trade diversion, but this is not an overwhelming effect.

For non-trade policies there is no legal basis for the EU disciplining its PTA partners and, probably no willingness. There is talk of requiring the CEEC candidates for accession to adhere to the Maastricht criteria, but accession is very different from a PTA. Moreover, the history of Greek economic policy since 1981 suggests that, once inside the EU, the pressure for discipline weakens. The EMAs are fairly weak outside the trade area and make no demands, and hence create no case for discipline, in areas such as privatization and labour markets.

With regard to incentives for the partner's government, the position is less clear-cut. Fernandez and Portes (1998) show that a PTA has mixed effects on the incentive for macro discipline in areas such as exchange-rate policy. However, there is an incentive for policies regarding micro-efficiency since such efficiency will help partners reap benefits from the PTAs. However, given the partners' unwillingness to accept direct requirements in these directions, there is little reason to expect significant indirect effects.

Possibly the most persuasive source of increased macro and micro credibility is the financial aspect of the EMAs and, conceivably, the post-Lomé arrangements for the ACP countries. The EU Mediterranean programme offers substantial financial assistance overall, but makes no *ex-ante* country allocations. Rather it states that resources will be disbursed according to partners' progress in undertaking 'courageous' reforms, targeted at 'medium-term support of policy changes or the social cushioning of reforms' (Rhein, 1996). Rhein is optimistic that this will induce substantial reform in much, if not all, of the region. Aghrout and Alexander (1997) are less optimistic, using phrases like 'success (…) difficult to predict' and 'sensitive issues', and noting limits to, and differences in commitment of EU members to the process. While cash seems likely to help rather than hinder credibility, the experience of the Bretton Woods institutions suggests that it is far from sufficient, especially if the funding body is subject to internal divisions.

Overall, therefore, while a PTA will induce some credibility in trade policy, this is limited and will not, I suspect, spill over strongly to other areas. Moreover, money aside, credibility seems likely only to be created by genuinely binding and liberal PTAs. It is icing on the cake of a good agreement, not a free bonus from a bad agreement. In this light, it may be expected that the EAs probably induced a reasonable amount of credibility, the EMAs some, and the other PTAs very little. Certainly it is not to be expected that, for instance, the EU-Mercosur agreement will increase the macro-economic credibility of Mercosur countries. To the extent that partners have witnessed increased credibility, it has arisen mainly through their own efforts and policy and WTO bindings.

Investment and growth

Investment does seem to follow PTAs. The example of the EFTA countries losing investment flows following the announcement of the Single Market programme of the EU and re-capturing it when they signed the EEA or equivalent is telling (Baldwin, Forslid and Haaland, 1996). This turn-around reflected the EEA's assured market access to the EU, which allowed or perhaps forced EFTA firms to deepen their specialization and competitiveness in the context of the larger and more competitive market.

The other PTAs have probably had similar effects, but attenuated by their weaker assurances of market access and of fundamental reform. Thus the CEEC have tended to fare better than the Mediterranean countries and the ACP countries rather poorly. Relatively short-term investment has increased, for instance to exploit the more liberal market access for out-sourced clothing, but it is not clear that credibility has increased sufficiently to induce major changes in capital accumulation.

The EA and EMAs include investment chapters guaranteeing EU investors in the partner countries limited freedom of establishment, freedom of capital flows and disinvestment, freedom to repatriate earnings, and freedom of movement for skilled personnel. Where local conditions are attractive, for instance in Poland and Hungary, these arrangements stimulate investment flows from the EU, but where conditions are not attractive, for instance in Romania, the arrangements do not help much.

In the end the major economic returns to a policy occur if it can increase economic growth, and this is certainly a hope for developing countries that are partners in PTAs with the EU. The evidence that PTAs have such effects, however, is rather weak and *ex-post* evidence of growth benefits is only provided by Henrekson, Torstensson and Torstensson (1996) who find that the EU increased members' growth rates over the period 1976-85. Other studies such as de Melo, Panagariya and Rodrik (1993) and Vamvakidis (1998) find no such effects.

There are good reasons why policy reform should enhance growth and Baldwin (1989) shows how a PTA might increase medium-term growth by fostering capital accumulation. However, the latter is yet to be supported empirically[10] and policy reform is arguably equally available to a determined government without as with a PTA. Thus, any hope that signing a PTA with the EU will, alone, accelerate growth and development is bound to be disappointed. In the context of fundamental reform it might contribute, but only as a junior partner to the reforms themselves.

Institutions and domestic policy

Individual countries may copy institutions and domestic policy of other countries unilaterally, but having a PTA might help in three ways. First, the PTA might require the adoption of certain norms, as for example the EA and EMAs insist on EU competition policy and the EU-Turkey and EAs on EU regimes for intellectual property rights[11].

Second, a PTA might ease the politics of reform by broadening the debate and allowing losses in one dimension to be compensated by gains in another dimension. If the PTA is genuinely advantageous, the returns to fundamental reform - or costs of not reforming - may become larger and hence reduce the opposition to reform. Tunisian and Moroccan ministers saw negotiations with the EU as a way of maintaining a reformist and liberalizing momentum, believing that alternative means such as binding in the WTO were not sufficient[12]. Third, the EU might be a source of considerable technical assistance in reforming institutions in its own image.

Financial support

Financial support is closely allied with technical assistance for reform. The EU offers fairly generous support to its current PTA partners, certainly when compared with the USA, except for the EEA in which case the flow is towards the EU[13]. This is ostensibly to compensate for the costs of reform, but since reforms are expected to pay for themselves in net present value terms, this is more an excuse than a reason. Part of the finance could be seen as compensation for the costs of trade diversion, but it can be argued that much of it is just a generalized development-orientated transfer.

Political security

Aside from the very real political benefits of prosperity, some partners see a relationship with the EU as a means of bolstering their political identity and integrity. Although the PTAs are not defence treaties, they do at least signify recognition by a relatively powerful force. This is probably relevant in the Mediterranean as a bulwark against international spillovers of fundamentalism or violence and possibly also against civil disruption. More obviously, in the early 1990s the CEEC craved arrangements with the EU as a bulwark against any backlash from Russia. Similarly Slovenia sought foreign recognition to differentiate it from the rest of Yugoslavia.

Another aspect of politics concerns democracy and human rights. To the extent that a PTA with the EU depends on maintaining democracy, and to the extent that the PTA is beneficial, governments can bind their own and their successors' hands. This is a political analogue of the credibility argument above and depends on exactly the same factors, the willingness and ability of the EU to use its influence. In the question of accession the EU has been quite direct - as was the case with Turkey and Latvia - and this was also the case with regard to the question of very basic reform, for instance when making trade agreements with Russia and Ukraine conditional on progress towards the market and democracy, and eschewing Libya in the Mediterranean. Whether it would be prepared to rescind or suspend a PTA for these reasons, however, remains to be seen.

5. Conclusion

This chapter has reviewed the wide variety of returns to their trade arrangements that the EU and its PTA partners seek. It has been suggested that notwithstanding some cases in which these objectives have been realized, disappointment seems likely in many cases. For the EU the objectives are primarily political rather than narrowly economic whereas for the partners they are primarily economic. The trade-offs the partners face - in varying degrees in different agreements – entail access to EU markets[14], credibility and investment, finance and institutional and political support on the one hand, versus the pain of reform, transfers of tariff revenue, a narrowing focus of trade relations and trade diversion on the other. The balance varies case by case, but for some partners it seems likely that larger economic benefits would stem from a stronger effort at domestic reform coupled with a more multilateral approach to opening their economies. Unless one believes that policy-making is biased or misinformed in some way, one must conclude that the attractions of the EU agreements are based on their requiring less reform and/or offering more financial support than the multilateral alternatives do.

Notes

[1] I am grateful to the editors, an anonymous referee, Bernard Hoekman and Won Chang for comments and inputs, and to Mary Ann Arouna and Moonhui Kim for logistical support. The first draft of this chapter was prepared while the author was research manager in The World Bank. The views expressed here are of the author's and may not reflect those of the World Bank and its staff, and its member governments.

[2] The remainder of this section is based on Commission of the European Communities (1997) and Pelkmans and Brenton (1997).

[3] The Israel FTA makes some progress in these areas.

[4] The current debate about how and when the first phase CEEC accedants will be ready for full membership encompasses an attempt to identify this price.

[5] This came in 1993 at the Copenhagen Council - see Winters and Wang (1994).

[6] The ongoing discussions about renewing Lomé reflect these developments more clearly.

[7] Wang and Winters (1998) did identify a few goods for which an African country was the EU's principal market in 1995, but most were very minor in terms of output and employment: the exceptions were one type of drilling equipment and one class of passenger ship.

[8] In this last case, however, development and stability are also significant.

[9] Indeed, one sometimes hears suggestions that the EU encourages partners to keep their tariffs up - e.g., in Estonia.

[10] Also as Walz (1997) shows a trade-diverting PTA could reduce growth rates.

[11] The EEA also harmonizes these dimensions, but the developed-country partners probably do not require external bindings to do so.

[12] Private communication from Mustapha Nabli and statement by Hassan Abouyoub, during the World Bank Conference 'What Policy Mexico Should Know about Regionalism', Geneva, May 1998.

[13] However, the EU is unlikely to be so generous in its new defensive agreements with the Western Hemisphere.

[14] In some cases - e.g., the Mediterranean - the EU is committed to providing unrequited preferences indefinitely, and thus the WTO is the only threat to access; in others - e.g., the ACP countries - the EU threatens eventually to abolish such preferential access.

References

Aghrout, A. and M.S. Alexander, 'The Euro-Mediterranean New Strategy and the Mahgreb Countries', *European Foreign Affairs Review*, Volume 2, 1997.

Baldwin, R., 'The Growth Effects of 1992,' *Economic Policy*, Volume 9, 1989.

Baldwin, R., *Toward an Integrated Europe*, Centre for Economic Policy Research, London, 1994.

Baldwin, R., ' A Domino Theory of Regionalism' in: R. Baldwin, P. Haaparanta and J. Kiander (eds), *Expanding Membership in the European Union*, Cambridge University Press, Cambridge, 1995.

Baldwin, R., J. Francois and R. Portes, 'The Costs and Benefits of Eastern Enlargement: The Impact on the EU and Central Europe,' *Economic Policy*, Number 24, April, 1997.

Centre for Economic Policy Research, 'Is Bigger Better: The Economics of EC Enlargement,' *Monitoring European Integration*, Number 3, London, 1992.

Commission of the European Communities, *WTO Aspects of EU's Preferential Trade Agreements with Third Countries*, Brussels, 1997.

Commission of the European Communities, *Communication from the Commission to the Council and the European Parliament: Guidelines for the Negotiation of New Cooperation Agreements with the African, Caribbean, and Pacific ACP Countries*, Brussels, 1997.

De Melo, J., A. Panagariya and D. Rodrik, 'Regional Integration: An Analytical and Empirical Overview,' in: J. De Melo and A. Panagariya (eds), *New Dimensions in Regional Integration*, Cambridge University Press, New York, 1993.

Djankov, S. and B. Hoekman, 'The European Union's Mediterranean Free Trade Initiative,' *World Economy*, Volume 19, 1996.

Falvey, R., *Factor Price Convergence*, mimeo, International Trade Division, The World Bank, Washington, D.C., 1995.

Fernandez, R. and J. Portes, 'Returns to Regionalism: An Analysis of Nontraditional Gains from Regional Trade Agreements,' *The World Bank Economic Review*, Volume 12, 1998.

Finger, J.M., M.D. Ingco, and U. Reincke, *The Uruguay Round: Statistics on Tariff Concessions Given and Received*, The World Bank, Washington, D.C., 1996.

Galal, A. and B. Hoekman, *Regional Partners in Global Markets: Limits and Possibilities of the Euro-Med Agreements*, Centre for Economic Policy Research, London, 1997.

Grilli, E., *The European Community and the Developing Countries*, Cambridge University Press, Cambridge, 1993.

Haaland, J. and V. Norman, 'Global Production Effects of European Integration,' in: L.A. Winters (ed.), *Trade Flows and Trade Policy After 1992*, Cambridge University Press, Cambridge, 1992.

Henrekson, M., J. Torstensson and R. Torstensson, 'Growth Effects of European Integration,' *European Economic Review*, Volume 4, 1996.

Hindley, B., ' The Regulation of Imports from Transition Economies by the European Union,' in: P. Ehrenhaft, B. Hindley, C. Michalopoulos, and L.A. Winters, *Policies in Imports from Economies on Transition: Two Case Studies*, The World Bank, Washington, D.C., 1996.

Lopez, R. and M. Schiff, 'Migration and the Skill Composition of the Labor Force: The Impact of Trade Liberalization in LDCs,' *Canadian Journal of Economics,* forthcoming.

Luyten, P., ' Multilateralism vs. Preferential Bilateralism: A European View,' in: J. Schott, *Free Trade Areas and US Trade Policy*, Institute for International Economics, Washington, D.C., 1989.

Martin, P., *Trade and Migration: NAFTA and Agriculture,* Institute for International Economics, Washington, D.C., 1993.

Maskus, K.E. and D. Konan, 'Trade-related Intellectual Property Rights: Issues and Exploratory Results,' in: A. Galal and B. Hoekman (eds), *Regional Partners in Global Markets: Limits and Possibilities of the Euro-Med Agreements*, Centre for Economic Policy Research, London, 1997.

Nagarajan, N., 'Regionalism and the WTO: New Rules for the Games?', *Economic Papers*, Number 128, European Communities, Brussels, 1998.

Pelkmans, J. and P. Brenton, *Free Trade with the EU: Driving Forces and the Effects of 'Me-Too'*, Center for European Policy Studies, Working Document Number 110, 1997.

Perroni, C. and J. Whalley, *The New Regionalism: Trade Liberalization or Insurance?*, National Bureau of Economic Research, Working Paper Number 4626, 1994.

Rhein, E., 'Europe and the Mediterranean: A Newly Emerging Geopolitical Area?', *European Foreign Affairs Review,* Volume 1, 1996.

Schiff, M., 'Small is Beautiful: Preferential Trade Agreements and the Impact of Country Size, Market Share, and Smuggling,' *Journal of Economic Integration*, Volume 12, 1997.

Schiff, M. and L.A. Winters, 'Dynamics and Politics in Regional Integration Arrangements: An Introduction,' *The World Bank Economic Review*, Volume 12, 1998.

U.S. International Trade Commission, *The Impact of the North American Free Trade Agreement on the U.S. Economy and Industries: A Three-Year Review*, Washington, D.C., Publication 3045, 1997.

Vamvakidis, A., 'Regional Integration and Economic Growth,' *The World Bank Economic Review*, Volume 12, 1998.

Viner, J., *The Customs Union Issue*, Carnegie Endowment for International Peace, New York, 1950.

Wang, Z. K. and L.A. Winters, 'Africa's Role in Multilateral Trade Negotiations: Past and Future,' *Journal of African Economics*, Volume 7, 1998.

Winters, L.A., 'Expanding EC Membership and Association Accords: Recent Experience and Future Prospects,' in: K. Anderson and R. Blackhurst (eds), *Regional Integration and the Global Trading System*, Harvest Wheatsheaf, Hemel Hempstead, 1993.

Winters, L.A., 'Assessing Regional Integration Arrangements,' in: J. Burki and G. Perry (eds), *Trade: Towards Open Regionalism*, The World Bank, Washington, D.C., 1997.

Winters, L.A. and Z. K. Wang, *Eastern Europe's International Trade*, Manchester University Press, Manchester, 1994.

Yeats, A., 'Does the Mercosur's Trade Performance Raise Concerns about the Effects of Regional Trade Arrangements?' *The World Bank Economic Review*, Volume 12, 1998.

Annex 9.A.1. Economic statistics on PTA partners, 1995.

Country	GDP (million US $)	population (million)	GDP/cap (US$)	Imports (million US$) goods and services	goods	services	goods from EU
Iceland	6,980	0.27	25,852	2,237	1,598	639	1,050
Liechtenstein							
Norway	146,602	4.36	33,624	46,984	33,741	13,244	23,325
Total EEA	153,582	4.63	33,171	49,222	35,339	13,883	24,376
Switzerland	306,143	7.04	43,486	95,787	93,916	1,871	63,808
Turkey	172,114	61.64	2,792	41,124	35,187	5,937	16,862
Bulgaria	13,106	8.41	1,558	6,062	5,224	838	2,098
Czech Republic	50,816	10.33	4,919	30,726	25,162	5,564	12,847
Estonia	3,550	1.48	2,399	2,855	2,362	493	1,681
Hungary	44,254	10.22	4,330	16,205	15,297	907	9,515
Lithuania	6,026	3.71	1,624	4,902	3,404	498	1,356
Latvia	4,453	2.51	1,774	2,194	1,947	247	905
Poland	119,053	38.59	3,085	29,252	26,687	2,565	18,782
Romania	35,478	22.68	1,564	11,783	9,487	2,296	5,292
Slovak Republic	17,393	5.36	3,245	10,648	8,820	1,828	3,354
Slovenia	18,744	1.99	9,419	10,395	9,305	1,090	6,513
Total CEEC	312,872	105.28	2,972	125,023	107,696	16,327	62,341
Algeria	41,158	28.06	1,467	12,855	10,250[1]	2,605	6,699
Cyprus	8,788	0.73	12,039	4,414	3,314	1,100	1,910
Egypt Arab Republic	60,433	59.23	1,020	14,681	12,267	2,414	4,563
Malta	3,244	0.37	8,767	3,487	2,671	816	2,139
Jordan	6,646	5.44	1,222	4,905	3,288	1,617	1,227
Lebanon							3,167
Israel	86,731	5.54	15,655	41,867	26,834	15,033	14,717
Morocco	32,985	27.11	1,217	11,331	9,268	2,063	4,321
Syrian Arab Republic	49,153	14.19	3,464	19,297	4,001	15,296	1,620
Tunisia	18,003	8.96	2,009	8,800	7,459	1,342	5,643
Total Med countries	307,141	149.63	2,053	121,638	79,352	42,286	46,006

Table 9.A *(continued)*.

	GDP (million US $)	population (million)	GDP/cap (US$)	Imports (million US$)			
				goods and services	goods	services	goods from EU
Aruba					1,772		
Angola					1,468		1,146
American Samoa							
Antigua and Barbuda	494	0.07	7,052	445	302	143	95
Burundi	1,208	5.98	202	273	176	97	117
Benin	2,009	5.41	371	789	692	97	444
Burkina Faso	2,182	10.20	214	649	549	100	230
Bahamas, The	3,069	0.28	10,962	1,820	1,157	663	651
Belize	587	0.22	2,669	319	231	88	28
Barbados	1,864	0.26	7,170	1,026	691	335	128
Botswana	4,520	1.46	3,096	1,670	1,579	91	
Central African Republic	1,103	3.27	337				93
Cote d'Ivoire	9,993	14.23	702	3,570	2,474	1,096	1,708
Cameroon	8,277	13.28	623	1,608	1,109	499	811
Congo Rep.	2,098	2.59	810	1,429	651	779	267
Comoros	225	0.61	368	103	53	50	103
Cape Verde				287	232	55	211
Djibouti				205			143
Dominica	223	0.07	3,181	144	103	41	40
Dominican Republic	11,801	7.91	1,492	5,885	5,145	740	64
Ethiopia	5,502	56.68	97	1,324	1,137	187	694
Fiji	1,999	0.80	2,499	1,159	761	397	36
Gabon	5,108	1.08	4,730	1,848	899	949	607
Ghana	6,179	17.34	356	2,119	1,688	432	1,105
Guinea				1,014	622	392	
Gambia, the				232	163	69	66
Guinea-Bissau	446	1.07	417	151	59	92	66
Equatorial Guinea	164	0.40	410	196	121	76	
Grenada	276	0.09	3,070	164	125	39	22
Guyana	622	0.83	749	528	537	(9)	103
Haiti	2,329	7.18	324	766	517	248	130
Jamaica	5,251	2.49	2,109	3,529	2,620	909	344
Kenya	9,054	30.52	297	3,503	2,652	850	1,241
St. Kitts and Nevis	231	0.04	5,781	170			28
Liberia							1,809
St.Lucia				394	269	125	142

Table 9.A.1. *(continued).*

	GDP (million US $)	population (million)	GDP/cap (US$)	Imports (million US$) goods and services	goods	services	goods from EU
Lesotho	852	2.03	419	1,036			
Madagascar	3,160	14.87	212	1,002	628	374	273
Mali	2,369	10.79	220	991	755	236	338
Mozambique	1,499	17.42	86	955	705	249	208
Mauritania	1,058	2.28	464	509	293	216	365
Mauritius	3,973	1.09	3,645	2,468	1,812	656	648
Malawi	1,468	9.79	150	625	475	150	95
Mayotte							
Namibia	3,381	1.54	2,195	2,028	1,511	517	
Niger	1,650	9.15	180	369	306	64	173
Nigeria	65,615	111.72	587	7,851	7,230	621	2,858
Papua New Guinea				1,875	1,262	613	75
Reunion							2,175
Rwanda	1,326	5.18	256	398	214	184	83
Sudan	5,253	26.71	197	1,238	1,066	172	390
Senegal	4,437	8.35	531	1,821	1,243	578	654
St. Helena							21
Solomon Islands							5
Sierra Leone	941	4.51	209	177	168	9	119
Somalia							28
Sao Tome and Principe							35
Seychelles	508	0.07	7,259	306	214	92	75
Chad	1,012	6.33	160				104
Togo	1,307	4.08	320	671	386	285	306
Tonga							7
Trinidad and Tobago	5,151	1.26	4,088	2,092	1,868	223	328
Tanzania	5,145	30.34	170	2,140	1,340	800	455
Uganda	6,170	19.26	320	1,280	927	353	265
St.Vincent and the Grenadines	263	0.11	2,387	159	119	39	29
Vanuatu	238	0.17	1,397	130	79	51	11
Samoa	154	0.17	906	115	80	35	2
Congo Dem. Republic	2,609	45.45	57	613	397	216	503
Zambia	3,498	9.37	373	1,433	693	740	174
Zimbabwe	7,637	11.53	662	2,910	2,480	430	539
Total Lomé countries	217,487	537.93	404	72,304	57,011	17,534	24,012

Table 9.A.1. *(continued).*

	GDP (million US $)	population (million)	GDP/cap (US$)	Imports (million US$)			
				goods and services	goods	services	goods from EU
Chile	65,215	14.20	4,593	18,735	14,657	4,078	3,156
Mexico	286,167	90.49	3,162	79,425	72,453	6,972	7,401
Argentina	279,613	34.77	8,042	24,136	18,726	5,410	5,618
Brazil	704,168	155.82	4,519	66,815	49,663	17,152	13,700
Paraguay	8,982	4.83	1,860	4,601	2,797	1,804	343
Uruguay	18,045	3.19	5,657	3,686	2,711	975	598
Total Latin America	1,362,190	303	4,491	197,398	161,007	36,391	30,815
South Africa	130,589	41.24	3,167	33,345	27,128	6,217	13,321
Total	2,962,119	1,211	2,447	735,840	596,636	140,446	281,541

Memorandum item.

	GDP (million US $)	population (million)	GDP/cap (US$)	Exports to non-EU goods (US$m.)
European Union	8,445,699	372	22,696	711,174

Source: Data taken from The World Bank files.

10

THE EU-ACP RELATIONSHIP AFTER LOMÉ

CHRISTOPHER STEVENS

IDS
Brighton
United Kingdom

1. Introduction

It has been conventional for surveys of relations between the European Union (EU) and the Third World to focus on the Lomé Conventions, which link Europe in a trade and aid relationship to a group of countries now totalling 71[1] in Sub-Saharan Africa, the Caribbean and the Pacific, known collectively as the ACP. This focus was natural as Lomé not only represented the largest Union-level aid programme and its most extensive set of preferential trade arrangements, apart from those with the European Free Trade Association (EFTA)/European Economic Area (EEA), but also provided an extensive statement of the objectives of European development co-operation, which was conspicuously lacking in most of the Union's other actions towards developing countries[2].

This exclusive focus on the Lomé Convention is no longer appropriate and may soon be redundant: the EU now has a host of other preferential trade agreements (PTAs), its aid to non-ACP countries has been growing much faster, the Maastricht Treaty provides a broad statement of the aims of development co-operation, and the EU is proposing that the current, fourth, Lomé Convention will be the last. This last point illustrates how far the ACP have sunk in EU

P. van Dijck and G. Faber (eds.), The External Economic Dimension of the European Union, 223–243.
© 2000 *Kluwer Academic Publishers. Printed in the Netherlands.*

interest, and how much the international environment has changed since the first Convention was launched in 1975.

This chapter describes and analyses the evolving relationship between the EU and the ACP, and indicates the probable shape these relations will take in the first decade of the 21st century.

2. Lomé's changing context

At the heart of the EU's declining interest in the ACP is a fundamental change in Europe's economic and political priorities. A change in the structure of Europe's economy has led to a growing disparity between the focus of the formal development policies of the EU and its economic and political interests in the South. At the same time, the collapse of communism to the East and concern with political and demographic patterns in its southern neighbours have refocused political attention closer to home.

Over the past decades there has been a change in the relative importance of various sources for European growth. The distortions caused by the Common Agricultural Policy (CAP) have simply accentuated a trend away from the traditional colonial trade pattern of importing raw materials from the South and exporting manufactures to it. In its place, a trade has developed with parts of the South that emphasizes a two-way flow of manufactures and services. But the ACP are not well represented in this new trade pattern.

Most dynamic partners in the new pattern of trade have been, on the European side, the countries with relatively weak colonial ties, notably Germany and, in the South, the countries of East and South-East Asia. By contrast, formal development policy was fashioned in the 1970s and 1980s largely by the major ex-colonial countries France and the UK, and was focused on the recent colonies, particularly the ACP.

A tension has developed between the focus of formal policy towards the South and the focus of the EU's immediate economic interests. Up to now, the tension has been defused partially as each EU member state has retained control over many of the most potent commercial policy instruments. Export credits, investment promotion, debt rescheduling remain member states' responsibilities. However, as powers are transferred increasingly from national to Union level, this capacity to run an independent shadow policy withers and the emphasis of Union-level policy acquires a direct importance for national interests.

Such changes come at a time when the foundations of the Union's relationship with the South are being eroded. EU officials have managed over the years to fashion with some skill a quasi-foreign policy based on the limited range of Union-level instruments. Trade preferences bulk large in the relationship with the South. However, the value of trade preferences to the beneficiary is related inversely to the level of protectionism, at least if the matter is viewed only in a short-term, static perspective. The 1990s have been a decade of liberalization, reducing the vitality of any preferences. Further, and possibly terminal, erosion looks likely in the next decade.

Hence, the whole edifice built up over the years by the EU is subsiding gently as its foundations are weakened by liberalization. Since this is happening at a time when the pace of European integration is quite fast, it may be expected that a new edifice will be thrown up to replace the old. The Union institutions will acquire a wider range of powers. Among them, no doubt, will be instruments that are of value to the South and may be used to construct a new relationship, such as a common foreign and defence policy. But it does not follow that the new instruments will be used in support of the same objectives - or countries - as the old.

3. EU development co-operation policies and Lomé

When Lomé I was signed in 1975, the Convention stood apart from Europe's other links with developing countries. It provided the coherent policy and administrative framework that was so noticeably absent from other aspects of European-level development co-operation. Its extensive trade preferences created an innovative trade relationship contrasting with most of the rest of European commercial policy. The European Development Funds (EDFs) offered an aid framework that was more substantial in financial terms and more predictable than were the other Community-level aid mechanisms.

With the signing of the Maastricht Treaty, the proliferation of trade agreements, and the inexorable growth of aid funded from the EU budget, these unique features no longer apply. Indeed, elements of the Lomé Convention appear increasingly as an anomaly. The structural split, for example, between aid from the EDF and from the main budget is sidelining many of the world's poorest countries.

The Maastricht Treaty

The Maastricht Treaty has been innovative in establishing policy objectives for Europe's relations with developing countries and in setting out the relative roles of the Union and national tiers of government. Before then, Union-level development co-operation policies had been based on a hotchpotch of arrangements. Some were rooted in powers that had clearly been transferred from the national to the Union level, e.g. trade preferences. For others the justification and objectives of Union-level policy were more obscure, e.g. aid. As a consequence there was insufficient clarity on the relative roles of the Commission and national governments to sustain a coherent Europe-wide strategy of development co-operation. This absence of a general framework for development co-operation gave the full exposition of the Lomé text and its comprehensive set of supporting institutions a considerable importance. This has now changed.

The old regime, based to a significant extent on broad interpretation of clauses in the Treaty of Rome and administrative regulations, was superseded in Maastricht by a clearly defined set of objectives. Title XX of the Treaty (ex Title XVII) establishing the European Community (EC) provides the legal basis for Union-level activities. Art. 177 of the Treaty (ex Art.130u) includes the provision that

'Community policy in the sphere of development co-operation, which shall be complementary to the policies pursued by the member states, shall foster:
- the sustainable economic and social development of the developing countries, and more particularly the most disadvantaged among them;
- the smooth and gradual integration of the developing countries into the world economy;
- the campaign against poverty in the developing countries'.

The phrase 'which shall be complementary' has been taken to imply that development co-operation is not an area in which the principle of subsidiarity is dominant, i.e. aid is not an instrument that must be exercised at either a Union or a national level. On the contrary, the phrase provides legal justification to the view that there are 16 aid programmes, one each for the member states plus one for the Commission. Union-level aid policy is neither superior nor inferior to national policy.

How should these 16 aid programmes relate to one another? Art. 180 of the EC Treaty (ex Art.130x) calls on the 16 to co-ordinate. It specifies that '[t]he Community and member states shall co-ordinate their policies on development co-operation and shall consult each other on their aid programmes, including in international organizations and during international conferences. They may undertake joint action. Member states shall contribute if necessary to the implementation of Community aid programmes'.

Another consequence of the Maastricht Treaty for development co-operation, that is not specifically referred to in Title XX (ex Title XVII), concerns decision-making. Along with other areas of Union decision-making, action on development co-operation can be approved by majority voting in place of the unanimity previously required.

One very important exception to this rule, however, is the EDF. As an extra-budgetary arrangement, unanimity remains the rule. This difference in the structure of decision-making between aid for developing countries funded out of the European budget (majority voting) and out of the EDF (unanimity) has had important policy consequences.

Also excluded from Title XX (ex Title XVII) because they do not concern *developing* countries, and therefore still subject to unanimity, are the provision of economic aid to the countries of Central and Eastern Europe (CEEC) under the PHARE programme and the provision of technical assistance for economic reform and recovery in the former Soviet Union and Mongolia under the TACIS programme.

Variegated trade policy

Just as Lomé is now only one element of the development co-operation policies of the EU, so is it also just a part of a wider trade policy system that has grown up over time and is particularly complex. The criticism that it is difficult to justify under criteria of the World Trade Organization (WTO), as discussed below, is shared with many of the other elements.

The system provides different degrees of preference to various groups of developed and developing countries. The depth and breadth of these preferences are not necessarily related to any objective criteria, such as the level of development of the recipient country. When studying the trade policy of the EU, it may be helpful to distinguish three groups of countries, each of which accounted for approximately one-third of EU imports in 1995.

(1) The most favourable access is made available to the 121 developed, developing and transition countries that are covered by three different types of regime: the Lomé Convention for 70 ACP countries; bilateral agreements that are, or will soon become, reciprocal free-trade areas, with 31 countries, mainly in EFTA, the Mediterranean, CEEC and the Baltics; and the superior tranche of the Generalized System of Preferences (GSP) - the 'Super' GSP - available to nine least-developed countries, the five Andean Community countries and six Central American countries for agricultural products only.

(2) Next come 54 newly industrialized, middle-income and poor countries that benefit only from the standard GSP. Some of these countries have been graduated out of the GSP for some products.

(3) At the base, with the least favourable access, are five industrialized countries that receive *most*-favoured-nation (MFN) treatment by virtue of their WTO membership together with countries that are not members of the WTO but to which the EU offers MFN access autonomously.

4. The effectiveness of Lomé

Trade

At the time of signing, Lomé I was hailed as an innovative form of co-operation that would herald a New International Economic Order, yet the subsequent economic performance of the ACP has been dismal. Has it failed? This is an impossible question to answer, since the ACP's economic performance without Lomé might have been even worse. Nevertheless, it is important to identify what has gone wrong.

The marginalization of the ACP as a trade partner

The trends in trade between the EU and the ACP countries illustrate starkly both the extent of the decline and its implications for a relationship billed when it was negotiated as a 'partnership' of mutual interest. The reasons for this marginalization are such that there is unlikely to be an early return to the *status quo ante*.

A reflection of this changed economic interest is to be found in data on EU import shares as presented in Table 10.1. In 1976, the ACP were the second most important source of EU imports from the five developing country regions covered in the table, with over six per cent of the total. They were second only to the Mediterranean and more important than Latin America, East and South-East Asia, and South Asia. In 1996, by contrast, the ACP were the second least important source of EU imports from these five country groups, and the only group to witness a declining share.

Not only had imports from East and South-East Asia soared ahead, but the ACP had also lost position to Latin America, seen their share decline relative to the Mediterranean, and found South Asia emerging as a much closer competitor.

A similar pattern follows from the shares of EU exports to these five regions, presented in Table 10.2. Again, the ACP have slipped over the period 1976-96 from the second most important to the second least important destination of EU exports, and by 1995 the ACP share was less than half what it had been only a quarter of a century before.

Do preferences work?

One piece of conventional wisdom that is not supported by these data is that there has been an inverse relationship between preferences and trade performance. It is argued that because the ACP, with their substantial preferences, have lost market share whilst the East Asian countries and members of the Association of South East Asian Nations (ASEAN), with modest preferences, have an increased share, the preferences may have had a malign influence. There may be something to such an argument; the data in Tables 10.1 and 10.2 are too limited to undermine it, but it requires a broader perspective if it is to be supported. The ACP are not the only preferred group, and East Asia and ASEAN are not the only less preferred group. If the comparison is between the Mediterranean countries with high preferences and South Asia and Latin America with low preferences, it is not so clear that there is an inverse relationship. The methodological problem with an analysis concentrating on the ACP, East Asia and ASEAN is in disentangling market access from the domestic supply position, for which the two groups are almost complete opposites.

In the absence of a convincing, rigorous analysis, the argument that preferences are malign seems most likely to be correct in relation to the commodity protocols that have made traditional exports to Europe much more attractive than they would be otherwise. However, even if some ACP countries such as the Caribbean have allowed guaranteed high prices in Europe for sugar and bananas to dull their efforts to diversify, it does not follow that this is an automatic malign consequence of preferences. Mauritius has based its impressive export growth on exploiting to

Table 10.1. EU imports from developing regions as percentage shares of extra-EU imports, 1976-96.

	1976	1980	1985	1990	1996
ACP	6.3	7.0	6.6	4.4	3.8
Latin America	5.2	5.1	6.4	5.5	5.2
East Asian NICs/ASEAN[1]	4.5	5.3	5.5	8.3	11.8
Mediterranean	7.6	7.6	10.1	8.7	8.3
South Asia	1.2	1.0	1.1	1.5	2.3

Sources: Calculated from Eurostat, *EEC External Trade (Nimexe) 1976–1987*, Supplement 1 (CD-Rom), Luxembourg, 1991 and Eurostat, *Intra- and Extra-EU Trade (Annual Data - Combined Nomenclature)*, Supplement 2 (CD-Rom), Luxembourg, 1997.

Note[1]: Newly Industrializing Countries/Association of South East Asian Nations.

Table 10.2. EU exports to developing regions as percentage shares of extra-EU exports, 1976-96.

	1976	1980	1985	1990	1996
ACP	6.8	7.1	4.6	4.0	3.0
Latin America	5.2	5.3	3.6	3.8	5.8
East Asian NICs/ASEAN[1]	3.8	4.2	5.0	8.1	13.0
Mediterranean	11.8	12.0	10.8	10.8	11.1
South Asia	1.3	1.7	2.1	2.0	2.1

Sources and note: See Table 10.1.

the full two of the most valuable Lomé preferences: on sugar and on clothing. And Mauritius is not alone.

ACP economic decline

Part of the reason for these dramatic changes is economic mismanagement on the part of some ACP governments, but it is not the only factor. If the problems were just the result of errors in economic policy, then improved economic management might alter fundamentally the direction of change.

The deep-seated element is that the nature of the European economy has changed and will continue to change in ways that affect relative demand for the types of goods that the ACP are currently able to produce. Such changes are manifest in other countries of the Organisation for Economic Co-operation and Development (OECD) as well with the result that the foreign-exchange earnings of ACP countries are falling and, hence, so is their capacity to import.

The relative importance of merchandise trade in European growth is falling and, within merchandised trade, there has been a decline in the relative importance of primary products and an increase in the share of manufactures. The decline in the value of primary trade reflects and, in turn, influences the drastic fall in world prices for most of the ACP's primary exports over the last decade and a half. The declining share of primary products versus manufactures in EU imports is illustrated in Table 10.3. Whereas both shares were more or less equal at the time Lomé I was signed, by 1996 manufactures accounted for two-thirds, and primary products for only one-third of total non-oil imports.

It will come as no surprise to discover that the ACP are more heavily dependent on primary products in their exports to the EU than other developing countries are. Whereas commodities have fallen from over 60 per cent to under 40 per cent of EU imports from all developing countries over the period 1976–96, in the case of the ACP they have declined only marginally and are still around two-thirds, as shown in Table 10.4. The most dramatic decline has been witnessed by ASEAN, but even the Mediterranean countries have seen a substantial change in the commodity composition of their exports to the EU since Lomé I.

Aid

In short, the world has changed dramatically since Lomé I was signed, but the ACP have failed to change with it. In consequence, a relationship that could be described in 1975, with only a certain degree of hyperbole, as a 'partnership of equals' is by now clearly far from such an arrangement. Increasingly, it is a partnership of 'unequals'. Yet, the institutional framework for Lomé reflects its original ethos of equality. The loss of any semblance of equality may explain some of the stresses that are occurring within this framework, particularly in respect of aid.

There has long been criticism of the quality of 'aid administration' at the level of the EU, but it has increased in strength recently. The irony is that the criticism tends to focus on Lomé aid even though this is in general more effectively

Table 10.3. Commodities as percentage shares of
non-oil EU imports, excluding intra-
EU imports, 1976-96.

1976	1980	1985	1990	1996
51.4	45.5	42.7	35.1	31.4

Sources: See Table 10.1.

Table 10.4. Percentage shares of primary products in EU non-oil
imports from selected regions, 1976-96.

	1976	1980	1985	1990	1996
All developing countries	64	58	59	43	36
ACP	79	80	78	62	62
Mediterranean	55	52	46	34	29
ASEAN	73	63	59	37	25

Sources: See Table 10.1.

administered than is aid financed from the EU budget. This oversight - which stems probably from a lack of knowledge about budget aid and from a failure to appreciate its current importance - is unfortunate since the member states have more effective influence over the European Commission in respect of the budget than of the EDF.

Until now, the Commission has been a relatively modest channel for European aid spending. Throughout the period 1970–94 Commission spending was much smaller than total aid spending by the member states - less than 10 per cent -, and it tended to follow the same upward or downward trend as total European aid, since the member states are the ultimate source of all European aid and have various possible spending channels open to them.

At the 1995 Cannes Summit the EU took decisions foreshadowed at the 1992 Edinburgh Council. Their effect was to alter the proportions of the aid given by the European member states that are channelled through Union, multilateral and bilateral institutions, as well as the shares of aid going to Eastern Europe and the former Soviet Union, the Mediterranean countries, and Sub-Saharan Africa. The twin stimuli for the decisions were:

(1) the need to allocate the totals agreed for external spending at the Edinburgh Summit in 1992, and

(2) the requirement to agree the aid allocation for the second half of the ten-year fourth Lomé Convention.

At the December 1992 Edinburgh Council it was agreed that the EU's external spending could rise annually by up to six per cent in real terms for the rest of the decade. The principal candidates for such external expenditure are the economies in transition and some developing countries, principally those in Asia, Latin America and North Africa. The ACP countries are excluded from this increase as their aid is charged not to the budget but to the extra-budgetary EDF.

Although most of Union-level financial aid used to be channelled through the Lomé Convention, this is no longer the case as shown in Table 10.5. In the mid-1980s disbursements of financial aid from the budget were at only half the level of the EDF, but by the early 1990s budget disbursements were at nearly the same level. As the budgetary aid programme has grown, the extra-budgetary nature of the EDF has come increasingly to appear an anomaly. At the 1995 Cannes Council this proved to be a dangerous anomaly for the ACP: the EU used the opportunity created by the division to virtually freeze the level of aid to the ACP and to offset to a certain extent the Edinburgh commitment.

5. Stimuli for changing Lomé

The EU has proposed to continue the Lomé trade provisions only until 2005, and for them then to be replaced either by Regional Economic Partnership Agreements (REPAs) or the GSP. Regardless of whether this objective is achieved, the Lomé preferences are likely to disappear over the next 10–15 years. The first sub-section explains the role that disputes in the General Agreement on Tariffs and Trade (GATT)/WTO have played in the emergence of the REPA concept, why preferences will disappear, and the WTO options; the second sub-section examines the characteristics of the proposed REPAs.

The banana dispute

The proposal to replace Lomé grew out of the EU's discomfiture from the adverse rulings of a series of GATT/WTO dispute panels set up to adjudicate on complaints over its banana regime (for more details, see Stevens, 1996). The problem arose from the difficulty of balancing three sets of demands:

Table 10.5. Main components of disbursed EU aid, in millions
of current US dollars, three-year averages, 1986-88
to 1992-94.

	1986-88	1989-91	1992-94
EDF	1,070	1,500	2,099
Budget excl. food aid	514	950	1,787
Food aid	482	694	598

Source: OECD, European Community, Table 3, Development Co-operation
Review Series Number 12, Development Assistance Committee,
Paris, 1996.

(1) those arising from the changes required for the completion of the Single
European Market;
(2) the Union's treaty obligations under the Lomé Convention, and
(3) its obligations under the GATT/WTO.

The removal of internal trade barriers meant that the EU could not continue
to use its traditional instruments to implement its commitments under the Lomé
Banana Protocol to safeguard the traditional markets of Caribbean and African
producers - primarily in France and the United Kingdom. Instead it established a
new system of implementation involving a two-tier import tariff and licences for
importing companies, designed to allow the Latin American countries to continue
to supply their traditional share of the market while imposing a serious barrier to
attempts to increase their market share at the expense of preferred suppliers.

Five of the aggrieved Latin American exporters lodged complaints in the GATT
and later the USA lodged a complaint in the WTO. The GATT panels ruled in
the Latin American countries' favour. Since the EU had justified its actions in
relation to the Banana Protocol of the Lomé Convention, the panel in these
rulings moved beyond the specific case of bananas to question the GATT-
compatibility of the entire Lomé Convention.

The immediate problem for the Convention was overcome when the EU
obtained a GATT waiver for Lomé IV. But the waiver expires with the current
Convention (in February 2000) and the continuation of the banana dispute, that
has since pitted the EU against the USA, has raised European concern that any
successor arrangement be put on a more secure footing in the WTO.

Preference erosion

The problems experienced with the WTO over Caribbean and African bananas illustrated how difficult it is becoming to protect high-cost ACP producers from international competition. Liberalization will add to these problems. One of the most important Lomé preferences is exemption from the Multi-Fibre Arrangement (MFA). Under the Uruguay Round the MFA will be phased out by the end of 2004.

This will leave just one really important Lomé preference: guaranteed prices under the Protocols for certain temperate agricultural products, and tariff cuts for many others. These are valuable to their ACP beneficiaries only as long as the CAP maintains artificially high prices in Europe. The CAP has withstood many attempts at fundamental reform, but it would be imprudent for the ACP to assume that it will not succumb during the next decade to the concurrent onslaughts of its costs to European consumers and taxpayers, the demands of EU enlargement to the East, and the next Round of WTO negotiations. The remaining 5–10 year 'window of opportunity' must be grasped by as many ACP as possible. After it has closed they will face the harsh winds of global competition in all of their markets.

The requirements of the WTO

Faced with the twin challenges of WTO scrutiny and the decay of traditional preferences, the EU put forward REPAs as a basis for wider-ranging, internationally acceptable partnership more attuned to the 21st century. Since the EU has nailed its REPA flag to the WTO mast, claiming that change is required in order to satisfy the demands of the international community, it is important to understand the basis of such claims. This is not straightforward: assessing the impact of the WTO on the EU–ACP relationship and possible future variants requires a combination of legal and political analysis. Adjudication in WTO disputes relies on a legalistic interpretation of the relevant texts, but the broader issues of what is, and is not, permitted and whether or not complaints are made is a political affair.

The task is to transform Lomé and the EU's other accords so that they can hang on one of the pegs under which members may seek justification for discriminatory treatment of one group of trading countries *vis-à-vis* others (which is what preferences are). These are:

(1) if the countries concerned are creating a free-trade area (FTA) or customs union (CU) covered by Art. XXIV;
(2) if the trade partners are developing countries subject to 'special and differential treatment' covered by the 1979 Enabling Clause, and
(3) if a waiver has been obtained under WTO Art. IX (ex GATT Art. XXV).
Unfortunately all three have their problems.

Art. XXIV

The formal procedure for obtaining WTO approval for a free-trade area is fairly straightforward. Two salient requirements of Art. XXIV are that the free-trade area must be completed 'within a reasonable length of time' (newly defined in the WTO as a period that 'should exceed ten years only in exceptional cases') and that 'duties and other restrictive regulations of commerce ... are eliminated on substantially all the trade between the constituent territories' (GATT, 1947: Part 3, Art. XXIV, paras 5(c) and 8(b); WTO, 1995, p.32). The parties to the agreement should notify the WTO following signature.

The current procedure following the successful completion of a free-trade area is for it to be referred to the WTO Committee on Regional Agreements for consideration. This committee has a large backlog of agreements: it is still assessing accords notified before the completion of the Uruguay Round (and hence subject to GATT rules), and so has not yet begun to establish any guidance for the interpretation of the regulations under the WTO. On past form, it is unlikely to give a straightforward approval or disapproval of any agreement.

In the absence of clear guidance from the Committee, it would still be open to any aggrieved WTO member to file a complaint under the dispute settlement mechanism, as discussed by Mathis in Chapter 6 of this volume. For example, if the USA should consider that the EU–South Africa disadvantages its exporters, it might post a complaint. But this would be risky. There is very little guidance available on how the imprecise words of Art. XXIV are to be interpreted. As the banana dispute has shown, the WTO has given birth to a strong dispute settlement mechanism. Any country launching a complaint would have to weigh up the possible consequences of multilateral trade policy being established in a quasi-judicial framework rather than through inter-governmental negotiation. There could be far-reaching implications from this 'case law', and some of these might rebound on the complainant in unexpected ways.

On the other hand, the USA is not the only country that could lodge a complaint - any WTO member might do so. And not all countries facing trade diversion in either the South African or the EU market will necessarily attach much weight to the danger of a precedent being established. So any accord could be vulnerable to challenge.

In short, it is far from clear what the response in the WTO would be to any post-Lomé REPA, but the reception of the EU–South Africa FTA may show the way. This agreement which has been completed well in advance of the REPAs, is likely to be of such commercial importance for third parties that they will have to consider carefully their reaction to it. Once a precedent has been set, it is likely that it will be applied to less commercially important agreements such as the REPAs.

Special and differential treatment

The main problem with an EU attempt to justify any of its preferential accords other than the standard GSP in relation to the 1979 Enabling Clause is that they do not cover all developing countries. In this respect, therefore, Lomé is no different from the EU's bilateral accords that have not yet been transformed into FTAs and, arguably, the Super GSP, given that it is not limited to a recognized group of especially poor countries.

It would seem impossible to overcome this limitation unless:
(1) the liberality of the Lomé preferences were extended to all countries;
(2) some objectively defensible basis can be identified that justifies enhanced treatment for a group of countries comprised (largely) of the ACP;
(3) ACP access was reduced to the level currently available under the GSP;

The first seems very unlikely, since the EU has given no indication of a political willingness to extend deep preferences to the more competitive, larger developing countries. Any generalization would tend, therefore, to be downward unless the second option proves to be feasible. Only through fairly complex manoeuvres (for example that combine income, vulnerability and size criteria) can a group comprised largely of the ACP be created. The intrinsic 'special pleading' in such a measure might make it vulnerable to challenge in the WTO. A downgrading to the standard GSP would not only erode the ACP's margin of preference, but would also effectively increase the EU's absolute level of protection.

A waiver

The third option is the one adopted by the EU in 1994 to seek a waiver from the MFN rule under WTO Art. IX (ex GATT Art. XXV). A majority of the 28 waivers granted since the inception of GATT have involved preferences granted by developed to developing countries on a non-reciprocal basis. The Marrakesh Agreement has made more onerous the rules for approving a waiver than was the case under GATT (when the Lomé waiver was agreed). The level of support required for approval of a waiver has been increased from a two-thirds majority under the GATT to a 75 per cent majority under the WTO. Nonetheless, the provision is well used. Both the USA and Canada, for example, justify their preference agreements with the Caribbean in this way.

The evolution of WTO rules

Since WTO compatibility represents a problem for any successor to Lomé as well as for several of the EU's other accords, any successful outcome will have to be negotiated. This could take place as part of wider WTO negotiations. The WTO agenda for the next decade is not yet certain, but there are some moves to launch a Millennium Round of negotiations covering a wide range of subjects. It is also possible that some Contracting Parties (CPs) may become alarmed by the genie of dispute settlement uncorked from the bottle of the Uruguay Round. Even if neither of these occur, the WTO members are committed to commence negotiations on agriculture and Trade-Related Aspects of Intellectual Porperty Rights (TRIPs) at the turn of the century, and either of these might involve a dimension that brings into question Art. XXIV, Art. IX, special and differential treatment, and dispute settlement.

One outcome of the Uruguay Round was to begin a process, which many expect to continue, of changing special and differential treatment in relation to developing countries except least-developed countries. The 1996 Ruggiero proposal to 'bind' GSP rates for least-developed countries has taken this evolution of special and differential treatment a step further. It might be most appropriate to consider any reformulation of existing rules to accommodate better North–South preferences in the context of this process of redefinition of special and differential treatment.

6. What might a REPA involve?

Characteristics of REPAs

It is far from clear what will be involved in a REPA, and with whom they would be negotiated. The EU's views have evolved since the idea was unveiled in 1997 (EU Commission, 1997) and, of course, current positions may change during the negotiation of the Framework Agreement. But the following have been mentioned from time to time by the Commission:

(1) a REPA will apply primarily to merchandise trade;
(2) there would be modest, if any, improvements to ACP access to the EU market;
(3) reciprocity would be required of the ACP, but:
(4) it would not need to cover all trade (only 'substantially all');
(5) liberalization would be asymmetrical, with the ACP being able to use *at least* the ten-year time horizon mentioned in the Uruguay Round texts;
(6) the EU's partners would be whichever countries or groups of countries wish to enter into a REPA (i.e. while the EU has a preference for REPAs with groups of ACP countries, the possibility of bilateral deals is not ruled out).

In addition to the uncertainty over the characteristics of a REPA, the task of assessing their potential impact is made more difficult because implementation will overlap with multilateralism as noted above, and pressure may be brought to bear for ACP countries to generalize to other trade partners the liberalization they have agreed with the EU.

Types of effect

With these caveats in mind, the broad effects of a REPA can be identified, as can the factors that are likely to affect both the scale and direction of some effects. Traditional Vinerian trade theory is relevant to this analysis, as is more recent work on the effect of hub-and-spoke models in which investment and competitive advantage tend to be concentrated in the hub, i.e. the EU. But given the considerable uncertainties, it is hard to move far beyond these models to identify, empirically, which of the potential effects is the more likely.

It may be helpful to distinguish analytically between two of the types of effect: the competition effect and the fiscal effect.

The extent to which a REPA increases competition for domestic producers and for other third-party suppliers on the market of the liberalizing country, and hence results in trade creation and diversion, depends upon the extent to which tariff cuts are passed on in the form of lower prices. If there is a substantial price cut, then there *could* be increased competition for domestic producers (resulting in trade creation), and also the possibility of trade diversion from more competitive, but relatively discriminated against, third-party suppliers. But prices might not fall, or might decline by much less than the tariff cut. The extent of the fall will depend partly upon elasticity of supply and partly upon the competitiveness of markets. It is entirely possible to conceive of a situation in which a large part of the tariff cut was absorbed in higher profit margins by elements in the supply chain. This could still result in trade diversion (by making imports more profitable from the EU than from other sources), but it would tend to dampen any effects on domestic production. This, in turn, would mitigate both the adjustment costs of liberalization and the dynamic economic benefits flowing therefrom.

The fiscal effect is more straightforward to identify, although its scale is still uncertain. Governments that rely heavily on tariff revenue will need to find alternative sources of funding following liberalization. Since trade taxes are so commonplace in developing countries precisely because they tend to be the easiest to collect, it follows that alternatives will not necessarily be entirely satisfactory and that in consequence expenditure patterns may also need to be changed.

The scale of both types of effect will be influenced if liberalization within a REPA is extended to others. Such generalization could occur through multilateral trade negotiations, or from other regional agreements, such as the proposed Free Trade Area of the Americas (FTAA), which would involve the Caribbean ACP, or the Trade Protocol of the Southern Africa Development Community (SADC) that envisages free trade in Southern Africa. Or it could result from bilateral leverage by major trading parties to overcome discrimination. For example, the act under which the USA offers preferences to the Caribbean specifically requires the preferences to be withdrawn if the beneficiaries' trade policies discriminate in favour of the USA's competitors.

In any of these cases, broad liberalization would increase the likelihood of prices falling as a result of tariff cuts. This would tend to increase both the competition and fiscal effects. This, in turn, would enhance both the adjustment costs and the ultimate gains attributed by conventional theory to liberalization.

By the same token, the marginal impact of a REPA would be reduced if any of the other sources of liberalization were occurring at the same time. This is an important point, given that REPAs are not expected to result in substantial liberalization by ACP countries until 2010 or thereafter. By this time, it is not unreasonable to expect significant multilateral tariff cuts to have been agreed and regional liberalization to have affected many ACP countries.

7. Conclusion

The last years of the 20th century see the EU's external economic policy towards developing countries in a state of flux, epitomized by the negotiations for a successor to the Lomé Conventions. These negotiations illustrate both the declining importance of recent colonial links and the growing importance of the WTO as a forum for settling trade disputes.

The sharp decline in the economic importance of the ACP to the EU over the quarter century since Lomé I was signed is evident in the negotiations. The Commission's position is that traditional preferences have failed and that a new approach is required. As an increasing number of developing countries indicate an interest in FTAs with the EU, the constituency in support of old-style non-reciprocity has declined.

The catalyst that provoked a change in policy was the GATT/WTO banana dispute. An issue that was of minor trade importance to the EU (although not to the ACP) has produced acrimony and sabre rattling with its most important trade partner, the USA, and is not yet resolved. It has brought into question other areas of EU trade policy.

It has become clear that economically unimportant trade partners can provoke very important problems of trade diplomacy. Such a situation is inherently unstable. The EU's approach to negotiating a successor to Lomé indicates that it proposes to resolve the instability by altering its relationship with the ACP to reduce the danger of such problems being created in the future.

Notes

[1] Only 70 countries benefit from the Lomé trade and aid regimes; South Africa, the 71st member, does not.

[2] The appropriate European terminology has changed over the period covered by this chapter. For the sake of simplicity, the term 'Community' is used in references that clearly relate to the more distant past, while the term 'Union' is used for the current and more recent periods. The acronym 'EU' is used throughout, even for periods when 'EC' was the correct term.

References

EU Commission, *Green Paper on Relations between the European Union and the ACP Countries on the Eve of the 21st Century: Challenges and Options for a New Partnership*, Luxembourg, 1997.

GATT, 'The General Agreement on Tariffs and Trade', in: WTO, *The Results of the Uruguay Round of Multilateral Trade Negotiations: The Legal Texts*, Geneva, 1995.

OECD, 'European Community', *Development Co-operation Review Series Number 12,* Development Assistance Committee, Paris, 1996.

Stevens, C., 'EU Policy for the Banana Market: the External Impact of Internal Policies', in: W. Wallace and H. Wallace (eds), *Policy Making in the EU*, Oxford University Press, Oxford, 1996.

WTO, *The Results of the Uruguay Round of Multilateral Trade Negotiations. The Legal Texts*, Geneva, 1995.

11

TOWARDS A PAN-EUROPEAN-MEDITERRANEAN FREE TRADE AREA?

GERRIT FABER[1]

Economic Institute
Utrecht University
Utrecht
The Netherlands

1. Introduction

The European Union (EU) is rapidly changing the nature of its relationships with neighbouring countries. After the dismantling of the Iron Curtain, new co-operation agreements with Central and Eastern European Countries (CEEC) were concluded that were succeeded by Europe Agreements (EAs) in the first half of the 1990s. These agreements have the objective of creating free-trade areas (FTAs) in a period of ten years of time. Full membership of the EU is the ultimate objective of these countries. Most countries in the Middle East and North Africa (MENA) have long-standing, preferential relations with the EU. Here as well, the EU is changing the nature of the relationship towards the creation of reciprocal FTAs. Some of these countries have the possibility of becoming full members of the EU.

The EU's relationships with neighbouring third countries develop gradually. Two new aspects are becoming visible. First, reciprocity is a guiding principle in the new agreements. Second, the new bilateral agreements could eventually be merged into one integrated FTA. If all agreements and plans in this regard will be

P. van Dijck and G. Faber (eds.), The External Economic Dimension of the European Union, 245–269.
© 2000 *Kluwer Academic Publishers. Printed in the Netherlands.*

fully implemented in the coming decade, a large Pan-European-Mediterranean Free Trade Area (PAMEFTA) will come into existence with more than 750 million inhabitants living in 35 or more countries.

This trade arrangement will have large political effects as the core group - the present EU - will have a strong influence on the organization of society in the neighbouring countries, since the present generation of FTAs and the preparation for full EU membership involves much more than merely the abolition of border measures that hamper trade in goods. The integration agreements include also the liberalization of trade in services, the free flow of persons and capital, the adoption of EU product norms and standards and (parts of) common policies and the approximation of regulations in many areas. This aspect makes regional integration an instrument of liberalization that is more effective than multilateral liberalization under certain conditions. In state-managed economies, governments face severe problems in introducing and maintaining policy reforms to liberalize the economy. Unilateral steps taken in a non-discriminatory way, can easily be reversed as the pain is felt immediately and the benefits from liberalization only show up after some time, while external sanctions are weak or absent. Although the economic gains from regional integration may not exceed the gains from multilateral liberalization and probably will be smaller, the regional approach may have more leverage to ensure that policy reforms are not reversed (Fernández and Portes, 1998).

With the exception of the member countries of the European Free Trade Association (EFTA), EU's neighbours are or will be in a process of policy reform required from the perspective of long-term welfare growth. A successful growth performance is not only required to improve welfare in these countries, but is also a necessary condition for a harmonious and peaceful relationship between the EU and its neighbours. The merging of the bilateral FTAs into one comprehensive zone of liberalized economic interaction would enlarge the static and dynamic gains from integration.

This chapter addresses the question which conditions will have to be met to realize a PAMEFTA, and which problems will have to be dealt with in the integration process. As these conditions and problems are mainly present in the relations with the CEEC and MENA countries, the chapter will not devote much attention to the relations with the EFTA countries. The topic will be addressed in the following manner. To start with, the economic situation of the neighbouring groups of countries, and particularly the prospects for development and growth in the CEEC and the MENA countries will be reviewed in the next section. Section 3 gives an overview of the changing contractual relationships with the neighbouring countries. Different aspects of the potential PAMEFTA are analysed in subsequent sections: approximation and harmonization of regulation in Section 4, hub-and-spoke complications in Section 5, political shocks and economic integration in Section 6, and the 'locking in' of structural adjustment in Section 7. The final section brings together the major conclusions[2].

2. Economic condition of the EU's neighbours

Economic development and political stability are necessary conditions for the harmonious development of relationships between the EU and its neighbours. To clarify the type of problems that have to be addressed in order to create prosperity in the region, a brief review will be presented of the actual economic situation of these countries.

The neighbouring countries of the EU can be subdivided into three groups: the industrialized European countries that have chosen not to become full members of the EU - Iceland, Liechtenstein, Norway, and Switzerland - the CEEC and the MENA group. Table 11.1 shows that levels of welfare in neighbouring countries are far below the average level of high-income countries, with the notable exception of the EFTA countries. In many CEEC and MENA countries gross national product per capita measured at purchasing-power-parity prices (GNP PPP per capita) is less than 25 per cent of the EU level. However, there are large variations in income per capita in both groups of countries. Israel has a much higher level of income per capita than Egypt has, and the same holds for Slovenia and Albania.

Table 11.1 also shows that the recent economic growth performance of the CEEC and MENA countries has been far from impressive. While annual average growth of GNP per capita in the low and middle-income countries in East Asia and the Pacific was nearly 10 per cent during the period 1990-97, the EU's neighbouring countries recorded much lower growth rates and many experienced even negative growth. There may be specific explanations for these low growth rates including the breakdown of Comecon and the central planning system of many of its former member countries, and the economic consequences of the Gulf War, but that does not diminish the need for substantially higher rates of growth to bridge the gap with the EU.

Table 11.1. GNP per capita measured at PPP, in US dollars, in EU's neighbouring countries in 1997, and average growth rates of GDP per capita, in percentages, 1980-90 and 1990-97.

	GNP-PPP per capita	growth rates of GDP per capita	
		1980-90	1990-97
Egypt	2,940	5.3	3.9
Morocco	3,130	4.2	2.0
Syria	2,990	1.5	6.9
Jordan	3,430	2.6	7.2
Algeria	940	2.8	0.8
Tunisia	4,980	3.3	4.8
Lebanon	5,990	78.2	8.3
Turkey	6,430	5.3	3.6
Israel	16,960	3.5	6.4
Albania	..	1.5	1.8
Bulgaria	3,860	4.0	-3.5
Romania	4,290	0.5	0.0
Lithuania	4,510	..	-4.5
Latvia	3,650	..	-10.7
Poland	6,380	1.8	3.9
Estonia	5,010	2.1	-4.3
Slovak Republic	7,850	2.0	0.4
Czech Republic	11,380	1.7	-1.0
Hungary	7,000	1.6	-0.4
Slovenia	12,520	..	..
Norway	23,940	2.8	3.9
Switzerland	26,320	2.2	-0.1
EU*	19,964	..	..

Note: * Excluding Luxembourg
Source: The World Bank, World Development Report 1998/99, Oxford University Press, Oxford, 1998.

This does not apply to the remaining EFTA countries and from many perspectives they may even be considered ideal neighbours. They share with the EU a highly developed market economy and a stable political system, and EFTA countries enjoy levels of income per capita considerably higher than in the EU. They were in a position to accede to the EU, but have opted for free-trade agreements (FTAs).

The other two groups of neighbouring countries are very different in many respects. Since the end of the 1980s, both the CEEC and MENA countries have been in a process of restructuring their economies in order to stimulate economic growth and employment. Apart from similarities, there were significant differences between the two groups of countries at the moment they started reforms. The level of state intervention was high in both groups, particularly so in the CEEC countries. The CEEC had reached a higher level of industrialization and human-capital formation than the MENA countries. In addition, the CEEC applied very low tariff rates at the start of the reforms, contrary to many MENA countries that are dependent on import tax revenues to a large extent (Hoekman, 1995). As a result, trade liberalization will necessitate the expansion of the tax base of the economies concerned.

Prospects for high growth rates of income per capita depend on the quality and quantity of available resources. The growth rate of population in the MENA countries is much higher – over two per cent - than in the CEEC - less than one per cent and in some countries even negative - which necessitates a much higher rate of growth of employment in the former group. However, the low rate of population growth of the CEEC is linked with a rapidly rising share of pensioners in total population which may retard economic growth. The level of training and education of the labour force in the CEEC is high as compared with the MENA group, as Tables 11.2 and 11.3 show. Adult illiteracy rates in most North African countries are high, particularly so for females. In the CEEC, illiteracy rates are very low and secondary school-enrolment rates are 80 per cent or more, significantly higher than in many MENA countries, particularly so for females. These differences in the availability and accumulation of human capital play an important role in the competition between the two regions for exports of processed products. The exclusive advantages of proximity and access to the European market that the MENA countries used to have, is now shared with the CEEC. Additionally, wage differentials between the two groups are relatively small in view of the differences in human-capital availability, which gives the CEEC a competitive advantage relative to the MENA group in many processing industries.

It is generally recognized that foreign direct investment (FDI) is a crucial factor in the development process of both the CEEC and the MENA countries as they

Table 11.2. School enrolment and illiteracy rates in the MENA
countries, 1993 and 1995.

	secondary school enrolment as % of age group		adult illiteracy rate(%)	
	female	male	female	male
Egypt	69	81	61	36
Morocco	29	40	69	43
Syria	42	52	44	14
Jordan	54	52	21	72
Algeria	55	66	51	26
Tunisia	49	55	45	21
Lebanon	78	73	10	5
Turkey	48	74	28	8
Israel	91	84	..	..

Source: The World Bank, World Development Report 1997, Oxford University
Press, Oxford, 1997.

bring in new productive capacity, technologies and marketing channels. Table 11.4 shows the flows of FDI to the two groups of countries during the period 1985-96. The MENA countries attracted larger amounts of FDI than the CEEC during the period 1985-90 but in more recent years the situation has been reversed dramatically. At present, the CEEC attract an inflow of FDI almost double the amount attracted by the MENA countries. In the two regions, a few countries attract the bulk of investment: Turkey and Israel in the Mediterranean Basin and the Czech Republic, Hungary and Poland in the CEEC. In relative terms as well, the FDI in the CEEC are more significant than in the MENA countries. In 1995, FDI accounted for less than 1 per cent of GDP in all MENA countries except Israel (1.7 per cent); whereas this share was as high as 10 per cent in Hungary, nearly 6 per cent in the Czech Republic, 5 per cent in Estonia and 3 per cent in Poland and Latvia. It can be concluded that the level of FDI in most MENA countries is small compared to other developing countries and in relation to their capital needs[3]. In addition, most FDI in the CEEC are concentrated in services and manufacturing; while in the MENA group, a substantial share of FDI is allocated in capital-intensive development of natural resources, including fossil

Table 11.3. Secondary school enrolment in
the CEEC, as a percentage share
of the age group, 1993.

	female	male
Albania	..	..
Bulgaria	70	66
Romania	82	83
Lithuania	79	76
Latvia	90	84
Poland	87	82
Estonia	96	87
Slovak Republic	90	87
Czech Republic	88	85
Hungary	82	79
Slovenia	90	88

Source: The World Bank, *World Development Report 1997*,
Oxford University Press, Oxford, 1997.

fuels and pipelines[4]. Foreign investment is complementary to domestic savings and investment and in order to attain high growth rates, gross domestic investment rates should approach 25 to 30 per cent of GDP (Fischer, et al., 1996). As shown in Tables 11.5 and 11.6, some countries have realized these investment rates in 1995, including Romania, Estonia, the Slovak Republic, the Czech Republic, Algeria and Turkey. Not only the investment rates of the other countries are alarmingly low, but also gross domestic savings rates of many countries in the regions are low - below 20 per cent - and particularly so in MENA countries. This reflects the urgency of structural reforms in the countries concerned in order to attain long-run growth rates sufficiently high to narrow the welfare gap with the EU.

In terms of international trade with the EU, the CEEC have been very dynamic. Their exports to the EU increased from 23.7 billion ECU in 1990 to 50 billion ECU in 1996. Exports from the Mediterranean Basin to the EU amounted to 44.3 and 49.5 billion ECU in the same years. In the same period, exports from the EU to the CEEC increased from 24 to 71 billion ECU and to the countries in the Mediterranean Basin from 61.5 to 73 billion ECU. Thus, the

Table 11.4. Foreign direct investment in the MENA countries and in the CEEC, in millions of US dollars, 1985-96.

	1985-90	1991	1992	1993	1994	1995	1996*
MENA	1,973	2,175	3,224	3,182	3,762	4,045	5,019
North Africa	1,285	886	1,582	1,679	2,364	1,265	1,633
Turkey	340	810	844	636	608	885	1,116
Israel	155	350	539	580	442	1,525	2,015
Others	193	211	259	287	348	360	358
CEEC	449	2,448	3,520	5,362	5,059	11,963	9,956
Hungary	345	1,462	1,479	2,350	1,144	4,519	1,982
Poland	26	291	678	1,715	1,875	3,659	5,196
Czech Republic**	77	600	1,103	654	878	2,568	1,200
Others	1	95	260	643	1,162	1,217	1,578

Notes: * Estimated
      ** Before 1993: former Czechoslovakia
Source: UN, *World Investment Report,* New York, 1997

two groups have similar shares in the external trade of the EU: approximately 11 per cent of exports and 8.5 per cent of imports. If this pace will continue in the future, the CEEC will occupy a much more important position in the external trade of the EU in a few years time. Figures 11.1 and 11.2 offer an overview of changes in these shares in the long term. The EU has a persistent trade surplus with both groups of countries which amounted to 21 billion ECU with the CEEC in 1996 and to 23 billion ECU with the MENA countries (Eurostat, 1997). A segment of CEEC trade with the EU that has grown in particular is the outward-processing trade, and in 1994 the share of the CEEC in the total outward-processing trade of the EU had increased to 37 per cent (Henriot and Inotai, 1997 and Kawecka-Wyrzykowska, 1996).

It may be concluded that both groups of countries have a long way to go before their levels of income per capita approach the average level of the EU. As average rates of savings and investment and educational levels of the labour force are higher in CEEC than in MENA countries, their prospects for catching up with the EU are better than for most MENA countries. However, even under the assumption of the right macroeconomic policies, it would take a country like Poland almost two decades to reach the average income level of the poorer EU member states.

Table 11.5. Gross domestic savings and investment as percentage shares of GDP in the MENA countries, 1995.

	savings	investment
Egypt	6	17
Morocco	13	21
Syria	..	..
Jordan	3	26
Algeria	29	32
Tunisia	20	24
Lebanon	- 22	29
Turkey	20	25
Israel	13	24

Source: The World Bank, *World Development Report 1997*, Oxford University Press, Oxford, 1997.

Table 11.6. Gross domestic savings and investment as percentage shares of GDP in the CEEC, 1995.

	savings	investment
Albania	- 8	16
Bulgaria	25	21
Romania	21	26
Lithuania	16	19
Latvia	16	21
Poland	18	17
Estonia	18	27
Slovak Republic	30	28
Czech Republic	20	25
Hungary	21	23
Slovenia	21	22

Source: The World Bank, *World Development Report 1997*, Oxford University Press, Oxford, 1997.

Figure 11.1. Shares of the CEEC and MENA countries in EU
external imports, in percentages, 1960-96.

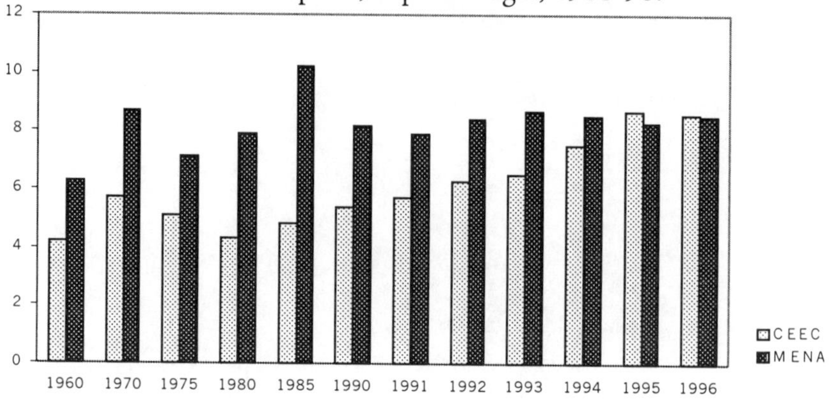

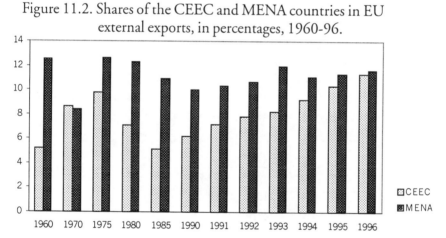

Source: Eurostat, *External and Internal Intra-European Union Trade Statistical
Yearbook 1958-1996,* Luxembourg, 1997.

Figure 11.2. Shares of the CEEC and MENA countries in EU
external exports, in percentages, 1960-96.

Source: Eurostat, *External and Internal Intra-European Union Trade
Statistical Yearbook 1958-1996,* Luxembourg, 1997.

3. Changing relationships

European Economic Area

Formal links between the EU and EFTA have been at a very low profile for a
long period of time. After the entry of Denmark, Ireland and the United Kingdom

Table 11.7. Countries with Europe Agreements.

	date of signing	date of application for full membership
Hungary	16 December 1991	31 March 1994
Poland	16 December 1991	5 April 1994
Czech Republic	4 October 1993	17 January 1996
Slovak Republic	4 October 1993	27 June 1995
Bulgaria	8 March 1993	14 December 1995
Romania	1 February 1993	22 June 1995
Estonia	12 June 1995	24 November 1995
Latvia	12 June 1995	13 October 1995
Lithuania	12 June 1995	8 December 1995
Slovenia	10 June 1996	10 June 1996

into the Community, bilateral FTAs for industrial products were negotiated by the EU and individual EFTA countries. The Single European Market project boosted the relationship with EFTA. In order to bring about free trade in the EFTA-EU region, EFTA had to accept large parts of the Internal Market programme (Maresceau and Montaguti 1995). This was laid down in 1991 in the Agreement on the European Economic Area (EEA). The most important characteristics of the EEA are:

(1) a free trade area for industrial products; as a result, the members of the EEA have their own trade policy *vis-à-vis* third countries;
(2) the harmonization of technical barriers to trade by adoption of EC norms and standards;
(3) liberalization of trade in services;
(4) full application of EC law in the area of competition law and other EC regulations, e.g. the protection of intellectual property rights;
(5) some areas have not been included in the EEA agreement, particularly agriculture, fisheries and the movement of labour.

The accession to the EU of Austria, Sweden and Finland has diminished the economic importance of EFTA considerably. Norway, Iceland and Liechtenstein are the remaining partners of the EC in the EEA, and Switzerland has a bilateral agreement with the EU that covers an FTA for industrial products and elements of the EEA.

Although the EEA is not very important for the EC in terms of trade flows, it is an interesting model in which the EC shapes its relations with neighbouring countries that do not or cannot become full members in the short run.

Eastern Europe

After the breakdown of the communist regimes in the CEEC, the reduction of trade barriers between these countries and the EU was accelerated and complemented with co-operation in many other areas. The EAs constitute the formal framework of this co-operation that will lead to FTAs in industrial products and ultimately will result in full membership of the EU. All countries with a EA have applied for membership of the Community as shown in Table 11.7. The European Council of Luxembourg decided in 1997 that the Czech Republic, Estonia, Hungary, Poland and Slovenia constitute the group with which the negotiations for membership should be opened.

As indicated above, the EAs provide for FTAs in industrial goods in ten years of time. For textiles, clothing and steel, free access to the EU was backloaded. At the beginning of 1998 the EU lifted tariffs and quotas for these products but safeguards may be introduced (Maresceau and Montaguti 1995, p. 1354). With respect to agricultural products, the EU and the partner country concerned will examine 'product by product' the possibilities of granting each other further concessions. Free trade is not the objective in this sector. However, in order to prepare the countries for complete membership, the agreements go well beyond the creation of FTAs for goods. First, improved reciprocal market access for services, workers and capital is covered as well. Second, in order to facilitate the liberalization of the circulation of goods, services, persons and capital, economic regulation in many areas in the countries concerned will be adapted to Community level. This applies for competition policy, government procurement, the protection of intellectual property rights and technical norms and standards.

In addition to the obligations following from the agreements, the CEEC will have to introduce the EC common policies before becoming full members. At present, a relatively large share of the CEEC population is employed in the agricultural sector at relatively low levels of productivity. A painful restructuring will have to take place before the CAP can be introduced. The CEEC are losing market shares, mainly to the EU, in their domestic markets and in the former

Table 11.8. Agreements between the EU and the MENA countries.

Country and date of signing	description of the agreement
Turkey (12 December 1963)	CU in three stages; last stage in force since 31-12-1996; possibility of membership; applied for membership on 14 April 1987
Cyprus (19 December 1963)	CU in two phases; applied for full membership on 4 July 1990
Malta (December 1970)	CU in two stages; applied for full membership on 16 July 1990
Tunisia (25 April 1976, 17 July 1995 respectively)	co-operation agreement with non-reciprocal trade preferences; new association agreement with free trade area
Israel (11 May 1975, 20 November 1995 respectively)	co-operation agreement with reciprocal free trade; new association agreement with free trade area
Morocco (27 April 1976, 15 November 1995 respectively)	co-operation agreement with non-reciprocal trade preferences; new association agreement with free trade area
Egypt (18 January 1977)	co-operation agreement with non-reciprocal trade preferences; association agreement with free trade area under negotiation
Jordan (18 January 1977, September 1997)	idem Morocco
Lebanon (18 January 1977)	idem Egypt
Algeria (26 April 1976)	co-operation agreement with non-reciprocal trade preferences; Barcelona declaration
Syria (18 January 1977)	idem Algeria

Soviet Union, their traditional markets (Henriot and Inotai, 1997, p. 190). A second demanding challenge will be to bring the environmental policies and practices of the East European countries up to EC standards. The same applies for areas such as consumer protection and measures to ensure health and safety at the workplace. The Commission published a White Paper on the approximation of laws and regulations in these countries that is required for full membership (Commission of the EC, 1995). The implementation of these new policies will require large amounts of money to invest in new capital equipment that embody cleaner and healthier technologies and to clean up the pollution of the past. It has been estimated that the costs involved in the introduction of the new equipment and in the harmonization of policies and legislation may well exceed 300 billion ECU (Ludlow, 1996).

Apart from a considerable renewal of public law, a transparent body of private law and a reliable judiciary are vital for the transition towards an 'EU style' mixed economy. Indeed, before the Eastern European states can become members of the EU, their economic systems and large parts of their laws and regulations must be modelled according to the EU system and perform satisfactorily[5]. This pre-accession situation resembles the EEA except for one big difference: the gap between the initial and the desired situation is very large in the case of the CEEC.

The Barcelona process

The relationships with MENA countries have always been of a rather diverse nature. Turkey, Cyprus and Malta have been promised long ago to become full members, be it at an unspecified moment in the future. The EC has concluded agreements for customs unions (CUs) with Turkey, Cyprus and Malta. In the 1970s, co-operation agreements have been concluded with the other countries in the region. The most important part of these agreements were the chapters on non-reciprocal trade preferences for access to the EC market. Israel has an agreement with reciprocal trade preferences. Moreover, the countries concerned have received financial assistance from the EU as well. Table 11.8 gives an overview of these relations.

In November 1995, a Euro-Mediterranean conference took place where the EU and the Mediterranean countries, including the Palestinian Authority, formulated the Barcelona Declaration, which gives new directions and creates new instruments for the EU Mediterranean policy (Rhein, 1996). In order to create an area of peace, stability, security, shared prosperity and mutual understanding, principles related to human rights, democracy and the rule of law are presented as guiding notions. The economic co-operation includes an FTA - involving the EU and all Mediterranean partners - co-operation in many policy areas and increased financial assistance by the EU. The amount of aid made available by the EU for the period 1995-99 amounts to nearly five billion ECU, and is explicitly aimed at facilitating structural reforms of the economies concerned[6].

The new approach is in the process of implementation and new 'Barcelona type' agreements have been concluded with Morocco, Israel, Tunisia and Jordan. Negotiations are under way with the other MENA countries. These new agreements can be characterized as bilateral FTAs including the liberalization of services and capital markets and the harmonization and approximation of economic regulation. Trade liberalization involves all industrial product and selected agricultural products. Given the non-reciprocal preferences already in existence, market access for the MENA countries improves only slightly, while the EC will get free access to the markets of the MENA countries (Aghrout and Alexander 1997; Hoekman 1995). The MENA countries will adopt many regulations that are common in the EU including competition policy, protection of intellectual property rights, technical norms and standards for products, rules for public procurement and rules for the financial sector. Co-operation in the area of the environment is aimed at sustainable development and the protection of human health. A general article indicates that approximation of legislation is necessary which will bring legislation of the country concerned 'closer to that of the Community'[7].

A Pan-European-Mediterranean FTA ?

It could be concluded from this brief overview that the EU is in the process of establishing a comprehensive FTA extending from the North Cape to the Sahara and from Central Europe to the Atlantic Ocean. Such a Pan-European-Mediterranean FTA (PAMEFTA) would have a population of 750 million, twice the size of the EU of 15 member states. The total GDP of this FTA would be about 15 per cent larger than the present GDP of the EU of 15 member states. This indicates a relatively small increase in purchasing power in the short run but a huge potential for increased welfare and demand in the longer run.

The next sections will deal with a number of conditions that have to be fulfilled before this PAMEFTA can become operational. These conditions range from rather technical reforms such as the adaptation of national regulation and the introduction of a unified set of rules of origin to the locking in of economic and political reforms in the neighbouring countries.

4. Approximation and harmonization of regulation

At the start of the European Community, a CU was established mainly by abolishing border measures among the member states. The Common Agricultural Policy (CAP) was the main exception. In those days, regional trade arrangements in the form of FTAs between the EU and third countries were relatively simple to introduce, particularly if trade in agricultural products was excluded. By abolishing import tariffs and measures having equivalent effects, free trade could be established. New members could accede by eliminating their tariffs and quantitative restrictions and adopting a fairly limited number of EC regulations. Periods of transition after accession enabled a smooth implementation of the *acquis communautaire*. Transition periods could be implemented as internal borders remained in place, thus enabling the new members to align agricultural prices in a gradual way and to introduce the free entry of Community suppliers in a phased manner. At the same time, the new members were restricted in their entry into the Common Market until the end of the transition period.

Since then, the integration process has been extended to include capital, persons and services. The ongoing process of economic integration and the growth in the number of areas of common policies has given rise to an ever larger quantity of regulation at the level of the EU. To bring about an integrated market without internal borders, regulations in many areas have to be harmonized. Consequently, the number of common policies has increased and market regulations by member states are increasingly constrained by EU rules.

The widening and deepening of the integration process have severe consequences for countries entering into regional free-trade arrangements with the EU. First, third countries that conclude FTAs with the EU will have to adopt a relatively large part of EU regulation into their national legislation. Obviously, candidates for full membership must apply the full body of EU rules and policies. The EEA Treaty has extended the Internal Market with all its procedures and harmonization to the countries concerned, despite the fact that the EEA is only an FTA in technical terms. In the framework of the Barcelona process the same approximation of laws of the MENA countries is planned to take place as indicated above, be it at a much slower pace. The second consequence is that a large part of the approximation of policies and regulations and the structural adjustment to the competition from the EU suppliers has to take place *before* a country accedes to the EU. As a result of the completion of the Internal Market, internal borders in the EU have vanished and new members fully enter into the Internal Market at the date of entry. For third countries having FTAs with the Community, there is not such a strict necessity to adopt the complete *acquis communautaire*, as borders between the EU and the FTA remain. However, it is very likely that there will be a link between the degree of approximation of the legislation of the third country to the Community level and the degree of free entry into the Internal Market. E.g., there is a correspondence between anti-dumping measures and competition policy. If a third country adopts and implements EU competition policy while there is reciprocal free access to markets, dumping is impossible. Price differences will give rise to arbitrage and to establishment of new competitors in markets where prices are high. Technical norms and standards constitute another illustration. If a third country does not use EU norms and standards or does not have test and certification procedures acknowledged by the EU, problems may arise at the entry of its products and services into the Internal Market, resulting in non-tariff barriers (NTBs).

Since the present candidates for full membership and for FTAs with the EU have economic systems and levels of welfare that are relatively far removed from the EU average, it will take a long time and many difficult political decisions before the Internal Market regime will be applied all over the Pan-European-Mediterranean region. It is only after this has been realized that PAMEFTA can come into practice.

5. Hub-and-spoke complications

A PAMEFTA does not only depend on the abolishment of tariffs and quantitative restrictions, and a sufficient harmonization and approximation of regulation of each individual partner country. The fact that this FTA consists of a large number of bilateral agreements with the EU gives rise to a hub-and-spoke system, with the EU being the hub and the neighbouring countries the spokes. In such a system there is no trade liberalization between the spokes. An additional complicating factor are the rules of origin which determine whether a product is deemed to originate from the FTA and is treated preferentially. Such rules are not required in a CU as all members apply a common external commercial policy. The EU has inserted rules of origin in all the agreements with neighbouring countries. Hub-and-spoke systems produce suboptimal economic and political results. Trade deflection and a lower level of specialization according to comparative advantages in the EU's partners in the East and South will limit the static and dynamic welfare effects of trade liberalization.

Major steps have been taken to merge some spokes into blocs: the Central European Free Trade Area (CEFTA), concluded in 1992, is to bring about free trade among the Czech Republic, Hungary, Poland and the Slovak Republic. However, CEFTA did not create a CEFTA-EU Free Trade Area, as CEFTA did not adopt the EU rules of origin (Enders and Wonnacott, 1996, pp. 258-59). However, the EU has reduced the negative effect of the hub-and-spoke system by including the possibility of cumulation of origin for all CEFTA countries. A Baltic Free Trade Area (1993) will do the same. An important step has been made with the agreement on Pan-European Cumulation between EU and CEEC, EFTA and EU, and EFTA and CEEC, leading to the same rules of origin in the countries concerned. Full implementation of this agreement will take away the NTBs resulting from differences in rules of origin and lack of cumulation of origin. The rules of origin as such remain barriers that hamper trade between the Pan-European FTA and third countries.

A comparable situation occurs in the MENA region. There are or will be bilateral FTA agreements between the EU and individual MENA countries but there is no trade liberalization among the MENA countries. The Barcelona Declaration calls for integration among all parties. At present, there is an initiative to liberalize trade among the Maghreb countries. An FTA among Israel and its Arab neighbours may have economic and political benefits if its introduction runs parallel to the FTAs concluded with the EU (Tovias, 1997). Generally speaking, there is little trade among MENA countries and one may question whether this volume would be much larger in case of full integration into a Mediterranean-EU FTA. In any case, increased competition among the spokes would improve the efficiency of the economies concerned, and thus have long term beneficial effects (Ekholm c.s., 1996). The new association agreements with Maghreb countries specify that the EU will cumulate origin over Algeria, Morocco and Tunisia under the condition that these countries agree on rules of origin for their mutual trade that are similar to the rules in use in their trade with the EU. In this way, the failure of the CEFTA members to establish a genuine EU-CEFTA FTA at an early date is less likely. In addition, the EU has declared that it will consider cumulation of origin between the MENA country concerned and a third Mediterranean country if the two agree to create free trade[8]. Cumulation of origin between EFTA, CEEC and a MENA economy, a necessary condition for PAMEFTA, is not accepted by the EU (Tovias, 1997, p. 21).

It may be concluded that the merging of the bilateral FTAs between the EU and its neighbouring countries is now well under way as far as the European part is concerned. Full membership will integrate the spokes into the hub as this implies a Common Commercial Policy (CCP). By merging earlier, the spokes could reap some benefits of full membership before they actually accede to the EU. For the MENA countries, the liberalization of trade among themselves and the adoption of the same rules of origin is necessary to abolish the hub-and-spoke pattern. Given the generally low priority of economic integration in the MENA region itself at present, this is not likely to occur in the short term. Eventually, the EU will have to accept that the logic consequence of its present policies is a PAMEFTA with similar rules of origin in every member state and with accumulated origin throughout the region[9].

6. Political shocks and economic integration

There is a close relationship between politics and economic integration. Economic integration often serves political objectives. In the case of Europe this has often been observed. The European Coal and Steel Community (ECSC) and the EEC have been created for political reasons. In fact, the Second World War and the ensuing Cold War created the conditions that made economic integration among the Six desirable for both the Western European countries and the Western world at large. The enlargement of the EU towards the East is the consequence of a political turnaround in the candidate member states. The demise of the communist order enabled - and forced - the countries concerned to change their political and economic system in a radical way. A return to the days of old was and is impossible. As economic co-operation in Comecon broke down, it was almost impossible to shift reforms into the future. Integration into the EU was attractive not only because of market access, but also for reasons of capital flows and financial support from the EU. More importantly, integration is linked to democratic systems, human rights and an open economic order. Integration in the EU will bring these countries firmly into the Western European family.

The MENA countries have not experienced a political shock that has forced them to change their political-economic systems fundamentally. In many of these countries, the traditional system of political and economic management has not provided the spread of welfare that many hoped for. Instead, stagnation and high levels of unemployment prevail in many of these countries. Some of the countries were able to use their natural resources to dampen the consequences of economic stagnation. As compared to developing countries in general, the MENA countries have been slow to integrate in the world economy (Otsubo, 1996, p. 25). In order to catch up, structural changes including trade liberalization, increased competition and adjustment of the exchange-rate policy are called for. New tax regimes will have to be introduced and investment in infrastructure will be required to attract foreign investment (Aghrout and Alexander, 1997). Such adjustments will involve losses of production and employment in sectors that were traditionally favoured and protected. It has been estimated that 60 per cent of the industrial firms in Morocco and Tunisia will not be capable to compete with freely imported EU products unless appropriate technological and marketing improvements are made by 2010 (Fontagné and Péridy, 1997, p. 16). On the other hand, the liberalization of economies gives rise to new economic interests: exporters and consumers will favour free trade and competition to the extent that they ascribe economic progress to the new economic regime. However, if the economic effects of structural adjustment are disappointing, or, more likely, if the costs of adjustment precede the benefits, reforms may come to a halt or be reversed. This is a real risk since the new agreements do not provide a significant improvement of the access to the EU market for MENA exports. There are no improvements in access for agricultural products which would have produced quick results. Additionally, MENA countries' exports of clothing will face more competition in the EU as a result of the liberalization of trade in clothing following the Uruguay Round and the FTAs with the CEEC.

As the MENA countries have not experienced a political shock that produced a blockade to the past, the possibility of a reversal of the reform process is real. This would simultaneously threaten the reciprocal free trade with the EU as PAMEFTA has the function of sanction supporting the reforms.

7. Locking in structural adjustment

The introduction of reciprocity in the trade relations between the EU and third countries has been interpreted as a strategy to lock-in policy reforms in those countries. Will the FTAs with the EU indeed bring structural reforms in the CEEC and MENA countries beyond the point of no return?

For the CEEC, the locking in effect of the EAs seems to be rather strong. In case of a reversal of the transition process, not only free entry into the Internal Market is at risk but the prospect of membership of the EU is put in jeopardy as well. As long as membership is a high political priority for the governments concerned, there is a strong incentive to continue the transition. Losing the prospect of membership would lower the political prestige of the country and its government in a dramatic way. There would be high economic costs as well: loss of exports, diminished attractiveness to foreign investors, and financial aid forgone. In addition, as there are no attractive alternatives for EU membership, the opportunity costs of continuing the way towards membership of the EU are low.

Like the CEEC, the MENA countries are dependent on the EU for much of their exports and their agricultural exports are particularly dependent on exceptions to CAP protection. The loss of these outlets would put a heavy burden on these economies. However, there are substantial differences in the lock-in effects of FTAs between these two groups of countries and the EU. First, there is no prospect of full membership for most MENA countries, which is an important message for foreign investors[10]. As indicated earlier, the prospect of membership plays a critical role in domestic politics of the CEEC. Second, with respect to FDI, it remains to be seen whether the new agreements will make a significant impact. After reviewing surveys among (potential) investors in Morocco and Tunisia, Page and Underwood (1997, pp. 109-10) draw the conclusion that

> 'European investor's perceptions of government commitment to trade policy and regulatory liberalization may improve as a consequence of the agreements. And perceptions of political risk may decline, but many of the major constraints identified by existing foreign investors - red tape, discretionary decisions, and legal problems - are not covered by the agreements and will require sustained efforts at administrative and legal reform'.

As far as the agreements do not have a clearly stimulating effect on FDI, their locking in function is weak. Third, given its dependence on imports of energy from certain countries in the MENA region, it is doubtful whether the EU would implement reciprocity to the full extent in case a MENA country reverses on the path towards liberalization. Fourth, the Arab-Israeli conflict may make economic relations across the Mediterranean subordinate to political arguments leading to diminished reciprocity. Fifth, the probability that the costs of liberalization will precede the benefits by a large time gap, particularly as a consequence of the failure of the EU to boost MENA exports in the short run, weakens the locking in function of the MENA agreements.

To conclude, the locking in function of the EAs is much stronger than the impact of the new agreements with MENA countries is likely to be.

8. Conclusions

The preceding sections have shown that the reform processes that are under way in the EU's neighbouring countries and in the relations between these countries and the EU may lead to a PAMEFTA. However, it will take a long time before reciprocal liberalization and harmonization of regulations will have been realized and the various bilateral agreements - the spokes - will have been integrated with the EU - the hub - into one Pan-European-Mediterranean Free Trade Area. Before the benefits from liberalization may be reaped, the costs of economic restructuring will affect the neighbouring countries. The agreements should facilitate the reform process and make a reversal unattractive. The question is: are the gains from participating in the PAMEFTA sufficiently large to overcome the pain of the reform process? This seems to be more likely for the CEEC than for the MENA countries for a range of reasons: on an average, the latter group of countries is at a lower level of income per capita, has not experienced the collapse of their political and economic system and does not have the perspective of full membership, with the exception of Cyprus, Malta and Turkey. In addition, the new reciprocity that the EU is introducing in its Mediterranean relations will mainly produce long-run benefits for the partner countries, while in the short run market access for products for which these countries have a large export potential, particularly agricultural products, will not be improved. The EU could make the agreements a stronger anchor for reforms by further opening its markets. The conclusion must be, that it is far from certain whether the Mediterranean part of PAMEFTA will be realized.

The EU hits the limits of its capability to pursue its foreign policy. Traditionally, the EU has realized its political objectives by creating economic gains by means of economic integration. This approach has been successful in the EU where economic integration has contributed to the establishment of peace and democracy in and among the member states. By expanding eastward, the EU will probably be able to continue the success of this approach. However, the establishment of an area of peace and stability across the Mediterranean area is an objective that may prove too arduous for the economic tools the EU is willing to use.

Notes

[1] The author thanks Matthijs Crietee and Jacob Kol for their comments on an earlier draft of this chapter.

[2] In order to keep the discussion in a time frame of about a decade, the study focuses on the relations between the EU and EFTA - Norway, Switzerland, Liechtenstein - the countries with Europe Agreements - Poland, Hungary, the Czech Republic, the Slovak Republic, Romenia, Bulgaria, Slovenia and the Baltic states - and the countries taking part in the Barcelona Declaration - Turkey, Cyprus, Malta, Tunisia, Israel, Morocco, Egypt, Jordan, Lebanon, Algeria Syria and the Palestinian Authority. The objective of free trade areas has been explicitly stated for these relations.

[3] With respect to Morocco, Fontagné and Péridy (1997, p. 69) conclude that 'FDI flows remain too small to have more than a negligable impact on overall economic growth'. For the Maghreb as a group, they argue that the level of DFI is very low, and that the outlook is not encouraging.

[4] In 1991 and 1992, almost 90 per cent of FDI in Tunisia was in energy, and mainly in the Algeria-Italy pipeline project (Fontagné and Péridy, 1997).

[5] The 1993 Copenhagen Council formulated three conditions for full membership of the CEEC. First, stable institutions that guarantee democracy, the rule of law, human rights and respect for the protection of minorities. Second, a functioning market economy and the ability to face the competitive pressures in the EC. Third, the capacity to meet the obligations of membership including those of the political, economic and monetary union (Bulletin of the EC 6-93).

[6] Critical assessment of the Barcelona process is given by Talahite (1996) and Mezdour (1996).

[7] E.g. Art. 52 of the EU-Tunisia Agreement of 1995.

[8] Protocol 4 to the Association Agreement between the EU and Tunisia. The Declaration of the EU is annexed to the Agreement as Declaration of the EU with respect to Art. 29.

[9] It is a different, but important issue that these rules of origin do not act as a NTB in trade between PAMEFTA and other countries.

[10] Turkey is a notable exception. However, the member states of the EU have left the date of Turkey's entry in so much doubt, that the incentive is much weaker than in the case of the CEECs.

References

Aghrout, A., and M. Alexander, 'The Euro-Mediterranean New Strategy and the Maghreb Countries', *European Foreign Affairs Review*, Volume 2, 1997.

Commission of the European Communities, *Bulletin of the European Communities*, Brussels, various issues.

Commission of the European Communities, *The Preparation for Integration into the Internal Market of the Union*, COM (95) 163 of 10 May, Brussels, 1997.

Ekholm, K., J. Torstensson and R. Torstensson, 'The Economics of the Middle East Peace Process: Are There Prospects for Trade and Growth?', *The World Economy*, Volume 19, 1996.

Enders, A., and R.J. Wonnacott, The Liberalisation of East-West European Trade: Hubs, Spokes and Further Complications, *The World Economy*, Volume 19, 1996.

Eurostat, *External and Intra-European Union Trade; Monthly Statistics*, Luxembourg, 1997.

Fernández, R. and J. Portes, 'Returns to Regionalism: An Analysis of Nontraditional Gains from Regional Trade Agreements', *The World Bank Economic Review*, Volume 12, Number 2, 1998.

Fischer, S., R. Sahay and C. Vegh, 'Economies in Transition: The Beginnings of Growth', *The American Economic Review*, Volume 86, Number 2, 1996.

Fontagné, L., and N. Péridy, *The EU and the Maghreb*, OECD Development Centre Studies, Paris, 1997.

Henriot, A., and A. Inotai, 'Economic Interpenetration between the European Union and the Central and Eastern European Countries', *European Foreign Affairs Review*, Volume 2, 1997.

Hoekman, B., *The WTO, the EU and the Arab World: Trade Policy Priorities and Pitfalls*, Discussion Paper Number 1226, Centre for Economic Policy Research, London, 1995.

Horovitz, D., '"Made in Europe": New European Rules of Origin and World Trade Liberalisation', *International Trade Law and Regulation*, Number 1, 1997.

Kawecka-Wyrzykowska, E., *Prospects for Trade Developments between Central and Eastern Countries and the EU,* paper for the Third ECSA-World Conference, Brussels, September, 1996.

Ludlow, P., *Preparing for Membership,* Centre for European Policy Studies, Brussels, 1996.

Maresceau, M. and E. Montaguti, 'The Relations between the European Union and Central and Eastern Europe: A Legal Appraisal', *Common Market Law Review,* Volume XX, 1995.

Mezdour, S., 'Opportunité Théorique d'une Zone de Libre-Échange Maghreb-UE', *Revue du Marché Commun et de l'Union Européenne,* Number 399, 1996.

Otsubo, S., *Globalization - A New Role for Developing Countries in an Integrating World,* The World Bank Policy Research, Working Paper 1628, Washington, D.C., 1996.

Page, J., and J. Underwood, 'Growth, the Maghreb and Free Trade with the European Union', in: A. Galal and B. Hoekman (eds), *Regional Partners in Global Markets: Limits and Possibilities of the Euro-Med Agreements,* Centre for Economic Policy Research, London, 1997.

Talahite, F., 'Le Partenariat Euro-Méditerranéen Vu du Sud', *Monde Arabe Maghreb Machrek,* Number 153, 1996.

Tovias, A., *Options for Mashrek-Israeli Regionalism in the Context of the Euro-Mediterranean Partnership,* CEPS Paper, Number 67, Brussels, 1997.

World Bank, The, *World Development Report 1997,* Oxford University Press, Oxford, 1997.

World Bank, The, *World Development Report, 1998/99,* Oxford University Press, Oxford, 1998.

12

THE EUROPE AGREEMENTS FROM THE PERSPECTIVE OF CENTRAL AND EASTERN EUROPE

Tibor Palánkai

Budapest University of Economic Sciences
Budapest
Hungary

1. Introduction

By the year 2000 the process of integration in the European Union (EU) will have reached a turning point. The introduction of the European Monetary Union (EMU) and the eastward enlargement require and bring about qualitative changes in the integration process itself. As a result of reforms and enlargements so far, the EU has changed considerably, but these processes have remained within the scope of common market integration based on the Treaty of Rome. However, the present institutional system of the EU was tailored for six countries. Although it was working tolerably with even 15 countries, it will not any longer do so with 20 to 25 member states.

The 1995 enlargement with Austria, Finland and Sweden did not involve substantial alterations in market competition since it did not increase considerably the size of the EU and trade with these countries had already been liberalized within the framework of the European Economic Area (EEA). Additionally, these three countries were on the whole net contributors - if only minimally – and not

P. van Dijck and G. Faber (eds.), The External Economic Dimension of the European Union, 271–291.

'jeopardizing' the EU budget. Finally, the three countries had already got ready for the EMU before it was introduced.

The Eastern enlargement represents an entirely new situation. The candidate member states will have to prepare themselves for the EU including the EMU, which will imply a harsh process of adaptation. Moreover, the EU itself is unable to implement this enlargement without the consistent realization of reforms of the common institutions, the Common Agricultural Policy (CAP) and the budget. By the year 2000, the European integration will thus have reached a decisive and critical stage and fundamental decisions have to be made regarding deepening and enlargement. The realization of these decisions is the task of the years to come, decisively setting the direction and fate of the whole European integration process, including the political and economic future of the Central and Eastern European Countries (CEEC).

According to their preambles the Europe Agreements (EAs), concluded in the first half of the 1990s, are preparatory phases for full EU membership. The European Council of Copenhagen of June 1993 has adopted the membership criteria for the CEEC:

(1) democracy, the rule of law, stability of institutions guaranteeing human and minority rights;

(2) a functioning market economy able to resist the pressure of sharp competition and market forces characteristic of the Union;

(3) fulfilling the obligations of membership, and the adoption of the objectives of the political, economic and monetary union, and

(4) full adoption of the institutional and legal systems of the EU, the *acquis communautaire*.

This chapter considers the EU's eastward enlargement from the point of view of Eastern Europe and investigates whether the EAs contribute in an adequate way to economic development of the CEECs required to fulfil the membership criteria mentioned above. The EU treats the CEEC in a uniform way to the extent that this is deemed possible. The chapter will present a general analysis, but the practical impact and consequences of certain measures are illustrated for the case of Hungary. The composition of the chapter is as follows. The next section will describe the content of the EAs. Section 3 will present an appraisal of the impact of these agreements on trade and foreign direct investment (FDI). The fourth section will discuss the opportunities for structural modernization of the CEEC, and the final section brings together the main conclusions.

2. The Europe Agreements

History

It lasted a long time before the contacts between the CEEC and the EU through the Council for Mutual Economic Assistance (CMEA) were affected by the détente, which started in the 1970s. CMEA countries had not accepted the common foreign trade policy of the EC and declined to place the mutual ties in the competence of the Commission of the European Communities. CMEA countries even denied the Commission diplomatic recognition. The policy of the CMEA countries had started to change after the death of Brezhnev in 1982, but substantive steps towards normalization were taken only after Gorbachov took office in 1985. Normalization and development of ties had quickened after the revolutionary changes of 1989. At the Paris Summit of the leading industrial powers in July 1989, a decision was made to launch PHARE, a programme to support Poland and Hungary[1]. All member countries of the Organisation for Economic Co-operation and Development (OECD) subsequently adopted the programme. The European Commission was asked to co-ordinate and run the programme and gradually the programme got fully under the control of the EU.

PHARE opened the possibility of bilateral credits and grants. As of April 1990, the programme has been extended gradually to other countries, with the exception of some Yugoslav republics. After the signing of the EAs, PHARE was integrated into the association constructions. For the countries of the Commonwealth of Independent States (CIS), the TACIS programme was launched at a later stage.

In addition, some trade-policy measures were attached to PHARE including most-favoured-nation (MFN) treatment and the abolishment of discriminative quotas that were put into effect as of 1 January 1990 instead of 31 December 1995. Moreover, the EU granted most CEEC treatment under the Generalized System of Preferences (GSP).

The possibility of association of the CEEC with the EC had been raised as early as the autumn of 1989. Based on Art. 310 of the EC Treaty (ex Art. 238), association was officially offered to these countries by the European Council at its Dublin Summit in April 1990. The offer of association was made 'to all the countries of Central and Eastern Europe'. Only later, following the differentiation of the region, the scope of the offer was limited to (then still) Czechoslovakia, Poland and Hungary. The Council adopted association guidelines required to start formal talks in December1990. In the meantime the term 'Europe

Agreements' was coined, the intention being to emphasize their particular significance and distinguished character. Talks came to a close in November 1991 and the three agreements were signed in December 1991[2].

Trade policy

The trade policy part of the 'association of the three' has been in force since March 1992, as a result of the Interim Agreement. In the case of Hungary and Poland, the other parts came into force in February 1994. Due to the separation of the Czech and Slovak Republics, their treaties of association were renegotiated after 1992.

The EU concluded similar agreements with Bulgaria and Romania in 1993, with the Baltic States in 1995 and with Slovenia in 1996. Apart from these 10 countries, most of the other former Yugoslav republics and Albania have only very little chance of realizing an EA and negotiations will not be on the agenda for the foreseeable future.

EAs show strong similarities regarding their main elements, but there are divergences as to the peculiarities and specific problems of the various countries. Like other traditional associations they aim at establishing free trade areas (FTAs). The agreements are committed to the 'four freedoms' but contain specific liberalization programmes for goods and capital only. Liberalization of the labour market is a remote goal.

With the exception of agricultural produce, the Agreements set the goal of establishing a complete free-trade area by 31 December 2000 for CEECs that were in the first group to conclude an agreement. For some countries specific rules apply for particular products, e.g. Poland is allowed to levy customs duties on cars until 1 January 2002. On a transitional basis, limitations have been maintained for industrial sectors, which are traditionally subject to special regulations such as metallurgy and the textile industry.

In the framework of the EAs, trade liberalization is realized on the basis of reciprocity. However, the FTAs are formed in an asymmetric manner. The association treaties set maximum transition periods of 10 years, in two consecutive steps taking five years each in principle.

To show the practical consequences of the EAs, the trade section of the Hungarian association will now be described in more detail. Our findings largely refer to the associations with the other CEEC as well. The access of Hungarian exports to the EU was improved in the following way. Quantitative restrictions that were imposed on industrial products making up nearly 55 per cent of Hungarian exports, were lifted on the day the agreement came into force, whereas the abolition of customs tariffs came in several steps after 1 January 1995. At the same time, customs duties imposed on the remaining 'sensitive products' were delayed in their abolition. As regards steel products - five per cent of Hungarian exports - all quantitative restrictions had immediately been lifted, whereas customs duties were reduced gradually and abolished completely by 1 January 1996. As regards textile products - 15 per cent of Hungarian exports - all quotas were lifted and freedom from customs duties came into force as of 1 January 1997. Processing trade was made duty-free immediately. Trade in agricultural products was not liberalized in a comprehensive manner but reciprocal special preferences have been granted for some products through favourable quotas and tariffs.

With respect to EU exports to Hungary, 'asymmetric' liberalization has implied that Hungary was granted a delay of four to five years to abolish trade barriers. Hungary started to increase its quotas on January 1st 1995 only and the use of these quotas will have to be abolished completely on 31 December 2000. The abolishment of customs duties for the major part of imports from the EU started on 1 January 1995, and will be continued stepwise until its completion by 1 January 2000. Within certain quantitative limits, Hungary treats agricultural imports from the EU favourably, particularly products that have played a significant role so far in the Hungarian market.

Hungary is entitled to protect its branches of industry by unilaterally introducing customs tariffs until the end of 2000. This safeguard can be applied in cases of structural transformation, when social tensions occur, to protect infant industries or to protect the balance of payments. These measures may not affect more than 15 per cent of imports and tariff rates may not exceed 25 per cent. The association agreement enables signatories to start dumping procedures, the only condition being that the Association Council is informed.

Foreign direct investment, services and labour

In order to stimulate FDI, the repatriation of profits and capital was guaranteed immediately[3]. The CEEC will gradually introduce EC regulations regarding the free movement of capital. During the transition period, existing restrictions may not be reinforced by new limitations. By 1995-96 convertibility had been realized in all associated countries. Regarding the right to establish firms, the Agreements introduced the general principle of national treatment.

As regards trade in services, the parties set liberalization as their objective, but left the necessary future decisions to the authority of the Association Council. The possibilities of liberalization in this area were outlined in the White Paper of 1995 (Commission, 1994, 1995).

Liberalization measures to improve labour mobility were left to the bilateral treaties to be concluded with the member states. Clearly, free movement of labour is only a possibility of principle and it was obvious for the CEEC that the EU could not be expected to offer any real opening strategy until its level of unemployment was reduced substantially. On the other hand, the Agreements guarantee that workers of associated countries are entitled to be granted social care[4]. To conclude, substantial liberalization of services and labour can only be expected when the CEEC become full members of the EU.

Special features of the Europe Agreements

EAs are characterized by a number of new features as compared to former associations. They introduce new elements to the association but in some other respects they are narrower and less generous than previous associations.

To start with, the Agreements include the objective of intensive political consultations and co-operation between the EU and the associated countries. Political dialogue and co-operation are based on shared values and aspirations including integration into the community of democratic nations, consideration of the interests of other partners, and enhancement of security and stability in Europe. This affects large areas of the economies, societies and cultures of the CEEC, thus aiming at their gradual integration in Europe.

Second, the Agreements emphasize the importance of political transformation: commitment to a democratic multiparty system and free and democratic elections, the rule of law, human rights, basic liberties and the principle of social justice, and a market economy. Starting with the second round of talks, mainly in the renegotiated Agreement with Slovakia, and later in the Agreements with Bulgaria and Romania, these objectives were translated into certain political conditions. Thus, respecting of minority rights was formulated in these agreements as a requirement.

Third, the Agreements envisage measures of harmonization in order to adapt the system of laws and regulation in the CEEC to EU norms that are applied in the Internal Market. This refers to areas such as the protection of consumers, competition, environment, and technical norms and standards. This is necessary for the CEEC in order to exploit the advantages of the liberalized trade in goods with the EU. The liberalization of services cannot be realized either without large-scale legal harmonization.

Fourth, the financial assistance committed in the Agreements are related to the framework of PHARE only. Most other association agreements contain concrete commitments for assistance such as the Lomé Conventions and the Mediterranean Agreements. No financial protocols were attached to the EAs. More will be said about this aspect in Section 4.

Fifth, the Agreements do not contain any concrete monetary prescriptions either, with the exception of financial support for currency convertibility. In the light of the Maastricht decisions with regard to EMU and the subsequent introduction of EMU in 1999, monetary policy performance and co-operation has been emphasized not only from the perspective of the member states but also of the CEEC.

3. Appraising the Europe Agreements

The Agreements concluded in 1990-91 mirrored the optimism of the early 1990s. At the time favourable growth rates were forecasted not only for the East but for the whole Continent as well. In 1990, a Commission report claimed that after the proposed market reforms would have been implemented, the region would quickly get out of the recession and would be able to realize an annual growth rate of five to six per cent (Financial Times, 1990). Many expected that the Internal Market measures in combination with the opening of the markets of the CEEC would have a strong dynamic effect on the whole European market. However, the economic development of the CEEC had been much less favourable in the first years of the association than expected during the negotiations in 1990-91 and the difficulties of transformation and consolidation were strongly underestimated on both sides. This can explain the modest concessions offered by the associations, but do not warrant them.

During the period 1989-94, the economies of the region were in a serious crisis. The transformation crisis reached its lowest ebb just in 1991-93, when the fall of production reached two-digit proportions. For instance, in Hungary gross domestic product (GDP), industrial and agricultural production had fallen by 20, 30 and 35 per cent respectively during the period 1989-94, and by 1993 unemployment had reached a level of 13 per cent. Inflation was reduced from the 1991 peak of 35 per cent to 23 per cent in 1992 and 1993, but the so-called moderate inflation rate as defined by Dornbusch and Fisher at 12-18 per cent per year was not reached until 1994 (Dornbusch and Fisher, 1993). Moreover, the balanced budget of 1990 could not be maintained and the deficit climbed to 8 per cent of GDP in 1993.

Since the economy of the EU went into recession as well in 1991-93, it was not surprising that the EU was not able during this period to contribute substantially to the stabilization of the region's economy and contribute to its growth.

It was feared that the rapid liberalization as laid down in the EAs might prevent the CEEC from protecting their economy against harmful outside competition. Due to the transformation, privatization, and the radical reorganization of enterprise structures, production structures had changed, considerable reconstruction projects were needed and new markets and relations had to be established. In large areas of the economy the new enterprises were facing the difficulties and syndrome of being 'infant industries' which proved to be more serious than expected at the time of the negotiations of the associations. This raised questions pertaining to the inadequacy of the period to postpone liberalization for four to five years or the lack of possibilities to protect enterprises as were provided by the Agreements.

After a difficult start, years of upswing followed after 1994. This resulted in a growth rate of four to six per cent in the CEEC and a quickening of the processes of structural and technological modernization.

Trade

The associations have had a positive impact on the development, transformation and modernization of the economies of the CEEC in several respects. These small countries are characterized by open economic structures and are highly dependent on international trade. After the collapse of the CMEA, they had to switch their trade from East to West, and the EU has been their main partner in this endeavour. During the 1990s the trade orientation of these countries towards the EU increased rapidly as illustrated in Table 12.1. Also, the shares of these associated countries in the external trade of the EU increased substantially as shown in Table 12.2.

Between 1989 and 1993, the share of the 10 CEEC in EU imports increased from 2.7 to 6.0 per cent, and in exports from 2.8 to 7.5 per cent, as shown in

Table 12.1. EU shares in foreign trade of the associated countries, in percentages, 1989, 1992 and 1996.

		1989	*1992*	*1996*
Poland	exports	32.1	58.0	66.2
	imports	33.8	53.2	63.9
Czech Republic[1]	exports	26.3	52.8	58.2
	imports	26.5	47.7	62.4
Slovakia[2]	exports	24.4	41.6	41.3
	imports	27.3	34.7	36.9
Hungary	exports	24.8	49.8	62.7
	imports	29.0	42.7	59.8
Romania	exports	25.2	32.1	56.5
	imports	5.7	37.2	52.3
Slovenia[3]	exports	51.3	54.9	64.6
	imports	56.9	50.1	67.6

Notes: [1] From 1993 including trade with Slovakia.
[2] From 1993 including trade with the Czech Republic.
[3] From 1992 including trade with the member republics of former Yugoslavia.
Sources: Wiener Institut für Internationale Wirtschaftsforschung, *WIIW Handbook of Statistics 1996,* 1997, and national statistics, see András Inotai, *Characteristics and New Trends of Foreign Trade between Hungary, the EU and the 10 Associated Countries, 1989-1997,* VKI and OMFB, Budapest, 1998.

Table 12.2. In some years, the EU had almost replaced the position of the CMEA. It should be noted that the radical re-orientation in trade of the CEEC to a large extent took place as early as 1989-92, before the EAs came into force in the field of trade on 1 March 1992.

The dynamics in trade flows between the two areas are shown in Tables 12.3 and 12.4. Under the circumstances of recession that afflicted both regions in 1993, growth of exports and imports not only slowed down, but the absolute value of trade flows even decreased considerably in some cases[5]. From 1994 onwards the business cycle has become more favourable and growth of trade

Table 12.2. Shares of the associated countries in EU foreign trade as percentages
of EU external exports and imports, 1989-97.

	EU exports				EU imports			
	1989	1993	1996	1997	1989	1993	1996	1997
10 associated countries	2.78	7.49	10.18	10.90	2.70	5.98	8.11	8.48
CEFTA 6[1]	2.42	6.87	9.22	9.81	2.59	5.39	7.24	7.56
Poland	0.96	2.36	3.18	3.47	0.86	1.80	2.11	2.11
Czech Republic	0.58	1.50	2.24	2.20	0.57	1.20	1.67	1.76
Slovakia	[2]	0.34	0.64	0.67	[2]	0.30	0.59	0.60
Hungary	0.72	1.37	1.60	1.89	0.58	1.03	1.52	1.73
Romania	0.17	0.53	0.71	0.70	0.57	0.38	0.62	0.66
Slovenia	..	0.77	0.86	0.88	..	0.68	0.73	0.70
Bulgaria	0.36	0.32	0.27	0.26	0.12	0.22	0.29	0.30
Estonia	..	0.10	0.27	0.33	..	0.06	0.19	0.21
Latvia	..	0.09	0.18	0.21	..	0.15	0.19	0.19
Lithuania	..	0.12	0.23	0.30	..	0.16	0.19	0.20

Notes: [1] The Czech Republic, Poland, Hungary, Romania, Slovakia and Slovenia
[2] Czechoslovakia
Sources: Eurostat, *External and Intra-European Trade, Monthly Statistics*, several issues and own
calculations, see András Inotai, *Characteristics and New Trends of Foreign Trade between
Hungary , the EU and the 10 Associated Countries. 1989-1997*, VKI and OMFB,
Budapest, 1998.

continued. The dynamism of trade with the EU contributed to the region's
economic growth, although trade expanded at a more moderate rate during the
period 1993-97 than was the case in the previous four years, notwithstanding the
liberalization resulting from the EAs. Likewise, the Agreements have had a dynamic
impact on exports from Romania and Bulgaria as shown in Table 12.3, although
the Agreements came into force only in 1994.

The positive impact of the EAs on the process of modernization of the countries
concerned is reflected in the changes in the composition of their exports to the
EU. In the case of Hungary, the share of machinery and vehicles in exports to the
EU increased from 23 to 51 per cent and the share of all products by manufacturing

industry increased from 66 to 80 per cent in the period 1993-97. Similarly, the proportion of machinery in total exports increased in the Czech Republic and Poland from 25 to 37 per cent and from 18 to 24 per cent respectively. The proportion of total manufactures in exports of most CEEC to the EU was about 80 per cent, as shown in Table 12.5.

The considerable modernization of the Czech, Hungarian and Polish export structures is obviously connected with the strong increase of FDI in these economies in recent years, as will be reviewed in more detail below.

So far, the years of the association have shown that the Agreements offered better opportunities for the EU countries to expand their exports than for the CEEC. Until 1990, the EU had a trade deficit with the East which fluctuated between 2.5 billion (in 1984) and 0.6 billion ECUs (in1989). During the 1990s the balance shifted from the 1 billion ECUs deficit in 1990 to surpluses which soared to 5.6 billion ECUs in 1993 and increased further in the years of the association, resulting in an accumulated trade surplus of about 64 billion ECUs over the period 1992-1997 (Inotai, 1998). This did not come as a surprise since previous experiences of associations had also shown that liberalization in the long run impaired the trade balance of less-developed countries. However, the extent of the shift in the trade balance was beyond expectation. In this context, the generosity of the agreements can be questioned.

The EAs include asymmetric concessions in the area of trade liberalization. In the framework of the Agreements, the EU has abolished all customs duties hampering trade. The average EU tariff level was not more than three to five per cent, which cannot be considered in itself a serious barrier to trade. Hence, its abolishment does not create a significant preferential advantage. However, the average tariff levels of the CEEC were much higher: in the case of Hungary, about 13 per cent in 1991, which was reduced to eight per cent in subsequent years. Consequently, with the association Hungary - like the other CEEC - offered more in terms of trade concessions than they received in return from the EU, notwithstanding the delay of some years. In view of the considerable trade surplus of the EU, it was less than warranted under these circumstances that the EU delayed the liberalization of 'sensitive products' such as steel and textile goods, in which associated countries had a substantial export capacity.

It must be noted that the direct effects of liberalization originating from the EAs have been quickly exhausted and that a dynamic export performance in the long run depends on structural modernization, as argued below. A liberal trade

Table 12.3. EU exports to the associated countries, in millions of ECUs, 1989-97.

	1989	1993	1996	1997	1993[1]	1997[2]	1997[3]
All exports outside EU	413,010	471,405	625,094	717,776	114	152	174
10 associated countries	11,484	35,302	63,618	78,267	307	222	682
CEFTA 6[4]	10,007	32,362	57,653	70,423	323	218	704
Poland	3,945	11,144	19,857	24,986	282	225	633
Czech Republic	2,385[5]	7,087	13,975	15,816	..	223	..
Slovakia	..	1,583	3,998	4,788	..	302	..
Hungary	2,988	6,447	10,001	13,539	216	210	453
Romania	689	2,513	4,445	5,005	365	199	726
Slovenia	..	3,618	5,377	6,289	..	174	..
Bulgaria	1,477	1,488	1,698	1,834	101	123	124
Estonia	..	492	1,697	2,347	..	477	..
Latvia	..	415	1,110	1,525	..	367	..
Lithuania	..	545	1,460	2,138	..	392	..

Notes: [1] 1989=100
[2] 1993=100
[3] 1989=100
[4] The Czech Republic, Poland, Hungary, Romania, Slovakia and Slovenia
[5] Czechoslovakia

Sources: Eurostat, *External and Intra-European Trade, Monthly Statistics*, several issues and own calculations, see András Inotai, *Characteristics and New Trends of Foreign Trade between Hungary , the EU and the 10 Associated Countries. 1989-1997*, VKI and OMFB, Budapest, 1998.

regime may contribute to the establishment of the required competitive environment.

Agriculture

The asymmetry in trade liberalization referred to above has occurred particularly in trade in agricultural products. Of all the CEEC, Hungary is the most dependent on agricultural exports and although the country committed itself to liberalize about 90 per cent of its total imports from the EU, the EU commitment has been limited to only 75 per cent of its imports from Hungary. As Table 12.6

Table 12.4. EU imports from the associated countries, in millions of ECUs, 1989-97.

	1989	1993	1996	1997	1993[1]	1997[2]	1997[3]
All imports outside EU	446,716	470,241	581,455	667,863	105	142	150
10 associated countries	12,082	28,099	47,128	56,656	233	202	469
CEFTA 6[4]	11,551	25,363	42,121	50,478	220	199	437
Poland	3,858	8,458	12,252	14,155	219	167	367
Czech Republic	2,558[5]	5,636	9,755	11,733	..	208	..
Slovakia	..	1,417	3,420	3,978	..	281	..
Hungary	2,587	4,878	8,827	11,548	189	237	446
Romania	2,548	1,796	3,597	4,405	70	245	173
Slovenia	..	3,178	4,270	4,659	..	147	..
Bulgaria	531	1,014	1,706	2,082	191	205	392
Estonia	..	296	1,089	1,497	..	506	..
Latvia	..	727	1,125	1,288	..	177	..
Lithuania	..	699	1,087	1,311	..	188	..

Notes and Sources: See Table 12.3.

indicates, access to the EU markets for agricultural products is much more difficult than access to the Hungarian market.

Hungary is at a disadvantage *vis-à-vis* the EU in the 'subsidy competition' as well. In 1990, the proportion of subsidies in the unit value of agricultural production was 48 per cent in the EU and only 18 per cent in Hungary and 17 to 18 per cent in the Czech and Slovak Republics. These subsidies make it difficult for Hungarian agricultural producers to compete in the external market and also in the domestic market. EU producers are subsidized to such extent that they can sell their products in the Hungarian market at a lower price than the production costs for the Hungarian producers. However, the CAP reforms will probably reduce the subsidy gap in the years to come.

Foreign direct investment

The EAs have improved the international position and image of the CEEC with respect to foreign investors and in international fora such as NATO, the OECD,

Table 12.5. Structure of EU imports of goods from the CEFTA
countries, in percentages, 1993, 1996 and 1997.

Countries	year	SITC groups[1]					
		0+1	2+4	3	5	7	6+8
All EU external imports	1993	7.5	6.5	13.1	7.0	31.0	31.3
	1996	7.9	6.5	13.8	7.7	32.3	29.2
	1997	7.2	6.4	12.6	7.6	33.8	29.3
CEFTA-6 together	1993	9.9	6.4	7.3	4.9	18.3	50.6
	1996	5.3	4.4	4.1	6.0	30.2	48.7
	1997	4.7	4.2	3.3	5.5	34.4	46.3
Poland	1996	7.3	4.0	7.0	5.3	22.6	52.2
	1997	7.0	4.0	6.5	5.0	24.3	50.8
The Czech Republic	1993	4.0	7.1	3.4	7.4	24.7	50.7
	1996	2.4	6.7	4.2	7.2	33.0	45.0
	1997	2.1	6.2	3.2	6.5	37.0	43.1
Slovakia	1993	14.9	6.8	1.8	8.8	23.4	42.8
	1996	1.5	4.7	2.8	8.1	29.9	51.7
	1997	1.7	4.8	2.0	7.4	35.6	47.5
Hungary	1996	9.7	4.5	3.4	6.0	42.1	33.0
	1997	7.4	3.5	2.1	5.5	51.4	29.0
Romania	1996	3.3	1.8	1.4	5.4	11.3	76.0
	1997	3.1	2.2	1.4	4.2	10.6	77.9
Slovenia	1996	1.4	2.4	0.2	4.1	37.3	54.0
	1997	1.4	2.6	0.2	4.1	37.8	53.2

Sources: Eurostat, *External and Intra-European Trade, Monthly Statistics*, several issues and
own calculations, see András Inotai, *Characteristics and New Trends of Foreign Trade
between Hungary, the EU and the 10 Associated Countries. 1989-1997*, VKI and
OMFB, Budapest, 1998.

Note: [1] Standard International Trade Classification (SITC)
SITC 0+1 foods, drinks, tobacco
SITC 2+4 raw materials
SITC 3 energy, fuel
SITC 5 chemicals
SITC 7 machinery and transport vehicles
SITC 6+8 processed industrial products.

the International Monetary Fund (IMF) and the World Bank. However, the agreements are not a sufficient condition for attracting FDI but they do contribute to a favourable environment. Over 90 per cent of the FDI destined to Eastern Europe including the former Soviet Union during the period 1988 – 1997 was directed towards the Czech Republic, Hungary and Poland. This is remarkable as wage costs in these countries are higher than elsewhere in Eastern Europe, while low wage costs are an important incentive to invest in this region.

Apparently, other factors are taken into account as well, such as the state of infrastructure, the development of capital markets and financial services, security and transparency of the legal system and the stability of the social and political environment. This may help to explain the limited FDI in Bulgaria and Romania despite their low wage costs. The case of Hungary may illustrate the importance of the EAs with respect to FDI. Until 1999, over 20 billion US dollars of FDI flowed into Hungary. It is obvious that this would not have happened without association. Moreover, these FDI enabled Hungary to take advantage of the Europe Agreement: about 70 per cent of industrial exports were generated by transnational companies operating in that country.

4. Structural modernization

The fundamental question of the EAs is how far they are able to promote the long-term structural modernization of the CEEC. Undoubtedly, the agreements provide significant impulses to modernization but at the same time they are far from being unambiguous and their full effects are expected to unfold after full membership only.

The CEEC underwent a rash industrialization programme in the 1950s and 1960s. However, from the 1970s onwards these countries have increasingly lagged behind large parts of the world economy, mainly because of shortcomings of the central-planning system including the lack of incentives for innovation and technological development, and the wasteful use of resources. Due to financial difficulties and restrictions, the level of investment declined or stagnated at a low level. Consequently, large-scale economic restructuring as was taking place in the OECD during the two decades before 1989, simply could not be taken into consideration in the CEEC. Part of the foreign loans received in the 1970s was spent on new industrial and technological projects but these investments did not produce real benefits in terms of technological innovations, due to the wrong

Table 12.6. Import tariffs in the EU and
            Hungary, in percentages, 1994.

Product	EU	Hungary
Slaughter cattle	156	21
Beef	244	21
Pork	61	21
Wheat	175	26
Chicken	45	26

Source: 'Agrárgazdasági Kutató és Informatikai Intézet',
        Világgazdaság, 22 July, 1994.

selection of targets and sectors and the wasteful use of resources. As a consequence, many countries became heavily indebted.

The relative backwardness of the industrial sector of the CEEC and the economic crisis were important factors that brought about a change of the system. Thus, in the early 1990s, the CEEC were facing the complex task of structural modernization. In order to diminish the use of energy and material in production and to improve competitiveness, the restructuring of the economy became a priority. Modernization of the physical infrastructure at the macro and micro levels could not be delayed. Moreover, programmes for cleaning up the polluted environment have required considerable resources as well in most countries.

The EAs have strongly promoted the transformation of the region. After 1990, this process has shown great dynamism in all CEEC, both regarding privatization and the establishment of market institutions, and the process has been strengthened particularly by the fact that it has become a criterion for full EU membership later on[6].

From the point of view of modernization, the EU is a natural centre of gravity or anchor for modernization for the CEEC. Most EU countries are highly developed and characterized by modern industrial structures and financial markets, and the region is integrated by means of a continental-wide infrastructure. The EU disposes of the technological capabilities required for the modernization of the CEEC and this applies to European firms operating in the global economy as well as to non-European companies operating in Europe.

However, the EU meets the requirement of dynamic markets that are important for modernization, only to a limited extent. Economic growth of the EU countries has slowed down since the 1970s and lags behind the growth rates of some other regions in the world economy such as the USA, and particularly China and other newly industrializing countries. The macro-economic achievements of the EU have deteriorated in other respects as well. In the early 1990s, the USA managed to return to the macro-economic parameters that were characteristic of the 1960s, but the EU has been considerably less successful in this regard. This is a restricting factor from the viewpoint of associations and particularly full membership. Nevertheless, the EU has become a dynamic market for CEEC exports in the course of the 1990s.

Apart from dynamic export opportunities, modernization of the CEEC requires substantial net resource transfers including official aid and private investment. Some of the countries in the region are already heavily indebted. For example, external debt per capita in Hungary was about 2,000 US dollars in the early 1990s and exceeded levels of indebtedness in many Latin American countries. No doubt, private investment is of fundamental significance for the financing of growth and for technological and structural modernization.

In view of the backward state of the infrastructure, however, there is a great need for inter-state resource transfers. This has been recognized from the outset, and as early as 1989 proposals were made for the creation of a 'Marshall-aid' programme for the countries of the region. However, these proposals have been rejected. The western countries did not dispose of the necessary financial means and at the same time the strategic interest in consolidating Central and Eastern-Europe decreased as a result of the collapse of the Soviet threat.

In contrast to all former associations that have offered financial aid in some form or other - particularly to the developing countries - the financial commitments of the EAs have remained rather modest. For example, Hungary received about 100 million ECUs annually in financial aid between 1990 and 1998, and more than 125 million ECUs per annum from the European Investment Bank (EIB) and the European Bank for Reconstruction and Development (EBRD) for investment in infrastructure and to support small businesses. These transfers represent less than 0.5 per cent of Hungarian GDP, only 10 per cent of the assistance granted to Greece and Portugal, and merely a fraction of what Germany's eastern provinces have been receiving. The CEEC can expect larger sums only in case of full membership.

5. Conclusions

The CEEC are in a process of transformation that has been changing their societies and economies in a radical fashion. Clearly, some countries have made more progress and enjoyed more gains from the transformation process than others. It was clear from the start that the primary responsibility for the restructuring process is with the CEEC themselves and that the relationship with the EU and the EAs in particular could be helpful but not decisive. This may be illustrated by the radical shift in the CEEC trade flows towards the EU that started to take place before the EAs came into force. However, the EAs have supported the process of modernization in a substantial way. By offering free access for the CEEC's exports, there was a direct economic stimulus. Moreover, free access and local supply conditions attracted FDI, which led to a further increase in exports and employment and a change in the composition of exports, reflecting the modernization of economic structures.

The contribution of the EAs to the restructuring and development of the CEEC has been substantial but could have been larger for three reasons. First, the EU has been limiting market access for sensitive products from the CEEC while the EU was running growing surpluses on its trade balance with these countries. For agricultural products, this even led to an asymmetry in trade liberalization for CEEC that are particularly dependent on the export of such products. Second, the EU has experienced relatively low rates of growth, which has limited its dynamic impact on the CEEC. Hence, CEEC should diversify their exports and look for other markets as well. Third, financial aid from the EU to support modernization has remained modest.

Moreover, the economic and political restructuring process taking place in the EU has complicated the EU-CEEC relationship. Structural weaknesses and interest groups opposing reform in both regions hampered trade liberalization and co-operation. Association agreements particularly dealt with trade questions and do not manage to shape the framework of an all-European policy serving structural modernization. Of course, there is an overall consensus regarding the idea of 'assistance through trade' and all sorts of trade promotion can be of fundamental significance for the region. Nevertheless, a comprehensive structural and modernization policy is needed on both sides and answers should be found as to how the 'structural crisis' is to be treated affecting both parts of the continent. The EAs and particularly the enlargement of the EU clearly offer opportunities to improve the global competitiveness of the continent as a whole as has also been indicated by Thurow in Chapter 2 of this volume.

Notes.

[1] The acronym PHARE is derived from *Pologne, Hongrie et Aide à la Reconstruction Économique*. The regional scope was widened later.

[2] The CEEC concluded parallel free trade agreements with the EFTA countries as well. Talks were over early in 1993, and agreements came into force as of 1 October, 1993. The agreements dealt with industrial products, and the processed produce of agriculture and the fisheries. With Austria, Sweden and Finland joining the EU in 1995, the significance of the EFTA treaties has largely diminished since they now only affect CEEC trade with Switzerland and Norway.

[3] Hungary had achieved this as early as 1986 in the framework of the new law on joint ventures.

[4] Hungary has such a bilateral agreement with Germany and Austria only.

[5] In 1993, Hungary's exports to the EU declined by about 20 per cent.

[6] The Copenhagen criteria.

References

Commission of the European Communities, *The Europe Agreements and Beyond: A Strategy to Prepare the Countries of Central and Eastern Europe for Accession*, Brussels, 1994.

Commission of the European Communities, *Preparation of the Associated Countries of Central and Eastern Europe for Integration in the Internal Market of the Union*, Brussels, 1995.

Dornbusch, R. and S. Fisher, 'Moderate Inflation', *The World Bank Economic Review*, Number 1, 1993.

Financial Times, 15 May, 1990.

Inotai, A, *Characteristics and New Trends of Foreign Trade between Hungary, the EU and the 10 Associated Countries, 1989-1997*, VKI and OMFB, Budapest, 1998.

Lutz, B., 'Helping Eastern Europe and the Structural Problems of the West', *Gewerkschaftliche Monatshefte*, Number 1, 1993.

13

MEETING ASIA AND LATIN AMERICA IN A NEW SETTING

PITOU VAN DIJCK

CEDLA
Amsterdam
The Netherlands

1. Introduction

The emerging economies in Asia and Latin America have become new centres of gravity in the world economy and have caused major shifts in world trade and investment flows, as shown by Van Dijck and Faber in Chapter 1 of this volume. Particularly in the Pacific Rim, purchasing power, investment and trade have grown at extraordinary rates during several decades of export-orientated economic growth. This successful growth performance was interrupted in 1997 by the Asian crisis but by now many countries in the region are recovering.

In Latin America, the economic crisis of the early 1980s induced radical change in economic policies along the lines of the Washington agenda. The comprehensive and rapid opening towards international markets of manufactured goods and investment since the late 1980s has made these economies more accessible to foreign traders and investors and stimulated domestic industry to export. However, the region's growth performance in the 1990s was rather volatile and less impressive than in Asia and notwithstanding relatively high average levels of income the overall purchasing power in Latin America as a region is more limited than in East and South-East Asia.

P. van Dijck and G. Faber (eds.), The External Economic Dimension of the European Union, 293–318.
© 2000 *Kluwer Academic Publishers. Printed in the Netherlands.*

In connection with the emergence of these economies, a range of policy initiatives has been taken at the multilateral and regional levels. Nearly all countries in these two regions have become members of the World Trade Organization (WTO). Their integration in the multilateral rule system has been one of the most significant achievements of the Uruguay Round and the deepening of their integration in the WTO will be among the major objectives of the Millennium Round, at least from the perspective of the European Union (EU).

Moreover, countries in both regions as well as outsiders have taken initiatives to co-operate and intensify their economic relations in many different ways, ranging from the creation of structures to facilitate exchange of information and co-ordination of policies to the establishment of preferential trade agreements (PTAs). A special case is the full integration of Hong Kong into China. An increasing number of countries participate in one or more PTAs with neighbouring countries or major trade partners outside the region. Particularly in Latin America, a complex cobweb of overlapping PTAs has been created in the 1990s to support the radical liberalization process. Partnerships among countries in the region and the Triad powers in PTAs may have significant trade-creation and diversion effects for participants as well as outsiders.

In this new setting the EU faces two challenges. First, to stimulate its own growth the EU needs to strengthen its position in Asia and Latin America. During the past decades, trade and investment between the EU and both regions have grown strongly and the share of these flows in the overall external economic relations of the EU has increased substantially. At the same time, however, the EU faces strong competition in these markets and its market shares in emerging markets have been declining. Strengthening the EU's position requires not only improved competitiveness and marketing at the level of the firm, but also EU initiatives to improve market access by lowering barriers to entry. No matter whether this will be negotiated in a multilateral or regional framework, it will require trade concessions on the side of the EU.

Second, the EU must respond to the policy initiatives of its major competitors in global markets, the USA and Japan, and the new regional superpowers in order to reduce the risk of becoming an outsider in these markets and to avoid the costs of trade and investment diversion.

This chapter analyses the new setting in which the EU has to design a new approach towards the Pacific Rim and Latin America, the policy choices that have been made to face the new challenges and the available options to intensify the relationships with these regions in the future. Sections 2 and 3 study the general characteristics of the new setting in which the EU has to make its strategic policy choices towards the two regions. Section 2 focuses particularly on the new multilateralism and Section 3 on the new regionalism. Section 4 presents the policy options available to the EU to intensify its relations with both areas. Sections 5 and 6 review the traditional and recent policy initiatives towards Asia and Latin America respectively. More specifically, the sections focus on the Asia-Europe Meetings (ASEM) and the PTAs between the EU and Mercosur, Chile and Mexico that are in the making. The final section presents concluding observations.

2. The new multilateralism

The setting in which the EU and the newly emerging countries in Asia and America attempt to intensify their relations changed during the 1980s and 1990s in two respects. First, most emerging countries significantly reduced their most-favoured-nation (MFN) tariff rates and deepened their commitment to the multilateral trade regime by offering more significant concessions in the Uruguay Round than ever before. Second, many countries in both areas and particularly in Latin America have been involved in the establishment of new PTAs among themselves as well as with their major trade partners among the Triad powers.

The growing commitment of emerging countries to a well-functioning multilateral trade regime reflects their higher dependence on trade for their growth and development. Since 1980 many countries in both regions acceded to the General Agreement on Tariffs and Trade (GATT) as was the case with Colombia (1981), Thailand (1982), Hong Kong (1986), Mexico (1986), Venezuela (1990), Bolivia (1990), Paraguay (1993) and several other countries. By now, nearly all countries in the two regions are members of the WTO, the major exceptions being China, Vietnam and Cuba.

Not only did the number of Contracting Parties (CPs) among developing countries increase but also their involvement in the process of trade liberalization through tariff binding has been intensified strongly. Traditionally, developing countries have enjoyed special and differential treatment in the GATT. Art XII on Restrictions to Safeguard the Balance of Payments, Art. XVIII on Government Assistance to Economic Development and Part IV on Trade and Development provide for a more flexible and less demanding participation in the GATT. Moreover, the so-called Enabling Clause of the GATT, on 'Differential and More

Favourable Treatment, Reciprocity and Fuller Participation of Developing Countries' allows them to enjoy preferential access to the markets of developed countries under the Generalized Systems of Preferences (GSP) without offering concessions in return. Also, they may notify PTAs among themselves under the provisions of the Enabling Clause as has been the case with Mercosur, which was notified to the GATT in February 1992 by Brazil. The Enabling Clause is less specific regarding the acceptable degree of tariff liberalization and the abolishment of non-tariff barriers (NTBs) than Art. XXIV is.

These special and differential arrangements allowed countries in Asia and Latin America to maintain a comprehensive and complex system of barriers against imports for several decades and to establish PTAs among them, which offered only little preferential margins to the partners. Strikingly, Brazil and India belonged to the founding fathers of the GATT in 1947 and were among the most protectionist countries in the world for many decades.

In several respects the Uruguay Round has changed in a significant way the position of developing countries and particularly newly emerging countries in the multilateral trade regime and contributed to their fuller integration in the world trade system. They accepted as a single undertaking the Multilateral Agreements on Trade in Goods, the General Agreement on Trade in Services (GATS) and the Agreement on Trade-Related Aspects of Intellectual Property Rights (TRIPs). Many provisions for special and differential treatment have been included in GATT 1994 and this holds also for the continued application of the Enabling Clause, but in several respects the degrees of freedom of developing countries have been reduced. Particularly the Understanding on the Balance-of-Payments Provisions of the GATT 1994, which relates to Art. XII and XVIII:B may increase discipline. Most significantly, all developing countries have schedules in the areas of goods with bound agricultural tariffs and many countries have bound a large part of their industrial tariffs as shown in Table 13.1.

In many cases, however, the actual tariff reductions and cuts in NTBs had taken place in the process of unilateral and autonomous structural adjustment, not so much as part of the multilateral negotiations in the GATT. Tariff ceilings in the GATT have been set at rates much higher than the rates actually applied. In Asia the percentage shares of imports with bound rates are smaller than in Latin America and the ranges of bound and applied Post-Uruguay Round rates are much wider. By comparison levels of applied tariff rates are low in South Korea and Malaysia and relatively high in Thailand. In most Latin American

Table 13.1. Tariff protection in Asia and Latin America.

	Imports with bound tariff rates (%)		Tariff rates (%) Post-Uruguay Round	
	Pre-Uruguay Round	Post-Uruguay Round	Applied	Bound
Latin America				
Argentina	17.1	100.0	10.3	31.0
Brazil	16.0	100.0	11.7	29.0
Chile	100.0	100.0	11.0	25.0
Colombia	4.4	100.0	10.9	39.7
Mexico	100.0	100.0	10.4	34.1
Peru	17.1	100.0	14.6	33.7
Venezuela	100.0	100.0	12.4	31.6
East Asia				
Indonesia	29.7	93.4	10.7	38.4
South Korea	21.3	83.2	7.7	16.4
Malaysia	1.6	77.4	6.4	9.3
Thailand	7.5	64.3	26.1	27.5
Latin America	50	100	11.7	32.7
East Asia	16	77	11.9	21.0
European Union	98	100	2.8	3.2

Notes: [1] Latin America: Argentina, Brazil, Chile, Colombia, El Salvador, Jamaica, Mexico, Peru, Uruguay and Venezuela.

[2] East Asia: Indonesia, Macao, Malaysia, Philippines, South Korea and Thailand.

Sources: J. Finger, M. Ingco and U. Reincke, *The Uruguay Round: Statistics on Tariff Concessions Given and Received*, as reproduced in: J. Nogués, 'Comment: The Linkages of the World Bank with the GATT/WTO', in: A.O. Krueger (ed.), *The WTO as an International Organization*, The University of Chicago Press, Chicago, 1998, and J. Finger and L.A. Winters, 'What Can the WTO Do for Developing Countries?', in: A.O. Krueger (ed.), *op.cit.*.

countries the use of NTBs has been restricted strongly and import tariff rates have been bound in the WTO for 100 per cent. The levels of bound tariff rates are rather high as compared to applied rates. As shown, post-Uruguay Round bound tariff rates in most of the large countries in Latin America are in the range of 29-34 per cent and applied rates are in the range of 10-15 per cent. This gives countries room to re-introduce barriers against imports to support their domestic industry or the balance of payments or, alternatively, to bargain for concessions in the WTO or PTAs.

3. The new regionalism in Asia and America

A second major element of the new setting in which future relations between the EU and emerging Asia and America will have to take shape, is the recent proliferation of PTAs in Latin America and to a lesser extent in East and South-East Asia. Figure 13.1 positions in a schematic fashion emerging Asia and America, two Triad powers and some other trade partners in this new setting.

It is remarkable to witness the rise of regionalism at the time that unilateral and multilateral liberalization have reduced the room to offer meaningful trade preferences substantially. Gravity models of international trade show that the impact of PTAs is additional to basic factors determining the size of trade flows such as gross national product (GNP) and population size of the trade partners, the degree of similarity in the structure of import demand and export supply or comparative advantage of potential suppliers and access to markets. The trade history of both regions shows that trade may expand strongly outside the framework of a PTA and that, alternatively, trade may be insignificant and stagnant notwithstanding trade preferences.

Regionalism in the Pacific Basin

In the case of Asia, economic links among the countries in the region have intensified because of high overall economic growth during several decades and a process of relatively early and gradual trade liberalization. Intra-regional trade in the Pacific Basin has been stimulated particularly by the high degree of complementarity between natural-resource poor, densely populated and industrialized economies such as Japan, South Korea, Taiwan, Hong Kong and Singapore, and natural-resource rich countries such as Malaysia, Indonesia and the Philippines. Moreover, intra-industrial patterns of specialization have developed between the industrially more advanced countries in the region and countries with a comparative advantage in labour-intensive production and assembly activities. In this vast region growth triangles may be distinguished of countries combining intensively different sources of comparative advantages (Chia Siow Yue and Lee Tsao Yuan, 1993). Informal networks and family ties rather than

Figure 13.1. The proliferation of preferential trade areas in Asia and America.

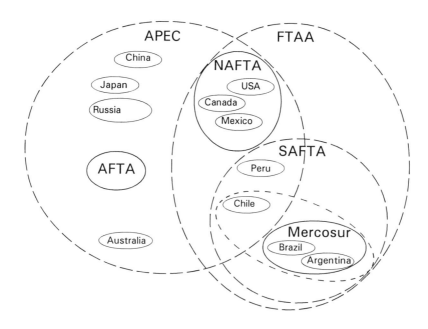

formal PTAs have played a significant role in shaping these intra-regional economic linkages (Noland, 1990).

So far, PTAs have hardly played a role in stimulating trade among Asian countries, as well as trade between Asia and the rest of the world economy, with the exception of the GSPs. Even ASEAN, prior to the promulgation of the establishment of the ASEAN Free Trade Area (AFTA) in January 1992, hardly contributed to intra-regional trade in South-East Asia. Also, the Asia-Pacific Economic Cooperation (APEC), formed in 1989, was initiated primarily to exchange information and facilitate policy co-ordination and harmonization, not so much to liberalize trade in a co-ordinated fashion, left alone to create trade preferences.

Against this background, the announcement of the initiative in January 1992 to establish a PTA among ASEAN countries - AFTA - reflects a significant change in policy direction. The initiative aims at reducing intra-group tariffs to 5 per cent within a period of 15 years. The ambition is to include all 10 countries in

South-East Asia and to liberalize markets for manufactures and agricultural products as well as financial services. In September 1994 it was agreed to shorten the timetable for cutting import tariffs above 20 per cent from 15 to 10 years with the deadline in 2003. Moreover, it was agreed to include agricultural products in the liberalization process. Also, ASEAN countries have aimed at the creation of an ASEAN Investment Area (AIA) to encourage foreign direct investment (FDI) by reducing barriers to the free movement of financial flows and by improving transparency.

More significant for the countries in the region as well as the rest of the world economy may be the future implications of unconditional or conditional free trade among APEC member countries as proposed at the APEC Summit in Bogor in November 1994. APEC has become an open economic association among an increasing number of countries and with a broadening agenda. Since its formation APEC-wide joint initiatives have been promoted to stimulate economic growth and improve the conditions for international trade and investment. Its creation has been prompted by the continuous integration process in Europe and the shift in US trade policy reflected by the Canada-US Free Trade Agreement (CUSFTA) of 1989 and the steps towards the North American Free Trade Agreement (NAFTA) in 1993.

Open regionalism has been the predominant approach towards trade liberalization in the region and distinguishes APEC from trade agreements such as the EU, NAFTA and Mercosur. Open regionalism is characterized by concerted unilateral trade liberalization on an MFN basis (Drysdale et al., 1998, p.6). As the Eminent Persons Group of APEC puts it in its Second Report (1994, p. 2), open regionalism is

'A process of regional co-operation whose outcome is not only the actual reduction of internal (intra-regional) barriers to economic interaction but also the actual reduction of external barriers to economies not part of the regional enterprise; ... '

In this perspective, open regionalism is, by definition, a building block for a liberalized global economy. Such a strategy has the advantages of avoiding the costs of trade diversion and the complications related to GATT Art. XXIV requiring that 'substantially all the trade' is liberalized in the region. More generally, open regionalism bypasses conflicts between multilateralism and regionalism at a large scale. At the same time, it opens the option of free-rider behaviour of non-members.

Three factors may complicate the realization of region-wide free trade or the establishment of a WTO-consistent PTA among APEC member countries. First, there are extremely wide differences among APEC countries in levels of economic development and degrees of competitiveness, economic organization and orientation. Apart from the USA and Japan, the group involves other high-income countries such as Canada, Australia and New Zealand, middle-income countries in Asia and Latin America such as South Korea, Malaysia, Thailand, Indonesia, Mexico, Chile and Peru, and countries in transition such as the Russian Federation, China and Vietnam. Consequently, countries differ widely in their capability to participate in a group-wise effort to liberalize trade. This is reflected by the different timetables for liberalization that have been proposed and the different priorities to include liberalization of agriculture in the APEC agenda. The USA, Canada and Australia insist on a comprehensive liberalization package but Japan, China, Taiwan and South Korea prefer a more exceptional treatment of the agricultural sector.

Second, a number of the Asian APEC countries have indicated at several occasions to have a preference for an exclusive East Asian Economic Group or East Asian Economic Caucus (EAEC) as proposed by Malaysia rather than the more heterogeneous group of APEC members.

Third, countries differ in their appreciation of the implications of open regionalism for non-members, which reflect in part differences in trade interests and strategic objectives. Japan and the newly emerging countries in Asia, particularly Indonesia, take the view that unconditional and non-discriminatory treatment of outsiders is preferable and Asian countries have confirmed their preference for MFN-tariff liberalization during the APEC Osaka Summit in November 1995. However, the USA, Canada and Australia prefer extension of concessions to outsiders on a reciprocal basis, to avoid giving the Europeans a free ride in the region.

In case APEC members would offer extension of benefits to non-members on the basis of reciprocity in order to avoid free rides, Art. I of the GATT on the MFN principle is violated since such a measure discriminates among non-members.

The USA in particular pushed strongly for trade and investment liberalization in APEC economies and managed to get the objective of free trade by the year 2010 for industrialized countries and 2020 for the rest of APEC accepted and included in the Bogor Declaration of November 1994.

Thurow has questioned the relevance of the decision to transform APEC into an area of free trade by the year 2020 suggesting that by implication there is no consensus on free trade in the region at an earlier time (Thurow, 1996, pp. 124-25. See also Chapter 2 of this volume).

Although APEC is not meant to become a closed block, the process of regional harmonization of trade and investment-related rules and standards may have significant consequences for the capability of outsiders to compete in the APEC region, even if free trade would be extended unconditionally to non-members. In case conditionality is introduced, rules of origin may limit the option for outsiders to gain from trade liberalization. Hence, there are good reasons for the EU to take complementary initiatives towards the APEC region.

Cobwebs of preferential linkages in Latin America

In contrast to Asia, Latin American has had a long history of establishing PTAs, which goes back to the early 1960s. The first wave of PTAs in the 1960s aimed at supporting a process of inward-orientated industrial development by protecting regional industry against outside competition. This policy kept external trade barriers high for a long time and liberalized intra-regional trade only to a limited degree. Notwithstanding the existence of a number of overlapping PTAs in the region, intra-regional trade as a share of overall trade tended to decline, particularly so during the 1980s.

From the early 1990s onwards, a second wave of PTAs swept the region and within a fairly short period of time a region-wide cobweb of preferential linkages has been established as also discussed by Ventura Dias in Chapter 14 of this volume. These PTAs aim at supporting the process of trade and investment liberalization, initiated in most countries only in the second half of the 1980s as part of structural reform programmes.

Renewed growth, overall liberalization and trade preferences have contributed to a strong increase in intra-regional trade in Latin America in the 1990s. It should be added, however, that there are also costs involved in this specific strategy. Although PTAs may have supported trade liberalization programmes, the emerging layers of preferential linkages with different rules of origins, preferential margins, exclusion lists and timetables contribute to the complexity of the liberalization process, may increase transaction costs and ultimately inflict welfare costs upon the region, as compared to an ideal process of unilateral or multilateral trade liberalization.

In this context Mercosur plays a crucial role since it involves two regional economic superpowers with a combined production of over 40 per cent of region-wide GNP measured at PPP prices. To the extent that Mercosur contributes to growth in its member countries, it may stimulate trade with the rest of the region but trade diversion may inflict welfare losses to trade partners,

Moreover, Mercosur is actively involved in shaping the trade and investment relations in the region by establishing special and preferential linkages with many countries inside and outside the region. In doing so, Mercosur has started to become the centre of a more comprehensive trade regime that will integrate a large part of the Latin American market. The priorities in this regard have been laid down in the Mercosur 2000 Action programme approved by the four heads of state in December 1995. Chile and Bolivia have become associate members of Mercosur in 1996 and 1997 respectively and it is expected that a PTA with Mercosur will be established by 2006. Moreover, Mercosur and the Andean Community signed a framework agreement in April 1998 which aims at launching a PTA by 2000. Also, Brazil has supported Venezuela to join Mercosur, and Mexico as well declared its interests in a special linkage with Brazil and Mercosur. In 1998 Mercosur and the Central American Common Market (CACM) agreed to set in motion a programme of tariff reductions in order to start a PTA among them. Finally, trade and investment agreements were signed with Canada. The extension of Mercosur and its new linkages with the rest of the region may be considered essential elements for the realization of one of Brazil's foreign policy initiatives, the South American Free Trade Area (SAFTA). Brazil announced in 1993 that such a PTA was to be created in 10 years of time. SAFTA aims at liberalizing trade among all members, not a hub-and-spoke model with bilateral linkages.

The new initiatives to establish preferential linkages between the USA and Latin America mark a major change in policy for all partners concerned. Traditionally, the USA supported multilateralism and only recently it has broadened its policy options by getting involved in the establishment of PTAs. By doing so, the USA makes progress in its international economic agenda less dependent on multilateral co-operation and creates a mechanism that provides it with more leverage over its economic partners as well as over multilateral institutions. The initiation of negotiations on a NAFTA and the announcement in June 1990 to create a Western Hemisphere Free Trade Area (WHFTA) not only created a new framework for hemispheric relations but was also a signal to the EU not to put progress in the Uruguay Round at risk.

Within a relatively short time span the USA established CUSFTA and NAFTA, took the initiative to create an area of free trade in the Pacific Basin among the countries associated in APEC and is the driving force behind a Free Trade Area for the Americas (FTAA).

The initial plan to establish free trade from Alaska to Tierra del Fuego in a WHFTA envisaged bilateral negotiations between the USA and individual countries or members of an existing PTA that were considered by the USA to be ready for a NAFTA-like arrangement. Chile and Argentina in particular indicated at the time to be interested in such an agreement.

Although the average MFN tariff rates of the USA are relatively low except for sensitive sectors, and Mexico and other Latin American countries have reduced their tariff rates significantly, trade and investment-diversion effects of these PTAs may negatively affect other trade partners and stimulate them to seek similar arrangements or compensation. Trade and investment diversion and the implications of stringent rules of origin of NAFTA on outsiders are discussed by Mathieson (1993) for Japan, Paemen (1996) for the EU and Frankel and Wei (1997, p. 87) for the East Asian developing economies. To avoid such effects, Thailand, South Korea and Singapore indicated their interest in participating in a NAFTA-like arrangement. According to the study by Hufbauer and Schott (1994, pp. 162 and 163) on the implications of a WHFTA for outsiders, trade-diversion effects for the EU will be concentrated particularly in the sectors of food, textiles, primary metals and chemicals.

In 1994, the USA initiated the plan for a FTAA during a hemispheric meeting of heads of states in Miami in 1994, aiming at hemispheric free trade by 2005. In the new approach all countries in the southern hemisphere will participate in negotiations on the comprehensive liberalization of trade among all of them. Such a strategy would deny the USA the potential advantages of the hub-and-spoke approach envisaged at an earlier stage. At the Trade Ministerial meeting in Belo Horizonte in May 1997 it was decided that the FTAA can co-exist with bilateral and sub-regional PTAs to the extent that the rights and obligations under these agreements are not covered by or go beyond the rights and obligations of the FTAA (Trade Ministerial Meeting, 1997).

The intensification of regional linkages between Mercosur and the rest of the region or the establishment of SAFTA will strengthen the position of the combined group of countries and particularly of Brazil in negotiations on the structure and the rules of a FTAA. Mercosur is at the heart of the Brazil's so-called building blocks approach of a FTAA to be built upon existing PTAs, not as an extension of NAFTA. In 1996, the USA proposed Brazil to form a strategic partnership to establish a hemispheric PTA by the year 2005.

Notwithstanding significant liberalization and structural reform in the countries in Latin America, only little progress has been made so far in establishing a hemispheric PTA. This has opened new opportunities for Brazil and the EU to establish preferential trade links with the countries in the region on terms that reflect more their own interests.

4. Strategic options for the EU

Essentially, the EU has four options at its disposal to improve access to the emerging markets and reduce the advantages that its main competitors may have created or are in the process of creating in these markets through the establishment of PTAs.

First, by speeding up multilateral rounds of trade liberalization to reduce the significance of preferential margins and essentially to undercut the rationale of regional preferential areas.

Second, by joining preferential areas of its main competitors. Of course, European firms have the option of joining by investing directly in the PTAs.

Third, by establishing its own PTAs with the same groups of emerging markets.

The fourth option is a sort of in-between approach by using effectively the offer of an unconditional extension of benefits, which members of a free-trade association may offer to non-members, or, alternatively, to respond to the option of a conditional extension of benefits of a regional PTA to non-members. The case of a PTA offering non-members unconditional extension of benefits conforms to the trade strategy of so-called open regionalism as proposed by some APEC countries.

When reviewing the recent initiatives of the Union, it may be noted that combinations of these options are being used. The initiative of the Commission to launch a new round of negotiations in the WTO reflects the EU priority to improve access to markets worldwide and will, if realized, reduce preferential margins of PTAs. Also, the Commission has taken policy initiatives towards emerging Asia and Latin America, the most significant of which are ASEM and the announced PTAs with Mercosur, Chile and Mexico. In addition, the

Commission has made a proposal to turn Lomé into several reciprocal PTAs, one of which involving the countries in the Caribbean.

5. Asia-Europe meeting

Europe and Asia have been too faraway for a long period of time, as Kagami indicates in Chapter 15 of this volume, notwithstanding the special arrangements made in the past to stimulate trade and investment between the two regions. The establishment of special and informal relations between the European Community (EC) and ASEAN goes back to 1972. By 1980 the EC-ASEAN Co-operation Agreement was signed with an emphasis on economic co-operation. This agreement has long served as the cornerstone of the EU's Asia policy (Dent, 1997-98). In the context of the agreement ASEAN received financial and technical assistance to promote trade with the EC, support for industrial and technical development, and project support in the areas of agriculture and transportation. Also, ASEAN countries benefited from the EC GSP. Moreover, the European Investment Bank (EIB) has extended its lending operations since 1993 to countries in Asia in the context of co-operation agreements. Apart from co-operation at the level of governments, dialogues were initiated between the private sectors of both regions. For an overview of traditional economic relations between the EC and ASEAN see Akrasanee and Rieger (1982).

Special arrangements to support economic relations had also been made with many other countries in East and South-East Asia. In April 1978 a trade agreement between the EC and China was signed which was replaced by the trade and co-operation agreement of September 1985. Relations between the EC and Japan were intensified by the EC-Japan Joint Declaration of 1991, which deals with co-operation in the areas of technological and industrial development. Moreover, a trade and co-operation agreement between the EU and South Korea was signed in 1996 at the ASEM Summit in Bangkok in March 1996.

In 1994 the New Asia Strategy (NAS) was launched and endorsed by the European Council of Essen in December. The NAS was induced by several factors. To start with, changes in the economic setting as analyzed in the previous section, made a critical assessment of the adequacy and effectiveness of the traditional relations with the Asian region urgent. Also, the EC 1992 programme resulted in a uniform trade policy for the Community and created a new internal setting to design an external economic policy. Moreover, in the context of the EU's special and differential relations with countries around the world, a lack of balance was noticeable between the economic importance of regions and the content and significance of the Union's formal relations with them (Pelkmans, 1997).

The initiative to establish non-formal 'Pacific-style' ties between Asia and Europe came from the side of the ASEAN countries by the end of 1994. From the perspective of the EU, a broad policy dialogue with the Asian members of APEC would facilitate the implementation of the NAS. ASEM is meant to function outside formal regional structures such as ASEAN and the EU, and is not only a meeting at the level of governments but involves the business communities as well. Meetings among members of the private sector have been organized to facilitate trade, investment, technical and economic co-operation between large and smaller firms in both regions.

Clearly, neither the EU nor ASEAN seek to establish a PTA, both confirm their commitment to the strengthening of the multilateral rule of law in the areas of trade and trade-related matters, and both consider consultations and co-operation in that framework the most effective way to intensify their relations. In that respect, the NAS differs significantly from nearly all other initiatives the EU has taken in other parts of the world.

Both sides have an interest in enjoying the gains from trade and avoiding the risks of trade and investment diversion. Studies of the effects of European integration on Asia in the 1990s indicate that additional economic growth will stimulate demand for commodities that are traditionally imported from developing countries and that little trade diversion will occur. However, Asian producers of labour-intensive manufactured goods may have suffered from substantial trade-diversion effects of previous enlargements of the EU with Spain, Portugal and Greece. Enlargement with Sweden, Finland and Austria may have caused trade diversion for Japanese export industries in relatively skill-intensive sectors. The future enlargement with countries in Eastern Europe such as the Czech and Slovak Republics, Poland and Hungary may cause additional trade diversion. However, the longer-term dynamic effects of integration in Europe are expected to stimulate exports from Asia at rates that exceed trade-diversion effects (Frankel and Shang-Jin Wei, 1997, pp. 89-91).

So far, PTAs in Asia had only a marginal impact on trade and investment flows and did not affect the positions of outsiders negatively. However, the intensity of the trade links among the countries in East Asia and the APEC region exceed levels expected on the basis of gravity models, suggesting that an implicit Asian or Pacific trade bloc favours trade in a discriminatory fashion. Brown, Deardorff and Stern find that outsiders may gain from an East Asian PTA due to scale economies and increased product varieties, but the CGE model of Lewis, Robinson and Wang shows that the significant trade-creation effects of a potential APEC PTA is accompanied by trade diversion for the EU (Frankel and Shang-Jin Wei, 1997, pp. 94-104).

Rather than creating a 'Fortress Europe' and an inward-orientated Asian bloc, both sides strive for new openings and look for mechanisms to facilitate trade and investment through interregional consultations and initiatives, business exchanges and the creation of new private-sector partnerships. Hence, at the first ASEM Summit Asian participants have proposed trade liberalization in Europe parallel to that of APEC. Another form of co-operation may concentrate on the multilateral rule system. Less than two weeks after the first ASEM Summit, Sir Leon Brittan referred to the combined Europe-Asia effort to save the multilateral negotiations on financial services. In the same vein, the two regions could co-ordinate their efforts in future trade negotiations to liberalize trade in an wide array of services as well as agricultural products and to establish new rules and standards to facilitate trade, and to protect investments and intellectual property.

In view of the wide differences between the countries in both regions in a number of these policy areas - particularly non-discriminating rules for international investments and higher standards for internationally traded products - intensification of consultations may be helpful not only to strengthen interregional ties but also to support the multilateral system.

The Asia-Europe Vision Group (1999), which was established at the second ASEM Summit in London in April 1998, recommended that ASEM partners set the eventual goal of free trade in goods and services by the year 2025 by adopting a strategic framework for progressive trade liberalization among themselves.

6. The EU-Latin America PTAs

The special economic relationship between the EU and countries in Latin America has been based on special and differential trade arrangements, investment facilities and development aid. Countries in the Caribbean have participated in the Lomé Conventions and benefited from preferential access to the EU market and development aid. Some of them benefited particularly from the Sugar, Rum and

Banana Protocols and subsequent arrangements that safeguarded their shares in the European market. However, after the ruling of the WTO panel in favour of Latin American countries that suffer from discrimination in the EU banana market, future arrangements with the Caribbean countries will in all likelihood be less WTO-inconsistent than the current arrangements are. In the first decade of the 21st century, the preferential relationship between the EU and the Caribbean countries may take the shape of a WTO-consistent Regional Economic Partnership Agreement (REPA), as discussed by Stevens in Chapter 10 of this volume. Also, Latin American countries have received trade preferences in the context of the GSP of the EU with special schemes for Central America and the Andean countries with so-called special drug regimes.

Moreover, the EIB has made loans available in the context of co-operation agreements of the EU with Latin American countries since 1993, particularly to finance infrastructural projects. From 1988 the European Community Investment Partners (ECIP) programme has supported investment and co-operation through the creation of joint ventures, and since 1994 the AL-INVEST programme has supported co-operation between small and medium-sized firms in the two regions through its Eurocentres in Latin America.

Finally, the EU is the largest donor of development assistance to countries in the region. Over 60 per cent of all bilateral official development assistance (ODA) received by the region in the mid-1990s was donated by the member countries of the EU and the Commission through its co-operation funds. Particularly Central America and the Andean countries benefited from these aid flows. New forms of development co-operation have been introduced including external debt relief for countries in Central America. The Commission aims at concentrating ODA to the poorest countries in the region to enhance its effectiveness and efficiency (IRELA, 1999).

Apart from these initiatives in the economic sphere, the Union has intensified the political dialogue with Latin America under its Common Foreign and Security Policy (CFSP) and the framework agreements for co-operation with Mercosur, Chile and Mexico that have been signed in 1995, 1996 and 1997 respectively (IRELA, 1997).

The recent initiatives to establish PTAs between the EU and Mercosur, Chile and Mexico involve major policy changes but fit well with the overall long-term trade strategies of countries in both regions to organize trade and investment links in the context of PTAs.

Countries have different reasons to participate in PTAs as indicated by Winters in Chapter 9 of this volume. Economic objectives appear to be dominant not only in the smaller partner countries but also in the EU. From the perspective of the Latin American countries, such PTAs will improve their access to the large EU market and may reduce trade diversion of EU PTAs with Central and Eastern European countries (CEEC) and countries in the Mediterranean and North Africa (MENA) that have already or will receive preferential access to the EU market, and supply a similar range of primary products. In the case of Mexico, a PTA with the EU may reduce the overall dependence on the USA and more specifically the costs of trade diversion resulting from NAFTA.

From the perspective of the EU, the PTAs would provide producers of exportables with preferential access to over 70 per cent of the Latin American market and reduce actual discrimination and trade diversion that they suffer in the markets of Mercosur and NAFTA, and potential diversion effects of SAFTA or FTAA.

A PTA with Mercosur is particularly significant in terms of potential flows of exports of goods, services and investment. However, even without preferential access, the Mercosur market has been gradually liberalized by the reduction of the common external tariffs (CET). As shown in Table 13.2, the average CET rate will be 11.2 per cent and 11.5 per cent for manufacturing at the end of the transition period which will be in January 2001 for Argentina and Brazil and January 2006 for Paraguay and Uruguay. Among the most important exceptions are metal products and transport equipment. As noted earlier, applied rates in the Mercosur member countries are significantly below the levels at which they are bound in the WTO, thus allowing for upward adjustments without violating WTO commitments. However, the effective rates of protection in manufacturing may be significantly higher than nominal rates and the highest effective CET rate in 2006 will be 53.1 per cent for cars, trucks and buses (Laird, 1997, p. 15).

Notwithstanding substantial reductions in external trade barriers there is concern about trade-diversion effects, particularly in some capital-intensive sectors such as capital goods and transport equipment (Yeats, 1997) which are of major importance from the perspective of EU exporters and investors. In itself this provides a rationale for the EU to negotiate for preferential access. It should be noted, however, that transport equipment has not yet been integrated fully in the Mercosur CET regime. According to schedule, Brazil and Argentina must establish a Common Automobile Regime by the year 2000. In the preliminary agreement

Table 13.2. Final common external tariff (CET) of Mercosur, 2001/06.

	%
Total	11.2
Agriculture, hunting, forestry and fishing	7.0
Mining and quarrying	3.4
Manufacturing	11.5
Food, beverages and tobacco	11.6
Textile, wearing apparel and leather	17.1
Wood and wood products incl. furniture	10.5
Paper, paper products, printing and publishing	10.9
Chemicals	8.1
Non-metallic mineral products	10.9
Basic metal products	9.9
Fabricated metal products, machinery and equipment	13.3
Other manufacturing industries	16.6

Source: WTO Secretariat, as reproduced in: S. Laird, *Mercosur: Objectives and Achievements*, Staff Working Paper TPRD 9702, WTO, Geneva, 1997.

the external tariff has been set at 35 per cent, the maximum allowed in WTO. At the same time, these high rates of protection have induced foreign firms to invest in production facilities in the region.

An additional consideration to opt for a PTA with Mercosur may be rooted in the instability of the Brazilian trade regime. In the recent past Brazil has adjusted frequently its tariff rates (Tavares and Tineo, 1998). At the request of the WTO, the International Monetary Fund (IMF) investigated Brazil's import regime for the car industry in 1995. Measures to limit imports and control investment in the automotive sectors provoked complaints in the WTO by Japan and the USA in 1996 and the EU and USA in 1997, and more complaints were filed in other areas by the Philippines, Sri Lanka and Canada in 1996 (WTO, 1998).

Moreover, the EU has a large interest in the liberalization of services in Mercosur, particularly in the sectors of transportation, telecommunications, banking and insurance. The Mercosur Framework Agreement on Services follows the approach of the GATS. Mercosur aims at establishing free trade in services among its members that will continue to apply national regulation towards non-member countries. According to Art. V.1 of the GATS on economic integration, a special or preferential agreement must have 'substantial sectoral coverage' in terms of number of sectors, volume of trade affected and modes of supply and should not provide for the *a priori* exclusion of any mode of supply. Moreover, such an agreement must provide 'for the absence or elimination of substantially all discrimination' among the parties, including national treatment as stipulated in Art. XVII of the GATS. However, Art. V.3 provides flexibility regarding these conditions for developing countries that are members of such a PTA. This relatively unexplored and complicated domain of trade negotiations may be difficult to include in a comprehensive agreement particularly in view of the 'sensitive' character of specific services.

Mercosur member countries as well as Chile have strong comparative advantages in agriculture and cattle husbandry and their exports to the EU are concentrated in a limited range of product groups including soya and derivatives, livestock, meat and derivatives, fresh fruit, coffee and tobacco, and fish products. These agricultural imports are directly and indirectly affected by the complex set of measures and regulations of the Common Agricultural Policy (CAP) as discussed by Keyzer and Merbis in Chapter 7 of this volume. According to EU tabulations, 63 per cent of agricultural imports enter the EU market freely: 52 per cent under a MFN zero tariff rate and 10.5 per cent under a GSP zero tariff rate. Only between 10 and 12 per cent of total EU imports from Mercosur are sensitive agricultural and fishery products and all together, 14-16 per cent of all products imported from Mercosur are considered sensitive or potentially sensitive, including some industrial products. Among the most important of these sensitive products are beef products, selected cereals and sugar, and some fresh fruits. Calculations of the European Commission indicate that liberalization of imports from Mercosur and Chile would entail additional costs up to 14.3 billion ECU annually (IRELA, 1998, p. 1). According to the current interpretation of GATT/WTO Art. XXIV.8 'substantially all the trade' requires liberalization of 90 per cent of trade, implying that some import restrictions may be continued in a WTO-consistent PTA, but nevertheless a significant transformation of the CAP will be required to liberalize trade with Mercosur and Chile.

As compared to the market of Mercosur, the domestic markets of Mexico and especially Chile are much smaller and potential effects of liberalization of trade and investment will be less sizable. The integration of Mexico in NAFTA and its participation in APEC and several PTAs among countries in Latin America, as well as the association of Chile with Mercosur add to the economic significance of PTAs with these countries. It should be noted that even without tariff preferences, these markets are well accessible in view of the low average import tariffs applied as shown in Table 13.1. Chile intends to reduce its import tariffs further to 7 per cent in 2001.

The PTA in the making between the EU and Mexico aims at the liberalization of 'substantially all the trade' in goods, the progressive liberalization of trade in services, and the liberalization of capital movements and payments. Moreover, the agreement aims at the opening of government procurement, prevention of distortion or restriction of competition, and protection of intellectual property rights.

In the area of trade in services, the agreement must be in conformity with Art. V of the GATS. While the EU makes an exception for the audiovisual sector, it aims particularly at liberalization of professional services, basic telecommunications, financial services and transport services.

Contrary to the trade relationship with the countries in the Southern Cone, a PTA with Mexico does not require substantial adjustments in the agricultural sector of the EU, which has facilitated the rapid conclusion of the negotiations. In the case of Mexico however, differences between NAFTA's rules of origin that are very detailed and specific in some manufacturing sectors and the rules the EU prefers to apply, have been a complicating factor in the negotiations.

Negotiations resulted in an agreement on the reduction of EU tariffs on 82 per cent of goods imported from Mexico by July 2000 and elimination of tariffs on the remainder by 2007. Mexico will set a maximum tariff of 20 per cent on 60 per cent of industrial products imported from the EU until 2003, a reduction of the maximum tariff to 6 per cent on 70 per cent of industrial products imported from the EU in 2003. Remaining tariffs on sensitive products will be phased out by 2010.

7. Concluding observations

The analysis has shown that the EU has been rather late and slow in designing new policies and taking new initiatives to facilitate and stimulate economic relations with emerging markets in Asia and Latin America. To exploit fully the new opportunities in international trade and investment and strengthen interregional relations, the EU has a large interest in improving the functioning of the multilateral trade system. This objective may be realized in the following ways.

Probably the most significant contribution the EU can make in this regard is the full integration of its regime for the agricultural sector in a liberal multilateral trade regime as has been initiated in the WTO Agreement on Agriculture. Also, liberalization of its import regime for textiles and clothing according to the Agreement on Textiles and Clothing of the WTO may contribute significantly. CAP reform and abolishment of barriers against labour-intensive manufactured products would benefit particularly the emerging countries in Latin America and Asia, respectively.

Next, full compliance of PTAs in which the EU is involved with Art. XXIV and the Understanding on the Interpretation of Article XXIV of the GATT 1994, and with Art. V of the GATS may help to make regionalism and multilateralism mutually supportive.

Finally, by supporting and respecting the decisions of the Dispute Settlement Body (DSB) of the WTO the authority of the multilateral regime will increase. The complaints of Ecuador, Guatemala, Honduras, Mexico, the USA and Panama concerning the EU regime for the importation, sale and distribution of bananas are a case in point.

Comprehensive multilateral liberalization may deepen the relationship with emerging countries and provide an effective strategy to reduce the trade-diversion effects of PTAs for outsiders. The EU must be prepared to respond to the challenge of an APEC strategy of conditional open regionalism, as preferred by the USA, Canada and Australia, by liberalizing trade in industrial products in particular.

The worldwide proliferation of large PTAs underlines the urgency of scrutinizing the consistency of PTAs with WTO rules and more specifically to increase discipline in the application of rules of origin in PTAs beyond the requirements laid down in the Agreement on Rules of Origin in the WTO.

Apart from these initiatives at the multilateral level there is room for effective and efficient region-wise policy initiatives as well. The emergence of very large PTAs reflects intense competition among the Triad powers, particularly the EU and the USA. In case the USA would be successful in turning APEC into a preferential trade zone in the Pacific Basin, and at the same time in creating a free trade and investment area from Anchorage to Tierra del Fuego, it would have managed to put itself into the position of a giant hub with preferential access to the markets of Japan, China, and all emerging economies in Asia and Latin America except India. The US hub position would become even more articulated with a Trans-Atlantic preferential linkage.

The recommendation of the Asia-Europe Vision Group to take the initiative for non-discriminatory trade liberalization is particularly relevant in this context. Finally, the regional initiatives towards emerging Asia and Latin America may be very effective and efficient in reducing non-border barriers to trade and investment, enhancing transparency, establishing trade channels and creating investment opportunities for small and medium-sized firms, as has been the experience of the Internal Market programme of the EU itself.

References

Akrasanee, N. and H.Rieger, *ASEAN-EEC Economic Relations*, ISEAS, Singapore, 1982.

APEC, *Achieving the APEC Vision – Free and Open Trade in the Asia Pacific*, Second Report of the Eminent Persons Group, Singapore, August 1994.

Chia Siow Yue and Lee Tsao Yuan, 'Subregional Economic Zones: A New motive Force in Asia-Pacific Development', in: C. F. Bergsten and M. Noland (eds), *Pacific Dynamism and the International Economic System*, Institute for International Economics, Washington, D.C., 1993.

Dent, C., 'The ASEM: Managing the New Framework of the EU's Economic Relations with East Asia', *Pacific Affairs*, Volume 70, Number 4, Winter 1997-98.

Drysdale, P., A. Elek and B. House, 'Europe and East Asia: a Shared Global Agenda?', in: P. Drysdale and D. Vines, *Europe, East Asia and APEC - A Shared Global Agenda?*, Cambridge University Press, Cambridge, 1998.

Edwards, S., *Crisis and Reform in Latin America - From Despair to Hope*, Oxford University Press, Oxford, 1995.

Frankel, J.A. and S. Wei, 'The New Regionalism and Asia: Impact and Options' in: A. Panagariya, M.G. Quibria and N. Rao, *The Global Trading System and Developing Asia*, Oxford University Press, Oxford, 1997.

Hufbauer, G.C., and J.J. Schott, *NAFTA - An Assessment*, Institute for International Economics, Washington, D.C., 1993.

Hufbauer, G.C. and J. Schott, *Western Hemisphere Economic Integration*, Institute for International Economics, Washington, D.C., 1994.

IRELA, *XIII Interparliamentary Conference European Union-Latin America*, Base Document, Madrid, 1997.

IRELA, *Development Cooperation with Latin America: Will Europe's Role Diminish?*, An Irela Briefing, Madrid, 31 March 1999.

IRELA, *Preparing the EU-Mercosur Association – Benefits and Obstacles*, An IRELA Briefing (Updated Version), Madrid, 20 November 1998.

Laird, S., *MERCOSUR: Objectives and Achievements*, Staff Working Paper TPRD 9702, WTO, Geneva, June 1997.

Mathieson, R., *Japan and NAFTA*, The Pacific Institute, New York, 1993.

Noland, M., *Pacific Basin Developing Countries, Prospects for the Future*, Institute for International Economics, Washington, D.C., 1990.

Paemen, H., 'The EC and the WTO Agenda', in: P. van Dijck and G. Faber (eds), *Challenges to the New World Trade Organization*, Kluwer Law International, The Hague, 1996.

Pelkmans, J. 'A Bond in Search of More Substance: Reflections on the EU's ASEAN Policy', in: Chia Siow Yue and J. Tan, *ASEAN and EU – Forging New Linkages and Strategic Alliances*, ISEAS, Singapore, 1997.

Tavares de Araujo, Jr., J., and L. Tineo, 'Harmonization of Competition Policies among Mercosur Countries', *The Antitrust Bulletin*, Spring 1998.

Thurow, L.C., *The Future of Capitalism - How Today's Economic Forces Shape Tomorrow's World*, William Morrow and Company, Inc., New York, 1996.

Trade Ministerial Meeting, *Joint Ministerial Declaration of Belo Horizonte*, 16 May 1997.

US Department of State, *North American Free Trade Agreement*, Washington, D.C., 1992.

Yeats, A., *Does Mercosur's Trade Performance Raise Concerns about the Effects of Regional Trade Arrangements?*, Policy Research Working Paper Number 1729, The World Bank, February 1997.

World Bank, The, *The East Asian Miracle - Economic Growth and Public Policy*, Oxford University Press, Oxford, 1993.

Electronic sources

Asia-Europe Vision Group, *For a Better Tomorrow: Asia-Europe Partnership in the 21st Century*, Seoul, 1999 (www.mofat.go.kr/english/realtion/region/aevg).

WTO, *Second Ministerial Conference of the World Trade Organization*, Geneva, 18 and 20 May, 1998 (www.wto.org/anniv/press.htm).

14

MANAGING ACCESS TO MARKETS: THE EU AND LATIN AMERICA

Vivianne Ventura Dias

ECLAC, Division of International Trade,
Development, Finance and Transport
Santiago
Chile

1. Introduction

In the early 1990s, the European Councils of Corfu and Essen recognized that the diversity in levels of development among Latin American countries required specific actions within one integrated regional approach. The European Council approved a flexible policy framework adjustable to the different levels of development of each country or group of countries in Latin America[1]. As a result, countries in Central America and the Andean Community will be recipients of development aid, whereas more advanced countries such as Mexico, Chile, and the countries that form the Southern Common Market - Argentina, Brazil, Paraguay and Uruguay - may become suitable partners in activities of mutual interest (European Commission, 1995). Accordingly, several agreements were signed between the latter group of countries and the European Union (EU): an inter-regional economic and trade co-operation framework agreement with Mercosur in December 1995, a co-operation framework agreement with Chile in June 1996, and a political, trade and economic agreement with Mexico in 1997.

P. van Dijck and G. Faber (eds.), The External Economic Dimension of the European Union, 319–339.
© 2000 *Kluwer Academic Publishers. Printed in the Netherlands.*

The selection of countries was not fortuitous: Argentina, Brazil, Chile and Mexico account for roughly 78 per cent of all Latin American imports from the EU and 75 per cent of Latin American exports to the EU in 1997. Moreover, Brazil and Mexico together account for nearly 60 per cent of all Latin American imports from the European countries. Similar concentrations can be observed in investment flows.

This chapter examines the complex set of international economic relations within which the preferential trade arrangements between the EU and the advanced Latin American economies are being established. The European countries are in the process of simultaneously deepening and widening their integration process. The advanced Latin American countries are attempting to implement their own foreign-trade strategies that include the reinforcement of the regional integration process. In parallel, those countries are negotiating with other Latin American and Caribbean countries, Canada and the United States the establishment of a Free Trade Area of the Americas (FTAA). The EU and the USA are also negotiating agreements to liberalize their mutual trade. Moreover, all countries are involved in the launching of new trade negotiations in the World Trade Organization (WTO) to further liberalize trade and investment.

The following section will argue that in spite of trade liberalization, national governments exercise their power to control the access to and exclusion from their territories. Governments can choose from a set of trade liberalization arrangements, but there are few analytical propositions to guide them in the selection process, since traditional economic theory neglects important components of the international political economy. Section 3 will describe major asymmetries of trade and investment relations between Chile, Mercosur and Mexico with the European countries, which limit their bargaining power in the negotiations with the EU. Section 4 will briefly review the different strategies followed by Argentina, Brazil, Chile and Mexico to manage their integration into the world economy with the purpose of assessing how potential trade arrangements with the EU may fit in. Finally, Section 5 presents some considerations on potential obstacles to the negotiations of preferential trade agreements between Europe and the most advanced Latin American countries.

2. Access to markets: fair trade and reciprocity. Far from free trade?

Assuming that markets function properly and there are no obstacles to the entry and exit of firms, efficiency in production and commercialization is the major factor to determine the success of enterprises in domestic as well as international markets. In the real world of 'second-best' policies, however, national governments try to influence the level, direction and composition of international trade. States define and enforce property rights through which they exercise control on the access of private and public entities to their territories. Hence, market imperfections of governmental origin may prevent the price mechanism to allocate national resources according to comparative advantage and the potential gains from international specialization and trade to take place. Competition can also be hampered by actions of private agents, but these practices will not be dealt with in this chapter.

Given the predictable gains from trade, unilateral trade liberalization should be the expected outcome of self-serving governmental policies. Yet, since unilateral liberalization has been rather the exception in more than 150 years of modern international trade, the standard economic model is not very helpful in explaining why countries prefer to control the access to their markets through complicate administrative measures, rather than undertaking costless trade liberalization; and, moreover, why countries prefer bilateral and plurilateral agreements to regulate their trade relations with other countries rather than fully engaging themselves in multilateral and non-discriminatory trade liberalization.

The more recent literature on the political economy of trade considers that the gap between real world observations and the prescriptions of trade theory can be explained by factors that traditional trade theory does not take into account. This is to say that the context in which governments make trade-policy decisions involves important transaction and adjustment costs as well as distributive problems that are not taken into consideration in neo-classical trade theory (Baldwin, 1985).

Trade liberalization can be perceived as a goal mutually advantageous to the parties involved but that requires co-operation[2]. As in any collective action, there are incentives for countries to deceive their partners, since each signatory government has to face a constant pressure for protection from constituencies in its country. Trade-liberalization agreements are contractual arrangements that reduce uncertainty and limit asymmetries in information of trade partners (Yarbrough and Yarbrough, 1992). Yet, any of the possible trade-liberalization arrangements are subject to the normal transaction costs derived from contracting with imperfect information. In order to accomplish international co-operation it is necessary to achieve successful contracting in a particularly demanding strategic environment since countries can dispose of various trade liberalization alternatives to improve on their bargaining power vis-à-vis the other partners. As Keohane (1984, p. 54) proposed 'Co-operation should not be viewed as the absence of conflict, but rather as a reaction to conflict or potential conflict. Without the spectre of conflict there is no need to co-operate'.

Trade-liberalization arrangements are therefore institutions that render defection or violations to obligations more costly and therefore create more incentives for partners to co-operate. By defining means of enforcing contractual obligations, and by diffusing information on trade policies and instruments in member countries, any trade-liberalization arrangement can foster collective action and prevent strategic calculations to spread. This is true for all kinds of arrangements, with the exception of unilateral trade liberalization.

Since it requires no contractual arrangement, unilateral liberalization is costless to administer, but has no enforcement mechanism. Unilateral liberalization may help the country to reallocate its production structure according to international prices, and to reap the static effects of trade liberalization. Nevertheless, if trade partners do not spontaneously follow the country's move toward liberalization, its own liberalization will not assure the access of its products to other countries' markets.

Moreover, if the country is small in economic terms with no capability to influence prices and terms of trade, its own liberalization is not likely to have any 'demonstration' effect on other trade partners. Economic theory argues that small economies are better off by adopting unilateral trade liberalization because of the basic assumptions of competitive markets, and of free and costless access to markets.

Economic theory shows that under specific conditions and on the basis of specific assumption unilateral trade liberalization is a self-rewarding action. This leaves unexplained why the USA chose to promote trade liberalization through negotiated 'concessions' on a reciprocal basis: each tariff reduction had to be 'paid' by an equivalent tariff reduction. It is important to recall that the multilateral trading system is based on the principle of non-discrimination as laid down in the General Agreement on Tariffs and Trade (GATT)[3]. The same treatment should be accorded to national and imported products in domestic markets according to GATT Art. III on national treatment and trade concessions should be extended to all WTO members according to Art. I on most favoured nation (MFN). The GATT does not require reciprocity but the text of the agreement makes clear that negotiations are to be on a reciprocal and mutually advantageous basis. Also, the practice in GATT among major negotiating parties was to seek reciprocity in concessions from the 'largest supplier' of a good and those concessions were later to be extended to all Contracting Parties (CP) through the MFN clause[4].

In addition, the success of the first decades of the GATT in trade liberalization was attributed to specific historical factors rather than to a compelling belief in the benefits of free trade by governments. Those factors included the composition of the industries in which liberalization occurred, the domestic policies of industrial countries that accompanied liberalization in this period, and the structure of North-South trade[5]. Moreover, trade liberalization progressed in some markets while other sectors were 'temporarily' removed from the disciplines of the international trading system.

Conversely, there is a general agreement in the literature that narrowing gaps in productivity levels among countries, the development of international production and transnational corporations and more interdependence of markets made international markets a vital component of domestic growth. Hence, competition in international markets evolved into a fierce dispute while obstacles to the access to foreign markets became less transparent since standards rather than tariffs prevailed as instruments of market-access control.

Market access through all kinds of 'minilateralism' became the standard objective of trade policy of every government. After the completion of their extended internal market, European governments realized the importance of maintaining and intensifying the presence of European products, services, enterprises and technology in dynamic markets such as those in Latin America[6].

In the particular case of the USA, additional problems resulted from the erosion of the arrangements that had contributed to an effective transfer of power from the legislative to the executive branches of government to run trade policy in the national interest. The US Congress became increasingly dissatisfied with the results of trade policy and pressed the administration for a more active role in changing the direction and the content of US trade policy.

Since the beginning of the 1980s, members of the US government have expressed increasing demands for market access of their trading partners as well as for 'levelling the playing field' of international competition. Those demands were reflected in a strategy that Bhagwati called 'aggressive unilateralism'. Instead of unilateral liberalization, the USA decided to use access to its market as the carrot and stick to extract trade concessions from its partners. National legislation provided powerful and credible threats to persuade unwilling trading partners to co-operate in opening new areas of trade such as trade in services and to include new issues in trade negotiations such as the protection of intellectual property rights[7]. After the establishment of preferential trade agreements (PTAs) with Israel and Canada and the North American Free Trade Agreement (NAFTA), the Federal Administration showed its intention to move further along this route.

Fair trade and reciprocity became closely related and invaded the debate on trade policy. On the one hand, the defence of domestic interests against alleged unfair foreign-trade practices was transformed into the expected outcome of trade policy. On the other hand, reciprocity that was a driving force for freer trade in the early days of the GATT ended up being associated with equalizing production, distribution and marketing conditions abroad with those in the USA.

Therefore, reciprocity was converted into a notion about equal market access in terms of outcomes rather than - as it had been formerly understood - in terms of opportunities. The major risk is that emphasis on fair trade and unfair practices may lead to discrimination and quantity-orientated market-sharing arrangements. Consequently, trade policies shaped by those notions will tend to be more sector-specific and country-specific than in the past. Ultimately, concerns with this kind of reciprocity are more consistent with a system of managed trade than with a rules-based system of open and competitive markets for all (Low, 1993).

There is a general consensus among economists that regionalism is complementary to multilateralism since trade and investment liberalization at the regional level will eventually converge towards multilateral liberalization[8]. Nevertheless, it is well documented that policies implemented during the European regional liberalization process brought about severe distortions in trade flows as well as in the international specialization of various countries. Baldwin (1997, p. 885) argues that the EU's Common Agriculture Policy (CAP) stands as one of the exceptions to his assertion that regionalism is a powerful force for multilateral liberalization. To minimize the impact of some of the Community decisions on its partners, the EU chose to manage the access to its integrated market through trade arrangements in which different groups of countries were treated differently and within each grouping of developing or industrialized countries different treatments were accorded.

Latin American countries, and among them the internationally competitive producers of tropical and temperate agricultural products, were adversely affected by European policies in two ways. The CAP denied them the access their comparative advantage required, and preferential trade areas (PTAs) with third countries from which Latin American countries were excluded, put the latter countries in a disadvantageous position. The introduction of the Generalized System of Preferences (GSP) in 1971 only partially compensated for Latin American losses, since the quantity of goods that were exempted from customs duties were subjected to ceilings and many products were excluded from the scheme. More recently, the GSP was further reformulated to adjust to the Uruguay Round obligations of European countries to exclude the more advanced countries from its benefits according to the graduation principle, and to include social and environmental concerns as well as a safeguard clause.

It is in this context of defence of domestic markets that the negotiations for preferential trade arrangements between the EU and Mercosur, Chile and Mexico will take place. By definition, Latin American economies are small and are better served by a strong rule-based trading system built on a balanced set of rights and obligations than by free trade arrangements with more powerful partners. However, as small players, they can neither define the terms of the negotiations nor refuse the possibilities of negotiations opened by their partners.

3. Asymmetries in trade relations between the EU and Chile, Mercosur and Mexico

From 1985 to 1995, Latin American countries went through a painful process of adapting their economies to the new conditions of the international economy. The contraction in foreign private loans that followed the foreign-debt crisis forced governments to adopt severe fiscal and balance-of-payments adjustment programmes. All Latin American countries moved away from a development strategy based on discriminatory trade and investment policies to embrace a combination of privatization, deregulation and trade and investment liberalization. The final results in terms of the policies adopted were quite similar albeit nations such as Argentina, Brazil, Chile, Mexico and Uruguay differed in political and institutional settings as well as in timing and sequencing of the implementation of the mix of macro- and micro-economic policies. Unilateral liberalization reduced average and modal tariff levels and drastically eliminated several layers of administrative controls and other non-tariff barriers (NTBs) established in earlier periods (ECLAC, 1997).

The direct result of those reforms was the restructuring of industrial and trade structures of major Latin American countries. Most of the enterprises that had been shielded from competition for so long had difficulties to meet the competition under the new more open trade regime and chaotic macro-economic conditions. The general trend was the strengthening of the industries in which those countries had comparative advantages based particularly on their natural resource endowment. With the exception of Mexico and to some extent Brazil, processed and unprocessed agricultural and mineral products predominate exports of Latin American countries. Moreover, in the case of Chile, the resource-intensive sectors have attracted foreign direct investments from industrial countries. The composition of those exports did not prevent growth of Latin American exports, particularly in the second half of the 1990s.

The direct result of those reforms was the restructuring of industrial and trade structures of major Latin American countries. Most of the enterprises that had been shielded from competition for so long had difficulties to meet the competition under the new more open trade regime and chaotic macro-economic conditions. The general trend was the strengthening of the industries in which those countries had comparative advantages based particularly on their natural resource endowment. With the exception of Mexico, and to some extent Brazil, processed and unprocessed agricultural and mineral products predominate exports of Latin American countries. Moreover, in the case of Chile, the resource-intensive sectors have attracted foreign direct investment (FDI) from industrial countries. The composition of those exports did not prevent growth of Latin American exports, particularly in the second half of the 1990s.

Trade relations between Latin America and the EU have been characterized by a lack of dynamism and wide asymmetries over the past decades, as a result of which the share of the EU in Latin American exports and imports has decreased considerably: from 33 and 28 per cent respectively in the 1960s and 1970s to 14 and 17 per cent respectively in 1996. Moreover, the limited growth in overall trade between the two regions was related particularly to a significant increase of Latin American imports from the EU, whereas the increase in exports was small and partially explained by price increases in agricultural and industrial products.

From 1990 to 1997, exports from Latin America to Europe increased by 21 per cent only whereas imports increased by 161 per cent.

Those averages hide important differences among countries and groups of countries in Latin America, although the basic trends are similar. South American countries have maintained closer trade and investment relations with Europe than Mexico and the Central American countries have. Europe accounted for less than 10 per cent of Mexico's exports up to the late 1970s. In the early 1980s, this share increased to 16 per cent and in the early 1990s it stayed at above 12 per cent, mostly because of oil exports. However, after the implementation of NAFTA, this share declined dramatically to slightly over 3.5 per cent.

On Mexico's import side, the share of Europe was reduced from about 17 per cent in 1990 to slightly over 9 per cent in 1997. This reduced presence of European goods and services in overall Mexican imports, however, has been accompanied by a large increase in imports from Europe, when measured in absolute terms, and a widening bilateral Mexican trade deficit in the trade relationship with the EU.

Europe used to be an important trade partner of Mercosur and Chile but here again, its role has tended to decline in the course of time, which has mostly been due to unilateral European trade-policy decisions. In the 1960s and early 1970s, over 48 per cent of exports of Mercosur and Chile were destined to the market of the 15 EU countries, whereas in 1996 this was reduced to about 24 per cent.

Also, the share of Europe in Brazil's imports was reduced form 33 per cent in 1970 to about 18 per cent in 1980. However, in recent years this import flow boomed and by 1996 and 1997, Europe's share has increased to 26 per cent. Here again, the Latin American countries accumulated significant trade deficits in their bilateral relationship with Europe.

Moreover, there has been little change in the composition of exports of the countries in the Southern Cone to the EU. Brazil exports products that are less processed, dynamic and technology-intensive than the average composition of Brazilian exports. In addition, there has been an increase in the share of commodities and a decrease in the share of manufactured products in Brazilian exports to the EU.

As shown by Van Dijck and Faber in Chapter 1 of this volume, trade with Latin America is only of little importance to the EU in relative terms, be it that it has shown much dynamism in recent years.

Latin America is not important as destination for European investments either. Although total foreign direct investment (FDI) flows from all countries to Latin America have increased substantially during the 1990s, Latin America accounted roughly for 4 per cent of European FDI in 1995. However, Latin America accounted for 28 per cent of European FDI flows outside OECD countries, compared to just 12 per cent in 1992. These investments are concentrated in Mercosur and Mexico - 56 per cent of all European FDI flows between 1990 and 1996 were channelled to Mercosur, 13 per cent to Mexico and 7 per cent to Chile. The USA continues to be the single major investor in the region, and Latin America accounts for an important share of US capital outflows.

4. National strategies to further integration into world markets

The vast literature on trade and investment policies in Latin America has identified the following four major factors as driving forces behind the general movement towards liberalization of trade[9]:

(1) the disenchantment of Latin American societies and their governments with the negative effects of import-substitution policies;

(2) the possible demonstration effect brought by the success of Asian exporters;

(3) the dominance of the neo-liberal doctrine, and

(4) the pressures by multilateral institutions on Latin American policy-makers (World Bank, 1993).

There is also consensus that unilateral trade and investment liberalization was crucial to explain further developments in regional integration, such as the formation and consolidation of the Mercosur as well as the Mexican decision to formalize its economic integration with the USA through a PTA.

There are additional micro-economic and institutional elements that contributed to the acceptance of trade liberalization by domestic entrepreneurs. First, industrial and entrepreneurial development itself that was supported by the policies of import-substituting industrialization. Regardless of static inefficiencies, fiscal and monetary problems associated with protectionist measures and other policy instruments directly linked to the import-substitution strategy, public policies helped Argentina, Brazil, and Mexico to develop their industrial and technological capabilities. The domestic entrepreneurial capacity that was created since World War II could benefit at a later stage from the dynamic opportunities that were opened by regional integration in the 1990s. Second, the period from

1965 to 1985 witnessed the emergence of organizations, rules, norms and procedures that are required for effective market operations within and between countries.

Conversely, the low level of industrial development hampered Latin American integration during the 1960s and early 1970s. At that time, labour-intensive and unsophisticated production processes dominated the industrial structure and the economies were highly dependent on extra-regional imports of technology, machinery and intermediate goods. Also, countries in the region were at similar stages of industrial development and domestic entrepreneurs had little exposure to external markets.

In addition, the principal objective of foreign-owned - mostly US majority-owned affiliates in Latin America - was market penetration rather than overseas production for exports. The combined effect of their strategies was market segmentation at the expense of integration, and protected regional markets at the expense of liberalization (Mytelka, 1992).

Hence, the major obstacle to the process of integration was paradoxically the very problem for which integration was proposed to be the solution. Put differently, the low level of industrial and entrepreneurial development in the region was a critical impediment for effective regional integration. As Fishlow (1984) phrased 'Economic integration failed not because of the large costs inherent in trade diversion, but because regional trade tended not to be divertible enough'. Regional markets were proposed as instruments to expose private enterprises in member countries to competition in a relatively friendly environment but enormous uncertainties and transaction costs associated with doing business in those markets would render the instrument ineffective. These factors had not been taken into account in the 'voluntarist' integration proposals of the 1960s[10].

From 1985 to 1990 all major Latin American economies implemented a policy of economic liberalization of trade and capital flows. The major exception was Chile where the process of economic reform had started much earlier (Agosin and Ffrench-Davis, 1993, p. 44). Parallel to the broad movement of 'unilateral' liberalization, these countries were very active in the Uruguay Round of trade negotiations. For the first time, Latin American tariff schedules included the totality of their tariff items although the ceilings of their tariff bindings were considerably higher than the actual tariff levels reached at the end of the process of unilateral tariff reduction (ECLAC, 1997). Moreover, Latin American governments decided to balance the multilateral liberalization process with bilateral and subregional preferential agreements. Some of these agreements – such as NAFTA and most Mexico-based minilateral agreements - include broader agendas and higher levels of commitments than the Uruguay Round agreements do, but they are extended to a small number of countries only.

In many ways, regional initiatives in Latin America have been functional to the process of unilateral and multilateral trade and investment liberalization comprising a general strategy of open regionalism. Subregional free-trade arrangements lent credibility to domestic liberalization policies since binding commitments at the subregional level necessarily raised the costs of violating agreements to individual countries. They have also contributed to a more gradual opening of the economies and helped governments to identify the impact of exposing local industries to foreign competition.

In Mercosur, the establishment of an effective timetable for tariff reduction, which was automatically applied across sectors, sent a clear message to entrepreneurs in member countries that their governments were committed to open markets to foreign competition albeit at a controlled pace.

The Treaty of Asunción, signed March 1991, contained a programme of trade liberalization (Annex I, Art. 3), that defined a timetable of tariff reduction starting in June 1991 (with a reduction of 47 per cent) and ending at 31 December 1994 (with 100 per cent). A reduced list of exceptions for each country was defined (Art. 6). However, the list should be shortened annually by a given proportion defined in the treaty. The subsequent negotiations on a common external tariff (CET) reinforced that message.

One additional variable that provided impetus to regional integration in Latin America has been the process actuated by the USA at the end of 1993 with the purpose of invigorating inter-American relations through an informal machinery of high level summits (Feinberg, 1997). Inter-American relations had been dormant since the melancholic failure of the Alliance for Progress in the late 1960s. In the Miami Summit of the Americas, which took place in December 1994, presidents and heads of state of 34 countries of the Western Hemisphere promised to execute an overly ambitious programme of inter-American co-operation. The Miami Summit produced a declaration of principles and a plan of action that contained 23 initiatives and more than 150 action items. Those initiatives expanded the scope of the hemispheric agenda and introduced new topics for inter-American co-operation such as the defence of democracy and good governance, fighting corruption and poverty, environmental protection, money laundering, civil society and women's rights. Those commitments were later renewed in the Second Summit of the Americas that was held in Santiago de Chile in April 1998.

The completion of the NAFTA negotiations took place during the first year of the Clinton Administration. The preparations for an inter-American Summit started soon afterwards and were dominated by the eagerness of most Latin American countries to join the new PTA, or conversely by fears of losing preferential access to the US market. The only moderate opposition came from Brazil that consistently put forward the need to strengthen the negotiating capability of Latin American countries and to slow the pace of the FTAA negotiations. That strategy implied the reinforcement of Latin American and the Caribbean subregional integration schemes, and in particular, priority for the formation of Mercosur.

During the negotiations for the Miami Summit, Brazilian diplomats were extremely careful to protect the status of Mercosur as a customs union. The wording of the Miami Declaration was skilfully negotiated to give higher prominence to the dynamics of subregional and regional integration and to prevent Mercosur and other subregional integration schemes from being impaired by the US initiative. Later, the other members of Mercosur endorsed the Brazilian position that became the official position of the group, not just in the FTAA negotiations but also in other meetings on the broad Miami Agenda. Hence, Mercosur countries defended the preservation of the dynamics of intra-Latin American economic, social and political integration, which should be allowed to evolve in parallel to deeper inter-American integration.

Domestic opposition in the USA to the expansion of NAFTA and the continuous discretionary use of US anti-dumping legislation against Latin American exporters - particularly Brazilian steel and Chilean salmon - helped the Brazilian and Mercosur position to gain wider support in Latin America. Moreover, the Santiago Summit endorsed the decisions taken at the meeting of vice-ministers in Costa Rica, that only subregional schemes that would evolve into deeper integration schemes than the FTAA will continue after the establishment of the FTAA.

In many ways, the nature and speed of economic co-operation in Mercosur have been triggered by the preparatory work of the FTAA. The second Summit of the Americas in Santiago de Chile formally launched the negotiations for the FTAA and defined the negotiating machinery. In December 1998, the Trade

Negotiating Committee further detailed the rules and procedures for the FTAA negotiations.

There are nine negotiating groups: market access, agriculture, investment, services, government procurement, intellectual property rights, subsidies, anti-dumping and countervailing duties, competition policy, and dispute settlement; a consultative group on smaller economies, a joint government-private sector committee of experts on electronic commerce, and a committee of government representatives on the participation of civil society.

In spite of the lack of the fast-track negotiating authority to the Clinton Administration, the FTAA negotiations are following their course. It should be a 'single undertaking' by consensus. Put differently, as in the Uruguay Round, the negotiations will be settled only after agreements will be reached in all negotiations. Attention will be focused on the major negotiating groups of market access and agriculture.

In parallel to the FTAA negotiations, Mercosur and the Andean Group are progressing in their negotiations for a South American Free Trade Area (SAFTA). These negotiations will be protracted because of major asymmetries in the productive structure of the two subregions. Chile and Bolivia already have an extended PTA with Mercosur. As the import tariffs of these two countries are lower than the CET of Mercosur, they have no interest in joining the CU. Nevertheless, Chile and Bolivia participate in Mercosur Summits of heads of states that are held every six months.

5. Prospects for free trade between EU and Latin America

The overall revival of geography in global economic integration has turned the relationship between regionalism, minilateralism and multilateralism into a central topic of international political economy. The expansion and consolidation of the European Internal Market and the control of access to European markets through a web of PTAs, the adoption by the USA of a multi-track trade strategy in which PTAs have gained prominence, the emergence of new and reinforced integration schemes in Latin America including PTAs among Latin American countries and between Latin American and industrial countries, are defining an increasingly complex trading environment for enterprises.

So far, there are no indications that the current move will lead to the fragmentation of the international economy, but there is the risk of governments' preference for discriminating liberalization as a negotiated solution for market access. Alternatively, partial liberalization may also be seen as a powerful instrument of multilateral trade liberalization. Over the past decade, principles, rules and procedures have been advanced in bilateral and plurilateral negotiations in areas in which no previous multilateral obligations existed (Baldwin, 1997).

Several initiatives have been implemented since the 1980s with the purpose of the deepening relations between the EU and Latin America and increasing European presence in the region. The admission of Portugal and Spain to the EU contributed to deepen trade and investment relations between Europe and Latin America. In particular, high-level meetings such as the Ibero-American Summits of heads of state and of governments and the political co-ordination of the Group of Rio created a fluid communication between European and Latin American decision-makers.

Third generation agreements were signed between the EU and all Latin American countries and subregions but the formal negotiations for PTAs are still in their preliminary stages. In the specific case of Mercosur, the European Commission has made efforts to establish the first interregional association between an integration scheme and the EU with strong political content, advanced forms of economic and technological co-operation, and a process of gradual trade liberalization.

European decision-makers did not hide that they would have preferred to have just one institutional structure in the Southern Cone. Put differently, they would rather sign a single agreement with Mercosur-Chile (Marin, 1996). The bargaining capacity of Mercosur and Chile *vis-à-vis* the EU is limited. The EU accounts for over 20 per cent of the exports of the Southern Cone countries, but only 2 per cent of exports of the European countries are destined to this part of the Western Hemisphere. Copper, metallic minerals, cellulose, furniture and fish flour are the major Chilean exports to the EU. The average import tariff of those products in the EU is zero or close to zero. Among Mercosur's exports to the EU are particularly agricultural, agro-industrial and other traditional products. Over 50 per cent of the products subjected to customs duties have preferential access to these European markets through the GSP, although from January 1999 onwards, Brazilian agricultural and agro-industrial exports are eliminated from the GSP and several other products face a reduction in their preferential margins.

Mexico is a special case in view of the overwhelming presence of the USA in Mexican trade and investment, and the significant diversification of its exports including skill- and technology-intensive manufactured products. In 1997, nearly 60 per cent of Mexican exports to the EU consisted of such products.

Remarkably, the first product exported by the EU to Mexico, ranked by its share in total Mexican imports, was milk powder. Hence, European negotiations with Mexico may proceed faster than negotiations with the other advanced Latin American countries will.

The first round of negotiations concluded in the second week of November of 1998. Three working groups of technical character were created: access to markets, trade in services and capital flows, and institutional aspects of the PTA. A timetable for the first eight months of negotiations was also defined (see the webpages of Secofi).

The negotiations for PTAs between the EU and Mercosur and Chile will face several problems since the room for negotiations by the Union is limited by: (1) the existing agreements that Europe maintains with other regions; (2) the impact that the negotiations with future members of the EU will have on the revision of the CAP (Agenda 2000), and (3) the multilateral commitments coming from the Uruguay Round agreements and the future round of trade negotiations.

Mercosur countries and Chile are competitive producers of agro-industrial products. The outcomes of calculations of the impact of a PTA with Mercosur and Chile on the CAP depend strongly on inclusion of the actual or the potential volumes of traded agricultural products. According to a preliminary study presented to the European Commission in July 1998, the elimination of duties on agricultural and agro-industrial products from Mercosur and Chile would require additional 14,300 million of ECU annually. Other studies concluded that less than 14 per cent of products exported by those countries to the EU could be considered 'sensitive', and that less than 2 per cent could affect the EU 'negatively'. Moreover, those impacts could be balanced by potential export expansion for the chemical, automotive and services sectors (IRELA, 1998a, p. 1).

Some European countries have raised objections to negotiating agricultural trade liberalization with Mercosur and Chile before the formal negotiations on agriculture are launched in the WTO and before the Agenda 2000 will be fully implemented (EUROLAT, 1998). On the other hand, the governments of Argentina, Brazil and Chile have made it clear that no negotiation will proceed without the inclusion of agricultural and agro-industrial products.

All Latin American countries wish a more significant European presence in Latin America to balance the influence that the USA has traditionally exerted in the region. This may also involve the presence of the alternative European model to contrast with the market-dominant model that the USA has been pushing. Finally, the European economic and social model may provide legitimacy to the regulatory powers of states in order to define and enforce a socially required discipline to markets.

Notes

[1] The regional approach is conducted through the Group of Rio institutional machinery.

[2] The standard concept of co-operation in international relations is Keohane (1984, p. 51): 'Co-operation requires that the actions of separate individuals or organizations – which are not in pre-existent harmony – be brought into conformity with one another through a process of policy co-ordination. This means that when co-operation takes place, each party changes his or her behaviour contingent on changes in the other's "behaviour"'.

[3] The GATT was incorporated into the WTO Agreement of 1994 and is referred to as GATT 1994.

[4] The 1934 US statute that provided the original text of the GATT was entitled Reciprocal Trade Agreements Act, and it implied that tariff and other barrier reductions would be agreed on a mutual and equivalent basis (Jackson, 1989). Also, US negotiators published a periodic report showing that the amount of trade coverage of concessions received was not lower than the trade coverage of concessions granted (Dam, 1970, p. 60).

[5] Ruggie (1982) used the expression 'embedded liberalism' to explain the success of the first wave of liberalization in the GATT. Tussie (1989), and Reich (1983) referred to the characteristics of the industries with greater concessions in which intra-industry trade was predominant.

[6] European decision-makers have recently announced a strategic approach to trade relations within which the access to external markets is crucial (European Commission, 1996).

[7] For all the historical information on the drafting of the relevant legislation, see Bhagwati and Patrick (eds), 1990.

[8] Bhagwati and Krueger are major dissenters of this view.

[9] See ECLAC, 1998b for a complete bibliography.

[10] Rosenthal (1991) divided the 30 years of Latin American Integration in three periods: (i) the voluntarist period (the 1950s and the 1960s), (ii) the revisionist period (the 1970s and part of the 1980s) and (iii) the pragmatic period (from the late 1980s onwards).

References

Agosin, M. and R. Ffrench-Davis, 'Trade Liberalization in Latin America', *CEPAL Review*, Number 50, August, 1993.

Baldwin, R., *The Political Economy of U. S. Import Policy*, MIT Press, Cambridge, Massachusetts, 1985.

Baldwin, R., 'The Causes of Regionalism', *The World Economy*, Volume 20, Number 7, November, 1997.

Barbosa, R.A., 'Uma Estratégia de Promoção Comercial Brasileira para a União Europea', *Revista Brasileira de Comercio Exterior*, 1998.

Bhagwati, J. and H.T. Patrick (eds), *Aggressive Unilateralism, America's 301 Trade Policy and the World Trading System*, The University of Michigan Press, Ann Arbor, 1998.

Bouzas, R., 'El Mercosur: Estado Actual y Desafíos de Política', in: Departamento Nacional de Planeación/BID (eds), *Integración Económica en Perspectiva*, Santafé de Bogotá, 1996.

Dam, K., *The GATT: Law and the International Economic Organization*, University of Chicago Press, Chicago, 1970.

Destler, I.M., *American Trade Politics*, Institute for International Economics, Washington, D.C., 1992.

Devlin, R. and R. Ffrench-Davis, 'Towards an Evaluation of Regional Integration in Latin America in the 1990s', in: J.J. Teunissen (ed.), *Regional Integration and Multilateral Cooperation in the Global Economy*, FONDAD, The Hague, 1998.

ECLAC, *Open Regionalism in Latin America and the Caribbean*, Santiago de Chile, 1994.

ECLAC, 'Los Acuerdos de la Ronda Uruguay sobre el Acceso a los Mercados de Bienes: Desafíos y Oportunidades para América Latina y el Caribe', in: *Panorama de la Inserción Internacional de América Latina y el Caribe*, Edición 1997, Santiago de Chile, 1997.

ECLAC, *América Latina y el Caribe: Políticas para Mejorar la Inserción en la Economía Mundial*, ECLAC/ Fondo de Cultura Económica, México, D.F., 1998a.

ECLAC, *La Inversión Extranjera en América Latina y el Caribe, Informe 1998*, Document LC/G.2042-P, Santiago de Chile, 1998b.

EUROLAT Carta Informativa, Volume 5, Number 23, October-November, 8 November, 1998.

European Commission, *The European Union and Latin America (1996-2000), Towards a Strengthening of the Partnership*, European Commission Communication, October 23, 1995.

Feinberg, R.E., *The Summitry of the Americas: A Progress Report*, Institute for International Economics, Washington, D.C., 1997.

Fishlow, A., 'The Debt Crisis: Solution by Economic Integration?, in: J. Nuñez del Arco et al. (eds) *The Economic Integration Process of Latin America in the 1980s*, BID, Washington, D.C., 1984.

IRELA, *Inversión Directa Europea en América Latina, Tendencias y Aporte al Desarrollo*, Informe de IRELA, 3 November, 1998a.

IRELA, *Preparando la Asociación UE-Mercosur Beneficios y Obstáculos*, Informe de IRELA, 20 November, 1998b.

Jackson, J., *The World Trading System Law and Policy of International Economic Relations*, The MIT Press, Cambridge, 1989.

Keohane, R.O., *After Hegemony: Cooperation and Discord in the World Political Economy*, Princeton University Press, Princeton, New Jersey, 1984.

Krueger, A., *American Trade Policy, A Tragedy in the Making*, The American Enterprise Institute, Washington, D.C., 1995.

Low, P., *Trading Free, The GATT and U.S. Trade Policy*, The Twentieth Century Fund Press, New York, 1993.

Marin, M., 'America Latina y Europa ante el Siglo XXI', in: P. Leiva (ed.), *America Latina y la Unión Europea Construyendo el Siglo XXI*, Ediciones CELARE, Santiago de Chile, 1996.

Ministry of Foreign Relations of Brazil, *Boletim de Integração Latino-Americana*, various issues.

Mytelka, L., *South-South Co-operation in a Global Perspective*, Paris, OECD, February, 1992.

Ostry, S. and R.R. Nelson, *Techno-Nationalism and Techno-Globalism, Conflict and Cooperation*, The Brookings Institution, Washington, D.C., 1995.

Ostry, S., *The Post-Cold War Trading System, Who's on First?*, The University of Chicago Press, Chicago, 1997.

Pelkmans, J., *New Horizons for Integration on Dominos, Alliances, Inside and Outside Regionalism*, paper presented at the seminar 'Escenarios Estratégicos de la Integración en el Umbral del Siglo XXI: Perpsectivas Americanas y Europeas', CEFIR, Brasilia, 6-8 October, 1998.

Reich, R., 'Beyond Free Trade', *Foreign Affairs*, Spring, 1983.

Rosenthal, G., 'Treinta Años de Integración en América Latina', *El Mercado de Valores*, Number 7, April 1, 1991.

Ruggie, J.G., 'International Regimes, Transactions and Change: Embedded Liberalism in the Postwar Economic Order', *International Organization*, Volume 36, Number 2, Spring, 1982.

Tussie, D., *Los Países Menos Desarrollados y el Sistema de Comercio Mundial*, Fondo de Cultura Económica, México, D.F., 1989.

Tussie, D. and D. Glover (eds), *The Developing Countries in World Trade - Policies and Bargaining Strategies*, Lynne Rienner Publishers, Boulder, Colorado, 1993.

Valdes, J.G., 'Chile y su Política de Acuerdos Económicos Internacionales', on the website of the Chilean Ministry of Foreign Affairs, 1998.

World Bank, The, *Latin America and the Caribbean - A Decade after the Debt Crisis*, Washington, D.C., 1993.

Yarbrough, B.V. and R.M. Yarbrough (1992), *Cooperation and Governance in International Trade - The Strategic Organizational Approach*, Princeton University Press, Princeton, New Jersey.

Electronic sources

Website of the Brazilian Ministry of Foreign Affairs (http://www.mre.gov.br).

Website of the Brazilian Ministry of Trade (http://www.mdic.gov.br).

Website of the Chilean Ministry of Foreign Relations (http://www.minrel.cl).

Website of the European Commission (http://europa.eu.int/comm).

Website of the Mexican Ministry of Trade (http://www.secofi.gob.mx).

15

EUROPE AND ASIA: TOO FARAWAY?

Mitsuhiro Kagami

Institute of Developing Economies/JETO
Tokyo
Japan

1. Introduction

Marco Polo wrote in his book *The Travels of Marco Polo* at the end of the 13th century that Beijing was the centre of the world where thousands of precious goods were brought from all over the world to the Imperial Palace as a tribute and that Quanzhou was one of the two largest commercial harbours in the world where the volume of the pepper trade was one hundred times larger than in Alexandria (Aoki, 1969). In the mid-17th century European pepper imports from Asia reached approximately 3,400 tons, of which 1,800 tons was imported by the Dutch East Indies Company and 1,600 tons by the London East India Company (Yamada, 1994).

The above-mentioned historical description shows that there was a lively trade between Europe and Asia at the time. However, contemporary relationships between the two regions seem to be, relatively speaking, somewhat restricted and narrow.

The remarkable growth of the East-Asian economies during the 1980s and the first half of the 1990s was reflected in the expansion of trade and investment between the European Union (EU) and East Asia. The share of exports to devel-

P. van Dijck and G. Faber (eds.), The External Economic Dimension of the European Union, 341–351.

oping Asia in total extra-EU exports increased strongly during the 1990s and amounted to 17 per cent in 1997 as shown by Van Dijck and Faber in Chapter 1 of this volume. At the same time, however, the share of EU exports destined to Japan declined to less than 5 per cent. Also, the relative share of the EU in imports of Japan and of developing Asia declined. Moreover, in relative terms the EU became a less significant export market for these Asian countries.

During the East-Asian monetary crisis and the onset of the Asian recession, the combination of depreciating East-Asian currencies and buoyant European economies have helped to drive Asian exports only in certain areas including electronics and textiles. However, the European boom seems to be more vulnerable of any possible downturn in the US economy and the turmoil in Russia which is itself expected to worsen in 1999. This will also affect trade between Europe and Asia adversely.

European capital flows to Asia are small as well. Outflows of foreign direct investment (FDI) from five European countries (France, Germany, Italy, the Netherlands, and the United Kingdom) amounted to 113 billion US dollars in 1995, of which 48.3 per cent went to the EU itself, 21.9 per cent to the NAFTA region, 5.7 per cent to Asia including Japan, 4.7 per cent to Latin America and 1.5 per cent to Africa as shown in Figure 15.1. The Asian share is small albeit expanding, and was only 2.8 per cent in 1990. This shows that Asia plays a marginal role for Europe in terms of trade and investment. Put differently, European economic ties with Asia are not as important to Europe as Europe itself or its ties with the USA.

The combination of a crisis-stricken Asia and Europe moving towards full integration seems to weaken the mid-term perspective of closer economic ties between the two regions.

The next section of this chapter analyses the introduction of the new monetary unit, the euro, and its impact on the world economy. Subsequently, the Asian recession caused by the Asian monetary crises will be examined. Both phenomena seem to weaken the relationship between the two regions. Section 4 reviews briefly the functioning of ASEM and presents some reflections on future relations. Section 5 presents some final observations.

2. A new power: the EU's inward drive

The EU realized its goal of integration in 1993. This integration has been strengthened by the Economic and Monetary Union (EMU). On 1 January 1999 a monetary union has started with the introduction of the euro in 11 member countries and the establishment of the European Central Bank (ECB). Denmark, Greece, Sweden and the United Kingdom will not participate in the first round of the union. For the first time in history, regional integration has culminated in real economic and political unity.

Initially each country has to co-operate to strengthen economic unity in the Single Market. For example, different interest rates, i.e. high Italian versus low German rates, should be narrowed, although at present world pressure is to lower the German rate. Moreover, the Stability and Growth Pact requires member countries to maintain budgetary discipline by themselves and by means of surveillance and sanctions systems. Unity and integration are the principal goal of the region. Levelling off differences in economic conditions in the region and building coherent policies internally will make Europe strong. Such an endeavour for economic convergence will result in an inward-looking inertia.

The introduction of the euro and the full use of the new currency from 2002 onwards will produce the euro zone in Europe. Its merits include:
(1) avoiding exchange risks;
(2) reducing transaction costs, and
(3) harmonizing and stabilizing prices.

Together with the use of the euro, common rules for transactions, more harmonized taxation and integrated stock exchanges will certainly increase economic efficiency and expand business opportunities in Europe. Borderless economies are to be realized. As a consequence, trade and investment in Europe will be stimulated and 'Fortress Europe' will be reborn.

At the same time, the euro will soon gain a reputation as a world currency, reflecting the EU's economic strength and stability. Trading partners will use it as a means of exchange, in international capital transactions and as foreign reserve holdings. It has been suggested that by the end of 1995, 48 per cent of transactions related to capital exports were expressed in US dollars, and that 40 per cent of portfolio holdings and 83 per cent of all transactions in exchange markets used the US dollar as a counterpart (Santer, 1997). There is substantial leeway for the euro to be a major player in asset holdings. Its circulation will expand worldwide

Figure 15.1. Destination of foreign direct investment of the EU, in percentages, 1995[1].

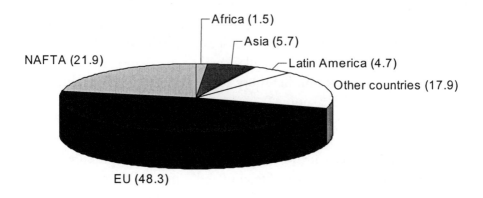

Note: Data refer to France, Germany, Italy, the Netherlands and the United Kingdom.
Source: OECD, *International Direct Invesment Statistics Yearbook*, Paris, 1997.

and it has been estimated that it will capture 30 per cent of exchange markets as against 50 per cent for the US dollar.

One of the main reasons for the East-Asian crisis was a dollar-dependent exchange system. Overvaluation of domestic currencies can be avoided by a currency-basket system with a mixture of the dollar, euro, and yen, reflecting the economic weight of the major trading partners. The role of the euro as a stabilizing factor for international exchange markets is thus vital.

By the same token, euro-denominated bonds will be bought by the Asian public as well as the Asian private sector. Actually, it has been reported that 20 per cent of the euro bonds issued by the Austrian government in October 1998 – with a total of 1.5 billion euros - were sold in Asia. The introduction of the euro is welcomed as a risk diversification measure.

3. Weakening Asia: monetary crises and recession

East-Asian countries have been suffering from recession caused by the Asian monetary crises which started in Thailand in June 1997, followed by Indonesia and South Korea. These monetary crises occurred for internal and external reasons.

Domestically, structural problems in the current-account deficits were the main cause and, externally, abrupt flows of foreign capital followed rapidly.

Current-account deficits arose from overvalued exchange rates and export-led industrialization strategies. The dollar-fixed exchange rates brought about an overvaluation of the East-Asian currencies as the US dollar appreciated. In general, this caused a widening of trade deficits. The East-Asian currencies such as the Thai baht were overvalued against the yen, too, which stimulated imports from Japan in particular.

At the same time, export-led industrialization emphasized FDI to operate in the host countries' export processing zones or industrial estates which offered foreign investors fiscal and financial incentives. Export promotion was successful but this type of industrialization was also import augmenting in order to meet the demand for capital goods and intermediate goods. These goods were all imported from the home countries of the multinational companies. Current-account deficits reached dangerous levels in many countries in the region and in Thailand it was nearly 8 per cent of GDP in 1996.

The current-account deficits have to be balanced by capital inflows which are categorized as FDI, loans and portfolio investment. Liberalization of financial markets led by international organizations such as the World Bank, the International Monetary Fund (IMF) and the World Trade Organization (WTO) accelerated capital inflows, especially short-term capital in the form of short-term lending and portfolio investment. Financial opening-up such as off-shore banking facilities like the Bangkok International Banking Facility, established in 1994, encouraged this tendency. Such short-term capital is quick to flow in but also quick to flow out. When the economic bubble bursts combined with political uncertainties which prevailed in different degrees in Thailand, Indonesia and South Korea, short-term capital fled in large quantities and hence foreign reserves shrunk abruptly.

External factors have also contributed directly to the East-Asian crisis. The emergence of global capitalism and the liberalization of financial sectors in recent times have created borderless economies and enabled money to cross national borders quick and easy. Voluminous funds represented by hedge funds flow in and out beyond the control of governments of developing countries. Nowadays foreign-exchange trading has reached 1,200 billion US dollars per day with hedge funds totalling as much as 400 billion US dollars. No developing country can escape the turmoil caused by sudden movements of these capital flows.

According to the IMF, net private capital flows to non-advanced countries - all developing countries, newly industrialized areas, and countries in transition - reached a peak of 241 billion US dollars in 1996 but fell back to 174 billion dollars in 1997 because of the East-Asian monetary crisis, as shown in Table 15.1. The average annual amount in 1984-89 was 15 billion US dollars so that net flows increased more than ten times during the last ten years. Asian figures show a sharp decline in net capital inflows from 102 billion US dollars in 1996 to a record-low level of 2 billion US dollars in 1998. A recovery is estimated in 1999 to 59 billion US dollars, equivalent to the 1993-94 level.

The IMF moved swiftly and rescue packages were arranged to deal with the East-Asian monetary crisis. Emergency loans were set for the crisis-stricken countries: 17.2 billion US dollars for Thailand in August 1997, 40 billion US dollars for Indonesia in November 1997, and 57 billion US dollars for South Korea in December 1997. Conditionalities of these loans included two main policy areas: demand control, particularly fiscal deficits, and financial reforms. Apart from the side effect of the ousting of Soeharto in Indonesia, these crises brought about a sudden halt to economic growth in the East-Asian region.

A credit crunch caused by weak banking systems with large bad debts and low world demand for manufacturing products, especially electronics, slowed down East-Asian production. It is estimated that four countries and one region in East Asia will record negative growth rates in 1998: Indonesia -13.1, Thailand -7.0, South Korea -5.0, Hong Kong -4.0, and Malaysia -2.9 - the first time in the recent history since the oil crisis in 1973, as shown in Table 15.2. Projections for 1999 are gloomy and growth is expected to be feeble. This will adversely affect trade and investment links between Europe and Asia for the immediate future.

Japan can play an important role in the recovery of East-Asian economies. Japan provided official as well as private rescue loans for the crisis-stricken Asian countries, the Japanese government pledged 4 billion US dollars for Thailand, 5 billion for Indonesia, and 10 billion for South Korea in the IMF-led rescue package. However, a more fundamental measure to support recovery would be an increase in Japan's demand for Asian products. This is delayed by slow decision-making by the Japanese government and prolonged financial reforms. The government of Japan finally decided to pour public money with a total provision of 520 billion US dollars, to restructure the banking sector and to boost the domestic economy after a three-month discussion in the diet which ended in October 1998.

Table 15.1. Net private capital flows in billions of US dollars, 1994-99.

	1994	1995	1996	1997	1998*	1999*
Total[1]						
Net private capital flows	160.5	192.0	240.8	173.7	122.0	196.4
Net direct investment	84.3	96.0	114.9	138.2	119.6	119.7
Net portfolio investment	87.8	23.5	49.7	42.9	18.0	34.4
Other net investment	-11.7	72.5	76.2	-7.3	-15.6	42.3
Net official flows	-2.5	34.9	-9.7	29.0	37.0	-8.9
Change in reserves	-77.2	-120.5	-115.9	-54.7	-67.1	-91.1
Asia						
Net private capital flows	63.1	91.8	102.2	38.5	1.5	58.8
Net direct investment	43.4	49.7	58.5	55.4	40.6	43.7
Net portfolio investment	11.3	10.8	10.2	-2.2	-7.0	5.3
Other net investment	8.3	31.3	33.5	-14.7	-32.1	9.8
Net official flows	6.2	5.1	9.3	17.7	24.7	7.0
Change in reserves	-39.7	-29.0	-48.9	-17.2	-24.4	-65.5

Notes: * Projection.
[1] All developing countries plus NIEs and countries in transition
Source: IMF, *World Economic Outlook,* Washington, D.C., April 1998.

The development of the securities and financial sectors is a reflection of the histories and traditions of each country. In the case of Japan, especially after the Second World War, the banking sector has been protected by the Ministry of Finance. The basic policy of the Ministry has been to avoid bankruptcy of major banks by using the so-called 'convoy-guard' method. Information on the financial conditions of the banks has not been disclosed to the general public, and has only been made available to the banks themselves and the Ministry of Finance. The outcome of this system has been the development of a secretive relationship which has fostered unfair practices. For example, banks provide posts for the bureaucrats of the Ministry after their retirement, the so-called *amakudari* or 'descendent from heaven'. Foreign banks have not been permitted to operate in Japan for a long time. Markets have also developed in a very distorted way. Bank lending has been heavily based on land collateral and not on business opportuni-

Table 15.2. Average annual real rates of growth of GDP, 1995-99.

	1995	1996	1997	1998*	1999*
China	10.5	9.6	8.8	8.0	n.a.
Hong Kong	3.9	4.6	5.3	-4.0	0.0
Indonesia	8.2	8.0	4.7	-13.1	-2.0
Korea	8.9	7.1	5.5	-5.0	2.0
Malaysia	9.5	8.6	7.8	-2.9	0.7
Philippines	4.8	5.5	5.1	1.0	3.5
Singapore	8.7	6.9	7.8	0.5	n.a.
Taiwan	5.9	5.4	6.6	5.2	n.a.
Thailand	8.8	5.5	-0.4	-7.0	1.0
Vietnam	9.5	9.3	8.5	6.0	7.0

Note: * Projection
Source: Database of the Institute of Developing Economies (IDE)/JETRO, Tokyo.

ties or performance. Therefore, banks faced accumulated bad debts after land prices fell sharply and the economic bubble busted in the mid-1990s.

Overlending dependent on high domestic savings through post office as well as bank savings became a common phenomenon of corporate finance. Thus, direct finance was ignored and securities markets left underdeveloped. In particular, the cross-holding of stocks by conglomerates of big companies and banks slowed the development of individual stock holdings.

Still at present, Japan's personal financial assets - approximately 8,900 billion US dollars - are mainly held in the form of savings deposits (53 per cent), while the share of securities represents only 12 per cent. Such a low percentage of holdings in securities means that the development of the stock and equity markets has stagnated. For example, in the USA the shares are almost exactly the opposite, 12 and 54 per cent respectively. The coming financial reform, the so-called 'big bang', is aimed at liberalizing the sector and correcting the skewed financial markets in Japan which is urgently needed after several bankruptcies and failures of large security companies and banks including Yamaichi Securities Co., Hokkaido Takushoku Bank, and Japan Long-term Credit Bank.

A nearly identical situation regarding the banking and equity markets can be seen in all East-Asian countries except Hong Kong and Singapore where free port status has been a long tradition. Less-developed financial markets cannot cope with rapid globalization and integration into the world financial system and the restructuring processes will take time, thus hindering the Asian recovery.

4. Linking the two regions: ASEM and its role

Between the two regions there exists a dialogue-based information-exchange system called the Asia-Europe Meeting (ASEM), which was proposed by Goh Chok Tong, Singapore's prime minister, whose inaugural meeting was held in Bangkok in March 1996. Its members include the15 EU countries, the European Commission, and 10 Asian countries including seven ASEAN countries, China, South Korea and Japan. The purpose of ASEM is to foster political dialogue, reinforce economic co-operation and promote co-operation in social and cultural fields. The London ASEM Summit in April 1998 reinforced a political dialogue for a partnership of equals between Europe and Asia. In the field of economic co-operation, two action plans were proposed, the Investment Promotion Action Plan and the Trade Facilitation Action Plan. The Third Asia-Europe Business Forum which is mainly based on initiatives of the private sector was held in parallel with the summit. Co-operation in social and cultural areas was also enhanced through several programs. In view of the East-Asian monetary crises, rescue measures such as the ASEM trust fund and the European Financial Expertise Network were initiated. The next steps for ASEM, according to the European Commission, include the adoption of an Asia-Europe Cooperation Framework to serve as a guide for the ASEM process between the London and Seoul Summit in the year 2000 and the launching of the ASEM Vision Group, the so-called 'Wise Men's Committee'.

The short- and mid-term prospects for the relationship between Europe and Asia are not so bright, but the long-term perspectives seem to be prosperous due to Asia's productive capacity and the huge potential demand as growth will recover in Asia.

An industrial base has gradually been established in East Asia and India, including electronics and car industries in ASEAN countries and computer software industries in India. Once the current recession is over, these industries and supply networks in the region may benefit from new business opportunities.

The prospects for new opportunities in China and India fascinate the business community all around the world.

To become superpowers in the 21st century, China and India must modernize their economies. China's banking system has large bad-debt problems, and the process of privatization of state enterprises has progressed slowly. Social-security systems are another major obstacle. India's liberalization process is also progressing slowly, the caste system hinders modernization and hunger among the poor still prevails in many regions.

5. Concluding remarks

The economic relationship between Europe and Asia will remain weak, although bilateral trade in percentage terms has been increasing over the last twenty years. The EMU will foster increased trade and investment inside an efficient 'Fortress Europe' and the East-Asian monetary crisis and recession will negatively affect trade and investment links between the two regions.

At the same time, the introduction of the euro brightens the future. A dollar-centred one-polar world system has been recognized as dangerous in the recent financial turmoil. The euro can substitute the dollar in international financial markets as well as reserve holdings to reduce risk and stabilize global financial markets.

In order to expand trade and investment between the two regions, the first requirement is recovery of the East-Asian economies. In this respect, Japan's role is important. Japan has to open further its market for Asian products. Moreover, it has to execute swiftly its financial 'big bang' to realign the financial sector. The recently-launched Miyazawa Plan - the fund of 30 billion US dollars provided by the government of Japan for five crisis-stricken East-Asian countries in the G-7 Finance Minister Meeting held in October 1998 - will contribute to the East-Asian recovery. Europe also has to abandon its attitude of 'benign neglect' towards Asian countries.

To finish on an optimistic note, it must be imagined that the relationship between the two regions will intensify with the emergence of two new super-powers, China and India, in the 21st century. Every modern-day Marco Polo is interested in the opportunities these countries may offer.

References

Aoki, T. *Toho Kenbunroku (The Travels of Marco Polo)*, Shakai Shisosha, Tokyo, 1969.

European Commission, *Building a Comprehensive Partnership with China*, communication from the Commission, Brussels, March 25, 1998.

Kagami, M., *Japan and Latin America*, mimeo, paper presented at the international seminar on 'South-South: Recent Developments in Relations between Latin America and Asia', organized by Leiden University, in Leiden and The Hague, 19-20 February, 1998.

Santer, J., *External Aspects of the Euro*, speech at Global 24 Conference, Frankfurt, 1 July, 1997.

Yamada, K., *Koryo no Rekishi (A History of Spices)*, Kinokuniya Shoten, Tokyo, 1994.

16

PREPARING FOR THE FUTURE

PITOU VAN DIJCK

CEDLA
Amsterdam
The Netherlands

GERRIT FABER

Utrecht University
Utrecht
The Netherlands

1. Policy making in a new setting

This volume has analysed the broad range of recent initiatives taken by the European Commission and the Council of the European Union (EU) to develop a common external economic policy. As put in Art. 2 of the Treaty on European Union (ex Art. B), the objective of the EU in the economic sphere is 'to promote economic and social progress and a high level of employment…' This comes close to the definitions of competitiveness as presented by Thurow and Kol. Moreover, Art. 2 of the European Community (EC) Treaty explicitly refers to 'a high degree of competitiveness' as a goal of the EC. Hence, when bringing together the main findings of the contributions to this volume, the emphasis will be on the contribution of these policies and initiatives of the Union to the competitiveness of the EU.

P. van Dijck and G. Faber (eds.), The External Economic Dimension of the European Union, 353–373.

During the last three decades of the 20th century, four major changes had a significant impact on the position of the EU in the world economy:
(1) the widening and deepening of the process of economic integration among the countries in Western Europe itself;
(2) the emergence of the Pacific Basin as a new centre of gravity in world trade and capital flows;
(3) the systemic change in Central and Eastern Europe as well as parts of Asia towards an open market economy, and
(4) the worldwide process of trade and investment liberalization.

At the end of the millennium, the EU stands out as a union of 15 member countries with a combined gross national product (GNP) measured at purchasing power parity (PPP) of 7.5 trillion US dollars, slightly smaller than the USA. The traditional dominant position of the countries at both sides of the Atlantic in the world economy, however, has been challenged by Japan and the emergence of a large number of countries in the Pacific Basin, including China and several generations of tiger economies that are connected by intensive intra-regional trade and investment relations. As compared to the Triad powers and particularly Western Europe, the newly emerging countries of East Asia have shown extraordinary dynamism over a prolonged period of time, interrupted only during the East-Asian crisis at the end of the millennium.

Apart from the megapoles in North America, Western Europe and East Asia, new growth poles are emerging in South Asia and South America where countries such as India and Brazil have started to open their fairly large economies only recently and are expected to play a more significant role in international markets in the decades to come.

The population of Western Europe has enjoyed high and rising standards of living: their average level of income per capita was over 3.2 as high as the world average by the end of the 20th century. According to Thurow and the definitions of competitiveness reviewed by Kol, such a high and rising standard of living, sustained in the long term, would reflect a high level of competitiveness of the Union. As the European Commission puts it (1998) 'an economy is competitive if its population can enjoy high standards of living and high rates of employment while maintaining a sustainable external position'.

When looking at the positions of the major areas on the world economic chess board, Thurow finds that Europe - including the EU, Central and Eastern Europe and Turkey, altogether nearly 900 million inhabitants - has a far stronger position than any group of people of more or less equivalent size: 'no region comes even close' in terms of income per capita, levels of education and skills, and infrastructure. A successful deepening and enlargement of the European integration process and the introduction of the euro will contribute to a strong starting position of Europe in the 21st century. Moreover, Europe's major industrial rivals, the USA and Japan suffer from serious weaknesses as Thurow has indicated. True as this may be, international statistics and ranking studies of the economic performance of countries provide evidence for some sobering reflections on Europe's position in the world economy.

When comparing the economic performance of the EU with its competitors in world markets, it follows that the USA and Japan have experienced a more dynamic overall economic performance during the last three decades of the 20th century and reached significantly higher levels of average income per capita than the EU. In other respects as well, the EU has been less successful than its main rivals. As Kol shows, the EU is behind the USA and Japan in its scoring on economic freedom and global competitiveness, and its creditworthiness is below that of the USA. A study by the European Commission (1997) shows that exports of the EU are concentrated in product groups with less dynamic international demand than exports of the USA and Japan. Moreover, several other regions in the world economy, particularly in East Asia, have been catching up with Western Europe and reduced the income gap significantly.

In the EU as in all the rest of the world, production and income are increasingly dependent on international markets. In this regard, some significant changes have taken place in the 1990s: the EU has become less inward-orientated and more dependent on external markets as reflected by the decline of the share of intra-EU trade in total EU exports from 66 per cent in 1990 to less than 61 per cent in 1997. Moreover, although the concentration of trade among the Triad powers is still strong - nearly 25 per cent of extra-EU exports in 1997 was shipped to the USA and Japan - the relative importance of the overall market of industrial countries (excluding intra-EU trade) declined while the share in EU exports of the Central and Eastern European Countries (CEEC), emerging Asia and to a lesser extent Latin America increased strongly. By the end of the 1990s, the USA, developing Europe (including CEEC and Turkey) and developing Asia have become three major trade partners of the EU of more or less equal size when measured according to EU exports. Altogether, the combined exports of the EU to Latin America and developing Asia now equals the combined EU exports to the USA and Japan. So, not only has the EU become more outward-orientated but the direction of its trade flows has shifted towards newly emerging regions in Europe, Asia and Latin America. At the same time, however, the Union has been losing import market shares in its traditional markets as well as the newly emerging markets all over the world, which contrasts with a more dynamic and competitive performance of the USA in some major export markets.

The significant long-term developments with respect to the position of the EU in world income, international trade and investment flows are the context of the new initiatives to shape the EU's common external economic policy. Essentially, the following broad options to strengthen the competitiveness of the EU and to enhance its position as a trader and investor in the world economy have been investigated in this volume:

(1) deepening of integration among EU members;
(2) enlargement of the EU;
(3) strengthening of the multilateral trade and investment regimes, and
(4) establishing preferential trade areas.

Policy initiatives in these four areas are interrelated and take place simultaneously, resulting in a complex and congested agenda. The growing number of countries with a decisive say in multilateral and regional policy matters adds to the complexities involved in shaping trade and investment regimes for the future. The world all over, governments take initiatives to strengthen the competitiveness of their economies, to support the penetration of foreign markets and to reduce the risks involved in the process of liberalization and deeper integration, which in turn induces other governments to take initiatives from their side.

The areas in which the new initiatives are concentrated are presented in a schematic fashion in Figure 16.1. At the multilateral level, the Union was among the most significant Contracting Parties (CP) of the General Agreement on Tariffs and Trade (GATT) and has taken the initiative to start a new Millennium Round of the World Trade Organization (WTO).

In recent years the Union has intensified the regional dimension of its external economic policy by establishing different types of special and preferential relationships with developed and developing countries as well as countries in transition. The EU has extended a large part of its *acquis communautaire* to its highly-developed neighbouring countries in the context of the European

Figure 16.1. The external economic dimension of the EU.

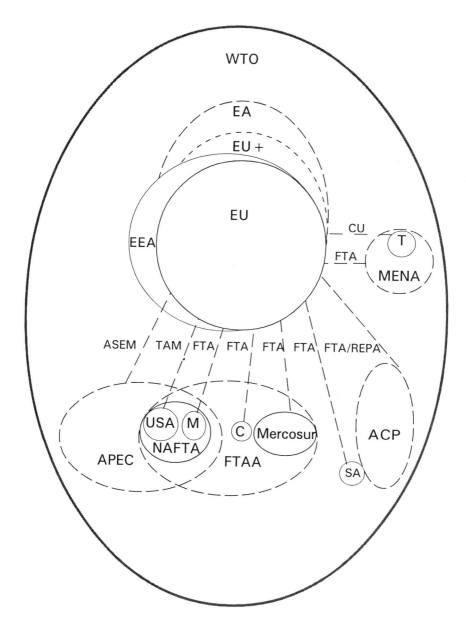

Note: C= Chile, EU+= EU plus next wave of new members, M= Mexico,
  SA= South Africa, T= Turkey.
  For all other abbreviations see text and List of Abbreviations.

Economic Area (EEA) and a bilateral preferential trade agreement (PTA) with Switzerland. The enlargement of the EU to the east and the intensification of the special relationships with the countries in transition in Central and Eastern Europe, as laid down in the Europe Agreements (EAs), dominate the policy agenda of the EU and require substantial adjustment in the decision-making procedures of the Union and in many policy areas including the Common Agricultural Policy (CAP) and the use of structural and regional funds. Also, the Union has been preparing to establish a special transatlantic economic relationship with the USA, its major trade partner.

Moreover, new reciprocal preferential trade agreements have been negotiated with countries in Latin America - Mercosur, Chile and Mexico - and in the Middle East and North Africa (MENA) as well as with South Africa. The agreement with Turkey has entered the stage of a customs union (CU). Finally, the Asia-Europe Meeting (ASEM) has been established as a framework for the intensification of economic relations with the newly emerging countries in East and South-East Asia. The findings of the studies in this volume regarding the recent external economic policy initiatives of the EU will be put together in the following sections.

2. Deepening and enlarging the Union

The deepening of the integration process among the EU members and the enlargement of the Union may generate large economic benefits, including the traditional static and dynamic effects of integration as well as non-traditional effects such as the 'locking in' of reforms and its impact on investors. To the extent that deepening and enlargement contribute to factor accumulation and total factor productivity, the process of integration contributes to the EU's competitiveness.

The establishment of the Internal Market and the Economic and Monetary Union (EMU) have increased competition or will do so in the future, which increases the level of welfare in the EU. Moreover, deepening expands the external powers of EU institutions. The Internal Market programme has increased the regulatory capability and powers of the EU institutions and this has an impact as well on the position of the EU in international institutions that deal with trade and investment regimes. If the euro will become a vehicle currency not only in Europe and its neighbouring regions in the east and south but in the major international markets as well, the EU will play a more decisive role in the international monetary relations and institutions.

Enlargement of the Union towards the east will have positive economic effects as well. As Palánkai shows, the EAs and the prospects of full membership have supported the economic transformation towards open and efficient markets, be it that the EU could do more in support. Ultimately, enlargement creates a more diverse supply of factors of production in an integrated market. However, deepening and enlargement may also induce inefficiencies in economic and political terms, as shown by several authors in this volume. The Common Agricultural Policy (CAP) stands out as the most prominent case of inefficient integration and its slow reform results from vested, sometimes contrary interests of producers and member states.

Reform of the CAP

The CAP underwent significant reform in 1992 with a shift from price support to direct income support, achieved by lowering the intervention prices and by compensating farmers via acreage and headage premiums, in combination with a set-aside scheme to reduce the production of cereals and oilseeds. Keyzer and Merbis conclude with the benefit of hindsight that the reform reduced tensions on international agricultural markets and virtually saved the Uruguay Round.

As the European Commission indicates in its Agenda 2000, a deepening and widening of reforms of 1992 is required because of the developments in the agricultural sector itself, the upcoming negotiations under the WTO and the planned accession of the CEEC. The recent proposals of the Commission to establish free-trade areas (FTAs) with countries that are major producers and exporters of agricultural products such as the member countries of Mercosur and Chile add to the urgency of reforms. According to the proposals of the Commission, the 1992 reform is pursued with a further reduction of the internal prices and an increase of acreage and headage premiums. Market conformity is improved by cutting the set-aside rate to zero and by allowing for some expansion of milk quotas. Agenda 2000 keeps the import regimes unchanged and focuses on a further reduction of export subsidies. Moreover, safety and quality concerns and rural policies are integrated in the Agenda.

As Keyzer and Merbis indicate, the proposals of the Commission to reform the CAP essentially reflect an extrapolative approach rather than a clear vision of the future of agriculture in the EU. More specifically, the proposals fail to take shifts in consumer preferences and concentration at the processing and distribution side into consideration adequately. They argue that society increasingly prefers high-quality products that meet consumer concerns and services to preserve nature and the landscape. If trade barriers are sufficiently reduced, agribusiness will shift bulk production of raw materials to regions where land is abundant, labour is cheap and reliable transportation is available. This implies a more comprehensive application of the principles of free trade in this sector and a deeper integration of the sector in the international division of labour.

The CAP has appeared to be a stumbling block for many of the initiatives of the EU for a new external economic policy. The Uruguay Round was kept on hold for three years and almost failed due to the inability of the EU to agree on a modest liberalization of the agricultural sector. Once more, the CAP may become a stumbling block in the Millennium Round under the WTO. As Keyzer and Merbis conclude, it is unlikely that the WTO negotiations can be successful without further CAP reform. Virtually all trade partners will resist maintenance of blue-box measures, that were introduced as part of the 1994 agreement under the GATT. At the same time, the European Commission is of the opinion that there is a strong need to defend and maintain a number of existing provisions in the Agreement on Agriculture under the GATT/WTO on which key elements of the CAP are built, including the blue box (European Commission, 1999a).

Moreover, the effectiveness of the EU's PTAs is limited due to the exclusion or exceptional treatment of agriculture. The new MENA agreements - to the extent they have been realized - are below their potential in terms of welfare and 'lock-in' effects. Ventura Dias and Van Dijck show that PTAs with Mercosur and Chile are delayed due to a lack of EU consensus on concessions regarding agricultural products, as a consequence of which the EU may not be able to prevent ending up at the exporting end of trade diversion caused by PTAs among countries in the Western Hemisphere.

Enlarging the Union

The enlargement of the EU will increase the number of member states to over 20 in the first decade of the 21st century. Apart from bringing benefits to the old and new members of the Union, this will also alter the nature of the Union. This is particularly due to the lower level of economic development of the new members as compared to the present members, which hampers them to adopt the full *acquis communautaire*. According to the classical school of European integration, these countries would have to adopt the full *acquis* at their accession as did Austria, Finland and Sweden. Long transition periods are not acceptable since they would cause disturbances in the Internal Market.

However, Andriessen argues that it is not realistic to keep the new entrants outside until they are capable to implement the full *acquis*. The political pressure on the EU to accept the new members in a few years of time is so strong that further postponement of accession will not be possible. Against this background, Andriessen proposes to formally accept the concept of differentiated membership, which exists already *de facto* in a number of policy areas, and distinguishes four policy zones.

Zone One would consist of the core group of member states which have accepted the entire *acquis* as well as the EMU, a compulsory Schengen, an adequate social policy and possibly more far-reaching rights of citizenship. Moreover, the institutional set up of this zone would be according to the first pillar, i.e. the EC. This first zone would have a more pronounced degree of identity and would serve as an example to the other member states.

Zone Two would be the present Union with its *acquis* and three pillars. Zone Three would include a number of new entrants which are essentially willing to accept the *acquis* but need derogations from important parts of it, such as full rights of citizenship, the Internal Market - perhaps with some important exceptions -, a full CU, full common policies on trade and competition, crime prevention, the free movement of persons and capital, compulsory monetary co-ordination, general convergence targets, social and environmental policies and other areas. Finally, Zone Four would include countries that are even at a much larger distance from membership than the countries with which negotiations have been opened.

Such a differentiated membership would also be reflected in differentiated powers and responsibilities of member states in the EU institutions but the implications of such a differentiated membership are not yet fully understood. It might be the case that the countries in Zone One will be so coherent that they are able to use their economic and other foreign-policy instruments in a very effective manner, but increased differentiation may as well give rise to fragmentation and may reduce the capability of the EU to act internationally.

The EU is ill-prepared for the coming enlargement. During the preparations the focus has been narrowed down to the budgetary and institutional aspects.

As Andriessen argues, the negotiations on the financing of the budget and the distribution of transfers should have been seized as an opportunity for fundamental debate on the method of allocating regional funds. Yet, the system as it exists at present will be maintained for the present 15 member states, while national limits are proposed for the new members. This puts the regional policy upside down as transfers should be paid according to an objective yardstick of need, to be applied to all member states.

With regard to the preparation for enlargement of the EU institutions, not much was realized by the Intergovernmental Conference (IGC) that resulted in the Treaty of Amsterdam in 1997. The Treaty has not realized the required breakthrough in institutional capacity and the principle that decisions are made by qualified majority except under extraordinary conditions has not been accepted. Also, a procedure to weigh votes in the Council of Ministers more adequately and to limit the number of European Commissioners could not be settled. Instead, the position of the Commission has gradually weakened since the Maastricht Treaty, according to Andriessen. The point is illustrated by the fact that not the Commission has been promoted to High Authority for the Common Foreign and Security Policy (CFSP) in the Treaty of Amsterdam.

Steenbergen arrives at slightly different conclusions. The Maastricht Treaty in 1991 provided the regime whereby the Union can participate in international economic agreements and policies and which entitles the Union to deal with virtually all other aspects of international relations, although the effectiveness of the EU outside the economic sphere is likely to remain small. At the IGC of Amsterdam some minor adjustments were made. Perhaps most notable is the obligation to have an integrated external policy, covering all aspects of external relations. This is a significant change of the EU's regime for its external relations, according to Steenbergen. Overall, the Treaty of Amsterdam has safeguarded to some extent the capacity of the Union to act, while stimulating at the same time the continued development of a coherent and integrated foreign policy of the Union and its member states.

From the above the following conclusions may be drawn pertaining to the deepening and enlargement of the Union. First, deepening and enlargement offer the prospect of intensified competition, a larger market size and a more diversified supply of factors of production. This will spur efficiency and enhance the competitiveness of the EU.

Second, countervailing factors are at work as well. The deep integration in the sector of agriculture hampers an efficient type of allocation and, moreover, prevents the Community from realizing trade agreements that may generate optimal results.

Third, the EU is not well prepared for enlargement. Differentiated membership seems to be inevitable. If well organized, fragmentation could remain limited as the core group is likely to be homogeneous. However, differentiation could also take place in a more erratic fashion through varying coalitions of member states, thus hampering the realization of coherent EU policies.

Fourth, the Amsterdam Treaty did not substantially improve the institutional capacity of the Union in its external relations.

Deepening and enlargement offer good prospects for improving the competitiveness of the EU. To reap these benefits, the EU needs to curtail the common policies that are inefficient and to build an institutional capacity that allows it to be flexible and effective internally as well as in its external relations.

3. Strengthening the multilateral system

The countries of the EU and the Commission have been actively involved in the design and execution of the agenda of the GATT and its successor, the WTO. Contrary to the expectations of many observers, the completion of the Internal Market did not result in a 'Fortress Europe' as the external trade barriers of the EU were reduced as well in the first half of the 1990s.

The average tariff reduction agreed by the EU in the Uruguay Round was somewhat larger than the reductions agreed by the USA and Japan, and 100 per cent of the post-Uruguay Round import tariffs of the EU have been bound. After implementation of the agreements reached in the Round, the simple average most-favoured-nation (MFN) tariff rates of the EU will be bound at 3.2 per cent and the applied rate will be 2.8 per cent, equal to the rates applied by the USA and Japan (Finger and Winters, 1998).

However, tariff barriers and quantitative controls are still largely in place to protect the agricultural sector as well as specific industrial activities such as textiles and clothing industries. As indicated earlier, conflicts on liberalization of agriculture and particularly the reform of the CAP seriously threatened the successful conclusion of the Uruguay Round. Moreover, many different types of regulations constrain international trade in services and the free movement of service providers. The EU stance in these areas will be of crucial importance to the future of the WTO.

The EU has been among the initiators to launch a new multilateral round of trade negotiations under the WTO and the European Council unanimously supported this initiative in 1998 and 1999. From the perspective of the Commission, success in the negotiations on the liberalization of agriculture and services can only be achieved in the context of a broad and time-bound framework of negotiations. However, the broad agenda that is proposed by the Commission may be too complex and comprehensive to deal with in a short period of time. The Commission proposes four major issues on the preferred agenda of the Millennium Round:

(1) to secure further trade liberalization and create improved conditions for competitiveness;

(2) to strengthen the WTO and make it 'a truly universal instrument for the management of international trade relations';

(3) to enhance the developmental role of the WTO, and

(4) to ensure that the WTO addresses issues of broad concern such as health, environment and social concerns.

The objective of sustainable development is conceived as a central benchmark of the Millennium Round as is reflected in the Commission's proposals for the agenda in the area of agriculture which emphasize the multifunctional role of agriculture including the preservation of human, animal and plant life or health, animal welfare, food safety and quality.

In the area of trade and development, the Commission takes the position that all developed countries should offer tariff-free treatment on 'essentially all products' from the least-developed countries to be implemented by 2003, as the EU itself has done since 1997. More generally, the Commission favours a fuller integration of developing countries in the WTO, be it that special and differential treatment may be required.

The broadening of the agenda is also reflected by the prominent inclusion of proposals for a multilateral framework for investment and competition policies. After the failed attempt by the member countries of the Organisation for Economic Co-operation and Development (OECD) to establish a Multilateral Agreement on Investment (MAI), the Commission has taken the position that the WTO is the only multilateral forum that can fully take into account the interests of both developed and developing countries in their position as home and host countries to international investors (European Commission, 1999a, b).

So far, the Commission has made no proposals related to the functioning of PTAs and their relationship with the multilateral regime, notwithstanding the large increase in the number of PTAs and the large share of world trade under such agreements. This is remarkable in view of the importance of compatibility of the initiatives of the EU in the area of special and preferential trade policies with the multilateral trade regime of the GATT/WTO.

The first two banana panels under the GATT have made it clear that the absence of an affirmative recommendation of a regional initiative by the GATT/WTO under Art. XXIV leaves room for a panel examination that can challenge all or part of such an initiative. To qualify for such an affirmative recommendation, the condition of 'substantially all the trade' should be fulfilled. Non-reciprocal arrangements such as the preferences under the Lomé Convention in no way can be brought under Art. XXIV. In the interest of all, the WTO must develop guidelines to review FTAs and CUs. As a starting point, a percentage guideline may be used of no less than 80 per cent of all intra-regional trade - the EU's traditional position in this matter - or 90 per cent as used as a point of reference in the negotiations on a PTA with the Mercosur - or perhaps as high as 95 per cent.

The absence of proposals in this area may reflect satisfaction with the progress made so far to close the loopholes in Art. XXIV of the GATT, but it may also suggest that the EU as well as the USA and other members of the WTO have calculated a benefit in the status quo whereby maximum flexibility is reserved for future initiatives in this domain, as suggested by Mathis. At the same time, however, a continuing absence of guidelines on PTAs increases the latitude for conflicts with trading partners who have chosen to use this trade strategy more actively than they used to do in the past. As Mathis concludes, at least the Union will benefit from framing its external regional policy in the WTO by taking into account not only the prospects of its own regional initiatives but also the implications of the initiatives of other countries.

4. The regional dimension

Traditionally the EU has supported the establishment of PTAs among countries around the world and has made extensive use of this specific trade-policy instrument throughout its existence. There used to be three layers of preferential treatment of third countries. First, the Lomé Conventions, which provided 71 countries in Africa, the Caribbean and the Pacific (ACP) with almost free access to the market of the EU with the exception of temperate-zone agricultural products for which special Protocols were established. Second, PTAs with most MENA countries, which provide for free access to the EU market with exceptions for sensitive manufactures and agricultural products. Third, the unilateral Generalized Systems of Preferences (GSP). The common characteristic of these preferential agreements was non-reciprocity, implying that the developing countries involved were not required to offer preferential access to the EU in return.

The EU policy towards PTAs has recently changed in two respects. First, non-reciprocal systems are giving way to reciprocal arrangements with the probable exception of a GSP for least-developed countries. Second, PTAs and special trade and investment arrangements are now being negotiated with many more countries than before. The shift towards reciprocity should be seen in the context of the changing position of the EU in the world economy and the intensification of multilateral rule enforcement. Also, the extensive use of trade preferences should be put in the context of the process of globalization and intensified international competition.

When analysing the regional dimension of the external economic policies of the EU, several economic and non-economic objectives and motives may be distinguished. On top of traditional static Vinerian economic effects of trade creation and diversion, non-traditional short-term and longer-term effects may be aimed at, including the exploitation of economies of scale and the stimulation and diversion of investment. The size of the effects depends not only on the trade potential of the participating countries, the preferential margins and the comprehensiveness of the agreement, but also on the specific model that has been used to establish the PTA. In case the EU would be successful to manage itself into the position of a giant hub with a unique access to the markets of a large number of economies, this would add to its attractiveness as an investment location and support the potential of its industries to exploit economies of scale and increase their competitiveness.

Apart from these economic objectives, several significant non-economic objectives may be distinguished. Winters refers to Viner's (1950) classic work on CUs indicating that in the asymmetric cases the larger partner was nearly always seeking political benefits while the smaller partner had economic objectives. In view of the relatively limited size of most partners involved in the traditional PTAs with the Union, it is reasonable to assume that economic motives are not the only and probably not even the most important objectives. Winters distinguishes four sets of motivations for the EU for its various PTAs: community with its neighbours, their stability and development, and most recently, the defence of markets. These motivations are mixed in different proportions in the various agreements. The non-economic motivations are particularly dominant in the EU's preferential relationships with its neighbours to the east and south. Altruistic concerns and development-orientated objectives may have played a role in the Lomé Conventions that used to combine non-reciprocal trade preferences with development assistance. The series of PTAs that the EU has started to negotiate more recently with distant partners such as South Africa and several countries in Latin America, and the special relationship with countries in East Asia, framed in the context of the ASEM, aim more specifically at securing (preferential) market access and creating a 'level-playing field'. In cases where partners participate already in PTAs or are in the process of negotiating PTAs with EU competitors, a PTA may undo or prevent discrimination in trade and investment. As Van Dijck shows, the negotiations of the EU with Mexico, Mercosur and Chile aim at reducing the trade-diversion effects of the North American Free Trade Agreement (NAFTA) and Mercosur, and the potential trade and investment-diversion effects of a Free Trade Area of the Americas (FTAA) which is negotiated by the countries in the Western Hemisphere.

The motivations of the partners of the EU are probably more related to their economic interests and include improved access to the large export market of the EU, support for the liberalization of imports in their own markets, improved policy credibility, increased investment and growth, support for the development of institutions and domestic policy, financial support and political security. Winters suggests that, notwithstanding some cases in which these obligations have been realized, disappointment seems likely in many cases.

The transatlantic relationship

Rood observes that the relationship between the EU and the USA is rather symmetrical or slightly asymmetrical to the disadvantage of the Union, in contrast to all other special external relations of the EU that are characterized by a certain degree of asymmetry in favour of the Union. In the words of Henry Kissinger, the EU and the USA have had a 'troubled partnership' with many strategic and economic conflicts. Disputes on bananas and hormones are just two recent cases in a long list of trade conflicts.

The transatlantic cohesion has been at risk due to the change in strategic setting with the end of the Cold War, the alleged re-orientation of the USA from the Atlantic Basin towards the Pacific Basin, and the shift in US economic strategy from multilateralism towards multilateralism *cum* regionalism, as reflected by a series of initiatives in the 1990s to establish special and preferential trade and investment relations with countries in the Western Hemisphere and East Asia.

In response to these forces of fragmentation a new institutional setting for consultation and co-ordination was called for and resulted in an agreement on a New Transatlantic Agenda in 1995 and a Joint EU-US Action Plan. From the European perspective, these initiatives offered the opportunity to influence US trade policy, especially to restrain its inclination for unilateralism and regionalism, and to reinforce the US commitment to multilateralism. The predominance of the economic dimension in this relationship is reflected by several proposals made by the European Commission to create a Transatlantic Marketplace (TAM) and even a Transatlantic Free Trade Area (TAFTA).

Stronger co-operation between the world's two largest economies and largest traders and investors may help to develop a transatlantic framework of public policy and may further worldwide liberalization in the old and new areas of the GATT/WTO. A successful outcome of the Millennium Round will depend to a large extent on the ability of the EU and the USA to co-operate. This, however, requires that they are capable to solve their disputes over specific trade issues and particularly agriculture. At the same time, an exclusive partnership between these two economic giants may threaten multilateralism, according to Rood.

Close encounters with the neighbours

The EU is in the process of concluding reciprocal trade agreements with nearly all of its neighbouring countries. After full implementation, these agreements could be merged into one Pan-European-Mediterranean Free Trade Area (PAMEFTA) including at least 35 countries in Western, Central and Eastern Europe as well as the Middle East and North Africa. The present EU will exercise a strong influence on the organization of society in the partner countries as the trade arrangements will require the partners to adopt all or part of the EU laws and regulations.

A successful PAMEFTA may be instrumental in the creation of a zone of prosperity and stability at the external borders of the EU. However, the chances that the Mediterranean part of PAMEFTA will be realized successfully are much smaller than the chances of success for the East and Central European parts. As Faber argues, the approximation in the MENA countries will require a much longer period of time than the merging of the Central and Eastern European countries into an FTA with the EU. Moreover, economic co-operation among MENA countries has been very limited so far. Also, the breakdown of Comecon forced the CEEC to change their economic strategy in a radical way while the MENA countries are reforming gradually with a larger probability of policy reversals. Finally, the 'lock-in' effect of the EAs with the prospect of full membership is much stronger than the impact of the new generation of Mediterranean Agreements, particularly since the access for the MENA countries to the market of the EU has not improved.

According to Palánkai, the EAs have been an important stimulus for the economic development of the CEEC by providing free access to large parts of the exports of these countries to the market of the EU and by promoting foreign direct investment (FDI). However, the policy initiatives of the CEEC have contributed as well to the significant shifts in the export-orientation of these countries from east to west, which started already before the first EAs came into effect. Although EAs have contributed in a positive way to the transition in the CEEC, the EU could have done more by providing more financial support and by being less restrictive towards so-called sensitive products.

Beyond Lomé

The special relationship of the EU with the group of 71 countries in Sub-Saharan Africa, the Caribbean and the Pacific, known collectively as the ACP, belongs to the initial cornerstones of the external economic dimension of the EU. The relationship involved two components: trade and aid. In analysing this relationship, Stevens finds that the Lomé Convention does not fit the present situation. The EU is not particularly dependent on raw material supply by these countries any longer, and the ACP do not offer a significant export market for the EU either. Moreover, the development record of the Convention has been disappointing.

In the trade area of the Convention, the EU offers non-reciprocal preferences. These preferences have been eroded due to the lowering of the EU's MFN barriers to trade as indicated earlier. However, ACP countries still enjoy substantial preferential margins for certain agricultural products, textiles and clothing. The phasing out of the Multi-Fibre Arrangement (MFA) as agreed in the Uruguay Round and the liberalization of the CAP will erode these preferential margins as well. Moreover, the stricter application of GATT/WTO rules will make the continued application of this preferential system beyond a transition period of five to ten years virtually impossible. Stevens argues that this transition period is a window of opportunity that must be grasped by as many countries of the ACP group as possible. As he puts it: '[a]fter it has closed they will face the harsh winds of global competition in all of these markets'.

Emerging markets

In view of the emergence of East Asia and, to a lesser extent, Latin America as new centres of gravity in the world market, the EU has taken initiatives to strengthen its relationships with both groups of countries, be it that these initiatives were taken rather late. Overall economic growth combined with the reduction of import barriers have stimulated trade between the EU and these areas. At the same time, however, countries in both regions are involved in a series of initiatives to participate in FTAs and CUs which may generate diversion effects to the disadvantage of the EU.

So far, the principles of 'open regionalism', characterized by concerted unilateral trade liberalization on an MFN basis, have dominated trade policies in East Asia, the major exception in the area being the establishment of the ASEAN Free Trade Area (AFTA). The USA has managed to get the objective of free trade by the year 2010 for industrialized members and 2020 for the rest of the Asia-Pacific Economic Cooperation (APEC) included in the Bogor Declaration of 1994. The USA, Canada and Australia prefer extension of concessions to outsiders on a reciprocal basis, to avoid giving members of the EU in particular a free ride in the region. Japan and the newly emerging countries in the region prefer unconditional liberalization and non-discriminatory treatment of outsiders. Even if APEC would liberalize in a non-discriminatory manner, regional harmonization of trade and investment-related rules and standards may have significant consequences for the capability of outsiders to compete in the APEC region. Consequently, there are good reasons for the EU to take initiatives towards the APEC region.

The Asia-Europe Meeting (ASEM) is the new framework to intensify the relationship between the EU and Asia. As indicated by Kagami and Van Dijck, ASEM does not aim at a PTA but at facilitating trade and investment at the level of the regions and at strengthening an open multilateral trade regime. ASEM offers a framework for interregional consultations, business exchanges and the creation of new private-sector partnerships. Two action plans have been proposed to promote trade and investment.

At the first ASEM Summit in 1996 Asian participants proposed trade liberalization by the EU parallel to liberalization by APEC. In 1999, the Asia-Europe Vision Group recommended that ASEM partners set the eventual goal of free trade in goods and services by the year 2025 by adopting a strategic framework for progressive trade liberalization among themselves.

In contrast to Asia, Latin American countries have strengthened their liberalization efforts by establishing complicated cobwebs of special and preferential linkages among themselves as well as with Asia, North America and the EU, as discussed by Ventura Dias and Van Dijck. The new initiatives to establish FTAs between the USA and Latin America mark a major policy change for all countries involved. The recent initiatives of the EU to establish PTAs with Mercosur, Chile and Mexico aim at reducing the potential trade-diversion effects of PTAs, from which the EU may suffer.

The emergence of these very large PTAs reflects intense competition between the EU and the USA. In case the USA would be successful in turning APEC into a preferential trade zone and in creating a PTA encompassing all of North and South America, it would have managed to put itself into the position of a giant hub with preferential access to the markets of East Asia and the Americas. The US hub position would become even more articulated with a transatlantic preferential linkage. The EU can deny the USA the potential advantages of such a position by establishing PTAs with the partners in the US-dominated PTAs that have been established or are in the making and by supporting the multilateral reduction of import barriers. Both strategies have been initiated but the simultaneous introduction of initiatives at different levels and with several groups of partners makes the process extremely complicated. Here again, the reform of the CAP is required to allow the EU to offer meaningful concessions to the members countries of Mercosur and Chile.

5. Final observations

At the end of this lengthy presentation of the many dimensions of the external economic policies of the EU, some final reflections are in place of a more general character. The first observation relates to the capability of the Union to implement change at the required speed. In the past, the external economic policy of the EU rested particularly on the discriminatory use of non-reciprocal preferences in agreements with the ACP countries and countries in the Mediterranean area. The Union started to prepare new initiatives long after it had become clear that the effectiveness of the traditional agreements was limited and that it was required to devote more attention to other regions in order to serve its own interests well. The past has shown that in a Union with 15 member states, it is hard to implement fundamental changes rapidly. The slow reform of the CAP and continued protection in other areas are cases in point. A further enlargement of the EU without appropriate adjustment of its institutional capacity does not bode well for the future capability of the Union to adapt to its changing environment at the required speed.

The second observation pertains to the effectiveness of the policy instruments that the Union has at its disposal. To realize its political objectives, the EU has always made use of trade-policy instruments, particularly in the context of PTAs. This approach was successful in supporting peace and democracy in the member countries of the Union. By expanding eastward, the Union will probably continue the success of this approach. However, establishing an area of peace and prosperity across the Mediterranean area may prove to be a task too arduous for the economic means the Union is willing to use. This applies even more to political objectives with respect to geographical areas outside the 'natural' sphere of influence of the Union. If the Union aims at realizing foreign-policy objectives beyond the improvement of its own competitiveness, the limited effectiveness of its instruments will be an immediate constraint.

Moreover, the successful development of the multilateral trade regime, to which the EU has contributed in a substantial way, reduces at the same time the effectiveness of PTAs as it limits the margin to offer trade preferences. The more comprehensive the agenda of the WTO and the larger its disciplinary powers, the less effective PTAs will be as an instrument to realize foreign-policy objectives in the future. New instruments are not yet at the disposal of the Union but will be required soon.

References

European Commission, 'The European Union as a World Trade Partner', *European Economy*, Reports and Studies Number 3, European Communities, Brussels, 1997.

European Commission, *The Competitiveness of European Industry*, European Communities, Luxembourg, 1998.

Finger, J. M., and L. A. Winters, 'What Can the WTO Do for Developing Countries?', in: A. O. Krueger, *The WTO as an International Organization*, The University of Chicago Press, Chicago, 1998.

Viner, J., *The Customs Unions Issue*, Carnegie Endowment for International Peace, New York, 1950.

Electronic sources

European Commission, *The EU Approach to the Millennium Round*, Communication from the Commission to the Council and to the European Parliament, http//europa.eu.int/comm/dg01/0807/nr.pdf, September 1999 (a).

European Commission, *The EU and the Millennium Round: More Trade Based on Better Rules*, http://europa.eu.int/comm/dg01/mren.pdf, October 1999 (b).

INDEX

A

ACP 2, 29, 31, 33, 42, 47,
131-133, 135, 136, 140,
141, 144, 149, 162, 198,
201, 206, 207, 213, 217,
225, 226, 230-233, 235,
237, 239, 241-243, 359,
368, 371, 372, 374

Acquis Communautaire 98-104,
107, 109-112, 199-202, 262,
274, 358, 363
  derogation of 100, 103, 109,
  111, 113, 363

Africa
  North Africa 2, 19, 59
  Sub-Saharan Africa 7, 19, 26,
  32, 162, 234, 371

AFTA 207, 301, 372

Agenda 2000 41, 105, 106, 153-
161, 166, 169, 170, 336,
361

Agreement on Pan-European
  Cumulation 264

Agribusiness 41, 155, 165-168,
170, 362

Agriculture 28, 36, 107, 122,
138, 150, 154, 159, 163,
165, 167, 169, 199, 201,
203, 205, 209, 240, 257,
284, 292, 303, 308, 314,
326, 334, 336, 361, 362,
365, 366, 370

AIA 302

AL-INVEST 311

Albania 249, 276

Algeria 12, 253, 264, 269

Alliance for Progress 332

Andean Community 164, 230,
305, 321, 334

Anti-dumping 19, 32, 200, 209,
210, 262, 333, 334

ANZCERTA 158

APEC 6, 37, 55, 180, 186, 187,
208, 301-304, 306, 307,
309, 310, 315, 316, 359,
372, 373
  Bogor Summit 186, 302, 303,
  372
  Osaka Summit 303

Approximation 20, 138, 248,
249, 259, 261-263, 371

Arab countries 200

Argentina 12, 18, 299, 301, 306,
312, 321, 322, 327, 330,
336

ASEAN 207, 231, 233, 301,
302, 308, 309, 351

ASEM 37, 207, 208, 297, 307-
310, 344, 351, 359, 360,
369, 373
  Bangkok Summit 308, 351
  London Summit 310, 351
  Seoul Summit 351
  Vision Group 310, 317, 351,
  373

Asia
  Central Asia 58
  East Asia 6, 7, 11, 12, 16, 18,
  43, 88, 226, 231, 249, 295,
  299, 300, 303, 306, 308-
  310, 343, 348, 351, 356,
  357, 360, 369, 370, 372,
  373
  South Asia 6, 7, 231
  South-East Asia 6, 7, 11, 12,

LEGAL ASPECTS OF INTERNATIONAL ORGANIZATION

1. S. Rosenne: *Procedure in the International Court.* A Commentary on the 1978 Rules of the International Court of Justice. 1983   ISBN 90-247-3045-7
2. T.O. Elias: *The International Court of Justice and Some Contemporary Problems.* Essays on International Law. 1983   ISBN 90-247-2791-X
3. I. Hussain: *Dissenting and Separate Opinions at the World Court.* 1984 ISBN 90-247-2920-3
4. J.B. Elkind: *Non-Appearance before the International Court of Justice.* Functional and Comparative Analysis. 1984   ISBN 90-247-2921-1
5. E. Osieke: *Constitutional Law and Practice in the International Labour Organisation.* 1985   ISBN 90-247-2985-8
6. O. Long: *Law and Its Limitations in the GATT Multilateral Trade System.* 1985   ISBN 90-247-3189-5; Pb: 0-86010-959-3
7. E. McWhinney: *The International Court of Justice and the Western Tradition of International Law.* The Paul Martin Lectures in International Relations and Law. 1987   ISBN 90-247-3524-6
8. R. Sonnenfeld: *Resolutions of the United Nations Security Council.* 1988   ISBN-90-247-3567-X
9. T.D. Gill: *Litigation Strategy at the International Court.* A Case Study of the Nicaragua versus United States Dispute. 1989   ISBN 0-7923-0332-6
10. S. Rosenne: *The World Court.* What It is and how It works. 4th revised ed. Prepared with the assistance of T.D. Gill. 1989   *For the 5th revised ed., see below Volume 16*
11. V. Gowlland-Debbas: *Collective Responses to Illegal Acts in International Law.* United Nations Action in the Question of Southern Rhodesia. 1990   ISBN 0-7923-0811-5
12. Y. Beigbeder: *The Role and Status of International Humanitarian Volunteers and Organizations.* The Right and Duty to Humanitarian Assistance. 1991   ISBN 0-7923-1190-6
13. A.B. Avanessian: *The Iran-United States Claims Tribunal in Action.* 1993 (also published in *International Arbitration Law Library*)   ISBN 1-85333-902-4
14. R. Szafarz: *The Compulsory Jurisdiction of the International Court of Justice.* 1993   ISBN 0-7923-1989-3
15. Y.Z. Blum: *Eroding the United Nations Charter.* 1993   ISBN 0-7923-2069-7
16. S. Rosenne: *The World Court.* What It is and how It works. 5th revised ed. 1994   ISBN 0-7923-2861-2
17. P.H.F. Bekker: *The Legal Position of Intergovernmental Organizations.* A Functional Necessity Analysis of Their Legal Status and Immunities. 1994   ISBN 0-7923-2904-X
18. S.A. Voitovich: *International Economic Organizations in the International Legal Process.* 1994   ISBN 0-7923-2766-7
19. S.A. Alexandrov: *Reservations in Unilateral Declarations Accepting the Compulsory Jurisdiction of the International Court of Justice.* 1995   ISBN 0-7923-3145-1
20. M. Hirsch: *The Responsibility of International Organizations Toward Third Parties.* Some Basic Principles. 1995   ISBN 0-7923-3286-5
21. A.S. Muller: *International Organizations and their Host States.* Aspects of their Legal Relationship. 1995   ISBN 90-411-0080-6
22. T. Kanninen: *Leadership and Reform.* The Secretary-General and the UN Financial Crisis of the late 1980s. 1995   ISBN 90-411-0102-0
23. C. Tomuschat (Ed.): *The United Nations at Age Fifty.* A Legal Perspective. 1995   ISBN 90-411-0145-4

KLUWER LAW INTERNATIONAL – THE HAGUE / BOSTON / LONDON